What History Tells

GEORGE L. MOSSE SERIES IN MODERN EUROPEAN CULTURAL AND INTELLECTUAL HISTORY

What History Tells

George L. Mosse and the Culture of Modern Europe

Edited by

Stanley G. Payne

David J. Sorkin

John S. Tortorice

THE UNIVERSITY OF WISCONSIN PRESS

The University of Wisconsin Press
1930 Monroe Street
Madison, Wisconsin 53711

www.wisc.edu/wisconsinpress/

3 Henrietta Street
London WC2E 8LU, England

1   3   5   4   2

Printed in the United States of America

Library of Congress Cataloging-in-Publication Data
What history tells: George L. Mosse and the culture of modern Europe / edited by Stanley G.
Payne, David J. Sorkin, John S. Tortorice.
p. cm.—(George Mosse memorial series in modern European cultural and intellectual history)
Includes bibliographical references.
ISBN 0-299-19410-8 (cloth: alk. paper)
ISBN 0-299-19414-0 (paper: alk. paper)
1. Mosse, George L. (George Lachmann), 1918–1999.
2. Europe—History—Historiography. 3. Nationalism—Europe—History—19th century. 4.
Nationalism—Europe—History—20th century. 5. Historians—United States—Biography. 6.
Jews—Germany—Historiography. I. Payne, Stanley G. II. Sorkin, David Jan. III. Tortorice,
John S. IV.
Series.
D352.9 .W43 2004
940'.07'202—dc21
2003007692

Contents

Foreword

Walter Laqueur

George Mosse was one of the most influential historians of his generation, as is evidenced by the contributions that comprise this volume, written by colleagues and students of George's who are among the leaders in their profession. His interests spanned various countries and periods—seventeenth-century England and nineteenth-century Germany, the two world wars and cultural history. Later he focused his attention on the nationalization of the masses, the cult of fallen heroes, fascism, German Jewish history, and the Holocaust.

Why a historian chooses to study one topic rather than another is of interest; accident plays a role, as do intellectual influences experienced at university, travel, or a sudden discovery in a library or the archives, but also apparently a certain predisposition, a fascination with a certain subject, which is difficult to trace but still very real. In his autobiography George occasionally hints at what made him opt for one topic and then another.

Perhaps one should not try to analyze these questions too deeply. In the final analysis they are not of paramount importance, and the historian might have been unaware, at least in part, of the impulses that steered him or her in a certain direction. That George should eventually have devoted most of the years of his creative life to issues of the twentieth century certainly does not come as a surprise, for the events of the 1930s and 1940s were overwhelming for those who lived through them.

It is often the assignment of the writer of a foreword to summarize briefly the contents of a book, but this is next to impossible in the present case, both because George was a man of many (and sometimes disparate) parts and because it has been done admirably by the contributors in the essays that follow, which survey both the state of their specialized fields and George's contribution. I shall recall instead George's role as editor of the *Journal of Contemporary History,* which has served for more than thirty-five years as a platform in the field of twentieth-century history, publishing well over a thousand articles with the emphasis on European political and cultural history in the age of fascism. When I asked George to be coeditor I did so not because of personal friendship or because we agreed on all essential issues. My reasons were more prosaic: George was deeply involved in and loved university life. He went to many conferences, served on many committees, and knew virtually everyone who was someone. My own inclinations and interests were and have remained different. I had certain ideas as to the directions in which we should proceed, but I fear that without George's knowledge of who was who and who could do what, these ideas would have remained for the better part a dead letter.

At the time George and I first met, our interests were close. He worked on his *Crisis of German Ideology,* I on a history of the German youth movement. Although the *Jugendbewegung* was not exactly identical with the German *völkisch* tradition, parts of it were, and in any case it was an important section of life reform, a topic close to George's heart. We had reached our topics in very different ways. George began professional life as a historian of early modern English history, which was of no interest to me. I had never even heard about *The Holy Pretence,* let alone of Sir Thomas Smith and Sir Edward Coke. I had attended a school in Nazi Germany for five years and graduated in 1938, so I had absorbed in my teens much of the zeitgeist as well as many of the books (above all, third-rate novels reflecting the prevailing mood) that George studied with such gusto at the time.

We were more or less the first in our respective fields. The *Jugendbewegung* had been forgotten, and the *völkisch* movement was generally regarded as a disreputable and relatively unimportant part of the German intellectual tradition. It was only in the subsequent years that dozens, if not hundreds, of books on these subjects were written, that conference and exhibitions were arranged dealing with these topics. To be present at the creation had its compensations, even though the immediate reception of George's book *The Crisis of German Ideology: Intellectual Origins of the Third Reich* in Germany was not overwhelming. I was warned that in view of my background I was less than ideally suited to understand a phenomenon that was so essentially German that no foreigner could fathom and describe it. But I cannot complain about the subsequent reactions, which were without exception friendly and positive, if with an admixture of some regret: Why was a "foreigner" needed to write the definitive story of such a quintessential German movement?

In the years that followed, our interests parted. George focused on the nationalization of the masses and the history of sexuality, worked on his cultural history of modern Europe, and eventually pioneered work in fields that seemed strange and incomprehensible to me: Why this morbid preoccupation with military cemeteries? My own interests were in the fields of Russian history and political violence. There was, to be sure, a certain coalescence with George's studying Max Nordau and my studying Zionist history in general.

I leafed through George's books of the 1970s and 1980s, but I did not read them and I suspect he did not closely study mine. This may explain why we never quarreled in our collaboration over the decades—it was not only the sweetness of his character and my own great tolerance (or unwillingness to mount the barricades because of one article or another).

But this is not the end of the story. In the months after George's death I became preoccupied with what he had written about fallen heroes, for it helped shed light on certain contemporary issues such as the cult of suicide terrorists not only in the Arab world but also, even more prominently, in Sri Lanka and other countries. The cult of fallen heroes goes back to time immemorial; it can be found in earliest Greek history (Simonides on the fallen Spartans at Thermophylae), the Jewish zealots who fought at Masada, and the Nordic sagas, which deal with little but acts of heroism— dying in battle and being taken to Asgard, the palace of the gods, with its 540 doors. The legends of the early Middle Ages are in a similar vein with the Chanson de Roland as a prominent example. The mixture of religion and nationalism as far as motives are concerned is interesting: they were fighting not only for la douce France but also for their religion against the pagans. Legends of this kind from Wilhelm Tell to Ivan Susanin can be found in the history of every people, and it was only during the Enlightenment that these traditions went out of fashion. But not for long: in the romantic age they returned with a vengeance, with Germany again as an obvious example. George quotes Theodor Körner, who wrote on the eve of a battle against Napoleon in which he lost his life, "Happiness lies in sacrificial death." Hölderlin was a greater poet than Körner, and he was not known as an aggressive militarist, but in an earlier poem (1797) entitled "Death for the Fatherland" he wrote exactly in the same vein.

I remember the inscription "Dulce et decorum est pro patria mori" (Horace) in the assembly hall of our school, and I suspect it appeared in schools all over Germany. This was in remembrance, above all, of the heroes of Langemark in November 1914, when many thousands of young students had tried to storm the enemy lines in Flanders, singing "Deutschland Deutschland über alles" at a time when this was not even the national anthem. Indoctrination (then and now) was supposed to create the impression that the fallen symbolized the triumph of youth and that they were not really dead but merely sleeping in the lap of Christ (or Muhammad). Graves and cemeteries became shrines of national worship.

The heroes had not died in vain but lived on in eternal life in the tradition of "Ich hatt' einen Kameraden," Uhland's famous poem that ends, "Kann dir die Hand nicht geben, Bleib du im ew'gen Leben" ("I cannot give you my hand, may you rest in eternal peace" bringing up the idea of eternal life), just as the Horst Wessel song maintains that those who were shot by the enemy continue to march with the living brownshirts in their columns, in spirit if not in body.

Under Nazism the heroic tradition of self-sacrifice became central to the essence of the regime, and this perhaps more than anything else led analysts to interpret Nazism as a political religion. At the same time, Nazi propagandists were instructed to explain to the bereaved that there was no need to mourn, since mourning was destructive to national morale; one should be grateful that loved ones had been given a chance to make the supreme sacrifice for a higher ideal. They were not suffering pain but were living on in eternity.

These ideas were reflected in hundreds of poems written not only by party hacks but also by more serious writers such as Ernst Bertram, the friend of Thomas Mann and one of the leading Germanists of the period. The cult of fallen heroes also figures prominently in the ideology and practice of other fascist movements, particularly the Rumanian Iron Guard, and in the writings of José Primo de Rivera. It takes a central place in the writings of postwar neofascists such as Julius Evola, one of their many gurus. It was customary on ritual occasions that when the list of those assembled was read out, the fallen were included and someone answered with "present" when the name was called. The similarity with the present cult of suicide bombers is startling. The Koran and the Hadith warn against mourning fallen heroes, seeing their sacrifice as a joyous occasion and instructing families to be proud, not dejected. There is the same belief that they were warriors in a holy struggle, that their group was cruelly oppressed and that their sacrifice was not only desirable but imperative. It was commonly believed that the collective (the religion, the sect, the nation, the race) was infinitely more important than the individual. A whole generation had been indoctrinated in this spirit, and many followed the call to give their lives when it came. It was not limited to one specific culture—mention has been made of the Liberation Tigers of Eelam (Sri Lanka); the kamikaze pilots could serve as an earlier example. Kamikaze missions were seldom if ever decisive. They did not prevent German defeat in World Wars I and II nor Japanese defeat in the World War II, and they are unlikely to succeed in terrorist campaigns.

There are other intriguing phenomena that would have been of great interest to George, the student of the history of sexuality. This refers to the awards waiting for the fallen warrior, for paradise, as the Hadith says, is under the shade of the sword. The martyrs were not only entitled to intercede for seventy of their relations to enable them to join them in paradise, which was described as a place of wonderful gardens, of streams with clear water, and overhead a jeweled dome of pearls and rubies extending from Damascus to southern Yemen. The martyrs were reclining on thrones and eating and drinking meats and fruit with happiness and with many servants at their beck and call. Above all, there were seventy (or perhaps seventy-two) virgins ready for them, in addition to the wives they had had on earth.

Those who have grown up in a post-heroic age find it difficult to understand the fallen warriors and their cult. It is to George Mosse's credit that he gave much thought to these problems, to religion, and to the patriotic uses of the cult of fallen heroes, and that he did pioneering spade work at a time when these subjects seemed of little contemporary relevance.

George Mosse, as initially pointed out, did pioneering work in a number of fields; others have followed in his footsteps since and many specialized studies have appeared in his wake. History is constantly written and rewritten and it has been said that the average life span of even a fine study in the field of history is little more than a decade, for it is bound to be superseded by more recent research, new material and a variety of considerations. But this is less true in the field of intellectual history in which

George specialized throughout most of his life. How to measure the influence a study has had? There is no foolproof way to do so, sales figures certainly do not tell the story. But there still are certain yardsticks, and the fact that so much of George Mosse's work is still in print many years after and that his very first book, *The Holy Pretence* which originally appeared more than fifty years ago is republished as these lines are written is as good a measurement as any.

Preface

Stanley G. Payne, David J. Sorkin, and
John S. Tortorice

During his long and prolific career, George L. Mosse ranged farther over the fields of early modern and modern European history than almost any other historian of his time. Beginning as a specialist in the era of the English Reformation, he later turned to modern European cultural history and helped to open a whole series of new areas for research. From 1960 through the 1990s, Mosse anticipated and helped to lead a wide variety of new trends and subspecialties, including the new cultural history; the comparative study of fascism; the history of racism, political symbolism, and mass movements; the history of monuments and of mourning; ethnic and Jewish history; and finally the history of sexuality. No other Europeanist historian of the second half of the twentieth century left a greater imprint on the course of historical scholarship, and none worked in a greater number of thematic areas.

In addition to the legacy of his scholarship, his many thousands of undergraduate students, and the thirty-eight historians who completed their doctoral work under his direction, George L. Mosse bequeathed his extensive family estate (finally restored by the German government) to the endowment of the George L. Mosse Program at the University of Wisconsin–Madison. The Mosse Program is dedicated to maintaining an extensive schedule of exchange fellowships for graduate students and junior faculty between the University of Wisconsin and the Hebrew University in Jerusalem, as well as to fostering its own publication series and a variety of other activities to sponsor historical research and teaching in the areas of Mosse's specialties. This is the first volume in the series to be published under the auspices of the Mosse Program. Following his death in January 1999, in view of the depth and breadth of Mosse's legacy, some of his closest colleagues and students saw a clear need to investigate the character and extent of his influence on diverse fields of early modern and modern European history. The result was the conference "An Historian's Legacy: George L. Mosse and Recent Research on Fascism, Society, and Culture." It was held at the University of Wisconsin-Madison on September 7–9, 2001. This conference was funded as the annual Burdick-Vary Symposium of the Institute for Research in the Humanities at Wisconsin, with generous additional aid from Wisconsin's Anonymous Fund. We wish especially to acknowledge the indispensable contribution of Loretta Freiling, the administrative assistant of the Humanities Institute, who, with her experience, care, and energetic supervision has played such a vital role in the Institute's conferences over the years.

The chapters of this volume are drawn from papers presented originally at the conference in 2001. They explore most, though not quite all, of the major themes of Mosse's work and help to explain its genesis, its unique character, and also some part of its impact on the world of historical scholarship. They also constitute a scholarly tribute to the passing of an unforgettable teacher, scholar, colleague, and friend.

What History Tells

Introduction

Steven E. Aschheim

George Mosse died on 22 January 1999. The present collection of essays, as well as the remarkable (September 2001) conference upon which it is based, seeks to delineate and critically assess his work, person, and legacy.[1] The essays gathered here succeed rather grandly in these aims, and little would be served by simply rehashing them. The task of these introductory remarks thus becomes one of attempting to assemble some kind of a composite picture of the man, the thought, and his epoch that emerges from these reflections.

The first, and quite overwhelming, impression concerns the extra-ordinary range of Mosse's oeuvre and the depth and variety of his influence—intellectual as well as personal. Through the pages of this collection we are made privy not only to George's substantive and meth-odological contributions to the general field of cultural history but also to his more specialized writings on the politics and theology of the early modern period; the Reformation and Christian casuistry; Jewish history and anti-Semitism; fascism, Nazism, and the Holocaust; monuments and mass politics; war and commemoration; intellectuals, liberalism, and "ir-rationalism"; racism, stereotypes, and visual culture; respectability, sexu-ality, and nationalism. The present volume documents and attempts to place these works within their historiographical and biographical context and traces the manifold ways in which George presciently influenced the subsequent course of these various historiographies—sensitizing them to new questions, exposing previously hidden connections, hinting at novel areas of research, nudging them on to redefine their agenda. At the same time, many of these pieces possess a critical edge. George, no doubt, would have chuckled and approved, for he encouraged criticism of his work (almost) as much as, a little wondrously, he might have appreciated the present homage.

Whether exposed to these manifold writings or his person (or both),

everyone, it appears, had his or her "own George." Perhaps this should
not be too surprising given his irrepressibly "peripatetic" nature. George
traversed diverse terrains of knowledge just as eagerly and restlessly as he
traveled over continents seeking (until the very end) new experiences and
horizons, establishing acquaintances, and—in quite unique fashion—
making new friends. "A rolling Mosse gathers no stones," Roger Griffin
wittily but accurately notes in his essay.[2] George's almost childlike open-
ness, his restlessness and insatiable curiosity—combined with Prussian
self-discipline and tough-mindedness—were essential ingredients of this
creativity and influence. No wonder he became a master analyst of the dialectic between "nervousness" and "self-control" in the modern world.

The volume, then, reveals Mosse's work and person in its manifold
roles and guises. He was, indeed, distinctively all of these and yet, somehow, always more than the sum of these parts, never simply reducible to
any one of them. George, to employ a phrase he loved to use, was "a fully
furnished house." But, of course, it was the complexities—and sometimes the contradictions—that made his mansion so distinctive and full of
surprises. David Sabean and Johann Sommerville, for instance, remind us
of the "Protestant" or "Christian" George. Given his self-proclaimed ad-
herence to the Enlightenment—he specifically requested, after all, that
God not be mentioned at his funeral—this is well worth remembering.
Whenever I upbraided him for his rationalist prejudices—he always referred to religious people as "pious"—he would retort: "I was a Christian
theologian, you know."

As David Sabean pointed out in his oral presentation to the conference, George's lecturing technique—integral to his pedagogic genius—
was partly based upon the structure of the Protestant sermon. Sabean is
also, surely, correct to identify Mosse's emphasis on the humane element
in Christian thought as part of his ongoing examination of the tension between practical life and ethical values. Beyond this, one must underline
the point that Mosse endowed religion with a formative and ongoing role
that few liberal rationalists (at least in previous decades) were wont to do.
As Johann Sommerville demonstrates, he was a pioneer in tracing the
new realism in seventeenth-century politics, and indeed the roots of the
Enlightenment, not just to nascent secular forces but to sources within
the framework of Christian theology itself.

Indeed, as several commentators in this volume note, many of
George's insights into the role of myth and symbol in modern mass poli-

tics derive from earlier work on religious belief systems and their relation to external events. Consonant with his sensitivity to religious forms, as early as his seminal 1963 Stanford seminar on fascism George was already referring to its "liturgical functions."[3] *The Nationalization of the Masses*—essentially a study in the modern sacralization of politics—later simply elaborated upon and systematized these insights. In typically unorthodox fashion, he located the origins of these sacral politics on the Left in the putatively rationalist French Revolution (in 1989 he followed this up in a study that pursued the hidden and surprising connections between "Fascism and the French Revolution").[4] But the main focus of *The Nationalization of the Masses* was obviously on the mobilizing dynamics and symbolic representations of the political Right. Highlighting "national self-worship," its mass meetings and festivals, the secularization of "holy flames, flags, and songs," Mosse's study sought ultimately, as he put it, to uncover "the organic development of the Nazi cult and its essentially religious nature."[5] But George applied such notions far more generally. When I met him in 1968 he already delighted in teasing his Israeli friends with the provocative but illuminating insight that Masada was secular Zionism's "holy mountain." "Every nationalism" (and, in his inimitable voice with its characteristic inflection,[6] to bring home the point he would repeat the phrase three or four times), "every nationalism, every nationalism has its holy mountain, Steve."

It is worth noting that the later work beginning with *Fallen Soldiers* (1990)—the pioneering and influential nature of which is analyzed here in the essays by Jay Winter and Emmanuel Sivan—is similarly sensitive to the religious dimension and its politico-nationalist annexation. "The Myth of the War Experience," as George termed it, was, he observed, to a great extent suffused with Christian themes and symbolism. The confrontation with and, above all, the transcendence of mass death was inextricably tied to "the traditional Christian means of consolation, the belief in the death and resurrection of Christ . . . the burial and commemoration of the war dead were analogous to the construction of a church for the nation. . . . War was made sacred, an expression of the general will of the people."[7] The subsequent works on sexuality similarly emphasize the role of pietism and evangelicalism in the making of middle-class respectability and attitudes toward masculinity.

In contrast to Mosse's "Christian" dimensions, his connection to Israel and the crucial importance of the "Jewish" components in both his work and his identity have long been recognized and analyzed, not least in his autobiography, where George renders this a fundamental part of his own "outsider" identity (a point to which I shall presently return).[8] In this volume, Shulamit Volkov has brilliantly analyzed some of the historiographical biases and limits as well as the insights and achievements that ensued from George's engagement with the Jewish experience. Here I want to confine myself to pertinent points arising from the fine contribution by Saul Friedländer. That this should have been the keynote speech of the conference was entirely fitting, for although George's political awakening, his antifascism, was sparked not by the German experience but rather by the Spanish Civil War,[9] Nazism was nevertheless the defining existential moment in his life, and it was the Holocaust that constituted the central historiographical conundrum.

Friedländer acutely notes that although George never wrote about the Final Solution "in any detail, [it] was nonetheless the visible center of his research." Let me suggest that the reason for the absence of such "detailed studies" in George's works derives from the wider perspective he adopted. He was less interested in the operational dynamics, the "how" of the Holocaust—which I think, with all due respect, he would have regarded as more or less a "technical" question. "All my books," he declared in 1985, "in one way or another have dealt with the Jewish catastrophe of my time which I have always regarded as no accident, structural fault or continuity of bureaucratic habits, but seemingly built into our society and attitudes towards life."[10] This marked his approach throughout and would apply as much to such later works as *Nationalism and Sexuality* and *The Image of Man,* which seemed to go well beyond Jewish victims and considerably broadened the scope of affected "outsiders." Ultimately, the Mossean project amounted to a cumulative, ever-expanding examination of the manifold, yet always interrelated, components of the prehistory of these atrocities, the cultural and attitudinal building blocks that rendered it a conceivable option. George viewed fascism, Nazism, and the Final Solution as the (not necessarily inevitable) culmination of deeper immanent trends, perceptions, and processes operating in Western and Central European culture—albeit in their most radical and corrupted form. (This is not to say that his cultural history revolved exclusively around such negative dimensions. In manifold ways he also explored the humanizing potential of the continuing, if always fragile, Enlightenment heritage and some of its liberal and Left offshoots.)

I want here to examine a related and more general point mentioned in passing by both Saul Friedländer and Walter Laqueur but which is in need of elaboration. Friedländer notes that the leading postwar German historians, "this new left-oriented generation—the Wehlers, the Mommsens, the Broszats, the Schieders—had little interest in the kind of cultural history that Mosse excavated." In a similar spirit, Laqueur asks why, when it came to George's pioneering work on the *völkisch* tradition and his own early study on the German *Jugendbewegung*, foreigners were needed to write the definitive stories of such quintessential movements.

The word "foreigner" in this respect is, I think, misplaced. There is perhaps more significance than meets the eye in the title of one of George's book-length interviews, "Ich Bleibe Emigrant."[11] This is singularly relevant, for I would argue that the very creation of a new kind of encompassing cultural history—distinctively removed from traditional, elitist *Ideengeschichte* with its inbuilt bias toward abstract ideas and a progressive Hegelian rationality—was, to a large degree, the product of George's German Jewish émigré generation, those to whom Germany was not at all foreign but deeply familiar and, yet, which experienced rejection firsthand. The underlying issue that confronted its members was how to account for the cultural roots and core dynamics of Nazism, the unprecedented eruption of the barbaric into their own putatively civilized world. This was not merely an academic problem but one that was inextricably linked to the impact of these events on their own lives. For all their differences, people such as Fritz Stern, Walter Laqueur, Peter Gay, and George Mosse were instrumental in shaping our understanding of the broader bases of fascism, Nazism, and totalitarianism. They did so, moreover, by placing "culture" and the dialectics of "irrationalism" at its center. (Later, of course, these thinkers—each in his own way—also pursued other issues, but all in such a way that they constantly expanded upon the horizons and subject matter of this new kind of cultural and intellectual history.)

Why did this not take place in Germany? Why, indeed, was there a clear *resistance* to this discipline, when it so illuminated the crucial cultural, ideological, and existential underpinnings of these developments and the modes by which both German and European identities and self-representations were integrally tied into them? It is not as if postwar German historians did not seek to explain the roots of Nazism. Indeed, these social historians were animated by a critical sense of the German past. They were the prime formulators of the *Sonderweg* thesis, a narrative that viewed German history as a record of its crippling deformations. Yet from the beginning, they were wary of the cultural-intellectual approach, regarding it as tainted by the idealist-elitist political traditions of historians like Friedrich Meinecke and Gerhard Ritter. They associated this way of thinking as in some way linked to Germany's disfiguration. In their eyes *Kulturgeschichte* became a kind of instrument or symptom of National Socialism, not a useful tool for analyzing it. In its stead they placed at the explanatory center social, economic, and political "structures" and "processes." Without ever really explaining why this should be so, the analysis of "society" was regarded as critical and "progressive," while the study of ideas was taken to be somehow reactionary and conservative.

This kind of social history, to be sure, did light up some important institutional aspects of the German past, but the concentration on these impersonal forms also served to elide those existential, ideational, and attitudinal realms in which choice, decisions, and personal responsibility played a cardinal role. Theirs was an allegedly critical history, but one that was devoid of real sting because of the absence of cultural and ideological analysis. This is the reason why, on reflection, I reacted so flatly to these works. They lacked urgency, electricity, relevance. They always seemed to miss their self-proclaimed target. How could one critically address this past without taking into account the self-representations, the re-formations of identities, the prejudices, emotions, and, indeed, minds of those who made it? It may very well be that these painful issues of personal agency and belief, the need to account for and come to terms with the Nazi past without laying blame directly on the generation of their "fathers," prompted the German social historians to go in this "structural," impersonal direction.

Even if, as Friedländer notes, there was a fairly prolonged period of gestation, it was the émigré historians who discerned the crucial importance of these cultural and existential dimensions and integrated them into the historical narrative. They were able to do this partly because they were free of the potentially apologetic biographical constraints of their German counterparts; partly because they had experienced the harsh realities of these ideologies on their own persons; and partly because, coming out of the German Jewish intellectual milieu, they were peculiarly sensitive to the cultural dimensions of experience (*German Jews beyond*

Judaism, indeed, makes this predilection, with all its strengths and weaknesses, the very core of a reconstituted modern German Jewish identity).

If this analysis accounts for the paucity, at least in the earlier years, of positive responses to George's work in Germany (a phenomenon noted by numerous contributors to this volume), it also explains the resonance it had for so many of us who found in his works (as well as in that of some of the other émigré scholars) a relevance and excitement so conspicuously absent in these other tomes of social history. George's books, lectures, and conversations always addressed themselves to questions of our own contemporary self-understanding, and his forays into the German and European roots of Nazism and its atrocities, his preoccupation with *the* great issue of the twentieth century, seemed critically linked to that self-understanding. His expansion of the boundaries of cultural and intellectual history and his refusal, as Robert Nye argues in his contribution to this volume, to "privilege ideas or movements in any hierarchy of significance, giving Hegel, say, pride of place over Father Jahn, or ranking Richard Wagner over Karl May" only added to the novelty and plausibility of his explorations.

Those explorations always came back to Nazism and its atrocities, as Saul Friedländer correctly surmises. Still, I would want here to make a certain qualification to his thoughtful conclusion:

Couldn't it be, therefore, that the past [Mosse] strived to exorcize by understanding it was even more present in his life than he recognized? Could it be that aside from intellectual understanding, something in and of that past fed both the anxieties, the fear and the restlessness and *also* the powerful constancy of his quest, something that George shared with many Jews of his generation and beyond? And couldn't that unacknowledged source of anxiety *and* of energy have been an intangible yet unmasterable sense of guilt for having survived the destruction of his world and the murder of his fellow Jews?

This is indeed an intriguing suggestion. It may well account for some of the deeper wellsprings of George's being (although it is not clear how one can verify or refute such speculations into the unconscious). Still, if we leave it at that, we miss, I think, certain characteristics that were quintessentially distinctive of George. He did, to be sure, regard himself, as we have seen, as an emigrant, yet this was never tinged with a refugee psychology or a sense of victimhood: "I do not belong," he emphasized, "to a more recent generation where victimization is a badge of pride rather

than a frustration or a test of character."[12] Peter Gay could describe his experiences under Nazism, his enforced exile, and the deposits it left on him
as "the story of a poisoning."[13] George, on the other hand, seems to have
experienced exile as a kind of liberation, his initial statelessness an opportunity for both personal expression and intellectual development. The
Nazi years certainly preoccupied him deeply, yet he was remarkably free
of bitterness. He never acted like, or presented himself as, a survivor. If
there was "an intangible yet unmasterable sense of guilt," it was exceed-
ingly well hidden. Indeed, what made him so distinctive and attractive
was the sense of joy and discovery he brought with him, his gregarious-
ness, his often outrageous hilarity and endless curiosity. It was these qualities, rather than intimations of survivor guilt, that prompted his Israeli
friends to comment: "We in Jerusalem measure time according to before,
during and after George's visit!"

Still, given this volume's attempt at an overall assessment, we must
come to terms with George's self-proclaimed sense of being an outsider
(always channeled creatively into his academic frame and given ultimate
expression in his final works). This outsiderdom, as *Confronting History*
makes clear, was in part chosen, a value, the option of being "an intellectual not tied down to time and place."[14] The other dimensions of that
identity—the Jewish and homosexual parts—were more complex in
provenance and expression. Rather surprisingly, while the Jewish and intellectual aspects are well covered in this volume, the proceedings almost
entirely ignore the question of his homosexuality.[15] Clearly, George's emphases in the memoir render this dimension central to both his work and
his person. Perhaps the reluctance to deal with it here is testament to the
ongoing power of the very "respectability" that George exposed but
which, as he recognized, still possesses considerable, if somewhat diminished, force.

Still, as David Gross has recently noted, there is something not quite
right about George's self-representation as an outsider. In terms of most relevant objective criteria—birth, wealth, privilege, professional success—
George, he insists, was actually very much an "insider." Being an "outsider"
was more of an existential and conceptual stance than a sociological fate. It
allowed him a certain critical freedom, a resistance to the conformist nor-
malcy necessarily exerted by society. It was precisely the taut complexity of
this position that rendered it so creative. George "was firmly in the establishment," Gross remarks, "yet not really part of it; he was 'respectable,' but

at the same also a 'critic of respectability.' Rather than being disconcerted by these ambiguities and apparent contradictions, Mosse fed off them, and even made them a spur to his best historical work."[16]

The seminal 1963 Stanford seminar on fascism and Nazism, which Emilio Gentile outlines in his essay in greater detail, is fascinating not only because almost everything George subsequently said on the subject was already embryonically there but because the very critical responses and intensely contested discussions it evoked revealed a crucial part of George's makeup. (The list of participants in the seminar was impressive. In attendance were Hugh Seton-Watson, Karl Dietrich Bracher, Juan Linz, Gordon Craig, James Sheehan, Gavin Langmuir, and Michael Ledeen, among others.) If Gordon Craig would have directed the following remark to anyone else one might have been surprised: "George, you really got me tonight. I think I may almost agree with you."[17] But here it appears entirely natural, at one with the kind of friendly, sometimes humorous, yet ruthlessly honest dialogue that George, inimitably, encouraged. This is because, like many of the historical characters he studied, he intensely disliked what he called a "wobble." "Ever since I can remember," he wrote, "I have disliked anything mushy, from personal attitudes, to human bodies, to ripe fruit. This preference did not mean opposition to compromise and accommodation—after all, I consider myself a liberal—but rather a demand for strong personalities who could hold their own, however much their firmly held opinions might grate upon me."[18]

Both in his person and in his work, George sought to combine this critical individualism with the values he perhaps most admired in the Enlightenment and German Jewish heritages: their conceptions of friendship, the attempt at all times to personalize relationships and to preserve their integrity against all opposing forces.[19] As these proceedings demonstrate, George was both an extraordinary and complex man and historian. It is perhaps most appropriate, however, that I should conclude this essay with "George the friend," for he embodied this capacity uniquely and magnificently. The world has been diminished by his departure.

Notes

1. A considerable literature on George Mosse already exists. For my own analysis see "George Mosse at Eighty: A Critical Laudatio," in my *In Times of Crisis: Essays on European Culture, Germans, and Jews* (Madison: University of Wisconsin Press, 2001), 155–77.

Given this body of work, I will try to focus here on those aspects that specifically emerged during the course of this conference.

2. Griffin's observations as to George's peripatetic predilections are remarkably perceptive, especially given the fact that he was not personally acquainted with George.

3. See the seminar "What Is Fascism?" 7 October 1963, 4. These seminars remain unpublished. I thank John Tortorice for giving me access to them.

4. See the essay by that name in his *The Fascist Revolution: Toward a General Theory of Fascism* (Howard Fertig: New York, 1999).

5. See *The Nationalization of the Masses: Political Symbolism and Mass Movements in Germany from the Napoleonic Wars through the Third Reich* (New York: Howard Fertig, 1975), 10.

6. See the marvelously evocative piece by Paul Breines, "Finding Oneself in History and Vice Versa: Remarks on 'George's Voice,'" in the special issue: George L. Mosse Memorial Symposium, *German Politics and Society* 18, no. 4 (2000): 3–17.

7. George L. Mosse, *Fallen Soldiers: Reshaping the Memory of the World Wars* (New York: Oxford University Press, 1990), 32–33. See also chap. 3.

8. From *The Crisis of German Ideology* (1964) on, almost all of George's work dealt in way or another with Jewish issues. In *Confronting History: A Memoir* (Madison: University of Wisconsin Press, 2000) he discusses both the academic and personal dimensions of his Jewishness. See too my article "George Mosse and Jewish History" in the special issue of *German Politics and Society.* An earlier piece with the same title, written by Zeev Mankowitz, appears in *George Mosse: On the Occasion of His Retirement—17.6.85* (Jerusalem: Hebrew University of Jerusalem, 1985), xxii–xxv.

9. See Mosse, *Confronting History,* 104. Anson Rabinbach places this into historical perspective in "George Mosse and the Culture of Antifascism" in the special issue of *German Politics and Society,* 30–45.

10. See Mosse's response in *George Mosse: On the Occasion of His Retirement,* xxviii.

11. See Irene Runge and Uwe Stelbrink, eds., *"Ich bleibe Emigrant": Gespraeche mit George L. Mosse* (Berlin: Dietz Verlag, 1991). The other book-length interview was conducted by Michael A. Ledeen, *Nazism: A Historical and Comparative Analysis of National Socialism* (New Brunswick: Transaction Books, 1978).

12. Mosse, *Confronting History,* 5.

13. See Peter Gay, *My German Question: Growing Up in Nazi Berlin* (New Haven: Yale University Press, 1998), ix.

14. Mosse, *Confronting History,* 217. Mosse goes on to add that this ideal of the "free-floating" intellectual "did not work in practice."

15. At the end of the conference, a rather puzzled Robert Nye pointed this out to me and wondered why it should be so. At the time I resisted his assertion that the question of George's homosexuality had been elided, but upon reading the papers I think Nye was quite correct.

16. See the insightful piece by David Gross, "Between Myth and Reality: George L. Mosse's Confrontation with History," *Telos,* no. 119 (Spring 2001). The relevant passages appear on pages 162–64.

17. Seminar of 18 November 1963, "The Problem of National Socialist Morality," 9.

18. Mosse, *Confronting History,* 207.

19. See his "Friendship and Nationhood: About the Promise and Failure of German Nationalism," *Journal of Contemporary History* 17 (1982): 351–67; and Mosse, *German Jews beyond Judaism* (Bloomington: Indiana University Press, 1985), esp. 32.

Part 1
Mosse on Early Modern Europe

George Mosse and *The Holy Pretence*

David Warren Sabean

In 1980, around the time Seymour Drescher, Allan Sharlin, and I were putting together George Mosse's Festschrift,[1] George sent me a copy of his 1957 book *The Holy Pretence*, subtitled *A Study in Christianity and Reason of State from William Perkins to John Winthrop*. He wrote on the jacket, "I (but hardly anyone else) consider it one of my most important books." Indeed, while his first book on English seventeenth-century constitutional thought, *The Struggle for Sovereignty in England*, was widely reviewed and highly praised, this book found only two reviewers and little positive comment. Up to the time George published *The Holy Pretence* in 1957, nearly all of his published research—the exceptions being two articles, one on a French seventeenth-century Calvinist and the other, oddly enough, in the *Economic History Review* on post–Corn Law politics—had dealt with late-sixteenth- and seventeenth-century English constitutional and political thought. The same year he published *The Holy Pretence*, George came out with an article in the *Leo Baeck Institute Year Book* entitled "The Image of the Jew in German Popular Culture: Felix Dahn and Gustav Freytag." That article, of course, signaled a change in the direction of his research, although it took a whole decade for his teaching to shift to match his new project(s). After 1957 there were occasional articles—one or two a year—until his pathbreaking *Crisis of German Ideology* appeared in 1964. By 1980, when he still saw *The Holy Pretence* as one of his best books, he had published *Nazi Culture, Germans and Jews, Nationalization of the Masses, Towards the Final Solution, Masses and Man*, and about 140 other pieces, mostly on racism, fascism, and nationalism.

In this essay I am interested in the meeting, in this hinge year of 1957, of two seemingly quite diverse projects, one brought to fruition and the

15

other just being tried out. I am also tantalized by Mosse's own estimation of *The Holy Pretence*, which George clearly saw as central to his intellectual biography. In his memoir *Confronting History*, after talking about the moment in 1933 of leaving Germany, he wrote: "All I have done since and all I have published has had a political agenda."[2] I think one central aspect of *The Holy Pretence* has to be found in its form of political analysis. But why did he not start right away with the roots of German fascism? There are several reasons, but in his memoirs he points to the influence of William Lunt at Haverford, under whom he did his senior honors thesis: "The subject which would determine my scholarship for the next sixteen years I started to study under Lunt's direction." There was a strong element of apprenticeship in his training. He went on to say: "Both at Cambridge and at Haverford, Medieval and early modern history were the periods devoted to serious study."[3]

There is the famous anecdote about a colleague who passed judgment on this period of George's life in the following terms: "How come that you yourself are so interesting and your books are so dull?" His answer gives us an important clue to what he thought he was getting out of this earlier project: "But I did not find my books dull, and, indeed, from the beginning tried to apply to sixteenth- and seventeenth-century English history theoretical concepts which came from my German background and my quite un-English interest in theory."[4]

I suspect that one of the reasons for the poor reception of *The Holy Pretence* has to do with the fact that most of Mosse's questions and many of his comparisons come from a Central European or Continental European tradition. He far more readily cites Meinecke, Troeltsch, Croce, Spengler, Heuss, von Muralt, Praz, Pezzolini, Orsini, Laski, von Doellinger, Reuter, Albertini, Cassirer, and Niebuhr than he does any English secondary literature. It was never a book easily assimilable into an English political theory discourse.

It is not exactly clear what George meant by "theory" in the quote above. While we were preparing Mosse's Festschrift in 1980, Robert Nye wrote quite astutely: "I have always taken Mosse to be an intuitive sort of intellectual historian, feeling his way through his materials and reconstructing intellectual developments as they 'must' have occurred. On this view, empathy has been his most useful tool; in his hands, ideology appeals as much to deep emotional structures as to rational and cognitive ones."

In contrast, I had always perceived a strong theoretical substructure to Mosse's historical practice, although it was one that he did not usually make explicit. There was no particular concept that he underlined so as to call attention to an innovation, nor was there any extended theoretical apparatus. Reflecting on the problem precisely with reference to *The Holy Pretence,* he had this to say: "I have always approached history not as a narrative but as a series of questions and possible answers. . . . [But] I believe that historical narrative must provide the framework within which problems of interest can be addressed. I have always been grateful that my teachers in England, and the rigorous examinations I had to pass, gave me such a precise framework. Theory cut loose from its concrete context becomes a mere game, an amusement of no particular relevance."[5]

This last quote moves on several different registers, and the logic is not straightforward. I think George was arguing for two things at once. On the one hand, narrative provided for him the dimension of practice, while on the other hand, theory was useful for generating questions, rigorously linked to context. He uses narrative to structure what he has to say. Theory for him is not directly linked to the narrative but involves a series of meaningful questions that are often only loosely linked to the matter at hand or to the overarching story he is telling. The questions often seem unprompted by the material itself; they come at right angles, so to speak, to the text he is developing. They can arise from his extensive reading, from his experience, or from something suggested by his imagination— a leap, an analogy, a comparison—and any of these things can seem at once compelling for the reader and wildly out of place. He could be writing on some late-nineteenth-century text at the same time he was reading Philippe Ariès's *Centuries of Childhood,* the latter providing an insightful question, which he would sometimes make explicit and sometimes leave for the reader to guess where the flash of insight came from. There was no overarching "theory" here but rather a myriad of theoretical points and analytical critiques pushing their way into and opening up spaces in the plot he was constructing. The plot itself usually involved an expository reading of text after text, each one chosen for its thematic usefulness. He treated the texts of Western (German) thought much as a biblical expositor might treat Scripture, moving back and forth, explaining here and there, bringing the texts from quite different places into juxtaposition. He takes a theme, builds a central focus, and explores variations. I think George became ever more didactic as he matured, and the scope of his

later work was much broader, suited to a radical shift in audience. But he
honed his craft in *The Holy Pretence.*

There is another passage in the memoirs that is just as telling: "Such
influence as my work may possess . . . does not stem from concrete discoveries, but rather from the new insights it has managed to convey, how
it may have shifted our vision by giving some new perspective and dimensions to aspects of modern history." Just after this passage, Mosse
outlines some of the chief themes that run through his work, many of
them rooted in his earliest writings: "My work in early modern history set
forth some themes which were followed up later in my work on fascism
and National Socialism and have influenced most of my writings on a wide
variety of subjects. . . . [T]his is how I see my work, how it falls into place
in my own mind." One theme, the fate of liberalism, found first expression, he tells us, in *The Struggle for Sovereignty in England.* A second
theme, the nature of outsiderdom, he points out, was not developed in his
early modern work but emerged in his 1957 article on the image of the
Jew in the novels of Dahn and Freytag. Here, he says, the course "was
now set for the method I was to pursue to the end."[6]

What was that method? It concerns—and here I sketch in briefly—
how he deals with culture, with culture as a systematic way of perception
and a set of powerful symbols. Culture, to get back to another central concern, was always linked to the political, and his interest lay in describing
"habits of mind" that establish ways of living that in turn inform political
reality. A third theme that Mosse alludes to in his memoirs he describes
thus: "To my mind, the real breakthrough in putting my own stamp upon
the analysis of cultural history came with *The Nationalization of the
Masses,* published in 1975, which dealt with the sacralization of politics:
the Nazi political liturgy and its consequences." This book was a departure from his early work methodologically: "This was no longer a book in
the tradition of the history of political thought as I had been taught it at
Harvard by Charles Howard McIlwain; instead it used the definition of
culture as the history of perceptions which I had offered in my *Culture of
Western Europe.*" Still he saw links to his early work: "While my historical research has concentrated upon various modern belief systems, it
would undoubtedly be correct to see here a continuity between my work
on the Reformation and that on more recent history. I was familiar with
theological thought as well as religious practices and could bring this
knowledge to bear upon the secularization of modern and contemporary

politics. It was not such a big step from Christian belief systems, especially in the baroque period, to modern civic religions such as nationalism in its various forms."[7]

A last part of the puzzle: Mosse referred in *Confronting History* to a note by Steven Aschheim: "George Mosse's Europe has always been peopled by strange and powerful forces threatening to engulf its precious but fragile humanist heritage."[8] There is, I think, a tragic vision in Mosse's work that goes along with his moral injunction to think and act realistically and in just proportion. While *The Holy Pretence* ends with the question of how well his casuists kept the balance—"prudence" became policy under a different name, and the religious element of reason of state was often only a disguise for the secular concept—*German Jews beyond Judaism* begins with the thought that the "history of German Jews from one point of view is that of chasing a noble illusion."[9]

I would like to return to the question of why George considered *The Holy Pretence* so important. Beyond summing up his first sixteen years as a scholar, it had important thematic and stylistic (one could say methodological, but I think this is the better term) characteristics of his later work. I would like to tease out some of these points and, without being comprehensive, trace some of them to his later preoccupations. The first is a lifelong concern with finding a balance between contesting forces. George always thought that life's realities possessed powerful demands for people and that finding an ethical balance was crucial for living a moral life. He found unsatisfactory both the life of unexamined power and the life of the virgin moralist, unsullied by immersion in practical affairs. *The Holy Pretence* was an attempt to look at how a series of political thinkers and actors negotiated Christian morality and the practical exigencies of seventeenth-century state politics. George thought that intellectually the greatest challenge for all Christian ethicists of the period was the powerful work of Machiavelli.

I think there was always a didactic element in Mosse's work. And his approach to texts—teasing out the tensions in a particular context—is closely related to his pedagogical intent, which I want to emphasize again is always a running commentary on the possibilities in a particular situation for meaningful, effective, and above all moral action. As his work progressed, one can see as a continuous thread a commitment to humanistic—or perhaps better, humane—values. For Europe of the seventeenth century, his concern was with the humane elements in Christian thought

and political commitment. But what drives the analysis is the location of
tensions between practical life and ethical values. Reason of state, he argued, oriented the statesman toward the realities of political life, which
judges a ruler by success in the adept handling of political power.[10] Christian ethical thinkers were concerned with what happens to the ethics of
Christianity in real political action. Mosse passes out judgments on the
success of various writers in negotiating the tension. The attempts of Sir
John Melton, for example,[11] writing in 1609, were feeble in this direction.
Mosse condemned a series of writers for failing to assimilate political
thought within a Christian framework, and he admired the casuists who
at least made the attempt. The people he most admired were those who
did not shirk the issue and did not reject the concept of reason of state.
His hero seems to have been the Anglican bishop Jeremy Taylor, who offered for him the crucial value of balance. Taylor assimilated policy and
maintained that in the end the proper criterion for judgment was the purpose for which power was used. Mosse wrote: "As long as tensions between religious presuppositions and realities of life exist, such casuistic
thought will always have great relevance in attempting to adjust the
Christian tradition to various forms of worldly wisdom and secular neces-
sities. The problem involved is to keep the balance between the Serpent
and the Dove, so that neither obliterates the other: for the victory of the
Dove can lead to unbridled idealism, and the ignoring of secular realities;
while the victory of the Serpent means the total acceptance of what the
sixteenth century called 'Machiavellism.'"[12]

    This way of proceeding shows up continuously in Mosse's later work.
Here I will give only one example—from a key chapter in *The Culture of
Western Europe*, first published in 1961, five years after he reoriented his
research agenda. This chapter, "Freedom and the Intellectuals," dealt
with central issues of humanism and analyzed the writings of figures such
as Benda and Rolland, who at that point in Mosse's life were very attractive to him. Benda had the fatal flaw, however, of not figuring out how to
engage politics. In Mosse's words, he "attempted to exalt . . . the image of
a free, reasonable, and moral man who rejected petty hatreds of an age of
anti-humanism and unchecked passions." But this appeal to rationalism
amid anti-rationalistic cultural forces failed in ways that Mosse's holy pre-
tenders did not fail—it found no way to mediate between idea and reality. "Seen in the context of the ruthlessness of twentieth-century political
and social movements, [Benda's solution] implied a withdrawal from so-

ciety, a retreat and half acceptance by intellectuals of those forces inim-
ical to liberty." Taking up Weber, Troeltsch, Gentile, and Croce in turn,
Mosse weighs each in terms of his ability to fuse humanistic values with
effective political intervention. But he has a hero in Romain Rolland to
match the seventeenth-century Jeremy Taylor: "One leading intellectual did attempt to fuse the idea of freedom with an appreciation of the
social forces which were reshaping his times." While Rolland sympa-
thized with the revolution and understood the importance of changes in
class-structured power configurations, he balanced that concern with
an emphasis on individual freedom. What Mosse liked about Rolland,
an admittedly forgotten figure, was his dialectical spirit, combining op-
posites in dynamic tension: "Romain Rolland is practically forgotten today. Perhaps his ideals seem more utopian than Croce's because they
combined sympathy for social revolution with an emphasis on freedom
of the mind. It could be argued, however, that he is more germane for
the present world crisis than the liberalism of Croce. Of all the intellectuals, he alone grasped the full implications of the social crisis of his
times, and he alone refused to abandon the freedom intellectuals must
have while resolutely accepting a solution which involved the destruction of bourgeois society."[13]

Mosse makes a similar point in *Germans and Jews* about left-wing
intellectuals during the 1920s: "We must realize the dangers inherent in
idealism that stresses the purity of absolute values and is apt to retreat into
its own circumscribed world in the face of a reality that will not bend to
the intellectuals' desire." He continues, "These men were not content to
build bridges from the present to the future but rather sought to bypass
such dreary work and leap across the stormy river." Thomas Mann
emerges as the crucial figure who finally struck the necessary balance. His
"objective was always the inner freedom of man, and now he realized that
this freedom must be linked to society, that there must be a balance between the rational as exemplified in working through existing political society, and the irrational expression of man's metaphysical impulse. Thus
he was able to find his way into a concrete political organization rather
than regarding such collaboration with reality 'foreign and inconceiv-
able.'"[14] Another case in point comes from *German Jews beyond Judaism:*
"The failure of Zweig and Ludwig to make meaningful contact with popular culture sums up the position not just of these authors but of an articulate and influential segment of German Jews."[15]

A second aspect already found in *The Holy Pretence*, it seems to me, is fundamental to Mosse's writing through to the end. It is also central to his teaching and is part of the didactic tenor of his work. I am not sure if what I am after can be captured by a single word, but different aspects of what I see in his work shade over into each other. A common feature of a Mosse text is its surprising, unexpected, almost jarring juxtaposition of things that do not seem to belong together. The procedure throws fresh light on the feature under analysis. This can seem outrageous or far-fetched or even evoke irritation on the part of the reader. Another aspect of what I am getting at could be brought under the heading of paradox or dilemma. In trying to get his audience to react, to see that there is no easy judgment to be made about historical actors, or even to see that the wrong people do the right thing or the right people do the wrong thing, Mosse was always concerned to make his audience understand that practical, everyday life is less open to immediate penetration than outside observers like to think. Let me offer an example from *The Holy Pretence* of these two aspects of his expository method. An unexpected juxtaposition or bringing together of disparate objects comes in his discussion of the Puritan theologian and statesman John Winthrop. Mosse wanted to underline his contention that Winthrop was of great importance in the history of political thought. Then comes the unexpected leap: "In some ways [Winthrop] is in a common tradition with that great nineteenth-century statesman who also thought of himself both as a Christian and as a master politician—Otto von Bismarck." Mosse used the comparison to make his didactic point even when warning the reader that what he is doing is "dangerous." His point was to put Winthrop in his context all the more firmly and to provide a perspective from which to pass judgment on him. "The New England Governor would have agreed that [personal] responsibility meant the necessity of controlling political power in order to fulfill the duties implicit in [the] relationship to God. But on the key issue of the assimilation of political ideas into the framework of Christian ethics, there is a great difference between the Christian statesman of the nineteenth century and the Puritan of the sixteenth."[16]

A contrasting example can be found in *Germans and Jews* where he juxtaposes Buber's rediscovery of the Hasidim and the contemporary German revival of Meister Eckhart and Jacob Böhme, or again, Buber's use of mythos paralleling that of Möller van den Bruck, or Buber the friend of Eugen Diederichs, or the contention that preoccupation with

Nietzsche and Hölderlin would make stronger Jews.[17] The very title of a chapter captures the juxtaposition of disparate elements—"Fascism and the Intellectuals"—as does his quoting Walter Benjamin to the effect that above all in a study of Goethe one finds one's Jewish substance.[18]

The other way disparate elements are made to work in Mosse's writings can be brought under the rubric of irony. This is fundamental for both 1957 texts. In *The Holy Pretence* he points out that Machiavellianism was indignantly rejected by English divines, who in reality assimilated Machiavelli quite readily. Analyzing closely the Puritan political doctrine of "prudence," he finds just another sophistry for "policy."[19] In his article on the image of the Jew, he notes that Gustav Freytag hoped that Jews could rise above the stereotype which Freytag himself had helped to create. He points out that Julius von Eckardt, who deplored "creeping anti-semitism," had a high regard for Freytag for hating intolerance. After describing in detail the development of the nineteenth-century German stereotype of the Jew, he suggests that many German Jews transformed this stereotype to Eastern Jews.[20] And there are many more examples: "The world view of the anti-fascists was close to fascist idealism."[21] The fascist "spiritual revolution" was hopelessly middle class.[22] The attitude of the pacifist von Ossietsky bore a "haunting similarity to that held by Weimar volkish critics."[23] In *German Jews beyond Judaism* he makes the following ironic comment about his students of the 1960s: "The Weimar left-wing heritage was especially appropriate for the revolt of those who had not come from the working class." And the deepest irony of all: "It was the German-Jewish *Bildungsbürgertum* which, more than any other single group, preserved Germany's better self across dictatorship, war, holocaust, and defeat."[24]

Let me end by juxtaposing two texts, one from 1957 and the other from 1985. From *The Holy Pretence:* "Thinking themselves surrounded by enemies on every side, the Divines . . . had to come to terms with that fact of life which Machiavelli described in his axiom that a man who wants to do good must perish among so many men who are evil. . . . The problem involved is to keep a balance between the Serpent and the Dove, so that neither obliterates the other."[25] From *German Jews beyond Judaism:* "The attempt to humanize nationalism is one of the most important legacies of German Jewry. . . . This is a part of Zionist history which demands to be written, and although it was aborted when it clashed with political reality, it did represent one of the few attempts in recent times to steer a

national revival from a narrow and provincial vision to a larger humanist
ideal, calling on patriotism rather than a nationalism which had plunged
Europe into some of the bloodiest wars of its history."[26]

Notes

1. Seymour Drescher, David Sabean, and Allan Sharlin, eds., *Political Symbolism in Modern Europe: Essays in Honor of George L. Mosse* (New Brunswick, N.J.: Transaction Books, 1982).

2. George L. Mosse, *Confronting History: A Memoir* (Madison: University of Wisconsin Press, 2000), 78.

3. Ibid., 115–16.

4. Ibid., 116.

5. Ibid., 174.

6. Ibid., 175.

7. Ibid., 178.

8. Ibid., 180.

9. George L. Mosse, *German Jews beyond Judaism* (Bloomington and Cincinnati: Indiana University Press and Hebrew Union College Press, 1985), 12.

10. George L. Mosse, *The Holy Pretense: A Study in Christianity and Reason of State from William Perkins to John Winthrop* (Oxford: Basil Blackwell, 1957), 9.

11. Ibid., 26.

12. Ibid., 154.

13. George L. Mosse, *The Culture of Western Europe: The Nineteenth and Twentieth Centuries: An Introduction* (Chicago: Rand McNally, 1961), 311, 312, 321, 322.

14. George L. Mosse, *Germans and Jews: The Right, the Left, and the Search for a "Third Force" in Pre-Nazi Germany* (New York: Howard Fertig, 1970), 31, 32, 213.

15. Mosse, *German Jews beyond Judaism*, 40.

16. Mosse, *The Holy Pretence*, 103.

17. Mosse, *Germans and Jews*, 87, 88, 96.

18. Mosse, *German Jews beyond Judaism*, 14, 144.

19. Mosse, *The Holy Pretence*, 147.

20. George L. Mosse, "The Image of the Jew in Popular Literature: Felix Dahn and Gustav Freytag," in *Germans and Jews*, pp. 61–76 (First published in *Leo Baeck Institute Year Book 2* [London: Secker and Warburg], 218–27).

21. Mosse, *Germans and Jews*, 148.

22. Ibid., 169.

23. Ibid., 171.

24. Mosse, *German Jews beyond Judaism*, 71, 82.

25. Mosse, *The Holy Pretence*, 153–4.

26. Mosse, *German Jews beyond Judaism*, 77.

The Modern Contexts of George Mosse's Early Modern Scholarship

Johann Sommerville

George Mosse is famous as a historian of sexuality and of modern cultural and intellectual history. Most of his readers begin with his writings on the nineteenth and twentieth centuries, and many never discover that he was also a scholar of the early modern period. With me, things were the other way around. I knew him as an early modernist long ago and only much later found that he had not in fact died—or gone into administration—sometime in the 1960s but had moved into the late modern period.

When I first heard of Mosse, it was as a prolific and penetrating analyst of sixteenth- and seventeenth-century history, and especially of political thought and religious ideas. Like many English high school and undergraduate students, I was exposed first of all to his *Europe in the Sixteenth Century*, written in collaboration with H. G. Koenigsberger and originally published in 1968. As a graduate student I encountered a number of his articles dating from the 1940s and 1950s as well as two books that were closely linked to the concerns of those articles. One of these was Mosse's very first book, *The Struggle for Sovereignty in England, from the Reign of Queen Elizabeth to the Petition of Right* (1950). This volume revised and extended his Harvard doctoral dissertation of 1946. The second book was *The Holy Pretence: A Study in Christianity and Reason of State from William Perkins to John Winthrop* (1957). Most of what follows is about these two books. Mosse observed that books take on a life of their own after they are published and that what happens to them often bears little relationship to their author's intentions. The paragraphs below are about the contexts in which the books were written and the rather different contexts in which they have lived their more recent lives.

A glance at Mosse's very lengthy bibliography (over three hundred items) suggests that between 1957 and 1960 he shifted his interests from early modern Europe, and especially England, to more recent times, to German and Jewish history and to the histories of nationalism, racism, and fascism. That is not to say that Mosse stopped publishing on the early modern period after 1960. I have already mentioned *Europe in the Sixteenth Century,* which appeared in 1968 and went into a much-revised and expanded second edition in 1989. In 1970 Mosse's essay on "Changes in Religious Thought" appeared in the volume of *The New Cambridge Modern History* devoted to the early seventeenth century. After 1970, though, nearly all his writings were on the late modern period (and, indeed, the 1970 essay was completed in 1959; it holds the record among Mosse's works for the length of time it took to reach print). Between 1949 and 1970 Mosse published two scholarly monographs, two textbooks, and fourteen articles on early modern European history. In addition, he produced several articles on the teaching and study of history in general, and he coedited materials for teaching Western civilization. When I was a graduate student this seemed to me like a reasonable output for a scholarly lifetime, and I assumed that Mosse's career had ended around 1970. It therefore came as a distinct surprise to me when I applied in 1988 for a post teaching early modern British history at the University of Wisconsin to discover that Mosse was not only alive and active but also on the search committee.

Although Mosse's interests shifted from the late 1950s, some themes are constant in his work on the modern and early modern eras. One is a stress on the need for solid empirical foundations as the basis for interpretation. A second is an emphasis on the importance of ideas in shaping historical action and on the irreducibility of ideas to social, political, or economic substructures. Particularly revealing on Mosse's attitudes in the 1940s and 1950s are two articles in *Social Studies* for 1949 and 1957, about teaching history to freshmen. The earlier article stressed the need to avoid the higher flights of theoretical fancy until we have firm factual knowledge. "Let us still teach the humdrum data," he advised, "before drawing inferences." "For the education of the citizen, towards which all general education strives," he wrote, "the terra firma of reality is vastly more important than the scholastic deduction from speculative and metaphysical absolutes." He did not think that we can recover reality with full and perfect objectivity, for he was well aware that no one is completely objective: "I know full well that all teaching of history implies interpretation, and that even Ranke interpreted while he extolled objectivity." But we can be more objective or less objective: "This is a matter of degree and not of absolutes." His message in 1949 was that we should try to be more rather than less objective and that in teaching freshmen we should prefer empiricism to theory, reality to metaphysics. He also stressed that American students should be taught about the European as well as the American past, since "the student is part of the tradition of both continents," and he insisted that social and economic history are not the only varieties of the subject worth teaching: "political history, though it may be the superstructure of economic and social movements, does influence and even help to determine the life of nations."[1]

By 1957, Mosse had come to attach rather greater importance to theories, metaphysics, and ideologies in the teaching of history to freshmen. He had not changed his mind about the need for historians to ground their conclusions on facts and to try to be objective. He certainly had not been converted to the thesis that there are no facts and that all metaphysical theories about the past are therefore equally acceptable. But he had come to believe that ideologies have in the past been of the utmost consequence in shaping action. And he had become convinced that a cardinal error of most American history textbooks was that they paid little or no attention to ideas: "Almost none of our texts," he declared, "show any realization that ideas can be weapons." The key reason for this failure, he argued, was to be found in American pragmatism, and particularly in the textbooks' assumption that "what moves history is the political and social-economic surroundings in which the struggle for life has its setting." Writers of American history books, he contended, reduced historical explanations to material terms and distorted or omitted ideas.[2]

He gave a number of examples, some pointing forward to his later researches, others referring to work he had already done on the early modern period. It was impossible, he asserted, to grasp why people in eastern Germany were taken in by the patently self-aggrandizing claims of the Communist Party if we did not appreciate the force of nationalism. To understand nationalism, he said, we need to read the novels of Gustav Freytag and others, and he reported that such literature had already been used successfully in undergraduate courses without producing, "as far as I know, any latter day National Socialists." Freytag's work featured in another article that Mosse published in 1957 and also in *The Crisis of German Ideology*, first printed in 1964. When Americans talked about puritanism, said Mosse, they tended to omit its religious elements and concentrate on its economic aspects, with the result that the freshman was "apt to leave our texts and courses thinking that the most important fact about Calvin is that he allowed usury." The textbooks, he affirmed, shied away from puritan theology "as if it were something un-American to have believed in original sin." By distorting puritanism, writers disguised from students important truths about their culture, for "Puritan ideals . . . are still a greater part of our lives than the differences between joint stock and proprietary colonies—a textbook favorite." Again, American scholars had little to say about "the question of religion and political morality which is currently occupying some of the best minds among our colleagues in Europe." The old explanation of the rise of absolutism in early modern Europe was in terms of "an alliance between King and middle classes," but this was inadequate, and it was clearly necessary to give weight to "concepts like 'reason of state' and 'sovereignty' which formed men's thinking and many men's actions in the process, concepts which became a very essential part of European political equipment." Mosse's first book was, of course, about sovereignty, and his second was about reason of state and the links between religion and political morality.[3]

In his early work on sovereignty and on reason of state, then, Mosse took very seriously ideas to which most American historians paid little attention, and the same was later true of his writings on such themes as fascism and German national consciousness. According to Mosse in 1957, there was one exception to the general American "fear of ideologies," for writers were happy enough to discuss freedom and democracy and their origins. What the textbooks especially avoided, he said, were "those abstractions which are 'pessimistic' about man and thus lead to absolutism rather than to democracy." There was evidence to support such claims. Mosse's own doctoral adviser was Charles Howard McIlwain, who wrote passionately about freedom and constitutional government in a number of works. McIlwain was a Pulitzer Prize–winning historian of early modern English and American constitutional and legal history, and political theory. He came to believe that states are ultimately governed either by force or by law. The rights of individuals and minorities, he claimed, can only be safeguarded where law rules, for any person or group who is above the law can trample on everyone's freedoms and reduce people to the position of slaves. Freedom can be preserved only if government is subjected to constitutional laws that it cannot change. According to McIlwain, it was in medieval England that constitutional government especially flourished, and from the English that other countries later learned constitutionalism. The United States, in particular, had taken key concepts and institutions from the English. But England itself had not proved faithful to its medieval past. In the early seventeenth century, King James I and his supporters had broken with older ideas by asserting that the king was an absolute monarch, above the law. His parliamentary critics responded by reasserting the supremacy of the constitution. Conflict on these points led to civil war under James's son Charles I. In the course of time, parliamentarians themselves abandoned their constitutionalism and opposed royal sovereignty not with constitutional law but with parliamentary sovereignty.[4]

Parliament's sovereign power was established in practice after 1689, argued McIlwain, and received its classic theoretical formulation in a book by John Austin published in 1832. For Austin, the sovereign in any state stands above the law, and law is nothing more than the command of the sovereign. In McIlwain's opinion, Austin's ideas constituted a "truly slavish theory of the state" that justified the oppression of minorities by the sovereign, whether that was a king or a majority of the people. Historically, the concept of sovereignty had been used to defend inequitable British policies toward the American colonies and toward Catholics and Dissenters at home. More recently, said McIlwain in 1939, an Austinian theory of sovereignty had underpinned Mussolini's suppression of nonfascist unions and associations in Italy. Sovereignty, he said, was no more acceptable in the hands of a government supported by the people than in those of a hereditary monarch. It was an "arbitrary government based on popular support which lately tore up the Weimar Constitution." The "best present-day representative" of Austinianism, he concluded, "is Herr Hitler."[5]

In McIlwain's scheme of things, the history of seventeenth-century England was of vital importance, for there the pernicious idea of sovereignty had first taken root. The notion that the king possessed sovereignty, he said, was clearly expressed by James I at (and just before) the very beginning of the century, and then by Filmer and Hobbes. McIlwain was less precise about when the theory of parliamentary sovereignty first arose, but he made it clear that the crucial period was after and not before 1640. During the political breakdown and Civil War of the 1640s, he claimed, Parliament in fact acted as a sovereign legislature, and this led to the formulation of "the doctrine of legislative sovereignty." Two of his students investigated the origins of English thinking on sovereignty in greater detail. One was Margaret Judson, who published *The Crisis of the Constitution* in 1949. The other was Mosse, whose *Struggle for Sovereignty* appeared the following year.[6]

Judson accepted McIlwain's basic framework, with a few modifications. She gave a precise date to the appearance of the doctrine of parliamentary sovereignty: 1642, when Henry Parker's *Observations upon Some of His Majesties late Answers and Expresses* was published. This accorded well with McIlwain's thesis that it was the political breakdown of the 1640s that led people to assert parliamentary sovereignty. However, whereas McIlwain had seen the period before 1640 as an age of conflict between royal absolutists and devotees of medieval constitutionalism, Judson contended that things were not so straightforward. Her book was a long and nuanced analysis of English political thought in the early seventeenth century, concluding that before 1642 people asserted neither parliamentary sovereignty nor—with very rare exceptions—the king's sovereignty. According to Judson's account, there were differences of principle among people in England before the Civil War, but they tended to be on matters of detail, not on the nature or location of sovereignty. It was the Civil War itself that subverted the old constitution and ushered in the new theory of legislative sovereignty.[7]

Judson's account left it rather unclear why civil war had broken out in England in 1642, or at it least implied that the war was not principally a consequence of ideological divisions. Mosse's *Struggle for Sovereignty* argued very differently, claiming that the war stemmed from political conflict that had roots in long-standing divisions over principle and that the concept of sovereignty lay at the very center of these divisions. Mosse's book was not in any straightforward sense a response to Judson, for her work was published too late for him to make much use of it, and his preface notes that their books "have different approaches and tend to different conclusions." Mosse did indeed differ from Judson—and also from their mentor, McIlwain. Judson and McIlwain dated the rise of parliamentary sovereignty to the years after 1642, but Mosse said that the idea was lucidly expressed in 1610 and that it became increasingly influential thereafter. From 1610 onward, he claimed, conflict between king and Parliament was "clearly inevitable." Judson thought the ideas of both royal and parliamentary sovereignty were rare before 1642; Mosse argued that they were common. McIlwain stressed the importance of

England; Mosse observed that the English derived the notion of sovereignty in considerable part from the Frenchman Jean Bodin, and he noted the impact of Continental thinkers on puritanism. McIlwain passionately criticized the Austinian (and Hobbesian and Filmerian) doctrine of sovereignty, suggesting that it had led to Hitler; Mosse adopted a calmer and more detached tone, though he did note that Harold Laski had suggested that the formal lack of rights of English individuals against the state could lead to problems at times when rapid change caused social divisions, and he described judicial review—which was incompatible with parliamentary sovereignty—as "the citadel of American constitutionalism." Mosse traced the idea of judicial review back to Sir Edward Coke, the great lawyer and legal scholar who was arguably the principal defender of medieval constitutionalism in the early seventeenth century. While McIlwain had stressed the prevalence of constitutionalist thinking as the main bastion against ideas of royal sovereignty before 1642, Mosse argued that the concept of parliamentary sovereignty was already significant, pointing out that Coke himself never fully determined whether Parliament was superior to the common law and the Constitution or vice versa. McIlwain linked the opposition of lawyers to the encroachments of royal power with puritanism. Mosse doubted that Coke's views had anything to do with puritanism.[8]

In *The Holy Pretence,* Mosse investigated the teachings of puritan and other clerics on politics and morality. Conventionally, secular Machiavellian ideas, which permitted the state to bend moral rules in the name of necessity or reason of state, had been contrasted with the rigid, otherworldly morality of the puritans. Mosse argued that through the medium of casuistry the puritans and other Christians themselves developed a morality that accommodated expediency. Puritans, he said, worked out "a theology which was well attuned to political action, and flexible enough to use all sorts of holy pretences." Whereas most historians linked "the emergence of a greater realism, both in the attitude towards nature and towards politics," with "the rise of secularism and the new sciences," Mosse suggested that "such a realism" sprang also "from changes within the theological framework itself, rather than from forces in opposition to it." The roots of the Enlightenment were to be found in Christian theological writings such as those of the Calvinist Jacques Saurin, who argued in the early eighteenth century that lying was justifiable in some circumstances. Deistic ideas could be traced back not just to Renaissance skeptics but also to radical puritans like the Leveller Richard Overton, who reached deistic conclusions from Christian premises, removing God from the world in order to absolve him from responsibility for human sinfulness.[9]

It is time to turn from Mosse's own aims and contexts to the later life of his writings. These—and especially *The Holy Pretence*—have been influential in work on casuistry, reason of state, and puritanism. Justin Champion and Richard Popkin, discussing the origins of deism and allied ideas in 1995, referred to Mosse's article on the subject as "still useful if little read." Historians of New England draw on Mosse's writings to document the influence there of English puritans such as William Perkins. The literary scholar Victoria Kahn, the historian of science Michael Hunter, and others have employed Mosse's work to substantiate points in connection with topics including the influence of Machiavelli, the ideas of Robert Boyle, and Shakespeare's *As You Like It*. Although *The Holy Pretence* is the most frequently cited of Mosse's early modern works, *Struggle for Sovereignty* has arguably had the most interesting fate, for after a long period of relative neglect it is now once again close to the center of debate over early modern English constitutional history.[10]

Mosse stressed the importance of ideologies in history, and McIlwain and Judson also—if in varying degrees—gave prominence to ideas as motors of political change in Stuart England. But in the 1950s and 1960s it was social rather than intellectual history that came into fashion, and for a long while scholars sought the origins of the seventeenth-century English Revolution in such phenomena as the rise of the gentry, the decline of the gentry, or the crisis of the aristocracy. By the 1970s this kind of approach had more or less played itself out, partly because no really convincing social explanation had been found for what happened in Stuart England, partly because class conflict was becoming outmoded as an explanation for political strife. In the 1970s and 1980s, political moderates in England came to see class hostilities as a leading cause of the country's economic problems. So-called revisionist historians—of whom Conrad Russell is the best known—began to argue that there had been no profound social conflicts in pre–Civil War England. They said that the war did not have long-term causes, whether social, economic, or ideological. According to the revisionists, there was no serious conflict in early Stuart England between advocates of royal absolutism and supporters of parliamentary sovereignty, for the English in fact virtually all endorsed their country's ancient constitution and rejected Continental ideas of absolute sovereignty. Revisionists were able to draw some comfort from Judson's work, which claimed that there had been few absolutists in early-seventeenth-century England. But they relied still more on John Pocock's *The Ancient Constitution and the Feudal Law*, published in 1957. A New Zealander by birth, Pocock did his doctoral work at Cambridge under Herbert Butterfield. As we saw, McIlwain linked the rise of sovereignty to despotism, fascism, and Hitler and linked English ancient constitutionalism to the preservation of freedom. In *The Englishman and His History*, published at Cambridge in 1944, Butterfield adopted a somewhat similar position, for like McIlwain he was concerned to defend ancient English constitutionalism. But the emphases of the two authors were very different. According to McIlwain, the constitutionalist tradition became corrupted in England during the seventeenth century with the reception of the concept of sovereignty; in America, however, the tradition survived, since judicial review trumped claims to sovereign power. Butterfield was not much interested in sovereignty or in the American constitution. His main contention was that the English had for centuries maintained a stable and free society while many other nations had undergone revolution and tyranny. The English, he claimed, were careful to avoid abrupt and revolutionary changes, preferring to retain their old traditions and to introduce reforms slowly and in piecemeal fashion. English political thinking centered on the concrete customs of the land, not on airy abstractions about universal rights and duties. Like Butterfield, Pocock asserted that early-seventeenth-century English thinking was rooted in the laws and customs of the realm, not in such abstract concepts as sovereignty or original contract. Both Butterfield and Pocock stressed the differences between the political ideas of English-speaking peoples on the one hand and those of the French and Germans on the other. One practical implication of this approach is to suggest that the English today would do better to ally themselves with peoples that share their traditions—such as the New Zealanders—than with the nations of Continental Europe.[11]

By the early 1980s, revisionism was well on the way toward becoming the new orthodoxy, despite the criticisms of such eminent historians as Christopher Hill and Jack Hexter. Over the last fifteen years or so, however, the revisionist position has come under vigorous attack, though it has been ably defended by scholars including Glenn Burgess, a New

Zealander who moved to England and gained his doctorate at Cambridge. In a series of books and articles, Burgess defended the basic claims of Russell and Pocock, including the propositions that England at the beginning of the seventeenth century was a harmonious society in which there were few divisions of political principle, and that English political thought was largely insular, rooted in the common law and ancient custom, and well calculated to promote consensus.[12]

As long as the focus of scholarly interest in seventeenth-century English history lay in the fields of social and economic history, Mosse's work was doomed to remain rather marginal. Once attention moved to ideology, his writings resumed their relevance. The intellectual historians John Salmon and Lisa Ferraro Parmelee, among others, have cited *The Struggle for Sovereignty* respectfully in the last few years. A more detailed and critical discussion of Mosse's book appears in the writings of the leading revisionist scholar Glenn Burgess. Burgess rightly notes that Mosse, unlike Pocock, did not take the common law to be pure custom, and he convincingly argues that Pocock was mistaken on this point, since lawyers asserted that the law was a product of reason as well as custom. But on other points Burgess rejects Mosse's arguments. Mosse claimed that when the English cited Jean Bodin it was usually in support of absolutist ideas. Burgess challenges the claim. Mosse argued that James VI of Scotland was an absolutist and that his ideas remained largely unchanged after he became king of England. Burgess takes issues with him on both of these points. More generally, Burgess's interpretation of early-seventeenth-century English history is diametrically opposed to Mosse's. While Mosse held that Bodin and other Continental theorists exercised considerable influence on English (and American) thought, Burgess and other revisionists stress the insularity of the English. Mosse contended that there were profound divisions among the English on fundamental questions of political principle and that conflict between king and Parliament was more or less inevitable by 1610. Burgess and other revisionists deny both that there were major ideological divisions and that the Civil War was inevitable until shortly before it actually happened, if then. Mosse emphasized the role of ideas in bringing political change. Most revisionists downplay ideology, and even Burgess—who does analyze ideas in detail—is more concerned with continuity than with change, and with suggesting that a conflict as serious as the Civil War can have— and did have—few or no ideological causes. Mosse argued that the concept of sovereignty was perfectly familiar across the political spectrum long before the Civil War but that disagreements over where it was located—in the monarch or in Parliament (the Crown and the two Houses)—caused conflict. According to the revisionists, there were precious few absolutists (of either the royal or parliamentarian variety).[13]

In the past decade and a half, the revisionist case has come under heavy fire, and Mosse's arguments seem not only relevant but also plausible. Many recent books and articles have put forward compelling arguments for questioning the idea that consensus prevailed in early Stuart England and that sweet harmony reigned in the ideological, social, and political spheres until the eve of the Civil War. Mosse's thesis that there were deep divisions of constitutional principle decades before the war is at least as convincing as the revisionist claim that there were none. Of course, much detailed research has been done since Mosse wrote, and not all of his judgments have stood the test of time. But his basic interpretation shows every sign of surviving vigorously in the twenty-first century.[14]

Perhaps still more valuable than the substantive conclusions Mosse reached, however, is the example he set on how to reach them. He was a historian of ideology who refrained from using his writings as a mere vehicle for promoting his own ideological agenda. While McIlwain spelled out the modern implications of his work and made plain his conviction that some past ideas were wickedly wrongheaded, Mosse brought detachment and even sympathy to his analysis of even such unpopular theories as royal absolutism. Like the best historians of ideas, he knew that ideologies are dangerous masters and that some values—like friendship and tolerance—are not worth sacrificing on their altar. Describing "the Mosse Milieu" in the 1960s, Paul Breines notes that Mosse engaged sympathetically with students whose views he did not share and that he did not allow ideological differences to get in the way of personal friendship. He comments—in words with which I will end—that "This historian of ideologies, who has unrelentingly stressed their primacy in history, has lived according to the assumption of their weakness in personal life."[15]

Notes

I am grateful to Paul Grendler for allowing me to read the typescript of his essay "The Renaissance and Cultural History: From Mosse to the Millennium," which contains valuable information on Mosse's approach to cultural and intellectual history and on the modern historiography of the Renaissance.

1. George L. Mosse, "Freshman History: Reality or Metaphysics?" *Social Studies* 40 (1949): 99–103, qtd. 100, 102–3, 101. Some remarks on Mosse's two articles in *Social Studies* are in Peter Novick, *That Noble Dream: "The "Objectivity Question" and the American Historical Profession* (Cambridge: Cambridge University Press, 1988), 312, 315.

2. George L. Mosse, "The Pragmatism of the Freshman History Course," *Social Studies* 48 (1957): 289–91, qtd. 289.

3. Ibid., 290, 291 (Freytag and nationalism), 290 (Calvin, original sin), 289–90 (absolutism, sovereignty, and reason of state). George L. Mosse, "The Image of the Jew in German Popular Culture: Felix Dahn and Gustav Freytag," in *Leo Baeck Institute Yearbook* 2 (London: Secker & Warburg, 1957), 218–27; George L. Mosse, *The Crisis of German Ideology: Intellectual Origins of the Third Reich* (1964; New York: Schocken, 1981), 20, 126–28, 163 (Freytag).

4. Mosse, "Pragmatism of the Freshman History Course," 290. Charles Howard McIlwain, *Constitutionalism Ancient and Modern* (Ithaca: Cornell University Press, 1940), 100 (England), 114–16 (James I). McIlwain, *Constitutionalism and the Changing World* (Cambridge: Cambridge University Press, 1939), 63–64 (emergence of parliamentary sovereignty).

5. McIlwain, *Constitutionalism and the Changing World*, 61–62 (1689), 57 (truly slavish theory; colonies, Catholics and Dissenters), 33 (Mussolini), 85 (Hitler).

6. McIlwain, *The High Court of Parliament and Its Supremacy: An Historical Essay on the Boundaries between Legislation and Adjudication in England* (New Haven: Yale University Press, 1910), 95–96.

7. Margaret Atwood Judson, *The Crisis of the Constitution: An Essay in Constitutional and Political Thought in England, 1603–1645* (New Brunswick: Rutgers University Press, 1949), passim, esp. 386, 423, 425. The standard modern account of Henry Parker and his thought is Michael Mendle, *Henry Parker and the English Civil War: The Political Thought of the Public's "Privado"* (Cambridge: Cambridge University Press, 1995). A good modern survey of political thinking in the English Civil War is John Sanderson, *"But the People's Creatures": The Philosophical Basis of the English Civil War* (Manchester: Manchester University Press, 1989).

8. Mosse, *Struggle for Sovereignty*, vi (his book and Judson's), 84 (parliamentary sovereignty in 1610), 107, 119, 128 (parliamentary sovereignty in 1620s), 88 (conflict clearly inevitable from 1610), 30–33, 37–38 (influence of Bodin), 178 (Laski), 179 (judicial review), 160 (Coke on parliament), 150 (Coke on puritan). McIlwain, *Constitutionalism Ancient and Modern*, 99 (common lawyers and puritans). Mosse, "Pragmatism of the Freshman History Course," 291 (influence of Continental thinkers on puritanism). Mosse also discussed Bodin's influence in England in "The Influence of Jean Bodin's *République* on English Political Thought," *Medievalia et Humanistica* 5 (1948): 73–83. Mosse saw Bodin as essentially an absolutist, who influenced royal absolutists in England, though some of these reduced the limitations on royal power, and especially the king's power over property, which Bodin derived from natural law: ibid., esp. 79–81; *Struggle for Sovereignty*, 422, 62, 106, 139. McIlwain saw Bodin not as an absolutist but a constitutionalist and stressed that in Bodin's theory the sovereign was subject to customary or even man-made constitutional rules: *Constitutionalism and the Changing World*, 38–39, 53, 55, 69, 72–74.

9. George L. Mosse, *The Holy Pretence: A Study in Christianity and Reason of State from William Perkins to John Winthrop* (Oxford: Basil Blackwell, 1957), 152. Mosse, "The

Importance of Jacques Saurin in the History of Casuistry and the Enlightenment," *Church History* 25 (1956): 195–210. Mosse, "Puritan Radicalism and the Enlightenment," *Church History* 29 (1960): 424–39, esp. 431–32, 436.

10. J. A. I. Champion with the assistance of R. H. Popkin, "Bibliography and Irreligion: Richard Smith's 'Observations on the report of a Blasphemous Treatise,' c. 1671," *Seventeenth Century* 10 (1995): 77–99, qtd. 90n. 5. Avihu Zakai, "Theocracy in New England: The Nature and Meaning of the Holy Experience in the Wilderness," *Journal of Religious History* 14 (1986): 133–51, refers to several of Mosse's writings on the English context of American puritanism. Edward H. Davidson, "John Cotton's Biblical Exegesis: Method and Purposes," *Early American Literature* 17 (1982): 119–38, qtd. 134n. 6, cites Mosse on Perkins's influence in New England. Mosse is cited in connection with John Winthrop in Scott Michaelsen, "John Winthrop's 'Modell' Covenant and the Company Way," *Early American Literature* 27 (1992): 85–100, qtd. 95n. 1. Another article on New England that draws on Mosse is Adam Seligman, "Inner-worldly Individualism and the Institutionalization of Puritanism in Late-Seventeenth-Century New England," *British Journal of Sociology* 41 (1990): 537–57, qtd. 554n. 11. Victoria Kahn draws on Mosse's writings in "Revisiting the History of Machiavellism: English Machiavellism and the Doctrine of Things Indifferent," *Renaissance Quarterly* 46 (1993): 526–61, qtd. 539n. 27, 545n. 36, and in "Political Theology and Reason of State in *Samson Agonistes*," *South Atlantic Quarterly* 95 (1996): 1065–97, qtd. 1093n. 37. Another article that refers to Mosse in connection with the influence of Machiavelli is Anne Jacobson Schutte, "An Early Stuart Critique of Machiavelli as Historiographer: Thomas Jackson and the *Discorsi*," *Albion* 15 (1983): 1–18, qtd. 1nn. 1–3. Narasingha Prosad Sil, "Political Morality vs. Political Necessity: Kautilya and Machiavelli Revisted," *Journal of Asian History* 19 (1985): 101–42, qtd. 111, uses *The Holy Pretence* in an Asian context. Michael Hunter refers to *The Holy Pretence* in "Casuistry in Action: Robert Boyle's Confessional Interviews with Gilbert Burnet and Edward Stillingfleet, 1691," *Journal of Ecclesiastical History* 44 (1993): 80–98, qtd. 81n. 2. Mosse's work is used to elaborate the context of *As You Like It* in Robert Schwartz, "Rosalynde among the Familists: *As You Like It* and an Expanded View of Its Sources," *Sixteenth Century Journal* 20 (1989): 69–76, qtd. 71. Some remarks on Mosse's interpretation of Anglican casuistry are in Johann P. Sommerville, "The New Art of Lying: Equivocation, Mental Reservation, and Casuistry," in *Conscience and Casuistry in Early Modern Europe*, ed. Edmund Leites (Cambridge: Cambridge University Press, 1988), 159–84, qtd. 180–81n. 40.

11. Judson is cited in support of revisionism by Conrad Russell, *Parliaments and English Politics, 1621–1629* (Oxford: Clarendon Press, 1979), qtd. 54n. 2, and by Glenn Burgess, *Absolute Monarchy and the Stuart Constitution* (New Haven: Yale University Press, 1996), 93, 113–14. Herbert Butterfield sets out his views in *The Englishman and His History* (Cambridge: Cambridge University Press, 1944), passim. J. G. A. Pocock's account of the insular common-law mind of most Englishmen is found in *The Ancient Constitution and the Feudal Law: A Study of English Historical Thought in the Seventeenth Century: A Reissue with a Retrospect* (1957; Cambridge: Cambridge University Press, 1987), 30–69.

12. Criticisms of revisionism include J. H. Hexter, "Power Struggle, Parliament, and Liberty in Early Stuart England," in *Journal of Modern History* 50 (1978): 1–50; Hexter, "The Early Stuarts and Parliament: Old Hat and the Nouvelle Vague," *Parliamentary History Yearbook* 1 (1982): 181–216; Christopher Hill, "Parliament and People in Seventeenth-Century England," *Past and Present* 92 (1981): 100–124; Derek Hirst, "Revisionism Revised: The Place of Principle," *Past and Present* 92 (1981): 79–99; Richard Cust and Ann Hughes, eds., *Conflict in Early Stuart England: Studies in Religion and Politics,*

1603–1642 (London: Longman, 1989); and J. P. Sommerville, *Royalists and Patriots: Politics and Ideology of England, 1603–1640* (London: Longman, 1999). Among the relevant writings of Glenn Burgess are "The Divine Right of Kings Reconsidered," *English Historical Review* 107 (1992): 837–61; *The Politics of the Ancient Constitution: An Introduction to English Political Thought, 1603–1642* (London: Macmillan,1992); and *Absolute Monarchy and the Stuart Constitution.*

13. J. H. M. Salmon, "The Legacy of Jean Bodin: Absolutism, Populism, or Constitutionalism," *History of Political Thought* 17 (1996): 500–522, qtd. 514. Lisa Ferraro Parmelee, *Good Newes from Fraunce: French Anti-League Propaganda in Late Elizabethan England* (Rochester, N.Y.: University of Rochester Press, 1996), 98, 191. Some other examples of recent references to Mosse's *Struggle for Sovereignty* are Michael Ross Fowler and Julie Marie Bunck, "What Constitutes the Sovereign State?" *Review of International Studies* 22 (1996): 381–404, qtd. 399n. 86, and Craig M. Rustici, "'The Great Sophism of All Sophisms': Colonialist Redefinition in Bacon's *Holy War*," *Renaissance and Reformation/Renaissance et Réfpre* 16, no. 4 (1992): 49–72, qtd. 71n. 46. Glenn Burgess, "Common Law and Political Theory in Early Stuart England," *Political Science* 40 (1988): 4–17, qtd. 5 (common law, custom, and reason); *Absolute Monarchy and the Stuart Constitution*, 26–27 (James I), 64–65, 79 (Bodin). Mosse, *Struggle for Sovereignty*, 88 (conflict inevitable after 1610). The ideas of Mosse and Burgess on Bodin are discussed in D. Alan Orr, *Treason and the State: Law, Politics, and Ideology in the English Civil War* (Cambridge: Cambridge University Press, 2002), 34

14. An interpretation of the period that in many ways coincides with Mosse's is in Sommerville, *Royalists and Patriots,* which draws on Mosse's *Struggle for Sovereignty* at 228 and points out some of the problems involved in Burgess's account at 228–62.

15. Paul Breines, "The Mosse Milieu," in *History and the New Left. Madison, Wisconsin, 1950–1970,* ed. Paul Buhle (Philadelphia: Temple University Press, 1990), 246–51, qtd. 250.

Part 2
Mosse and Fascism

A Provisional Dwelling

The Origin and Development of the Concept of Fascism in Mosse's Historiography

Emilio Gentile

I too wanted to be an intellectual not tied down to time and place, solely guided by his analytical mind—something of an eternal traveler, analyzing, observing, suspended above events. My view of history encouraged such an attitude, since it recognized the need for empathy even with those considered evil and dangerous.

George L. Mosse, *Confronting History: A Memoir*

The "Mosse Revolution"

George L. Mosse developed his interpretation of fascism over the course of a long and productive career of research and reflection that spanned nearly four decades. It is significant that the last book he published, *The Fascist Revolution*, is a collection of the essays that marked, between 1961 and the late 1990s, the various stages in the development of his interpretation of fascism. In its introduction, Mosse synthesized the results of his research and the criteria that had inspired and guided it, and he reasserted the validity of the cultural approach he had introduced in the study of the fascist phenomenon. With legitimate pride he indicated in his cultural interpretation of fascism one of the factors responsible for the progress achieved by historiography "in our understanding of fascism as it existed in its epoch, overturning most older interpretations and reevaluating its consequences,"[1] because "the cultural interpretation of fascism opens up a means to penetrate fascist self-understanding, and such empathy is crucial in order to grasp how people saw the movement, something which cannot be ignored or evaluated merely in retrospect. . . .

Cultural history centers above all upon the perceptions of men and women, and how these are shaped and enlisted in politics at a particular place and time."[2]

Mosse conducted his research primarily in the area of Nazism, but he always had, as frame of reference and orientation, a comprehensive view of the fascist phenomenon, for he was convinced of the existence, between the two world wars, of a European fascism made up of movements that shared many features. Mosse was equally convinced, however, that among the various fascisms there were important and substantial differences, even between its two main expressions, Italian fascism and Nazism. Specifically, Mosse felt that racism and anti-Semitism were not basic elements in all fascist movements, whereas they were essential in Nazism. In the latter case, moreover, Mosse long insisted—with a certain inclination toward the theory of *Sonderweg*—on the specificity and uniqueness within the fascist phenomenon, due to the peculiarity of the *völkisch* ideology, of racism and anti-Semitism, even though he rejected the "from Luther to Hitler" formula and categorically ruled out the notion of the inevitability of Nazism determined by German history.

Such was the framework within which Mosse developed his concept of fascism. To the formulation of a general theory of fascism he devoted only a few specific essays: the chapters on fascism and Nazism in *The Culture of Western Europe,* published in 1961 and republished in 1974, with a substantially revised chapter on fascism; the article "The Genesis of Fascism," published in 1966 in the first issue of the *Journal of Contemporary History;* and, above all, in the long essay "Toward a General Theory of Fascism," published in 1979. However, even when they do not deal directly with fascism or Nazism but rather with nationalism, racism, the myth of the war experience, sexuality, or masculinity, all of Mosse's books and articles on contemporary history include observations that have broadened, rectified, nuanced, or fine-tuned his definition of fascism, without, however, modifying the basic structure of his view of the whole phenomenon as he had outlined it as early as 1961.

In Mosse's historical writings, the development of the concept of fascism can be divided into two main phases. The first belongs to the years from 1961 to 1966, during which Mosse laid out the basic principles of his interpretation, focusing primarily on the problem of ideology and culture, a problem he envisaged at the time in mainly traditional terms, that is to say, as a complex of ideas representing an interpretation of life and a solution to the problems of existence formulated by means of *verbal* expression. The second phase—in my view, the more innovative one—falls between 1969 and 1975, when mass politics becomes the central problem of his analysis of fascism, with the reformulation of the concept of culture in the sense of a vision of the totality of life interpreted through myths, rituals, and symbols in which visual and aesthetic representation and political style acquire decisive importance.

Critically reconstructing the development of the concept of fascism in Mosse's work is a complex task that cannot be fully accomplished within the limits of this essay. Here I shall deal only with those moments in the development of his concept of fascism that I consider most important, both on account of their originality and because of the influence they have had on the study and, above all, on our own perception of fascism as a historical phenomenon. Mosse contributed significantly to renovating the study of fascism and, above all, to modifying substantially our historical perception of it. He introduced new perspectives and concepts, such as "new politics," "nationalization of the masses," and "antibourgeois bourgeois revolution," just to recall those that by now have been permanently incorporated in contemporary historiography and are profitably used even by historians who do not fully share Mosse's interpretation of fascism. I believe we can speak without exaggeration of a "Mosse revolution" in the historiography on fascism, a revolution consisting first of all in the novelty of his method of analysis, which in turn was a consequence of a way of envisaging history and the historian's task which has been an integral and essential part of the "Mosse revolution." This method is a cultural approach that gradually developed in Mosse's historiography alongside the concept of fascism and his understanding of history and the historian's role. For this reason it will be necessary to link the evolution of the concept of fascism with the evolution of Mosse's historiography. One final preliminary remark regarding Mosse's work on fascism. I believe that the cultural approach to the problem of fascism was for Mosse not merely the consequence of a methodological choice but also the consequence of an existential need that we must keep in mind, as an inescapable starting point of our inquiry, in order better to understand the genesis, the development, and the character of his concept of fascism.

The Fascination of the Persecutor: Between
Autobiography and Historiography

For Mosse, understanding fascism—its origin, its nature, its significance in contemporary history, and above all why it fascinated millions
of people—was a cultural, moral, and political challenge that engrossed
him both as a man and as a historian. The fundamental question that inspired his research was always the same: how fascism "could attract so
much popular support and govern by consensus for some time after it
took power."[3] Mosse was a victim of Nazism who wanted to know the fascination of his persecutor by penetrating inside his mind, by studying the
ideas, the mentality, the principles, the values, the myths, and the symbols
through which he interpreted himself and reality, prefigured the world he
wanted to bring into existence, and defined the forms and the methods of
action aimed at making it a reality. In that question there was not only the
need for rational knowledge but also the impulse of an emotional involvement that went beyond the condition of victim in that it made him,
in a certain sense, a participant in the irrational presuppositions that were
at the origin of the fascination of the persecutor and of the mass consensus that the latter had generated. In his memoirs Mosse recalls how, as a
boy in the Salem boarding school, he had shared the myths of German nationalism that paved the way for the triumph of Nazism: "The school also
gave me a first taste of nationalism, which at the time I found congenial;
there was a danger that it might provide the belief system I so sadly
lacked. . . . When as a historian much later I wrote about German nationalism, I did have an insight into its truly seductive nature."[4] He tells us,
moreover, that he personally experienced—in Germany, France, England, and Italy—the involvement of the individual in the exciting rhythm
of mass movements,[5] which was one of the primary causes of fascist se-
duction, and that he even felt the charismatic fascination of Nazi rallies.
He was fourteen or fifteen years old, he said in a 1990 interview, when he
watched Nazi demonstrations in front of his family's home in Berlin. "The
impression was so great, in fact, that I ran away from home, it must have
been in 1932, and went to a Hitler rally. I must admit, even today, that it
was an experience. I was swept away. First there were the masses of
people; that was very captivating to be in the middle of it all. But it was
also Hitler, if I remember correctly."[6] Finally, Mosse has admitted in his
memoirs that even as an adult he could feel the emotion of myths and rit-

uals that his rationality as a historian rejected and had tried to demystify, convinced as he was, as he wrote in *Masses and Man,* that it was "the task of the historian to destroy old myths in order to encourage new confrontations with reality."[7]: "I knew the danger of being captured by images and liturgy and had written often enough about their use in manipulating people, but I myself was far from immune to the irrational forces which as a historian I deplored—especially when it came to that group which I regarded as my own."[8]

By becoming a historian of himself and of his own work, Mosse in his memoirs explicitly formulated his historiographical "creed": "As a trained historian I have some practice in attempting to go back in time to see how people living then understood their world. I have always believed that empathy is the chief quality a historian needs to cultivate. Empathy means putting contemporary prejudice aside while looking at the past without fear or favor."[9] Further on he reiterates this concept even more explicitly and decisively: "It is my firm belief that a historian in order to understand the past has to empathize with it, to get under its skin, as it were, to see the world through the eyes of its actors and its institutions."[10] His notion of history, stimulated by the impulse of his personal involvement in the tragedy of Nazism, "encouraged such an attitude, since it recognized the need for empathy even with those considered evil and dangerous."[11] In the chapter devoted to the historian's work, Mosse strongly reaffirmed his historiographical "creed":

History for me took the place of religion, with the advantage that history is open-ended and not exclusive, for one cannot understand one's own history or the history of one's ethnicity without trying to understand the motivation of others, whether they are friendly or hostile. A historian, if he is to get history right, cannot be bigoted or narrow-minded. Empathy is for me still at the core of the historical enterprise, but understanding does not mean withholding judgment. I have myself mainly dealt with people and movements whom I judged harshly, but understanding must precede an informed and effective judgment.[12]

In keeping with these theoretical premises, Mosse studied fascism on its own irrational and mythical terms without watering down in the least his antifascist convictions: "I hoped that the books which resulted would contribute to an understanding of National Socialism and fascism; books, in my view, are the true voice of antifascism today, when the immediate menace which had stimulated my earlier antifascist involvement is long past."[13]

The intertwining of autobiography and historiography had a decisive importance on how Mosse analyzed and interpreted fascism. "The attempt to make sense out of the history of my own century," he wrote in his memoirs, "was also a means of understanding my own past."[14] This statement was in keeping with his concept of history. Mosse liked to quote the words of historian W. K. Ferguson: "What man is only history tells."[15] From Benedetto Croce's humanistic historicism Mosse had derived his "creed" as a historian: all human reality is history and nothing but history, and historiography is inseparable from the historian's personality.

Mosse was no theorist of history and historiography. Besides, by temperament he was more inclined to the all-embracing intuition of a problem or a phenomenon than to the detailed analysis structured in complex conceptual architectures. His innovations, it has been written, consist "in having a broad vision, in putting seemingly disparate topics together, in getting the big picture. He transcends the specificity of his researches to arrive at a synthetic analysis."[16] His historiographic style is characterized by evocative representation supported by very concise hypotheses and definitions and accompanied by demonstrative examples, without it being developed through a systematic conceptual argumentation. For this reason some have ascribed the originality of his investigations and of his ideas on fascism to an intuitive talent, to occasional "inspirations," or to fortunate discoveries of unexplored fields that other historians had either ignored or neglected. Unquestionably, Mosse had a remarkable intuition for identifying in historical phenomena basic problems, aspects, and connections that other historians were neglecting. His inexhaustible curiosity, his joyous passion for history, his desire to understand the totality of human experiences, even the most horrific—these were no doubt at the root of many of his findings. The novelty of his representation of fascism owes a great deal to his highly personal sensitivity, a sensitivity I would describe as that of an *artist of history* capable of evoking, in their context and in their own spirit, ideas, myths, mentalities, states of mind, the ways movements behaved, all of which were repugnant to his enlightened and liberal culture. He observed Nazism, fascism, nationalism, and racism with a predisposition I would go so far as to define as "Nietzschean"; that is to say, he placed himself, for knowledge's sake, beyond good and evil, or to be more precise, beyond his own concepts of good and evil. Mosse tried to place himself *inside* those movements in order to understand their views on life, their mentality, their world of ideas, myths, and values, setting them in their historical context, observing them through their own perceptions and mental attitudes, with a sort of "participating intuition." And yet, even though it was conditioned by his personal experience and taste, his cultural approach was the application of a rational method of historical analysis that acknowledged the presence and the power of the irrational in contemporary politics: "The chief problem facing any historian is to capture the irrational by an exercise of the rational mind. This becomes easier when the irrational is made concrete through rational acts within the terms of its own ideological framework."[17]

The Roots of a Cultural Approach

Mosse began to work on Nazism and fascism in the late 1950s, at a time when his major scholarly interests still lay primarily with the constitutional history and the political and religious thought of the sixteenth and seventeenth centuries. In terms of both content and style, his studies in early modern history have a quite different character from the studies in contemporary history he began publishing in 1957. And yet I believe there is a link between the historian of the political and religious thought of the sixteenth and seventeenth centuries and the historian of fascism, a link that establishes a continuity of development in terms of both problems and methodology. The problems and the movements Mosse dealt with always belonged to periods of social, political, and spiritual upheavals, periods that witnessed the confrontation of different views on life, the world, and politics, such as the confrontation between Christian tradition and Machiavellianism, the ideology of "reason of state" and the Enlightenment, or the "religious cataclysm"[18] represented by the Reformation which marked the passage from the Middle Ages to the modern era: "Such rapid changes in history," Mosse wrote in 1953 in *The Reformation,* "usually come about when the gulf between what is and what should be, between outward reality and the human condition, becomes painfully apparent. At that point a leader can spark an attempt to bring to an end the dilemma created by such a situation. Luther was such a leader and he as well as the other reformers found Europe prepared for their message."[19]

The passage I have just quoted already contained the nucleus of the cultural approach Mosse was to develop through his historiography on fascism. Historical knowledge meant for Mosse interpreting past phenomena in their historical context, examining them according to the mentality and the ideas of their time, without ever projecting on the past, retrospectively, problems and concepts that belonged to the historian's present world. "History must not be read backward," he wrote in 1957 as he took issue with the thesis that saw the origins of modern democracy in Calvinism: "If we define democracy as the election of their rulers by all the people, and the constant scrutiny by the governed of those so elected, a government so defined would have meant anarchy to men of the sixteenth century."[20] As a consequence, the historian's task was to understand how the people of that time perceived and interpreted the world in which they lived according to the prevailing ideas and values of their time, even if this might be far from easy when the historian had to face ways of thinking of the past that were different from his or her own mentality and from his or her own categories of interpretation of life: "in our more pragmatic age this seems difficult to understand, but the key role of what we now call ideology for men of the sixteenth century cannot be underrated."[21] The reference to "our more pragmatic age" is significant, for it echoes Mosse's polemical attitude vis-à-vis the positivism and pragmatism of that historiography which interprets historical phenomena only through rationalistic and utilitarian categories, political and economic, giving weight exclusively to power plays and class interests, while minimizing the role of ideologies which it views as a mere superstructure of economic reality or as instruments of a naked will to power.

I have argued that Mosse was no historical theorist, but that does not mean he was indifferent to the methodology of historical analysis. On the contrary, as I will show, the most innovative moments of his historiography on fascism were, from the start, preceded and accompanied by methodological reflections connected by the coherent development of some fundamental ideas. For instance, the concept of "historical continuity," the necessity of "a sense of constant historical development," which would prove of decisive importance in Mosse's interpretation of the place of fascism in European history, appears already in a 1949 article on freshman history where he criticized the tendency to interpret an entire epoch according to abstract "ideal types" in order to "synthesize the unsynthesizable," because "this search for the 'ideal type,' whether it be a man or a century, certainly neglects the elements of continuity and development which are involved in obtaining an historical perspective upon the present."[22] Over against a "metaphysical" history of "ideal types" Mosse defended the history of facts as the indispensable basis of every interpretation: "The facts are there. They cannot be ignored, and history without them may be a course in humanities or in speculative philosophy, but it is no longer history. Let us teach the humdrum data first before drawing inferences. . . . Any synthesis must be based upon the scope of facts, and the teaching of freshman history must still be largely a matter of putting across a solid framework of historical data." The article concluded hoping for a form of teaching capable of getting across "the many-sided problems of human behavior" and of providing the sense and the rhythm of history as "a continuous process," while grounding historical interpretations on the complexity of the human reality.

Mosse went back to discussing the methodology of history in 1957. The year is significant, for it marks a decisive turning point in the development of his historiography as it quickly followed his move from the University of Iowa to the University of Wisconsin, where Mosse was also asked to teach European cultural history of the nineteenth and twentieth centuries. In that year, in addition to the book *The Holy Pretence*, which still dealt with the history of the sixteenth century, there appeared his first study on the problem of Nazism in which he investigated the diffusion of the image of the Jew in the German popular culture of the nineteenth century through the novels of Felix Dahn and Gustav Freytag.[23] The publication of this article marked not only Mosse's entrance into the field of studies on Nazism and fascism but also the start of an important renovation in his method of historical analysis, a renovation determined, in my view, precisely by the necessity to confront phenomena such as anti-Semitism, National Socialism, and fascism with new categories, as he felt that those then prevailing in historiography were inadequate for understanding the nature of those movements. In that same year, in fact, Mosse also published a polemical article on the "pragmatic approach" then prevalent in American historiography, because he considered it "a kind of environmental determinism" based on the principle that "what moves history are the political and socio-economic surroundings in which the struggle for life has its setting. What this has meant is failure to deal with abstract thought and political rationalization."[24] The pragmatic approach, according to Mosse, had a "fear of ideology" and did not understand that "ideas can be weapons" and that "how men rationalize their actions often determines what actions they take." Mosse, on the contrary, deemed it necessary to introduce students to the knowledge of "categories of thought which have determined the outlook, and therefore also motivated actions of men in vital stages of their historical development," such as the idea of "reason of state" or nationalism. In the latter case, Mosse wrote, "we are dealing with a 'mood' rather than something that can be analyzed through political or economic factors alone." The knowledge of political and economic facts was not sufficient for understanding historical periods in which events were conditioned by decisive clashes between opposing ways of interpreting life and politics itself. "Sometimes evolutions in thought can have more long range importance than barricades and it may just be possible that to know about Thomas Hobbes is as important as to identify Marshal Radetzki." In this sense, Mosse stressed the importance of the study of popular culture which contributes to shape people's attitudes and reveals their perceptions of life and of the world in which they operate. From reading Freytag's novels, which had influenced the way of thinking of generations of Germans, the scholar, Mosse explained, could draw "a deeper understanding of German Nationalism . . . than from many a chronological and external account of its development."

Here it is evident how, in Mosse's historiography, the development of research has always been joined by the revision of the method of historical analysis through notations and reflections that defined his interpretative categories. The article on the image of the Jew was, in fact, the earliest concrete application of the method of historical analysis sketched in the article on the "pragmatic approach." Mosse demonstrated the importance of studying popular culture for knowing the formation and diffusion of stereotypes and attitudes that paved the way to the rise of Nazism and favored its success:

The creation of the image of the Jew ran outside any serious political and social analysis, and that was its power. It could in this way provide the emotional foundations for the totalitarian way of solving these problems. There must have been many others who, like Hitler, when faced with real problems, first awakened to the stereotype of the "Jew" and then built their ideology around it. To be sure, anti-Jewish feeling only acquires particular relevance when it is combined with political issues or when Jewish group interests conflict with other powerful interests, but it would not be able to acquire any relevance at all without the support and preconditioning of popular culture. That is why we must give more attention to such cultural investigations and modify our exclusive concentration upon social, political, or economic analysis. Only in this way will we be able to fathom the continued influence of anti-Semitism which seems in a distressing way to antedate and to outlast its immediate political or social relevance.[25]

This article is significant for our investigation because in it Mosse first analyzes the ideological dimension not in the traditional form of formally elaborated political or religious thought, as he had done in his earlier studies, but as the locus of formation of "stereotypes" and "attitudes" through novels that were of modest quality yet very popular. In this article Mosse used the concept of "attitudes," explicitly echoing the historian William O. Aydelotte, who had stressed the importance of popular literature for knowing "attitudes which, though they may be trivial in themselves, yet to the extent that they are widely shared, underlie and motivate basic historical changes." Here was the first important innovation in his methodology in connection with the study of the problem of Nazism. Another important element for the genesis of the concept of fascism that emerges from this article is the link Mosse ascertained between the formation of anti-Semitic stereotypes and "the need for integration" of the middle class as it felt threatened in an age of rapid economic and social transformations and aspired to find stability and security by strengthening its ties to the organic roots of the *Volk* against the disruptive forces of modernity that were identified with "this segment of the population as the rootless, unsettled class which defies integration with the *Volk*. This class includes the migratory worker, but also the journalist, the bureaucrat and, above all, the Jews."

In this way Mosse made his entrance in the historiography of Nazism and fascism, asserting in a clear and decisive manner the importance of seriously studying the ideological aspects of these movements, in sharp contrast to the entire traditional historiography, which ignored them as being devoid of importance or unworthy of serious consideration. Historians, Mosse wrote in 1958, "have never been at home in *outré* subjects, and no subject is more *outré* than the National Socialist view of Jew and Aryan. And then these views did not seem absurd at all to many respectable members of the community who embraced them. Such racial attitudes, ridiculous to most Western intellectuals, had been prepared by popular novelists for more than a century before National Socialism came to power."[26] Mosse believed that historians must take seriously the ideology of National Socialism, because it was the product of a current of thought that had taken shape long before the birth of the Nazi Party, and because, for this very reason, it had been one of the decisive conditions for its success. As Mosse wrote in 1961 in "The Mystical Origins of National Socialism":

Today we are forced to realize that a more complex cultural development gave its impress to that movement long before it crystallized into a political party. At the very center of this development were ideas which were not so much of a national as of a romantic and mystical nature, part of the revolt against positivism which swept Europe at the end of the XIXth century. . . . We are primarily concerned with the actual formation of this ideology from the 1880's to the first decade of the XXth century. This is necessary because historians have ignored this stream of thought as too outré to be taken seriously. . . . Historians who have dismissed these aspects of romanticism and mysticism have failed to grasp an essential and important ingredient of modern German history.[27]

In the articles written between 1957 and 1961 we can already clearly see the essential criteria of the cultural approach with which Mosse henceforward confronted the problem of Nazism and fascism. Those criteria can be summarized in the concept of "culture" defined "as a state or habit of mind which is apt to become a way of life intimately linked to the challenges and dilemmas of contemporary society."[28] Mosse proposed this definition in 1961 in the introduction to *The Culture of Western Europe*, where he presented for the first time his vision of fascism.

An Agent Provocateur in the Historiography on Fascism

The general interpretation of fascism which Mosse was proposing in that book subverted, like his previous articles, all the interpretations then generally accepted in the historiography, whether liberal or Marxist. To speak of the "subversive" character of Mosse's work may seem a paradox today, since Mosse is now a well-known and highly respected historian. His cultural approach has become almost a fad, and like all fads it is often adopted by imitation without critical reflection. Yet his current reputation should not make us forget that for a long time his ideas on fascism and his way of interpreting it, through a cultural approach that took seriously the ideas of fascism and Nazism, were received with some diffidence by many historians, both Marxist and liberals, and that diffidence has not disappeared even in our own day. At least up to the early 1970s, Mosse's interpretation of fascism did not meet everywhere with a generally favorable reception. In 1963, when Mosse conducted a seminar on the intellectual origins of National Socialism organized by Stanford University, most of the participants "shot down" his theories, as he himself put it, adding the humorous comment that "somebody asked me whether I felt like the Christians among the lions, and I don't know how they felt."[29] There are other, more recent examples. In Italy Mosse is now a highly respected author. He used to say that Italy was one of the countries where his books have met with the greatest success. Nevertheless, in 1968, when the Italian translation of *The Crisis of German Ideology* was first published, it was virtually ignored and soon ended up on the shelves of remainder bookstores, not to be republished until 1994. Even his interpretation of fascism as "new politics," which he had proposed in *The Nationalization of the Masses* and had published in Italian in 1975, was "unanimously rejected" by the so-called progressive Italian historiography, as one of its representatives was later to recall.[30] In Germany, too, the acceptance of Mosse's works has been slow to come: the hegemony of social history, to a large extent influenced by Marxism, was not favorable to his cultural history.[31] In France, where presumably the historiography of the *Annales* ought to have produced a favorable response to his approach to cultural history, not one of Mosse's books on fascism and Nazism has yet been translated; only recently have *Fallen Soldiers* and *The Image of Man* come out in French translation. As late as the 1980s a French historian, who a few years later was to become a much acclaimed spokesman of anti-communist revisionism, refused to publish Mosse's article "Fascism and the French Revolution," considering it too favorable to fascism.[32] I do not think it would be a paradox to say that had Mosse himself not been a victim of Nazism, he might have been accused of being a revisionist historian in the derogatory sense of the word—that is to say, an apologist of fascism—because he had taken seriously the ideas and myths of fascism, had wanted to study fascism on its own terms, and, in his definition of fascism, had used such concepts as "culture," "democracy," "revolution," "consensus," and "participation."

In order to understand the motivations behind the diffidence or the hostility toward the interpretation of fascism set forth by Mosse since the early 1960s, one must keep in mind the vision of that phenomenon which dominated the historiography between the late 1950s and the mid-1970s—in the period, that is, during which Mosse formulated his most original ideas of his interpretation of fascism. Fascism, according to the prevailing interpretations of that time, was a total historical negativity, an aberration away from the development of European society and culture. A fascist ideology and a fascist culture did not exist. Fascists were thugs and opportunists at the service of class reaction and in the defense of vested interests. Their leaders were demagogues without principles and without morality, driven only by a naked and brutal will to power as an end in itself. Fascist regimes were occupation governments forcibly imposed on a hostile populace that had been subjected to the manipulation of propaganda. Fascism, in the end, had not had a historical individuality of its own, like liberalism, democracy, socialism, or communism, but had only been an "anti-movement," a "revolution of nihilism."

Mosse was the first historian to call into question the validity of this view of fascism as well as the methods then prevailing in liberal and Marxist historiography, exclusively focused as it was on the analysis of the political struggle and the class struggle. Toward them he assumed the role of an "agent provocateur, constantly provoking the establishment, breaking taboos in order to arrive at answers to problems,"[33] as he wrote in his memoirs. And vis-à-vis the representation of fascism that prevailed at the start of the 1960s, the general interpretation of fascism he proposed in *The Culture of Western Europe* was most certainly intended as provocation. Placing fascism squarely inside the European society and culture of the nineteenth and early twentieth centuries was the most important innovation of this interpretation. "Fascism was to climax many habits of mind which grew up after the age of romanticism,"[34] Mosse stated, thus laying the fundamental pillar of his concept of fascism that would remain unchanged in the entire course of its development. For Mosse fascism was neither an aberration from the course of European history nor the sudden irruption of a movement void of ideas, a "revolution of nihilism" exclusively prompted by a naked and brutal will to power, a contingent reaction triggered by World War I. Mosse saw in fascism, as a general phenomenon embodied primarily in Italian fascism and in National Socialism, the product of cultural, political, and moral currents that had accompanied the transformation of society and of the ways of life in the age of the traumatic upheavals caused by industrialization, modernity, and the birth of mass society. Moreover, fascism had been successful not only thanks to its resort to violence but also because it had known how to effectively interpret—through its ideology, its organization, and the charisma of its leader—the longing for security, authority, and belonging strongly felt by many alienated people in an age of rapid changes, people who were disoriented and deeply troubled by the challenges of modernity. Millions of people saw in fascism the solution to the dilemmas and conflicts of modernity, a promise of security, stability, and order that parliamentary institutions no longer seemed capable of providing. Fascism promised to put an end to alienation by reintegrating the individual in the collectivity of the nation while sacrificing the individual's freedom. For these reasons, Mosse argued that fascism was anti-parliamentary but not anti-democratic, in the sense that it represented a form of popular participation alternative to parliamentary democracy. Popular consensus to fascism and the forms in which consensus was obtained became other fundamental pillars of his interpretation. At this point, however, it is appropriate to let Mosse himself speak:

There can be little doubt about the popularity of fascism, especially in the beginning. . . .

The new leaders would depend not on the shifting allegiances of political parties but on "intuition." . . . Intuition would guide the creation of a state in tune with the "spirit" or the "race" of the people. Sorel termed this whole process that of the creation of a "myth" which gave a group cohesion and enabled it to fully utilize its energies. Human beings acted upon illogical premises; therefore the creation of a "myth" would stimulate their will for action. . . .

Not surprisingly the "myth" as both a faith and a passion fused into a kind of mysticism. . . .

This fusion bestowed upon the people a sense of commitment and belonging which destroyed that alienation from society which many men had felt so deeply. It was no small part of fascism's attraction. This sense of belonging was concretized in an orgy of uniforms which raised the status of even that man who performed the most humble tasks. . . . Though fascism did not modify the class structure, its social paternalism gave the workers something more than the previous parliamentarian regimes. In reality, the real wages of workers dropped and the rich got richer. But through the corporate structure, through such organizations as those mentioned above, the worker felt himself a valuable and integral part of the whole. . . . This kind of ideology was closely tied to action; the pragmatic impetus for fascism was always present. The governing elite's merits were gained through action. . . .

Direct action was more valuable than writing, for this was only of merit if it was part of the myth-making process, a work of propaganda. . . . Fascist meetings were religious rites in which allegiance to the myth was reaffirmed in a spectacular visual manner. . . . Fascism acted out its ideology through dramas in which all the devoted participated and renewed their fervor. . . . This was probably the only original cultural contribution the fascist regime has made.[35]

I have quoted at length because here, in my opinion, Mosse laid out the foundations of the concept of fascism that he would develop in subsequent years. It is important to note that the excerpts I have quoted remained almost completely unchanged in the later editions of *The Culture of Western Europe* published in 1974 and 1988, even though, as early as the second edition, the chapter on fascism had been largely revised and expanded, whereas the chapter on Nazism had remained nearly unchanged. This confirms that the ideas expressed in 1961 represented for Mosse a definitive component in his interpretation of fascism.

Confronting Modernity

For nearly two decades after 1961, Mosse devoted himself wholeheartedly to the study of National Socialism and fascism, and these were the subjects of an intense scholarly production. To this period belong the works that have contributed most to the "Mosse revolution" in the historiography on fascism: *The Crisis of German Ideology: Intellectual Origins of the Third Reich* (1964); *Nazi Culture: Intellectual, Cultural, and Social Life in the Third Reich* (1966); *Germans and Jews: The Right, the Left, and the Search for a "Third Force" in Pre-Nazi Germany* (1970); and *The Nationalization of the Masses: Political Symbolism and Mass Movements in Germany from the Napoleonic Wars through the Third Reich* (1975). The subsequent works on racism, nationalism, the myths of war, experience, sexuality, and masculinity, even though they all added some new element to the definition of fascism, have not introduced, in my view, important innovations, nor have they modified the overall orientation of his interpretation. Even Mosse's final book, *The Fascist Revolution*, offers no innovations but only confirms the ideas and the method formulated between 1961 and 1975 in the wake of the interpretation outlined in *The Culture of Western Europe*.

The novelty of those works consisted first of all in the century-long perspective within which Mosse examined fascism, placing it in the course of European history in the nineteenth and twentieth centuries. Through empirical research, carried out on the basis of his new cultural approach, Mosse showed that fascism could not be understood as just an "anti-movement"—that is to say, as a contingent reaction caused by World War I and by Bolshevism, as an aberration from the historical progress—but was the "climax" of cultural and political movements that had already taken roots in European society and culture before World War I. From this vantage point Mosse has always viewed fascism as the extreme outcome of a century-long process he summed up in the image of the conflict between liberalism and totalitarianism, between enlightenment and romanticism, between rationalism and irrationalism, between the individual and the masses. And in this conflict Mosse saw the fundamental significance of fascism in contemporary history.

At the root of this general view of contemporary history was an anthropological approach to the human condition in the age of modernity that was the underlying motif in all Mosse's writings on fascism and played a decisive role in orienting his cultural interpretation of this phenomenon. Mosse's vision of modernity is important for our discussion, for his concept of fascism derived from and was always conditioned by his vision of the condition of modern man, so that the two phenomena are intertwined in a bond that makes them complementary and inseparable. Mosse's view of modernity would deserve a special analysis in order to trace its genesis, its variations, even its contradictions, in connection with the development of the concept of fascism, but here I must limit myself to sketching only one essential aspect, namely, that which refers to what we may call the anthropological reactions of modern man to modernity.

According to Mosse, during periods of rapid transformations, human beings feel largely at the mercy of impersonal forces that, while deeply changing the reality in which they live, upset their existence, overturn their belief system, and throw their categories of good and evil into disarray. To all this they react by trying to recover stability and security in a wholesome and happy world, and in order to realize this aspiration they are willing to submit to the authority of anyone who they believe has the power to bring about a better life. This had happened at the start of the modern age, at the time of the Reformation, and the same had occurred in the nineteenth and twentieth centuries, as Mosse explained in the introduction to *The Culture of Western Europe,* when he formulated in essential, yet nearly definitive, terms his vision of man in the face of modernity:

Looking over the span of cultural history with which we are concerned, it would seem that men constantly longed for an authority to which they could relate themselves. Moreover, they saw this authority in terms of hope for a better life and a happier future. These longings took the form of rejection of present reality, leading to the contention that the future could not be constructed from the existing human situation. Throughout history there have been men who, like the Puritans, wanted to "build Jerusalem without tarrying," but in the modern age this desire seemed to provide much of the general mood of the times. There is a reason for this. These last centuries were periods of rapid change as Europe was becoming both urban and industrialized. In this period many people felt pushed to the wall, while others beheld changes they could not understand and problems which defied solutions. More men were alienated from their society than ever before in human history. No wonder that they longed for a more hopeful future, and it is not astonishing that they conceived of this future as outside the present reality of European life.[36]

Nearly two decades later, in 1980, Mosse reformulated this interpretation in the introduction to *Masses and Man,* where he discusses fascism as an extreme manifestation of nationalism, used by men and women "in order to keep control over their lives":

From the end of the last century onwards, these lives were lived in an ever more complex and impersonal society where all seemed in motion. This was a nervous age, as contemporaries saw it, threatening to wipe out traditional distinctions between the normal and the abnormal, the permitted and the forbidden—a time when human discourse threatened to break through all that was held sacred and private in life. . . . Men and women longed for a new wholeness in their lives; they reached out for totality.[37]

"Hunger for totality" in nineteenth- and twentieth-century Europe was, according to Mosse, a reaction against modernity, the opposition to everything disruptive that modernity represented: the rapid transformation of reality caused by industrialization and urbanization; the crisis of centuries-old institutions and values; the breakdown of traditional roles; and the alienation of the individual, who was freed from the traditional community only to be subjected to the anonymity of mass society. From here was derived, according to Mosse, many people's decision to recover a new whole feeling of belonging and fulfillment, even at the cost of renouncing their freedom, in order to be reintegrated into an organic collectivity. The aspiration to "a fully furnished house" was, according to Mosse, the fundamental reason for the acceptance of fascism by millions of men and women, who chose fascism because its ideology reflected their myths, their stereotypes, and their sense of the difference between good and evil, and, at the same time, looked to fascism as an effective and exciting solution for winning the confrontation with modernity.

According to this view of modern man, which we could label the Mosse theory of "confronting modernity," Mosse thought it entirely logical to place the ideological dimension and culture (in the sense in which he defined them, namely as an "attitude toward life") at the center of his analysis of fascism, without, however, underestimating or minimizing the importance of objective reality. "I said very carefully that it [ideology] alone doesn't explain everything; you have to bring in the concrete factors,"[38] Mosse stressed in his 1963 Stanford seminar on the intellectual origins of National Socialism. And nearly two decades later, in the introduction to *Masses and Man,* he reiterated this methodological conception:

In any analysis of the past, what counts is the objective reality and human perceptions of it. . . . However much they may be limited by objective reality, men and women do have choices to make. Indeed, that reality tends to be shaped by the perceptions men and women have of it, by the myths and symbols through which they grasp the existing world. Myths and symbols serve to internalize reality and to infuse it with fears, wishes, and hopes of man.[39]

The dialectic between perceptions and reality constitutes the methodological structure of Mosse's approach to fascism, but his historiography is exclusively meant to analyze the first term of the dialectic, to the point of seeing in the ideological dimension the very essence of fascism, the primary factor for defining its nature.

We have thus reached a crucial point in our inquiry, namely, the relationship between fascism and ideology, which is at the root of Mosse's concept of fascism. In order to appreciate the importance of this relationship we must keep in mind that the elaboration of the interpretation of fascism in Mosse's historiography takes place under the impulse of circular connections among the concept of ideology, the method of analysis, and the interpretation of the nature of fascism, in the sense that each element, while undergoing modifications and development, influences and modifies the others. This applies, first of all, to the way ideology is understood. It was through the study of fascism that Mosse was led to redefine his concept of ideology and to revise his methodology, but this change, in turn, influenced the elaboration of his interpretation of fascism in essentially ideological terms.

The Primacy of Ideology

The most important change, during the first phase in the development of Mosse's concept of fascism, is already apparent in 1963 during the seminar he directed at Stanford. I shall devote special attention to that seminar, not only because the text of those lectures has remained unpublished and is therefore unknown to most of Mosse's readers, but above all because Mosse anticipated at that time, in a more or less elaborate form, almost all the fundamental ideas of his interpretation of National Socialism and of fascism in general, ideas he would later expound in *The Crisis of German Ideology,* in "The Genesis of Fascism," and in *Nazi Culture,* and which would then remain as pillars of his concept of fascism. In that same seminar, Mosse explicitly formulates a new orientation regarding the cultural approach. We can therefore consider the 1963 seminar as a central moment in the development of both his methodology and his interpretation of fascism.

Mosse explicitly placed at the center of his analysis of fascism, which served as a framework for his lectures on various aspects and themes of the intellectual foundations of National Socialism, the importance of ideology understood as "the formation of basic attitudes towards politics, towards life,"[40] explaining that by "attitudes" he meant "the images people have of politics, that's after all what determines their actions."

I believe that the important thing about people's attitudes are the kind of images people form of reality. I don't think these images necessarily have a direct tie with reality, though reality must always be a part of them. . . . The stereotype always has a basis in truth. But it doesn't have to have a whole basis of truth. . . . And especially I think in a tight situation these images become aggravated into a kind of wish fulfillment, into a flight from reality, a flight into metaphysics.[41]

At the same time, however, we must notice that Mosse had modified his own concept of ideology by resorting to Sorel's idea of "myth," which he now considered more adequate for identifying the specific ideological dimension of fascism—its irrationalistic character and its twofold nature as a movement that exalts the past while rushing toward the future. In the context of fascism, Mosse states, "ideology must be based upon man's irrational feelings, his supposed historical experience—the past—translated into wish fulfillment for the future. That is what the 'myth' does. The past is tied to the future, not as it actually was, which is irrelevant, but as it exists in man's irrational unconscious."[42]

Another important innovation in the method of analysis of fascism that we find in Mosse's discussion at the Stanford seminar is the adoption of the concept of "institutionalization of ideology": "I consider ideologies only as historical forces if they do become institutionalized,"[43] that is to say, when ideology becomes "objectified" through cultural institutions, art, literature, and popular culture, thus spreading myths and moral and aesthetic stereotypes that shape people's attitudes toward reality and orient their choices among the forces in the field. This indeed happened in Germany with the *völkisch* ideology that had been institutionalized through the educational systems and popular culture and thus became a system of beliefs, based on racist and anti-Semitic myths and stereotypes, long before the birth of National Socialism as a political party. "My theory about this is that all these ideas are so important because they did become institutionalized before the war"—that is, they shaped millions of people's attitudes toward life and politics long before the war.[44]

On the basis of these methodological presuppositions, Mosse, in the introductory lecture, presented his definition of fascism as a general European movement, even though the case he examined was only National Socialism, which he presented as a movement that had had its own coherent vision of life, and he argued that the presence of this positive ideology had been the main reason for its success. In open polemic with the thesis proposed by Ernst Nolte in *Der Faschismus in seiner Epoche,* published that same year, Mosse stated that fascism could not be considered only as an "anti-movement," as a reaction to the Marxism produced by the crisis that followed World War I, because such an interpretation "denies ideological sincerity to the movement, and moreover makes it entirely a product of the post-1918 era," whereas he was firmly convinced that fascism had "a clear ideological base emerging from the problems of the very times from which this movement grew: the 80's and 90's of the last century. It is, I believe, this historical background which is important," and by this he meant to refer to "a general atmosphere leading to certain intellectual presuppositions," which was a decisive condition for the birth and success of fascism, while rejecting "at once the idea that all of the history of one country culminated in fascism and National Socialism, that there was an inevitability about it."[45]

By asserting the primacy of the ideological dimension in his analysis of fascism, and in the definition of its concept as well, Mosse explicitly placed in the background the organizational dimension and structural factors: "I am not convinced that the party and the structural factor are as important as the ideological factor."[46] And in the conclusion of his seminar he reiterated: "I do not see how in dealing with fascism we can get away from the primacy of the ideological component."[47] In that sense, he also meant to refuse to consider the political action of fascism only as a pure and simple manifestation of a political opportunism void of ideas and to explain its success only in terms of propaganda, organizational techniques, and terror, but he reaffirmed the primacy of the ideology that supplies the presuppositions and the goals of political action. Referring in particular to Hitler, Mosse reiterated even in this case the primacy of ideology as he spoke of an "ideological pragmatism": "The ideology gave him the presuppositions and gave him his goal, and that in the reaching of this goal he used political opportunism. . . . But what gave him this drive was an intellectual commitment. Hitler was, if you like to put it that way, an intellectually committed person."[48]

A "Revolution of the Soul"

Besides the affirmation of the primacy of ideology, the other major novelty proposed by Mosse in the 1963 seminar, and probably the most disconcerting one for most of the participants, was his definition of fascism as "a truly revolutionary movement." Indeed, Mosse opened his first lecture with a strong statement, the same statement he would repeat at the start of the concluding chapter of *The Crisis of German Ideology* and of the article "The Genesis of Fascism," as if this were the slogan that summed up the originality of his interpretation: "our century has seen two and not one revolutionary movements: Marxism and Fascism. We shall therefore deal with fascism as a serious movement of a revolutionary nature. We will deal with this from the ideological point of view."[479]

Here the reference to ideology was linked not only to Mosse's methodology but also to his original concept of fascism as revolution. He explains that fascism had been "a singularly ideological kind of revolution."[50] It was "a revolution of a special sort, really a flight into ideology, an irrational ideology to be sure, but one which was supposed to affirm the basically human and dynamic against present fossilized society. The human was defined through aesthetic criteria, spiritual criteria: the human soul." The chief protagonists of this revolution were young bourgeois who rebelled against their parents and against the conventions, the materialism, and the artificiality of bourgeois society, who cultivated the ideal of the "genuine," of creative spontaneity, and of sentiment against rational intellectualism, who had a romantic nostalgia for a preindustrial world that was retrieved through the myth of the native landscape and a "nature mysticism": "The fight against materialism as they saw it meant a new and increasing concern for the connecting link between politics and aesthetics, so that alienated industrial man (bourgeois) could become organic and whole once more."[51] The new man of fascism "was 'drenched by the idea' for which he was impassioned; in tune with nature and its genuine life spirit, handsome in body, an organic man." Those young bourgeois in revolt against the bourgeoisie gave birth to new forms of political organization coherent with their ideology, "a voluntary association of men linked by shared soul experience and eros. The soul experience was founded on a shared 'genuineness' bound up in a common mystical experience of *Volk* and landscape. This meant a new sense of community, for which this youth longed, where community was an 'experience' and not an artificial creation (*Erlebnis und kein Begriff*). Living the common experience took precedence over thinking about it." And from this community there emerged spontaneously the figure of the leader viewed as "*primus inter pares,* for he merely gave expression to the basic emotional but concretized experience."[52]

The fascist revolution wanted to realize a "revolution of the spirit" without modifying the basic structures of bourgeois society; it wanted to install a new hierarchy of values and functions without upsetting class divisions. That too was, for Mosse, a fundamental aspect of his interpretation of fascism, an aspect on which he insisted with special emphasis. "I make this point, for, however outre, however opposed to our way of thought, this was a searching, above all by youth in its beginning, which became an alternative revolution to Marxism in our age." The peculiar sense of this "ideological revolution" was not only its dynamism but also the determination to keep it under control. The fascists exalted the impetus of the revolutionary thrust, but at the same time they wanted to put an end to chaos and "to find a definite base, to tame this dynamic in the name of security and of belonging. They wanted both to be revolutionaries and [to put] an end to human alienation."⁵³

With this qualification Mosse introduced another important concept of his interpretation of fascism, namely the "taming of revolution," which oriented his definition of the fascist revolution and the formulation of the relationship between fascism and the bourgeoisie in a new version, different from that given by Marxism but equally intended to affirm their substantial identification, not in the class structure or in the theory of fascism as the tool of capitalism, but in their morality. In spite of its revolutionary drive, Mosse explained, fascism pursued the affirmation of basic values, "honesty, bravery, lack of dissimulation," which coincided with the values the bourgeoisie had cultivated and institutionalized during the nineteenth century. In words that must have sounded no less disconcerting to many of the participants in the seminar, Mosse argued that the fascist ideological revolution "turned out to be the ideal bourgeois revolution, a revolution in ideology and not in social and economic fact," thus setting up one more fundamental pillar of his concept of fascism as a general European movement, which he synthesized in these words in the introductory lecture:

It was a revolutionary movement which had its immediate origins in the rejection of the materialism of the *fin de siecle*. Because it centered its revolt against it, it turned toward the aesthetic, romantic, literary, the "myth," rather than toward the concrete and practical means of change. It became a "displaced" revolution, an anti-bourgeois revolution which the bourgeoisie could fully accept. It came to objectify itself through the search for new forms of organization (I have mentioned the Bund) and ideals of beauty which became the stereotypes. It came to infiltrate social institutions, above all education in Germany, even before the first World War. Moreover, it combined the Nietzschean ecstasy with its taming.⁵⁴

At the conclusion of this first presentation of his theory, after receiving a first volley of criticisms from the members of the seminar, Mosse reformulated his definition of fascism in general by stressing its peculiar revolutionary nature:

All right, may I give you a definition of fascism again. And you can shoot it down again. I would say that fascism, fully blown, is a mass movement, a mass movement which organized the proletariat, as you said, in a mass form, as an explicitly revolutionary movement. But a revolution which does not mean to and does not change the existing class or social structure. . . . It is a revolution of the soul, they were revolutionizing the soul. They operated with this kind of concept. I'm not saying they didn't want power. Everybody wants power. . . . It's a revolution to create a new mind, a new man . . . they talked not so much about the new society, these fascists, they talked about the new fascist man, and I think this is very important.[55]

The revolutionary character and the aspiration to create a new man did not, however, diminish the decisive importance of the role played by a preexisting tradition of ideas that were widespread among the populace, by an ideology that had become institutionalized before World War I, as a fundamental condition that explains the success of fascism:

I have never denied that only after 1918 did these ideas become attached to a politically effective mass movement, nor have I denied the importance of the war. But I still believe that the formation of the attitudes of so many people have deeper and longer historical roots, that the images which they have received led them to the Right when they could have gone to the Left, that National Socialism had an attractiveness beyond the mere techniques of organization—which themselves had a liturgical quality about them.[56]

And yet, precisely when referring to the German case, in his conclusions Mosse set another pillar of his interpretation of fascism, namely the specificity of National Socialism within the framework of the fascist phenomenon, a specificity due to the peculiarity of the *völkisch* ideology and of its institutionalization, which was not found in other fascisms. Just as racism and anti-Semitism were not present or predominant in all fascisms, as they were in National Socialism, so was the opposition of various fascisms to modernity diverse. The attitude toward modernity seemed to be characterized in the various fascist movements by common features. "All of fascism was tradition oriented. It wrote its message not upon history considered as a progressive dialectic, but upon history considered nostalgically. The old glory had to be recaptured." The anti-modernity of fascism, however, did not manifest itself as a total refusal, because "this never meant that all modern advances in technology and psychology could not be used in the service of this goal as means, but never as ends." Nonetheless, Mosse further explained, in Germany "this anti-modernity became more emphasized than in other fascisms, . . . here the doctrines of nature, of the German faith, of the peasant, and all that this implied, gave it a much greater consistency in that direction." In his conclusions Mosse criticized himself for having excessively molded his concept of fascism on the German experience and stated that the Italian case would have been a more fitting model for such a definition:

> Most of western fascism looked to the Italian and not the German model. This is highly significant. For the growth of the *voelkisch* ideology separated Germany from the West; it provides the crucial moment in this separation. I would now hold that Italian fascism can provide a more general context for a definition of the movement than the German model, for here the *voelkisch* ideology was missing in favor of a more direct state nationalism. I believe that my exposition of fascism at our first meeting was based too much upon the German model. The important point instead concerns precisely the difference between National Socialism and the other fascist movements, which is symbolic for the gulf between this Germanic ideology and the West.[57]

In his concluding lecture, Mosse reiterated in the strongest terms the presuppositions of his interpretation based on the conviction that in order to understand fascism and to identify the common elements shared by the various movements that constitute the fascist phenomenon, it was necessary to place ideology at the center of analysis; ideology, for its part, could not be reduced to anti-communism or to the opportunistic mask of a pure and simple will to power, just as the success of fascism could not be explained only on the basis of organizational efficiency or the use of terror:

> I still hold that more links fascism than merely anti-Communism or the use of techniques of organization. . . .
> We must still return to a nationalism which sees the organization of the new nation under the primary aspect of ideology. This primacy of ideology meant flexibility in the economic and social realm, it meant the absolutism of a leader who incorporated the "idea." The organization was never allowed to touch the leadership ideal. We must not magnify it to this extent, in spite of its importance as a means for national revival. Fascism, to my mind, was not so much a "flight from freedom," for it redefined freedom, but a flight into ideology.[58]

The reference to the primacy of ideology led Mosse back to the problem of methodology and to the definition of his approach to the problem of fascism through the study of ideology in order "to find out attitudes," with emphasis on "continuity through the ideology's penetration of institutions."[59]

Mosse frankly declared his belief that "for National Socialism, indeed for all fascisms, the history of ideas as I have defined it provides a fruitful approach," and he was obviously pleased, given his spirit of "agent provocateur," to underscore that his conception "is perhaps a little unorthodox in the context of what used to be considered in America the history of ideas," because he did not study ideas for their intrinsic value but rather, as he put it, in order "to find out attitudes":

> We thus come to the problem of methodology. The history of ideas by itself cannot explain events satisfactorily. It is essential to define the "myth" (in the Sorelian sense) by which men live, but why men adopt this myth must be answered from the concrete circumstances of historical development. . . . This is an approach to the history of ideas which denies the intrinsic value of ideas. Instead it attempts to see how, through the formation of attitudes, they penetrated into the realities of history.[60]

In this way Mosse laid out the foundations for a new type of cultural history that was unmistakably distinct from the history of ideas understood as the analysis of formal theoretical thought, after Arthur O. Lovejoy's manner, and moved toward the formulation of a history of "attitudes" such as they express themselves through stereotypes and collective myths that the historian must analyze not on account of their intrinsic originality and theoretical coherence but in order to understand the attitudes that orient people's choices when faced with the challenges of objective reality in a given historical situation. In the course of Mosse's investigations, even this approach, while preserving its fundamental presuppositions, underwent modifications that influenced the elaboration of his views on fascism, thus confirming the close interdependence (what I have called "circular connection") in his historiography among research, methodology, and theoretical elaboration as inseparable aspects of his interpretation.

Fascism between Dynamism and Conservatism

Between 1964 and 1966, Mosse further elaborated the general features of fascism that he had discussed in the Stanford seminar, keeping at the center of his interpretation the ideological dimension investigated primarily through the ideas and political thought of intellectual groups. In the writings published during this period, however, we can trace the way in which Mosse, by combining research and theoretical reflection, further elaborated his concept of fascism while simultaneously redefining the criteria of his methodology. Even at this stage of his investigations, which were devoted primarily to National Socialism, Mosse stressed the specificity of the German case as represented by racism and anti-Semitism, because neither of these elements "was a necessary component of fascism. . . . It was only in central and eastern Europe that racism was from the beginning an integral part of fascist ideology." Not even mass terror, nearly everywhere linked to racism, can be "a part of the definition of fascism as a European-wide movement. Hannah Arendt is wrong in this regard and forced to concentrate solely on the German example. There is a difference between fascist violence and street fighting on the one hand and mass terror on the other which is explained partly by the predominance of the racial and anti-Jewish direction of the movement in central and eastern Europe."[61] As a consequence, within the broad fascist phenomenon, Mosse wrote in his conclusions to *The Crisis of German Ideology* (1964), "the German variety came to be unique. It was unique not only in the way it managed to displace the revolutionary impetus, but also in the primacy of the ideology of the Volk, nature, and race. . . . The divergence of German fascism from the other fascisms reflects the difference between German thought and that of the other European nations."[62]

In this book Mosse studied the intellectual origins of the Third Reich through the process of the institutionalization of the *völkisch* ideology and viewed National Socialism as the climax of a historical development inherent to the German ideological tradition of opposition to modernity. The very structure of the book, as evidenced in the headings of the parts in which it was divided, exemplified his theory: Part 1, "The Ideological Foundations"; Part 2, "The Institutionalization of the Ideology, 1873–1918"; Part 3, "Toward National Socialism, 1918–1933." Mosse demonstrated what had been, before the birth of the National Socialist movement, the penetration of ideas, myths, stereotypes, and nationalist, racist, and anti-Semitic attitudes of the *völkisch* ideology both in high culture and in popular culture, permeating the school system, academic and professional institutions, and youth movements.[63]

Until then historians had not understood this fundamental aspect of National Socialism's success, "for they regarded the ideology as a species of subintellectual rather than intellectual history. It has generally been regarded as a façade used to conceal a naked and intense struggle for power"[64] or as "an aberration, something abnormal and indeed satanic." In this way they denied a factual reality, namely that "many of the men and women who came to hold these ideas were normal in any usual definition, people whom one might have considered good neighbors."[65] National Socialism won the consensus of many intellectuals and of many respectable and normal people because it was considered the most effective interpreter of their desire for securing bourgeois morality and respectability on solid foundations by restoring order and security in a society that would be healed and sheltered from the evils of modernity. Those respectable and normal persons ensured the triumph of National Socialism because they saw in it the defense of their interests and values against the chaos of modernity, the revolt against the decadence of society, and the realization, through a "German revolution," of their utopia of a tidy and happy world, firmly rooted in the eternal truths of nature and race. National Socialism embodied for them "the 'ideal' bourgeois revolution: it was a 'revolution of the soul' which actually threatened none of the vested interests of the middle class" while it concentrated its hatred against "another enemy within," the Jew, who "stood for modernity in all its destructiveness."[66] In this way, Mosse concluded, an ideology "that was only vaguely relevant to the real problems confronting the German people ultimately became normative for the solutions to those problems. . . . It was the genius of Adolf Hitler to wed the Volkisch flight from reality to political discipline and efficient political organization."[67]

Mosse reaffirmed these key concepts in *Nazi Culture* (1966), where he illustrated, with an anthology of documents, the main aspects of the intellectual, social, and cultural life of the Third Reich. This book can be considered a companion to the previous work and, at the same time, a development and a deepening of his cultural approach to the definition of National Socialism as a spiritual revolution. In this instance, too, we have, rather than a mere repetition, a reformulation of his interpretive concepts, with the addition of new ones. Mosse, for instance, insisted here on the concept of the "totality" of culture and on the identification of National Socialist morality with bourgeois respectability, and this would become later on one of the new pillars of his definition of fascism. Both National Socialist morality and bourgeois respectability, Mosse stated, merged in the Nazi vision of politics as a totality that aimed at embracing and permeating everything with its ideology in order to realize in the totalitarian state, through the "nationalization of the masses," the "good society" of the Aryan people, a society molded according to the anti-Semitic, racist ideology and bourgeois morality:

This society would not allow for the differentiation between politics and daily life which many of us naturally make. . . . Hitler's aim was to construct an organic society in which every aspect of life would be integrated with its basic purpose. . . . Politics was not just one side of life or one among many other sciences; it was instead the concrete expression of the Nazi world view. This world view was held to be the very crux of what it meant to be a German, and therefore politics was the consciousness of race, blood, and soil, the essence of the Nazi definition of human nature.

This is what Hitler meant when he talked about the "nationalization of the masses"; will and power were the keys to winning the hearts of the masses, for they could lead the people back to the consciousness of their race. Such a total view of politics meant—as it was called after January 1933—*Gleichschaltung,* "equalizing the gears" of the nation. All individuals and all organizations in Germany had to be "nationalized" in the sense of making them subject to party control. . . .

This was the totalitarian state, and the Nazi party, like the spider in its web, controlled all the lifelines of the nation.[65]

Mosse underscored the peculiarity of the German case and of the *völkisch* ideology in order to ascribe to National Socialism a unique place within the fascist phenomenon, but in doing so he did not intend "to deny that all fascisms had certain features in common," notably the attitude toward modernity, the spirit of rebellion against industrial society, and the actualization of an ideological revolution, what he then called "a displaced revolution" derived from "a common need to transcend a banal bourgeois world":

All fascisms attempted to capture and direct bourgeois dissatisfaction with existing industrial and political reality, a dissatisfaction which began to take a concrete revolutionary form in the late nineteenth century. . . . Fascism was far from being purely nihilistic; indeed, the discovery of a positive ideology was what enabled some fascists to succeed while their more "negative" ideological *confrères* failed. . . . Fascists everywhere spurned existing social and economic systems in favor of an irrational worldview which sought both individuality and belonging at a new level. This irrational worldview was itself objectified in the form of a new religion with its own mysticism and its own liturgical rites. . . . [a religion that] at the same time preach[ed] revolution. Existing society was supposedly rejected *in toto* and fascist thought centered instead upon the "new fascist man."[69]

Mosse elaborated further on these observations in "The Genesis of Fascism," published in 1966 as an introduction to the first issue of the *Journal of Contemporary History,* which was devoted entirely to international fascism. In this article Mosse emphasized in his definition of fascism the attitude toward modernity, the mystique and the aesthetics of politics typical of all fascist movements, and the relationship between revolutionary dynamism and conservatism that was inherent in fascist regimes and set them apart from traditional reactionary and authoritarian regimes. From the very start of the article Mosse reiterated his conviction that fascism had been a revolutionary movement alternative to the revolutionary movements derived from Marxism and that this made fascism a phenomenon substantially different from reaction. "Fascism and reaction had different visions, and the two must not be confused," he wrote. "Reaction rejected all revolutions, opted for the status quo, and looked back to the ancien regime for its models."[70]

Diversity was at the very root of fascism, even though, in the course of its development, it may have appropriated some of reaction's values and ideas. At the origin of all brands of fascism, according to Mosse, there was an emotional and intellectual revolt against industrialization and urbanization as these threatened to sweep the individual into anonymous conformism. The driving motivations behind all fascisms were "a desire to break out of the fetters of a system which had led to such an impasse," "the urge to recapture the 'whole man' who seemed atomized and alienated by society," and the attempt "to reassert individuality by looking inwards, towards instinct or the soul, rather than outwards to a solution in those positivist, pragmatic terms which bourgeois society prized."[71] Born of the late-nineteenth-century generational revolt against bourgeois society, fascism was a movement of young people of bourgeois extraction who aspired to a sense of community within the organic unity of the nation. "Thus they were quite prepared to have their urge to revolt directed into national channels, on behalf of a community which seemed to them one of the 'soul' and not an artificial creation. . . . Returned from the war, they wanted to prolong the camaraderie they had experienced in the trenches. Fascism offered it to them."[72]

Starting from this premise, Mosse reformulated his concept of the "revolution of the soul" by offering further elements for defining the peculiarity of the fascist revolution on the basis of the premises from which it started, the ideas that guided it, and the goals it wanted to achieve:

The revolution of youths of a virile activism ends up as a revolution of the "spirit," asserting the primacy of ideology. It is the shared world-view which binds the Nation together and it is this which must be realized. The world-view restores the dignity of the individual because it unites him with that of his fellow men.

Fascism did stress the aim of social justice. . . . The political and social hierarchies were to be open to all who served. . . . Economic hierarchy was also preserved, but within this framework a note of social justice was struck: Mussolini had his Charter of Labor and other fascisms drew up similar documents. Once more this meant the primacy of ideology, ending spiritual alienation as a prerequisite for improving economic conditions. . . . Fascism was a revolution, but one which thought of itself in cultural, not economic terms.

In spite of the working-class support it attracted in the more backward countries, in the West this was primarily a bourgeois revolution. The bourgeoisie could have a revolution as an outlet for their frustrations, and at the same time rest assured that order and property would be preserved.[73]

Even in the reformulation of his definition of fascism as an "ideal bourgeois revolution," Mosse introduced a new problem, one that he had defined as the process of "taming the revolution," a process he considered peculiar to fascism in power. This new concept was important for understanding both the internal dynamic of fascism itself as a revolutionary movement that had to face the necessity of satisfying its promise of order and stability that guaranteed the consensus of the middle classes, and its rapport with the masses, which fascism intended to integrate in the organic unity of the race or the nation. "The key to fascism is not only the revolt but also its taming. For the problem before the fascist leaders was how to make this attitude towards society effective and to counter the chaos which it might produce." Moreover, the dynamic impulse of fascism had to be reconciled with the promise of putting an end to the chaos of modernity and of restoring order and hierarchy according to the terms of its ideology, while integrating the masses in the organic community of the nation. According to Mosse, Sorel and Le Bon had shown fascism how to domesticate the revolution and to integrate the masses by the use of myth, the conservative irrationalism of the crowd, and the fascination of the leader:

The appeal must be made to this irrational conservatism and it must be combined with the "magic" influence of mass suggestion through a leader. . . . The conservatism of crowds was reborn in fascism itself as the instinct for national traditions and for the restoration of personal bonds, like the family, which seemed fragmented in modern society. . . . But the taming was always combined with activism and this kind of conservatism inevitably went hand in hand with the revolution. . . . All European fascisms gave the impression that the movement was open-ended, a continuous Nietzschean ecstasy. But in reality definite limits were provided to this activism by the emphasis upon nationalism, racism, and the longing for a restoration of traditional morality.[74]

All these elements, which combined to elaborate a general theory of fascism, were for Mosse a clear confirmation of the autonomous nature of fascism as a historical phenomenon endowed with its own individuality, with a "positive ideology" that had won the consensus of millions of individuals. This aspect was for Mosse fundamental for understanding fascism and could be neither denied nor ignored, even though, in the end, the experiment aimed at realizing the fascist myth of a better world and shared by millions of respectable, normal individuals produced suffering, destruction, and death for millions of other human beings who were considered beneath respect and abnormal:

> The fascist revolution cannot be understood if we see it merely in negative terms or judge it entirely by the dominance which national socialism achieved over it by the late 1930s. For millions it did satisfy a deeply felt need for activism combined with identification, it seemed to embody their vision of a classless society. The acceptance of the irrational seemed to give man roots within his inner self, while at the same time making him a member of a spontaneous, not artificial community.
>
> The negative side of fascism triumphed in the end. . . . The answer was war upon the internal enemy, the adoption of racism; but another general solution lay in the realm of foreign policy. The activism must now be tamed by being directed towards the outside world. . . .
>
> The "new man" of whom fascism had dreamed went down to defeat, the victim of a dynamic which had, after all, not been satisfactorily curbed. The dream turned out to be a nightmare.[75]

The crucial question that Mosse intended to answer when he embarked on his study of fascism was why it had achieved consensus. At this early stage of his research he was convinced that he had found a persuasive answer, one he considered definitive in many respects, through the analysis of the ideological dimension. His investigations proved that, precisely in that area, National Socialism, far from being a merely contingent reaction to the postwar crisis and to Bolshevism, had deep roots in an ideological tradition that had shaped the attitudes of millions of Germans because it had been "institutionalized" long before World War I. For this reason the National Socialist message, rendered effective by Hitler's organization, political ability, and charismatic appeal, had been welcomed as an effective solution not only to the concrete problems of the German crisis but also for defeating the chaos of modernity and for ensuring a wholesome and happy life. And yet, it is noteworthy that, in his definition of fascism in general, Mosse did not make use of the concept of the "institutionalization of ideology" but rather referred to something generic and far from "institutionalized," namely a spirit of revolt, the desire to fight against the chaos of modernity in order to build a new organic totality within the myth of the nation. In this sense, what characterized fascism in general, according to Mosse's definition, was not the presence everywhere of an institutionalized ideology but rather a state of mind, an attitude toward life essentially based on the exaltation of the irrational over the rationality of modern industrial society. It seems evident here that, in the shift from the definition of National Socialism to the definition of the general features of fascism, the concept of "institutionalization of ideology" actually lost importance, precisely on account of the stated and proven uniqueness of the German case. Moreover, by insisting on the irrationalist nature of fascism, did not one run the risk of acknowledging the validity of the traditional interpretations that, precisely on the basis of its irrationalism, had defined fascism as a total historical negativity, a "revolution of nihilism"? It is probable that Mosse became aware of that risk and for that very reason was led to reflect on the nature of fascist irrationalism in order to reconsider the conceptual presuppositions of his cultural approach. In this sense I believe one can identify in 1966 a moment of transition between the two stages in the development of Mosse's concept of fascism, when a new course of investigations and reflections got under way that would culminate in 1979 in a fresh attempt aimed at the elaboration of a general theory of fascism. For reasons we will now see, this intermediate stage, which could be called a transition from ideology to liturgy, involves primarily questions of methodology and results in a substantial revision of the presuppositions of the cultural approach and of the very method for dealing with the cultural history of fascism.

From Ideology to Liturgy

I have the impression that in 1966, after he had brought to completion some important contributions to the development of his concept of fascism, Mosse found himself faced with a series of problems that led him to entertain doubts about the way he had studied and interpreted the ideological dimension of fascism. Even though he had freed the concept of ideology from its identification with theoretical rationalism by giving historiographical importance to currents of thought that traditional historiography had viewed as belonging to a "sub-intellectual sphere" undeserving of serious consideration, his analysis had been limited to the written expressions of ideology, which until then he had studied solely through the theoretical formulations of intellectuals. In this way, however, he must have realized that a conspicuous and important aspect of fascism—namely its ritual and symbolic apparatus, the mass ceremonies, and the very representation of ideology through myth—remained on the fringes of his cultural interpretation of fascism. Mosse himself, as he wrote the preface to a new edition of *The Crisis of German Ideology,* published in 1981, identified the methodological limitations of that book precisely in his failure to pay attention to the mass liturgy of National Socialism: "I had not yet realized that in the age of mass politics, symbols and political liturgies were of central importance in making abstract ideas effective and concrete. The National Socialists used these as a form of self-representation and through them Volkisch ideas were transformed into a new religion. As in all religions, ideals of beauty played a central role, and not least the ideal of classical male beauty."[76]

   Mosse had certainly not ignored this aspect in his writings on fascism, but he had interpreted these rituals, symbols, and mass ceremonies essentially as Machiavellian instruments of power, as techniques of domination used by governments to seduce and control the masses. He had accordingly made use of concepts such as "manipulation," "propaganda," and "technique of power"—terms that were typical of the pragmatic historiography he had criticized and upon which rested those interpretations of fascism as "revolution of nihilism" that he so strongly opposed, both because they prevented us from understanding the true nature of fascism as a system of power inspired and conditioned by a genuine system of beliefs and because they explained away the role of ideology as a mere tool "used" by the leaders for manipulating the masses. As he went more deeply into the study of National Socialism and reflected on the nature of fascism, Mosse must have become aware of this contradiction and, in striving to resolve it, began, almost imperceptibly, to modify his cultural approach, shifting attention from the ideas expressed by intellectual groups to the ritual and symbolic (and thus aesthetic) forms that affected the masses involved in implementing the fascist revolution.

An early sign that this process of revision was under way can be found in the conclusions to *The Crisis of German Ideology* where Mosse, in order to avoid the risk of lending support to the interpretation of fascism as a nihilist revolution, proposed a new interpretive formula that separated irrationalism from nihilism and conferred upon irrationalism a rationality of its own based on the logic inherent in the forms through which it expressed itself and grew into a concrete political movement.[77] I believe that this formula was the embryo from which grew the entire second phase of Mosse's historiography on fascism, the phase that I consider more original and fruitful. For this reason I think it is essential that we focus, however briefly, on this moment of transition.

To begin with, it must be noted that Mosse had derived this formula from the religious phenomenon where the irrational, as he explained, has "an internal logic of its own which [takes] on concrete, outward forms."[78] Mosse considered it wholly legitimate to apply this formula to National Socialism as well, because the latter, as "the whole Volkisch movement, was analogous to a religion." Later on, in his article on the genesis of fascism, Mosse developed this idea, pointing out that liturgy had a decisive role in the process of "taming" the fascist revolution after power had been seized:

The "cult element" was central to the taming process; it focused attention upon the eternal verities which must never be forgotten. . . . The liturgical element must be mentioned here, for the "eternal verities" were purveyed and reinforced through endless repetition of slogans, choruses and symbols. These are the techniques which went into the taming of the revolution and which made fascism, even that which leaned on a Christian tradition, a new religion with rites long familiar in traditional religious observance. Fascist mass meetings seemed something new, but in reality contained predominantly traditional elements in technique as well as in the ideology.[79]

And again, in *Nazi Culture* we find a new development in Mosse's reflection on the role of liturgy in the process of the institutionalization of myth and in the mass politics of the National Socialist regime.[80] The growing interest for liturgy clearly shows how, in 1966, Mosse had embarked on an important process of revision in how he tackled the problem of fascism, both in terms of the concepts he used and in terms of the definition of the very nature of the phenomenon. Almost without being fully aware of it, as he faced a question that was crucial for understanding and defining fascism, he opened a new perspective, and that new perspective would see him once again acting as an "agent provocateur," for the road Mosse had traveled after 1966 led him to break many historiographical taboos.

The crucial question Mosse found before him as he shifted his attention from ideology to liturgy, from intellectual groups to the masses, concerned the relationship between faith and pragmatism, between the "genuineness" of the system of beliefs expressed by ideology and the "manipulation" of the masses at the hands of the leaders expressed through rituals and symbols. In the Stanford seminar Mosse had tried to explain that relationship with the formula "ideological pragmatism," which, however, applied only to the interpretation of the role of the leader viewed as a man who believes fanatically in the ideas he wants to implement but at the same time resorts to any form of opportunism in order to reach his goal. Even the most brutal and naked will to power of the most unscrupulous opportunist, Mosse stated, is embedded in a historical context and is guided by an interpretation and an attitude toward life.[81]

Mosse had no doubt that Hitler had "skillfully used" the moral values, the nationalism, and the racist and anti-Semitic prejudices that were widespread among Germans, but he stressed that with the term "'used' we do not mean to imply that these ideas were not part of a worldview genuinely held by Hitler" and that one must keep in mind, in the relationship between ideology and political action, "the constant interplay between theory and application, but to this must be added the equally close interplay between genuinely held belief and its manipulation for the purpose of making it the sole national religion,"[82] as Mosse stated in *Nazi Culture*. And yet in that same book it seems evident that Mosse was beginning to doubt that the concept of "manipulation" was the most adequate for interpreting the liturgy and mass politics of National Socialism, for it was a concept that could lead to a misreading of his interpretation. I believe my observation is confirmed by the fact that, in his conclusions to that book, Mosse felt the need for a very significant clarification:

Yet we must always remember that there were many who were enthusiastic for the new order, to whom the Nazi ideology seemed to give a new meaning to life. . . . We can now see the Nazi assumption of power in its proper dimensions— as opening the gate through which this Nazi culture poured down upon the people. That it struck so many responsive chords is perhaps the greatest tragedy of all . . . but that millions should have identified themselves wholly and unconditionally with Nazi culture gives a seriousness to these documents which cannot be brushed aside as merely the creation of clever or successful propaganda.[83]

Closely connected to this clarification is the introduction, in the analysis of fascism, of another concept that surfaces through the transition from ideology to liturgy. I refer to the definition of fascism as religion. Already in the Stanford seminar Mosse had hinted at the religious character of fascism when he commented on Paul Hohenberg's remark that fascism was "a minor example of the sort of historical movements which try to revolutionize the mind, which are religious movements": "Yes, it is essentially a religious movement. But I wouldn't say very minor," Mosse replied.[84] Subsequently, as we just saw, the analogy between National Socialism and religion had been at the origin of the new formula of interpretation of the dialectic between irrationalism and rationality in the politics of fascism. We must now notice that in *Nazi Culture* Mosse no longer presents the similarity with religious phenomena as a mere "analogy" but rather as an integral part of the very essence of National Socialism: "National Socialism was a religion; the depth of the ideology, the liturgy, the element of hope, all helped to give the movement the character of a new faith."[85] Finally, in his review of the translation of Nolte's *Three Faces of Fascism*, published in 1966, Mosse extended this definition to fascism in general:

Fascism was a new religion (not ashamed to use traditional religious symbols) and it gave to its followers their own feeling of transcendence, to be sure, not transcendence in Nolte's definition, but this very definition can lead to a failure to understand the movement on its own terms, the meaning it contained for its followers. Fascism did hold that man will reach an absolute whole through the release of his creative instincts, that he will recapture his own personality. But its world-view also restrained the flight into transcendence, for it opposed the Messianic tradition. The limits were set by the "eternal truth" of man's rootedness in his nation or in his race, and this excluded the experiencing of universally valid ideas. Fascism gave a vision to its followers, but also security by setting a definite limit to the flight of the mind.[86]

On the basis of these considerations, which gave ever greater emphasis to the nature of fascism as mass movement, Mosse restated his opposition to an interpretation of fascism as mere anti-Marxism, because "Fas-

cism possessed a dynamic of its own; it put forward a solution to the problems of industrialism and modernity on its particular terms," and he extended his criticism to any interpretation that reduced fascism to an instrument of the leader, because "this undue emphasis upon the leader
ignores fascism as a movement," with all that this meant for understanding the phenomenon itself and its rapport with the masses, a rapport that
represented a fundamental element of its nature and, as a consequence,
of its definition: "Fascism, unlike reactionary movements, attempted to
involve all levels of the population with every facet of the new society. . . .
The fascist version of democracy needed 'myths' in order to manipulate
the masses, and found them in the appeal to a new kind of community
which would end alienation by common participation in the reawakening
of the nation and its struggles, symbolized by the leader."[87]

From all these new elements introduced by Mosse in the interpretation of fascism, the important role played in the development of his concept of fascism by the moment of transition from ideology to liturgy seems
beyond doubt. We are in the presence of another significant instance of
the circular connections among methodology, research, and interpretation, which, in my judgment, have always marked the most important
stages of Mosse's historiography and of the development of his concept of
fascism. Decisive in this instance was the influence of anthropology,
which helped Mosse to redefine his concept of culture by placing greater
emphasis, in the analysis of mass movements, on myths and symbols as
forms of interpretation of life and as forms of mediation between the human being and objective reality. Proof of the importance of this influence
is Mosse's 1969 article "History, Anthropology, and Mass Movements,"
which I consider the most significant among his contributions to the subject of historical methodology.[88]

Through a highly personal use of some anthropological theories of
Ernst Cassirer and Claude Lévi-Strauss on the role of myth and symbol
in the manifestations of collective mentality, Mosse revisited the reflections he had been pursuing during the last three years on the problem of
the irrational, liturgy, and mass politics. He formulated a new definition
of cultural history more suitable for understanding mass politics, a definition radically different from the traditional history of ideas which he himself had followed until then when dealing only with intellectual groups.
Now, Mosse stated, "the time has come to go beyond the study of such
elitist groups to a more thorough investigation of popular practices and

sentiments," because "in an age of mass politics and mass culture, the intellectual historian needs new approaches that take into account those popular notions that have played such a cardinal role in the evolution of men and society . . . in order to understand the nature and force of popular beliefs and predilections as expressed in politics and culture." All modern mass movements—not just totalitarian movements—influenced the masses "by using familiar and basic myths and symbols. These found expression within the literature of the movement and in its liturgy as well, in festivals, mass meetings and symbolic representations such as national monuments. Here indeed the great manifestations of society originate at the level of the unconscious as Levi-Strauss believes." Cultural historians must realistically recognize that in the age of masses "the irrational seems to predominate, and the historian needs different tools to capture the structure of the popular mind. Here anthropology can be of great help, for not only have anthropologists concerned themselves with the analysis of folkways and community customs, but their use of myths and symbols can provide useful ways to penetrate the mind of modern as well as primitive man." Even though historians could hesitate before this juxtaposition of modern man and primitive man, they could not ignore the fundamental role myths and symbols played at the collective level in shaping mentality and the attitudes of the masses. "The myths and symbols that modern mass movements use in order to manipulate their followers badly need historical investigation as myths and symbols."[89]

The dimension of ideology as expression of intellectual groups was thus definitively replaced, in Mosse's cultural approach, by the concepts of myth and symbol, because he considered them more adequate for making the historian penetrate inside the collective mentality of mass movements:

Historical analyses of the myths and symbols used by such movements are essential, and neither the history of ideas nor the sociology of knowledge will suffice any longer for the intellectual historian. Anthropology can be helpful; at least one must be familiar with its methods. . . . Beyond these considerations the intellectual historian interested in popular culture or mass movements is confronted with the necessity of fathoming the complexity of the human mind in its interplay with other factors that make up historical reality. He must draw general conclusions as to how the unconscious mind penetrates reality. It is here that the existence of myths and symbols can provide an entering wedge and keep him from sliding into an idealistic or materialistic posture. This presents an approach that can no longer be ignored if intellectual history is to advance beyond the history of intellectuals.[90]

This methodological article brought to a conclusion the transition from ideology to liturgy and opened a new perspective within which, between 1970 and 1979, there would unfold, with a rich series of publications, the second phase of Mosse's historiography on fascism centered not on ideology but on liturgy, the rituals and myths of mass politics, a phase that found its most original and innovative expression in the publication, in 1975, of *The Nationalization of the Masses.*

The writings Mosse published between 1969 and 1976, in a rapid annual succession that in itself reveals his intellectual commitment to the new fields of inquiry opened by the shift from ideology to liturgy, mark, in my view, the most productive phase in the development of his interpretation of fascism.[91] Moreover, during this phase we have new and more significant examples of the role constantly played in his work by the circular connections among methodology, research, and interpretation, just as we also find a confirmation of the thesis that Mosse's most original ideas on fascism did not spring out of some brilliant "intuitions" or sudden "illuminations" but were rather the result of reflections and hypotheses that had emerged from and been verified by empirical research that proceeded "by a wide variety of examples over a broad time span," within the framework of nineteenth- and twentieth-century European history. Even though the choice of those examples might seem "arbitrary and episodic," Mosse believed that "until more research is available, it seems best to point out some general trends and insights into the subject" in order "to stimulate additional work."[92]

Mosse's writings on fascism published during this period can be read as chapters of a single work devoted to the elaboration of the idea of the "new politics" and culminating in *The Nationalization of the Masses.* This book can be considered as the ripest product of Mosse's cultural approach, as the decisive moment of the renovation of his historiography that resulted from the shift from ideology to liturgy. He himself has emphasized in his memoirs the importance of this book, a book that has certainly been one of his most successful and most influential works, even when compared with another, and certainly influential, book such as *The Crisis of German Ideology,* which, however, as Mosse observed, "can still be read as part of a traditional history of political thought":

To my mind, the real breakthrough in putting my own stamp upon the analysis of cultural history came with *The Nationalization of the Masses,* published in 1975, which dealt with the sacralization of politics: the Nazi political liturgy and its consequences. The book's success was slow in coming, but eventually the work was regarded as innovative for no longer referring dismissively to Nazi propaganda but instead talking of Nazi self-representation, which interacted with the hopes and dreams of a large section of the population. This was no longer a book in the tradition of the history of political thought as I had been taught it at Harvard by Charles Howard McIlwain; instead it used a definition of culture as the history of perceptions which I had offered in my *Culture of Western Europe*.[93]

The conceptual frame of *The Nationalization of the Masses* was built around the idea of the "new politics," and it developed the interpretation of fascism as a secular religion. "This book," we read in the first chapter, "is concerned with the growth of a secular religion. As in any religion, the theology expressed itself through a liturgy: festivals, rites and symbols which remained constant in an ever-changing world. National Socialism, without doubt, illustrates the climax of the uses of the new politics."[94] The "new politics" had originated, at the time of the French Revolution, from the modern idea of nation and popular sovereignty. During the nineteenth and twentieth centuries it had taken root with the mass movements of both the Right and the Left, and ultimately it had given birth to the fascist political style. The fascist style, Mosse explained, "was in reality the climax of a 'new politics' based upon the emerging eighteenth-century idea of popular sovereignty" and on Rousseau's concept of "the general will":

The general will became a secular religion, the people worshipping themselves, and the new politics sought to guide and formalize this worship. . . . The worship of the people thus became the worship of the nation, and the new politics sought to express this unity through the creation of a political style which became, in reality, a secularized religion. . . . The chaotic crowd of the "people" became a mass movement which shared a belief in popular unity through a national mystique. The new politics provided an objectification of the general will; it transformed political action into a drama supposedly shared by the people themselves.[95]

A "New Politics" for Mass Democracy

Given the central place the idea of "new politics" occupies in Mosse's interpretation of fascism, it will be appropriate to retrace the origin and development of this new concept in his historiography. I will do so with a specific analysis in which I will highlight especially such aspects as are directly connected to the problem of fascism and to the renovation of the methodology of the cultural approach that Mosse started with his article on the connections among history, anthropology, and mass movements. The influence of anthropological thought in drawing Mosse's attention to the study of political symbolism seems evident. I believe, moreover, that Mosse was influenced by Thomas Nipperdey's seminal article on the uses of national monuments in nineteenth-century Germany.[96] Mosse found another important source of inspiration in the work of Johan Huizinga, who, in *The Waning of the Middle Ages,* had remarked, on the question of the relation between myth and symbol in the Middle Ages, that "having attributed a real existence to an idea, the mind wants to see it alive and can effect this only by personalizing it."[97] This same process of personification and concretization by means of symbols, was, according to Mosse, at the root of the "new politics" of National Socialism and, therefore, of fascism too and was typical of an age when masses were more attracted by visually represented images than by the written word: "All modern mass movements," Mosse wrote in 1976, "are apt to be visually oriented, focusing on symbols (e.g. flags of various colors), marches, and songs, which was also vital for National Socialism."[98] Another, more fruitful suggestion for Mosse's interest in political symbolism may have come from Rousseau's theories on civic festivals as necessary instruments for inculcating patriotism in the citizens, and probably also from Jacob Talmon's reflections on the role of religion in the origins of "totalitarian democracy."[99] Mosse himself has called attention to Rousseau in his memoirs:

I began writing *The Nationalization of the Masses* in 1972 while teaching in Jerusalem and living in the apartment of the historian Jacob Talmon, surrounded by the works of Rousseau and of the leaders of the French Revolution. Here the importance of myth, symbol, and the acting out of a political liturgy was brought home to me, especially by Rousseau, who moved from believing that "the people" could govern themselves through town meetings to urging that the government of Poland invent public ceremonies and festivals in order to imbue the people with allegiance to the nation.[100]

Beyond these strictly intellectual reasons, I think that even in this new phase Mosse's curiosity about the problem of myth and symbol in mass movements was stimulated by his own participation in a lived experience.

I have in mind above all the student movement of the 1960s, in which Mosse was personally involved as a faculty member faced with the student unrest at the University of Wisconsin in Madison.[101] The student revolt was certainly a concrete and actual instance of "new politics," the emergence of a new, antagonistic political style that, however, could draw on a long American tradition, both cultural and political, of civic and patriotic myths, rites, and symbols. I find more than merely chronological connections among the student revolt, the publication of the essay on the relationships among history, anthropology, and mass movements, and the study of the "new politics" that started from reflecting on the problem of a "third way" between Marxist materialism and capitalist materialism, something the rebellious students of the 1960s, too, according to Mosse, were searching for.[102]

Among the personal experiences that influenced Mosse's thought we can also include his encounter with Albert Speer, an encounter that enabled him to penetrate into the mentality of National Socialism and above into all its symbolic universe through the self-representation provided by the chief creator of Nazi liturgy, and one that drew his attention as a historian to an aspect that was crucial for understanding the nature and the essence of National Socialism and the reasons for its success.[103] "Obviously," Mosse wrote in 1976 in a review of Speer's journal, "none of the class analysis so popular today can discover the truth about National Socialism as it conceived of itself, as it represented itself and was accepted by the masses of its most fervent supporters (who should not, however, be confused with the passivity of the vast majority of the population). This is the National Socialism Speer tells about."[104] To Mosse, Speer's testimony seemed fundamental for understanding the vision Hitler and the Nazis had of themselves and of their movement, for "such a view determined the nature of Nazi politics and their accomplishment," and it was necessary to know it if one was to understand the power of attraction Hitler exerted on millions of individuals, "many of whom saw in his political liturgy the fulfillment of their needs." In this sense, the conversation with Speer and reading his journal not only influenced the shift of Mosse's historiography from ideology to liturgy but also helped to confirm his belief in the validity of his cultural approach:

The historian has to recapture their enthusiasm as they felt it at the time and not to impose his own abstract categories upon it thirty years later. Once we have understood Hitler and, through his taste and politics, those who were his devoted followers, we can begin to see whether ideas of class, social grouping and conventional politics fit the case. Most historians have put the cart before the horse, and Speer proved an invaluable corrective.[105]

Finally, I believe it was above all Mosse's reflections on the transformation of the nature of politics in the age of masses that led him to shift his attention from the ideas of groups of intellectuals, from the written word, to the images that visually represented myths and stereotypes, through the rites and the symbols of mass movements. As he wrote in June 1969 in the introduction to his collected essays published in 1970 under the title *German and Jews*, "In the 'age of the masses' the use of myths and symbols became of prime importance in forming political movements, and these had to rest on an unchanging appeal to man's equally unchanging wishes and desires."[106] The millions of men and women whom the Industrial Revolution was incessantly throwing onto the political stage represented masses of uprooted and alienated people who "longed for traditions to which they could relate, within which they could end their alienation from society and indeed participate in determining its fate."[107] The "age of the masses" (viewed by Mosse as the time when "the penchant of thinking in absolutes was not confined to intellectuals"[108] but spread to ever wider segments of the population as they became involved in politics) was another theme that he now placed at the center of his historiographical perspective, notably for the analysis of anthropological reactions to modernity. Mosse thus reconnected the problem of the masses to his concept of modernity, to "the existential dilemma of modern man," basically interpreted as the "quest for identity in a world in which the 'vulgar rationalization of life' threatens to swamp the individual personality, and the advances of technology as well as the progress of urbanization and industrialization produce a feeling of alienation. . . . This dissatisfaction with man's place in the world was a wholesale rejection of modernity and led to a flight from society and from the traditional pursuit of politics. The individual personality was suffocating, and the existing political parties provided no satisfactory alternatives."[109]

I think the problem of the "new politics" makes its first appearance in the introduction to *Germans and Jews* mentioned earlier. This book was a collection of essays whose common theme was spelled out in the subtitle: *The Right, the Left, and the Search for a "Third Force" in Pre-Nazi Germany.* There Mosse reformulated his concept of fascism, emphasizing now the idea of the "third force," that is, fascism as the expression of the search for an alternative to both capitalism and Marxism, and for an alternative to parliamentary democracy seen as the expression of a materialistic and alienating society. This search for a "third force" presented itself, in its nationalist version, as a movement of regeneration of the nation aimed at unifying it into a new, organic community symbolically incarnated in the leader and organized in a corporative state, but it was also represented by a new political style that made use of myths, symbols, and public festivals in order to involve the masses. Mosse traced the earliest historical instances of the new political style to the French Revolution and to the origins of German nationalism at the time of the Napoleonic Wars and, subsequently, to the revolutionary and counterrevolutionary movements of the nineteenth century: "both revolutionary and counterrevolutionary forces were to use public festivals as a means to control and manipulate mass movements. The abstract collectivity needed symbols to make its existence concrete and tangible to the mass of men."[110]

Rites, symbols, and public festivals became the instruments of new forms of mass democracy of both the Right and the Left, alternative to parliamentary democracy, which would pave the way for the birth and growth of fascism. In this instance, too, Mosse examines the problem of the "new politics" from a long-term perspective, stressing the importance of an already active and widespread tradition for understanding the birth and the growth of fascism. One of those traditions was Caesarism, which Mosse analyzed in a essay published in 1971, where the concept of the "new politics" was used for defining the role of rites, symbols, and public festivals in the relationship between the leader and the masses:

Caesarism as a concept is important in modern times because it became shorthand for a new political constellation arising during the nineteenth century. . . . A discussion of Caesarism leads necessarily to an analysis of the rise of mass democracy. New political instruments and new political myths were being forged in order to cope with the new élan of the masses. . . . The Roman ruler exemplified the symbiosis of leader and people which left no room for traditional institutions or individualism of any kind. But such confrontation needed its own political techniques to go beyond the plebiscite as both Napoleons had understood it. Such techniques became a secular religion within which Caesarism could play the role of unifying symbol of leadership.[111]

Another important example of the mass politics analyzed by Mosse were the rightist movements that tried to organize the working class with an ideology of anti-capitalist national socialism or social nationalism. These include, in Germany, the national socialist movement of Friederich Naumann, which, however, had but limited success, while the most important one, on account of the following it actually managed to achieve among the workers, was the syndicalist organization Les Jaunes, which was active in France during the Third Republic. Mosse was the first to draw attention to it in a 1972 article:

> Though conservatives were also involved, national socialists were in the forefront. Their dynamism was due not only to their concern with social questions and their nationalist mystique, but also to their anti-capitalism which they equated with anti-Semitism. National socialists were interested, above all, in national unity and rejected class war in favor of class collaboration without, however, approving the capitalist and bourgeois order in which they lived.[112]

Movements such as Les Jaunes prefigured, according to Mosse, some features of fascism and showed how the new mass politics did not preclude the possibility of mobilizing portions of the working class with the nationalist mystique. "Nationalism became the principal movement involving the people in the politics of their time," Mosse stated in a lecture on mass politics and the liturgy of nationalism given in 1972 at the University of Canberra.[113]

As he developed the concept of "new politics," Mosse also reconsidered the role of the intellectuals, emphasizing now not the ideas set forth in their writings but their contribution to the formation of the new political style for the age of the masses. The most significant example was the poet Gabriele D'Annunzio. Mosse discussed the role of the Italian poet in the formation of the new politics in a 1973 article, but he had already talked about him a year earlier, as he told me, at a conference at the University of Papua New Guinea. Regardless of the poet's political influence, Mosse used the D'Annunzio case to illustrate the process of transformation of politics into a secular religion intended for the new mass society:

> The poet played a meaningful role in the creation of the politics of the times and contributed something new, essential, and original to the art of governing. The reason that poets now got their chance to be politically effective lay in the changed nature of politics. . . .
>   Politics became a drama expressed through secular liturgical rites and symbols closely linked to concepts of beauty in which poetry felt at home. National festivals, often held under the stars, on sacred native ground, surrounded by

symbols such as the holy fire and the flag, constituted a political style essential to the building of nations, and here the poet could make a contribution to the political expression of a growing national self-consciousness.[114]

The reelaboration of Mosse's concept of fascism through the concept of the "new politics" appears already completed, in its essential elements, in the revision of the chapter on fascism prepared for the new edition of *The Culture of Western Europe* published in 1974, whereas, as I pointed out earlier, the chapter on National Socialism was left nearly unchanged. Here it is not possible to examine in detail the modifications, deletions, and additions made in the new edition, but a comparison of the two versions of the chapter on fascism shows clearly the substantial progress Mosse had made in his interpretation. Fascism was now presented as a "secular religion of myth and symbol which expressed itself in mass meetings and public festivals."[115]

This reformulation was consistent with Mosse's methodological revision of his cultural approach, for now, in the introduction to this new edition, he again set forth his definition of culture as an attitude toward life but shifted his attention away from the ideas of the intellectuals[116] to what he called the "general mood" of an age:

But what do we mean by a "general mood"? It consists of reactions to the complexities of daily life as well as of images of a better future. . . . Christianity had fulfilled the function of providing such myths and symbols for many centuries, but since the eighteenth century, at least, they began to be secularized—transposed upon a society which was becoming a mass society and upon politics which was becoming mass politics. Thus symbols like the sacred flame, the flag, and national monuments became the self-representation of the nation, the means by which the people represented and indeed worshipped themselves.[117]

This shift of attention from ideology to liturgy was warranted by the very nature of fascist ideology, as Mosse explained in the introductory chapter of *The Nationalization of the Masses:*

Fascist and National Socialist political thought cannot be judged in terms of traditional political theory. . . . The fascists themselves described their political thought as an "attitude" rather than a system; it was, in fact, a theology which provided the framework for national worship. As such, its rites and liturgies were central, an integral part of a political theory which was not dependent on the appeal of the written word. Nazi and other fascist leaders stressed the spoken word, but even here speeches fulfilled a liturgical function rather than presenting a didactic exposition of the ideology. The spoken word itself was integrated into the cultic rites, and what was actually said was, in the end, of less importance than the setting and the rites which surrounded such speeches.[118]

In adopting the concept of the "new politics," Mosse had found new arguments for reiterating one of the key elements of his interpretation of fascism viewed as the "climax" of cultural and political currents that already had an established and widespread tradition by the time fascism made its appearance as a political movement after World War I.[119] He now considered the tradition of the "new politics" as the crucial factor in the success of fascism and in the attraction it held for the modern masses who aspired to the totality of "a fully furnished house," where they could find stability and security in a world undergoing rapid transformation: "The longing for a healthy and happy world and for a true community exemplified by the aesthetics of politics in which all could join. What Levi-Strauss calls the 'cosmic rhythm,' which possesses mankind from the earliest times onward, we would define in a more pedestrian manner as the desire for permanent and fixed reference points in a changing world."[120] The "new politics" looked like the realization of a permanent order that involved the masses organized in an experience of participation through rites, symbols, and collective festivals which, together with the leader's figure, replaced parliamentary institutions by creating the sense of a "true democracy."[121]

In this function of mediation performed by the new political style, a decisive role was played, according to Mosse, by the idea of beauty and by the principles according to which it was defined as integral part of the vision of the ordered and happy world the masses longed for: "The 'aesthetics of politics' was the force which linked myths, symbols, and the feeling of the masses; it was a sense of beauty and form that determined the nature of the new political style."[122] Mosse was certainly not the first historian to look at fascism as a form of aestheticization of politics, but the originality of his interpretation consisted in reconnecting the aesthetics of fascist politics to a tradition that was not exclusively fascist but which had a history that went much farther back in history and reflected, as anthropological theory explained, fundamental needs of the human spirit. The "aesthetics of politics" did not merely express the snobbery of intellectuals who threw themselves "into the arms of fascism where they sought their heroes and a life removed from the ordinary drabness of bourgeois existence"; rather, it was "basic to the new politics, and appealed to the masses as well":

The longing for experiences outside daily life, experiences which "uplift," is basic to all religious cults and was continually transferred to the secular religion of politics. Even the bourgeoisie liked to infuse their ordered lives with the extraordinary and the uplifting. An examination of the European novel around the turn of the century has shown that the mystique of "living life to the full" had become a secularized myth in which domestic or public festivals symbolized the high point of existence.[123]

This aspiration to totality through the cult of beauty, too, was a form of transcendence in which, according to Mosse, the secular religious character of the new politics manifested itself. In this way the aesthetics of politics contributed to shaping the stereotypes that were used to define the ideal model of the national community, a community regenerated through the invigoration of its historical roots and rescued from the precipitous flow of time and the frenetic rhythm of modernity: "Calling to history was one way of organizing time, of coping with its speed. Thus the emphasis upon history was not only necessary for myth and symbol, but also served to preserve order within an ever faster flow of time. The Greek ideal of beauty which Winckelmann had put forward, embedded in history as it was, exemplified the noble simplicity and quiet greatness which contrasted so sharply with the speed and unrest of the present."[124]

The emphasis Mosse gave to the aesthetics of politics did not depend only on the consideration of the importance of "visuality" in the age of the masses but also derived from his conviction that, since the origins of the "new politics," there was a close link between the canons of a supposed timeless beauty, defined according to the neoclassical aesthetics of the idealization of Greek beauty, and the principles of an ethics, of an ideal of man and of human conduct, considered as being no less timeless, absolute, and eternal, which led one to identify the external beauty with the internal harmony of a virtuous individual. This ideal of beauty, intimately bound to the essence of the "new politics," also expressed an ideal of morality in which, according to Mosse, were reflected the fundamental principles of bourgeois morality sublimated as eternal values and placed by fascism itself at the basis of its vision of the new society and the new man. In his previous writings Mosse had already hinted at the idea that fascism was the realization of nineteenth-century bourgeois morality, in the wake of a tradition that dated back to the origins of modern nationalism.

In subsequent years Mosse developed his idea on the identity between National Socialism and bourgeois morality on the basis of his research on racism, on the relationship between sexuality and nationalism, and on the elaboration of the image of masculinity. He emphasized ever more strongly the importance of the link between the aesthetics of politics and bourgeois morality for defining the myths and symbols of the fascist vision of life and especially of the racism and anti-Semitism of National Socialism. In the end, this link became for Mosse the most distinctive element in his interpretation of fascism as "an anti-bourgeois bourgeois revolution,"[125] with the emphasis falling, however, on the bourgeois component, not so much in a social and economic sense as in a moral sense. The new man of fascism—such was Mosse's conclusive conviction—was "the ideal bourgeois."[126]

Against the New Positivism

The notion of "new politics" represents, in my view, the most original and innovative moment in Mosse's historiography on account of both methodology and the development of his concept of fascism. Mosse's methodology, however, raises an important question concerning the role that must be ascribed to the "new politics" in the interpretation of the nature of fascism, of its historical significance, and of the reasons for its success. This brings our inquiry back to the existential presuppositions, so to speak, of Mosse's interest in the problem of fascism and to the original question that had always driven his reflections: Why has fascism succeeded in attracting millions of individuals with its myths and its symbols? The answer he had provided, through his concept of the "new politics," implied a judgment on human nature. "Whether a liturgy can be regarded as still more basic than social forces depends upon our view of human nature. A belief in man's inherent goodness and rationality, for instance, would view the new politics as mere propaganda and manipulation," Mosse wrote in the conclusion to *The Nationalization of the Masses*.[127] It is clear that he did not share this belief and did not think it could serve as an adequate criterion of historical interpretation for understanding the confrontation with modernity in which millions of people were involved who aspired to live in a secured and ordered world that would be sheltered from the convulsions of a hectic age and from the precipitous flow of time.

On the basis of these presuppositions, Mosse was always convinced that the cultural approach he had adopted was the best way to understand the nature and significance of fascism, for it went beyond the interpretations that were one-dimensional or reduced everything to pragmatic and utilitarian motives. On this way of interpreting the mass politics of fascism Mosse's negative judgment was unequivocal. Applying the term "propaganda" to political liturgy, he had written in 1975 with reference to National Socialism, "is singularly inappropriate here, for it denotes something artificially created, attempting to capture the minds of men by means of deliberate 'selling' techniques. This is to misunderstand the organic development of the Nazi cult and its essentially religious nature."[128] And this negative judgment was reiterated even more clearly and decisively in his essay on the general theory of fascism:

> More serious is the contention, common to most theories of totalitarianism, that the leader manipulates the masses through propaganda and terror; that free volition is incompatible with totalitarian practice. The term "propaganda," always used in this context, leads to a misunderstanding of the fascist cults and their essentially organic and religious nature. In times of crisis they provided many millions of people with a more meaningful involvement than representative parliamentary government—largely because they were not themselves a new phenomenon, but were instead based upon an older and still lively tradition of popular democracy, which had always opposed European parliaments.[129]

The elaboration of the concept of "new politics" gave Mosse the opportunity to resume his polemics with the traditional historiography that started from rationalistic and pragmatic presuppositions and was thereby incapable of assessing the importance of the new political style for defining the nature of fascism and for explaining the reasons for its success. "Such a political style," he argued in his Canberra lecture, "has seemed vague and difficult to understand for those reared in the traditions of liberal or socialist thought. They continuously search for a logical political system and forget that men have been captured more often by theology than by the canons of classical political thought."[130] This pragmatic approach did not take into account the fact that during the nineteenth century, with the development of nationalism and mass politics, "an important change in the nature of politics" had taken place and that from it there had emerged "a new political style which operated within the framework of myths, symbols, and public festivals" and had transformed politics into a drama in which the masses were involved as an integral part of the nation. In the introductory chapter of *The Nationalization of the Masses* Mosse summed up all his criticisms of the traditional interpretations of fascism:

Theories about fascism itself have tended to ignore the importance of those myths and cults which eventually provided the essence of fascist politics. For those who thought of themselves as liberals or as belonging to the left, fascism often presented an aberration of history, an "occupation" of the country by a barbaric minority. The people were held captive and when left to determine their own destiny would return either to a renewed liberalism or to Socialist ideals. . . . But despite the fact that some who fervently held such views in the past changed their mind, this concept of fascism is still widespread.[131]

After 1975 Mosse did not do new research on fascism and National Socialism. His work over the next two decades represented a new phase in his historiography—and a productive one in terms of research and reflections—with original and innovative writings in which, however, fascism was viewed only as part of wider phenomena such as nationalism, racism, the myth of the war experience, sexuality and respectability, and the construction of masculinity. To be sure, Mosse's scholarly production after 1980 did include essays that shed light on specific aspects of fascism, but I believe these were further refinements, with a few modifications, of concepts he had already formulated rather than new contributions to or substantive changes from the whole conceptual structure he had achieved by the end of the 1970s. From this vantage point, as one looks back at the whole development of Mosse's concept of fascism, one can see, as it were, a "spiral-shaped" trajectory: it is a work of research and reflection that always goes back, in successive stages, to the same themes and problems, yet observes them, at each stage, from a higher standpoint, from a broader perspective, and hence with a more complex, enriched, and renewed vision, but one that is always organic and unitary, such as it looked at the end of the 1970s. Moreover, even considering the subsequent developments of his historiography, it was in this period that Mosse felt that by now he had reached a mature and fully comprehensive vision of fascism, so much so that he could attempt to define a general theory that he first proposed informally in the interview on National Socialism originally published in Italian in 1977, and then, more systematically, in the 1979 essay titled "Toward a General Theory of Fascism," even though that which Mosse elaborated was neither a theory nor a typology according to the method in use in the social sciences and in the more common theories of the so-called generic fascism but rather was a presentation of general ideas supported by historical examples derived for the most part from the Italian and German experience.

That essay, however, must be viewed as an integral, complementary part of the introduction to his collected essays, *Masses and Man*, published a year later. These essays, including the one on the general theory of fascism, dealt primarily, as the subtitle explained, with the "nationalist and fascist perceptions of reality." The introduction is important for our subject because it contained some elements for a further development of the concept of fascism as an "anti-bourgeois bourgeois revolution" within the framework of radical nationalism. In the essay on fascism, moreover, Mosse restated, in opposition to "a new positivism" that "has captured the historical imagination,"[132] a conclusive redefinition of his cultural approach to the study of the past based on the study of the "human perceptions filtered through myths and symbols that are at the core of our historical analysis,"[133] while, always true to this principle, he reiterated his conception of the historian's attitude toward the past: "We must not look at a historical movement mainly from the viewpoint of our political predilections, lest we falsify historical necessity."[134] The essays collected in *Masses and Man* demonstrated the productivity of this approach with a wealth of examples drawn from the nineteenth and twentieth centuries, from nationalism as well as from socialist and liberal humanism, from Nazi and fascist culture, and from Hebrew culture:

Here the historian becomes an investigator of myth. Not only nationalism but all modern ideologies have attempted to express themselves through symbols which men and women can grasp, which they can see and touch. The twentieth century, the age of mass politics and mass culture, has been visually oriented rather than tied to the written word. This visual orientation had always existed among a largely illiterate population, but now, with the refinement of photography, the film, and political ritual, it became a major political force.[135]

The 1979 essay and the introduction to *Masses and Man* can thus be considered the conclusion of Mosse's long work of research and reflection on fascism. Accordingly, our own inquiry, too, is approaching its conclusion. All that is left for us to do is to recall what Mosse considered "the building blocks" for a general theory of fascism such as it is formulated in the writings of this period. I shall not dwell on the blocks that had already become permanently embedded in Mosse's concept of fascism during the early phase of its construction, but I shall dwell only on the more innovative aspects that Mosse introduced at the end of this second phase of his historiography on fascism.

The Building Blocks

Mosse confirmed his vision of fascism as a general phenomenon consisting of national varieties that shared common elements but also had distinguishing features, and these had to be studied within their respective national contexts, such as the concept of revolution as "spiritual revolution," the nationalist or racist mystique, the search for a "third way" and the ideal of the organic corporative state, the revolutionary dynamism and the problem of "taming the revolution," the cult of the leader, the myth of the new man, and the assimilation of bourgeois morality and respectability into the ethics of the nation regenerated according to warlike and traditionalist models of masculine virility for men and of wifely and maternal dedication for women. Mosse still stressed both the diversity and the affinity of the various forms of fascism, but now he seemed less inclined to emphasize the uniqueness of National Socialism. Besides, he did not even reject a comparison between fascism and Bolshevism and between fascism and the revolutionary tradition of Jacobinism, something that had been missing in his earlier definitions. These movements shared common elements that made possible a comparative analysis in that they were all revolutionary movements which, albeit in different and distorted forms, appealed to the principle of popular sovereignty and proposed a mass democracy involving the masses with forms of participation alternative to parliamentary democracy. Mosse remained skeptical as to the validity of using the concept of totalitarianism when referring to these movements, because "it may serve to disguise real differences, not only between bolshevism and fascism, but also between the different forms of fascism. . . . Indeed, totalitarianism as a static concept often veils the development of both fascism and bolshevism."[136]

Mosse's polemic was clearly aimed at the theories of totalitarianism that centered solely on the definition of the totalitarian regime, a definition based upon concepts such as terror, manipulation, propaganda, and the monolithic cult of the leadership. However, he did not entirely reject other interpretations of totalitarianism which he himself, as we have seen, had endorsed as early as 1961, when he had emphasized "the longing for totality"[137] as typical of the aspirations of the modern masses, and fascism's ambition to respond to them by suppressing the distinction between public life and private life with the creation of a community held together by myths, rites, and symbols. With its ideal of totality, represented in myths and symbols, fascism had provided an answer to this aspiration: "large numbers of people today may still share those basic longings for wholeness and the need to objectify which seem an integral part of humanity. There is, even in our time, a longing for the totality of life which is closely related to myth and symbol."[138] Mosse was wary of the theories of totalitarianism, but he fully grasped the essential character of totalitarian reality when he asserted the importance of the concept of culture as totality for defining the nature of fascism:

Politics and life must penetrate each other, and this means that all forms of life become politicized. Literature, art, architecture, and even our environment are seen as symbolic of political attitudes. At times when parliamentary government does not seem to be working well, men are apt to return to the idea of culture as a totality which encompasses politics. . . . But what is often condemned as the politicization of all aspects of life is in reality a deep stream of history which has always condemned pluralism, the division of politics from other aspects of life.[139]

Viewed in these terms, totalitarianism, in the interpretation suggested by Mosse, was not just a structure of power but a response to demands of totality which, according to Mosse, had been shared by many people who, in the first half of the twentieth century, "increasingly perceived the world in which they lived through myth, symbol, and stereotype," predisposing themselves to welcoming the promise of totality represented by fascism.[141] Other novelties can be found in the definition of fascism as "climax" of earlier traditions and on the role of World War I. Mosse confirmed his theory that fascism, as a political movement, had emerged after World War I, but the materials that went into the making of its ideology, its culture, and its political style were in no way original, for they were already present in traditions that had been in existence before the rise of fascism as a political movement. Fascism, then, had not had an original ideology, but Mosse insisted that this feature had been one of the

main reasons for its success: "the lack of original ideas was not a disad-
vantage, as many historians have implied, for originality does not lead to
success in an age of democratic mass politics. The synthesis which fascism
attempted between activism and order, revolution and the absorption of
past traditions, proved to be singularly successful."[141] Mosse gave a more
effective reformulation of this concept by resorting to a new image for
defining fascism's attitude toward old traditions and other ideologies: "It
was a scavenger which attempted to annex all that appealed to people in
the nineteenth- and twentieth-century past: romanticism, liberalism, and
socialism, as well as Darwinism and modern technology. Too little attention has been paid to this scavenging; it has been subsumed under the so-
called eclecticism of fascism. But in reality all these fragments of the past
were integrated into a coherent attitude toward life through the basic fascist nationalist myth."[142] In this new perspective Mosse attenuated in part
his definition of fascism as an anti-modern movement, even though he did
not have the opportunity further to develop his interpretation of the relationship between fascism and modernity, and confined himself to recognizing that fascism—and especially Italian fascism, which had more organic ties with the intellectual avant-garde[143]—did not have a totally
negative attitude vis-à-vis modernization:

It was not afraid to annex modern technology if this could be embedded within
fascist myths. Indeed, the dictators were singularly perceptive in their appreciation of technological advance. . . . The newest technology was annexed to an ideology that looked to the past in order to determine the future. . . . Nationalism,
and even volkish thought, were not necessarily opposed to modernization, provided it was made to serve the ideology of the regime, which in turn justified it.[144]

The idea of fascism as "climax" of previous movements remained, at
any rate, the cornerstone of Mosse's interpretation, but now he attached
greater weight to the Great War's "crucial role"[145] in the formation of the
mentality, culture, and political style of fascism. Fundamental materials
for the formation of fascism were derived from the experience of that war,
such as camaraderie, the cult of fallen soldiers, and the myths of violence
and war. These materials, even when they were connected to ideological
precedents, such as the myth of the virile community of males taken as a
model for national regeneration,[146] were no longer merely intellectual experiences but were the result of concretely lived experiences, and this was
for fascism more important than the ideas handed down by tradition. "For

fascism," Mosse stated, "it was always 'the experience' that counted, and not appeals to the analytical intellect."[147] Fascism was "the continuation of the war experience in peacetime"; it "was based upon a strong and unique revolutionary tradition, fired by the emphasis on youth and war experience; it was able to create a mass consensus that was broken only by a lost war."[148] Mosse reiterated his definition of fascism as a revolutionary movement that had had its own autonomous dynamic force vis-à-vis Bolshevism, even though it shared with the latter some common features, just as it shared some features with the French Revolution, in spite of being ideologically at opposite ends from it.[149] Fascism, like Jacobinism and like Bolshevism, had realized, with the use of myths, rites and symbols, a form of popular participation that many people perceived as a more real and authentic expression of the nation than parliamentary representation. Fascism was a secular religion that had satisfied the need for faith, certitude, authority, integration, and the participation of millions of people who felt alienated in industrial society and were frightened in the vortex of modernity. "It was the strength of fascism everywhere that it appeared to transcend these concerns, gave people a meaningful sense of political participation (though, of course, in reality they did not participate at all) and sheltered them within' the national community against the menace of rapid change and the all too swift passage of time."[150] Fascism promised security and stability and fulfilled that promise by assimilating traditional values in defense of family, morality, and respectability. "The traditionalism of the fascist movement coincided with the most basic of bourgeois moral prejudices."[151] However, Mosse now added, this did not mean that fascism must be identified with capitalism and with the bourgeoisie as a social class; its interclass appeal must also be recognized: "Fascism thus attracted a motley crowd of followers from different backgrounds and of all classes, even though the bourgeoisie provided the backbone of the movement and most of its leaders."[152] As a consequence, every theory based exclusively on the interpretation of fascism according to class interests was for Mosse simplistic and a departure from historical reality, for it denied or ignored fundamental aspects of fascism as a revolution that conceived of itself in spiritual rather than social terms and tried to reconcile its revolutionary dynamism with the tradition more consonant with its own nationalism. In this instance, too, Mosse redefined with another telling image his interpretation of the peculiar nature of the fascist revolution: "Within its basic presuppositions of revolution, nationalism, and war experience, fascism contained two rhythms: the amoeba-like absorption of ideas from the mainstream of popular thought and culture, countered by the urge toward activism and its taming. Both were set within the nationalist myth, and the whole gave the proper attitude toward life."[153]

I have delineated the essential new elements Mosse inserted into the redefinition of the concept of fascism when he wanted to attempt to formulate the foundations of a general theory. At this point all I have to do is to leave to Mosse himself the task of summarizing this concept in his own words:

The building blocks for a general theory of fascism now seem to lie before us. Fascism was everywhere an "attitude toward life" based upon a national mystique which might vary from nation to nation. It was also a revolution, attempting to find a "third way" between Marxism and capitalism, but still seeking to escape concrete economic and social change by a retreat into ideology—the "revolution of the spirit" of which Mussolini spoke; or Hitler's "German revolution." However, it encouraged activism, the fight against the existing order of things. Both in Germany and Italy, fascism's chance at power came during conditions of near civil war. But this activism had to be tamed, fascism had to become respectable; for activism was in conflict with the bourgeois desire for law and order, with middle-class virtues that fascism promised to protect against the dissolving spirit of modernity. . . . The result was that activism had to exist side by side with the effort to tame it. This was one of the chief problems faced by Hitler and Mussolini before their rise to power and in the early years of their rule.

Fascism could create a consensus because it annexed and focused those hopes and longings that informed diverse political and intellectual movements of the previous century. Like a scavenger, fascism scooped up scraps of romanticism, liberalism, the new technology, and even socialism, to say nothing of a wide variety of other movements lingering from the nineteenth into the twentieth century. But it threw over all these the mantle of a community conceived as sharing a national past, present, and future—a community that was not enforced but "natural," "genuine," and with its own organic strength and life, analogous to nature. The tree became the favorite symbol; but the native landscape or the ruins of the past were also singled out as exemplifying on one level the national community, a human collectivity represented by the Fascist Party. . . .

. . . It was the only mass movement between the wars that could claim to have a largely cross-class following.

In the end the fascist dream turned out to be a nightmare. It is not likely that Europe will repeat the fascist or National Socialist experience. The fragments of our Western cultural and ideological past which fascism used for its own purposes still lie ready to be formed into a new synthesis, even if in a different way. Most ominously, nationalism, the basic force that made fascism possible in the first place, not only remains but is growing in strength—still the principal integrative force among peoples and nations. Those ideals of mass politics upon which fascism built its political style are very much alive, ready to absorb and exploit the appropriate myths. The danger of some kind of authoritarianism is always present, however changed from earlier forms or from its present worldwide manifestations.

Speculations about the future depend upon an accurate analysis of the past. This essay is meant to provide a general framework for a discussion of fascism, in the hope of leading us closer to that historical reality without which we cannot understand the past or the present.[154]

To Conclude: Not Just Culture

I hope I have retraced the development of Mosse's concept of fascism with a sufficient degree of impartiality. I believe that his concept of fascism is on the whole persuasive and that it stands, in many respects, as a definitive contribution to the historiography on fascism. There are, however, some aspects, both specific and general, of Mosse's interpretation and methodology that raise various problems, and these will have to be thoroughly discussed in another venue as part of a broader critical revision of Mosse's interpretation, because they are essential for understanding fascism. I have in mind, for instance, the relationship between fascism and modernity, the role of World War I, the relationship between the leader and the movement, and the problem of the political system of fascism. A critical revision of his ideas, by the way, is what, in my view, Mosse would appreciate as the best recognition of the value of his work, since he himself has been a constant critic of his own ideas. Since it is not possible to undertake such revision here, I shall limit myself to just three problems, which, however, I consider fundamental because they involve both Mosse's concept of fascism and his cultural approach to the problem of fascism.

One such problem arises from the definition of fascism as an "anti-bourgeois bourgeois revolution" and from the characterization of the new fascist man as the ideal type of bourgeois respectability. In his latest writings Mosse had gone so far as to assert a substantial identity between bourgeois respectability and fascism, an identity that historically, in my opinion, stood in sharp contrast to the very essence of fascism, with its culture, with its concept of man, of politics, of the national community, and of the totalitarian state. To say that fascism represented the ideal bourgeois revolution because it based its morality on the values of honesty, probity, diligence, and respectability—values that were the products of bourgeois morality—is tantamount to inserting conservatism, liberalism, and democracy in the genealogy of fascism. If we consider this genealogical descent with regard to Nazi racism and the genocide of the Jews, I share the critical objections raised by Steven Aschheim when he commented on "the most startling of all Mosse's theses: Nazism as the incarnation, the most extreme defender of bourgeois respectability," pointing out that bourgeois respectability, "while often illiberal, was seldom genocidal; and it is surely in the processes of corruption and radicalization that such a transformation was engendered."[155]

To define fascism as an "anti-bourgeois bourgeois revolution" and to state, at the same time, that the fascist revolution was the ideal bourgeois revolution amounts to making one part of the preceding definition irrelevant and removing one or its essential components, because one ends up ignoring the congeniality of anti-bourgeois polemic in fascism's fundamental attitudes that belonged to the essence of its origins and of its militaristic and collectivist nature and made it ultimately incompatible, despite the ambiguity of occasional compromises, with the bourgeois respectability of liberalism and conservatism and with the ideals and the values of morality that were prevalent in the democratic and liberal Western bourgeoisie. The identification of fascist respectability with bourgeois respectability underestimates the role the anti-bourgeois spirit played in fascism, not so much as shown in some anti-capitalist attitudes, which, in my opinion, were never very decisive, but rather on account of the collectivist essence, in the sense of the ideological and organic community, of fascist totalitarianism; on account also of the fascist concept of politics as a permanent militia and of its belligerent vocation. Fascism did share with the bourgeoisie some notions of morality and respectability, yet we must keep in mind that, beyond the consonance between bourgeois morality and fascist morality, there still lies a substantial difference between *respectability in civilian clothes* and *respectability in uniform,* and we must keep in mind that the latter, rather than the former, was the ideal of fascist morality. The new man of fascism was not the incarnation of traditional "respectability in civilian clothes," which was the ideal of the individualist and liberal bourgeoisie, but of the new "respectability in uniform" of the collectively organized man who was raised according to the principles of a militarist and belligerent morality which was the antithesis of everything that was typical of the "respectability in civilian clothes" of the bourgeoisie. Bourgeois culture did not identify its sense of belonging and of respectability with military style, whereas "respectability in uniform" represented for fascism an ideal of communitarian life explicitly and polemically anti-bourgeois, because with it fascism intended to combat and annihilate the claim that bourgeois civilization ensured a private dimension in familial and social existence, quite separate from and autonomous vis-à-vis politics.

To this critical observation another must be added involving another aspect of fascism, namely the militarization of politics, which, together with the sacralization of politics, has been a defining factor of all fascisms and which, in my view, truly represents one of the fundamental building blocks for a general theory of fascism, whereas it seems to me that it has been almost entirely left out of Mosse's concept. Mosse had intuited the importance of that problem when he wrote, in *The Culture of Western Europe,* that in fascism "the sense of belonging was concretized in an orgy of uniforms which raised the status of even the man who performed the most humble tasks,"[156] but in the later development of his interpretation this problem was neglected, just as the passage I have just quoted was deleted in the subsequent editions of the book. With the term "militarization of politics" I am not referring to a political movement that adopts a military model of organization but rather to a movement that conceives of politics itself as essentially and integrally military in both its values and its goals and which finds its realization in the "party as militia." The way fascists understood it, the militarization of politics was something quite different, despite a superficial resemblance, from traditional militarism, for the latter assumed, as a matter of course, a differentiation between the political dimension and the military dimension, between the citizen in civilian clothes and the citizen in uniform. The fascist militarization of politics suppressed this distinction when it asserted the identity of the citizen and the soldier in the truly fascist ideal of the citizen soldier, by which it meant that the entire individual and collective life must be organized militarily according to the principles and values of its integralist concept of politics. Militarization thus became, in fascism, a redefinition of the citizen's identity—a sharp antithesis to the bourgeois civilization, which had developed on the basis of the differentiation between the civilian and military dimensions.

Another and more important problem, of a more general nature, arises from Mosse's tendency to make use of the cultural dimension for the definition of his concept of fascism, which leads him to identify fascism with its self-representation and its political style. I have written several books on fascist ideology and culture that have drawn their inspiration from Mosse's work, and I thus cannot be accused of being an adversary of the cultural approach or of underestimating the importance of ideology in fascism. Nonetheless, I do not believe that in the elaboration of a general theory of fascism the primacy of ideology is to be preferred to the primacy of the economy or the social structure.

In the introduction to *The Fascist Revolution,* Mosse claims with legitimate pride the importance of the contribution his cultural interpretation of fascism has made to the progress of historiography and the growing success it has met among historians, especially of the new generation. And yet it seems to me that very success may also open the way to some serious risks that are already noticeable in the current tendency to give pride of place, in the analysis of fascism, to the cultural dimension, to give an exclusive primacy to ideology in the definition of fascism, to consider ideology as the essence of a fascism in its "pure state," excluding from the definition of a general theory of fascism the organizational and institutional dimension, as these are considered almost as places of degradation of the essence of fascism from the "pure state" of ideology to the incompleteness of practical reality. I think, however, that in so doing one inevitably slips into that category of historians Mosse himself had criticized, namely those who "were prone to look for a single key to unlock the secrets of fascism's existence and success."[157] But to pretend to extract only from the cultural dimension the blocks for building a general theory of fascism, leaving out of the construction other fundamental blocks that belonged to the organizational and institutional dimension: is this not a way of turning cultural history into another "single key"?

I do not believe that it is possible to elaborate a general theory of fascism by separating ideology from history, myth from organization, culture from institution. After all, the irrationality of fascist culture was politically effective not only because it fascinated the masses with myths, symbols, and rites but because it was joined to the rationality of the organization and the institution. Without the rationality of the organization and the

institution, without being a party and a regime, without becoming the ideology of a modern state, fascism would have probably remained an ideology at the margins of politics and history, confined to the fields of intellectual snobbery.

I consider this problem fundamental for understanding the nature of
fascism, for I do not think one can exclude the organizational and institutional dimension—that is, the reality of the party and the regime in the
concrete unfolding of their history—from any project aimed at the construction of a general theory of fascism unless that theory is willing to
be, pretentiously, a new one-dimensional theory.[158] Mosse himself has
warned against the tendency "to press history into the straightjacket of
single causes which are bound to make fact fit theory rather than have theory fit all available facts."[159] This does not mean that we must renounce
elaborating a general theory of fascism but rather that we must be aware
of the fact that such a theory can only be based on many-sided dimensions, just as the historical reality of fascism was many-sided. And it certainly does not help the quest for a rational understanding of the
significance of this phenomenon to force its historical reality into a one-
dimensional scheme, whatever that scheme may be, or to pretend that we
can enclose the concept that defines this complex reality within a single
formula. As Stanley Payne has commented: "Indeed, the uniqueness and
complexity of fascism cannot be adequately described without recourse
to a relatively complex typology, however laudable the principle of parsi-
mony may be."[161] I agree with this view without, however, thinking that
there will ever be some theoretical definition of fascism that could aspire
to become a perennial monument and that could presume to replace the
constantly active research and reflection. After all, as Mosse has observed,
and here I gladly let him have the last word for concluding this analysis of
his theory of fascism, "any general theory of fascism must be no more than
a hypothesis which fits most of the facts. We shall attempt to bring together some of the principal building blocks for such a general theory—
there seem to be enough of them to construct at least a provisional
dwelling."[161]

Notes

1. George L. Mosse, *The Fascist Revolution: Toward a General Theory of Fascism*
(New York: Howard Fertig, 1999), x.
2. Ibid., xi.

3. Ibid., xi.

4. George L. Mosse, *Confronting History: A Memoir* (Madison: University of Wisconsin Press: 2000), 70.

5. Ibid., 103–4, 108–9.

6. *George L. Mosse, "Ich bleibe Emigrant": Gespräche mit George L. Mosse,* ed. Irene Runge and Uwe Stelbrink (Berlin: Dietz, 1991).

7. George L. Mosse, *Masses and Man: Nationalist and Fascist Perceptions of Reality* (New York: Howard Fertig, 1980; reprint, Detroit: Wayne State University Press, 1987), 18.

8. Mosse, *Confronting History,* 191.

9. Ibid., 5.

10. Ibid., 53.

11. Ibid., 217.

12. Ibid., 172.

13. Ibid., 205.

14. Ibid., 176.

15. Ibid., 171.

16. James Wald, "Cultural History and Symbols," *New German Critique* 37 (Winter 1986): 182.

17. Mosse, *Masses and Man,* 15.

18. George L. Mosse, *The Reformation,* 3rd ed. (Hinsdale, Ill.: Dryden Press, 1963), 1.

19. Ibid., 2.

20. George L. Mosse, *Calvinism: Authoritarian or Democratic?* (New York: Rinehart, 1957), 1.

21. Mosse, *The Reformation,* 8.

22. George L. Mosse, "Freshman History: Reality or Metaphysics?" *Social Studies* 3 (1949): 99–103.

23. George L. Mosse, "The Image of the Jew in German Popular Culture: Felix Dahn and Gustav Freytag," *Leo Baeck Institute Year Book 2* (London: Secker & Warburg, 1957), 218–27.

24. George L. Mosse, "The Pragmatism of the Freshman History Course," *Social Studies,* 8 (December 1957), 289–92.

25. Mosse, "The Image of the Jew," 227.

26. George L. Mosse, "Culture, Civilization, and German Anti-Semitism," *Judaism* 3 (1958): 256–66.

27. George L. Mosse, "The Mystical Origins of National Socialism," *The Journal of the History of Ideas* 23.1 (January–March 1961), 218–27.

28. George L. Mosse, *The Culture of Western Europe: The Nineteenth and Twentieth Centuries: An Introduction* (Chicago: Rand McNally, 1961), 2.

29. George L. Mosse, "What Is Fascism?" one of the lectures given in *The Intellectual Foundations of National Socialism,* a seminar held at Stanford University, European Studies Seminar Center, conducted by G. Mosse, autumn 1963 (Stanford, Calif.: [n.p.], 1964), 34.

30. Maurizio Vaudagna, ed., *L'estetica della politica: Europa e America negli anni trenta* (Rome: Laterza, 1989), viii.

31. See Moshe Zimmerman, "Mosse and German Historiography," in *George Mosse on the Occasion of His Retirement, 17.6.1985* (Jerusalem: The Koebner Chair of German History/The Hebrew University of Jerusalem, 1986), xix–xxi.

32. Mosse himself told me of this episode, and there may be a trace of it in his records.

33. Mosse, *Confronting History,* 147.

34. Mosse, *The Culture of Western Europe*, 340.

35. Ibid., 341–48.

36. Ibid., 6–7.

37. Mosse, *Masses and Man*, 1, 11.

38. Mosse, "Fascism Once More," *Intellectual Foundations of National Socialism*, 15.

39. Mosse, *Masses and Man*, 14–15.

40. Mosse, "The Peasant and the Ideology," *Intellectual Foundations of National Socialism*, 33.

41. Mosse, "Conservatism," *Intellectual Foundations of National Socialism*, 22–23.

42. Mosse, "What Is Fascism?" 9.

43. Ibid., 3.

44. Ibid., 19; Mosse, "Conservatism," 35.

45. Mosse, "What Is Fascism?" 2–3.

46. Mosse, "Conservatism," 35.

47. Ibid., "Fascism Once More," 5.

48. Mosse, "Adolf Hitler," *Intellectual Foundations of National Socialism*, 26.

49. Ibid., "What Is Fascism?" 2.

50. Ibid.

51. Ibid., 5–6

52. Ibid., 8–9.

53. Ibid., 6.

54. Ibid., 12. Participants in the seminar included Gordon Craig, Hugh Seton-Watson, Karl Dietrich Bracher, Juan Linz, Sidney Verba and Paul Hohenberg.

55. Ibid., 30–31.

56. Mosse, "Fascism Once More," 2.

57. Ibid., 4.

58. Ibid., 5–6.

59. Ibid., 1.

60. Ibid., 6–7, 14–15.

61. George L. Mosse, "The Genesis of Fascism," *Journal of Contemporary History* 1.1 (1966): 25.

62. George L. Mosse, *The Crisis of German Ideology: Intellectual Origins of the Third Reich* (New York: Grosset & Dunlap, 1964), 315.

63. Ibid., 8.

64. Ibid., 1.

65. Ibid., 9.

66. Ibid., 7.

67. Ibid., 9.

68. George L. Mosse, ed., *Nazi Culture: Intellectual, Cultural, and Social Life in the Third Reich*, trans. Salvatore Attanasio et al. (New York: Grosset & Dunlap, 1966), xx.

69. Mosse, *The Crisis of German Ideology*, 312–13.

70. Mosse, "The Genesis of Fascism," 22–23.

71. Ibid., 14–15.

72. Ibid., 18.

73. Ibid., 19–21.

74. Ibid., 15–16.

75. Ibid., 25–26.

76. George L. Mosse, preface to *The Crisis of German Ideology: Intellectual Origins of the Third Reich* (New York: Schocken Books, Inc., 1981), vii.

77. Ibid., 317.

78. Ibid., 316–17.

79. Mosse, "The Genesis of Fascism," 17.

80. Mosse, *Nazi Culture*, 95–96.

81. George L. Mosse, *Germans and Jews: The Right, the Left, and the Search for a "Third Force" in Pre-Nazi Germany* (New York: Howard Fertig, 1970), 21.

82. Mosse, *Nazi Culture*, xl.

83. Ibid., 368.

84. Mosse, "What Is Fascism?" 32.

85. Mosse, *Nazi Culture*, xxxi.

86. George L. Mosse, "E. Nolte on *Three Faces of Fascism*," *Journal of the History of Ideas* 4 (1966): 621–63.

87 Ibid., 623–24.

88. George L. Mosse, "History, Anthropology, and Mass Movements," *American Historical Review* 75, no. 2 (1969): 447–52.

89. Ibid., 447–48.

90. Ibid., 452.

91. See the introduction to *Germans and Jews* (New York: Howard Fertig, 1970); "Caesarism, Circuses, and Monuments," *Journal of Contemporary History* 6, no. 2 (1971): 167–82; "The French Right and the Working Class: Les Jaunes," *Journal of Contemporary History* 3–4 (1972): 185–208; "Mass Politics and the Political Liturgy of Nationalism," in *Nationalism: The Nature and Evolution of an Idea*, ed. Eugene Kamenka (Canberra: Australian National University Press, 1973), 32–54; "The Poet and the Exercise of Political Power," *Yearbook of Comparative and General Literature* 22 (1973): 32–41.

92. Mosse, "Caesarism, Circuses, and Monuments," 168.

93. Mosse, *Confronting History*, 177.

94. George L. Mosse, *The Nationalization of the Masses: Political Symbolism and Mass Movements in Germany from the Napoleonic Wars through the Third Reich* (New York: Howard Fertig, 1975), 16.

95. Ibid., 1–2.

96. Thomas Nipperdey, "Nationalidee und Nationaldenkmal im 19 Jahrhundert," *Historische Zeitschrift*, June 1968, quoted by Mosse in *The Nationalization of the Masses*, 1–2.

97. Quoted by Mosse in "The Poet and the Exercise of Political Power," 33. Mosse acknowledged his intellectual debt to Huizinga in *Intervista sul nazismo*, ed. M. A. Ledeen (Rome-Bari: Laterza, 1977), 12.

98. George L. Mosse, "Albert Speer's Hitler, Spandau: The Secret Diaries," *Quadrant* 20, no. 10 (1976): 54.

99. Actually, in *The Nationalization of the Masses*, Mosse makes no references to Talmon's theory as found in *The Origins of Totalitarian Democracy*, probably because he viewed it as a theory formulated according to the traditional history of ideas and, as such, exclusively limited to the analysis of political theory while ignoring political style. On this, see Mosse's reflections on Talmon's work in George L. Mosse, "Political Style and Political Theory: Totalitarian Democracy Revisited," in *Totalitarian Democracy and After: International Colloquium in Memory of Jacob L. Talmon, Jerusalem, 21–24 June 1982* (Jerusalem: Israel Academy of Sciences and Humanities/Magnes Press/Hebrew University, 1984), 167–76.

100. Mosse, *Confronting History*, 177–78.

101. Ibid., 164.

102. Ibid., 183.

103. Ibid., 205.

104. Mosse, "Albert Speer's Hitler," 54.

105. Ibid., 55.

106. Mosse, *German and Jews*, 22.

107. Ibid.

108. Mosse, however, continued to pay attention to the involvement of intellectuals, as intellectuals, with fascism, as shown by his important contribution to *The Nature of Fascism*, published in 1968, in which he reiterated with new arguments his opposition to the still widely accepted interpretation of fascism "as an aberration from the dominant current of European history and thought." "Fascism and the Intellectuals," in *The Nature of Fascism: Proceedings of a Conference Held by the Reading University Graduate School of Contemporary European Studies*, ed. Stuart J. Woolf (London: Weidenfeld & Nicolson, 1968), 205–26.

109. Mosse, *Germans and Jews*, 4.

110. Ibid., 13.

111. Mosse, "Caesarism, Circuses, and Monuments," 167–69.

112. Mosse, "The French Right and the Working Class," 186.

113. Mosse, "Mass Politics and the Political Liturgy of Nationalism," 39.

114. Mosse, "The Poet and the Exercise of Political Power," 32–33.

115. George L. Mosse, *The Culture of Western Europe: The Nineteenth and Twentieth Centuries*, 2nd ed. (Chicago: Rand McNally, 1974), 335.

116. Mosse underscored the importance of the links between fascism, especially Italian fascism, and the cultural avant-garde: see "Faschismus und Avant-Garde," in *Faschismus und Avant-Garde*, ed. Reinhold Grimm and Jost Hermand (Königstein/Ts.: Athenäum Verlag, 1980), 133–48, later published as "Fascism and the Avant-Garde" in *Masses and Man*, 229–44; and "The Political Culture of Italian Futurism: A General Perspective," *Journal of Contemporay History* 25, nos. 2–3 (1990): 253–68.

117. Mosse, *The Culture of Western Europe*, 4.

118. Mosse, *The Nationalization of the Masses*, 9–10.

119. Ibid., 3–4.

120. Ibid., 211.

121. Ibid.

122. Ibid., 20.

123. Ibid., 21–23.

124. Ibid., 212–13.

125. Mosse, *Masses and Man*, 6.

126. George L. Mosse, *Nazism: A Historical and Comparative Analysis of National Socialism: An Interview with Michael A. Ledeen* (New Brunswick, N.J.: Transaction Books, 1978), 43. See also George L. Mosse, *Nationalism and Sexuality: Respectability and Abnormal Sexuality in Modern Europe* (New York: Howard Fertig: 1985), 153–80.

127. Mosse, *The Nationalization of the Masses*, 161.

128. Ibid., 10.

129. Mosse, *Masses and Man*, 161.

130. Mosse, "Mass Politics and the Political Liturgy of Nationalism," 40.

131. Mosse, *The Nationalization of the Masses*, 3–4.

132. Mosse, "Toward a General Theory of Fascism," in *Masses and Man,* 167.

133. Mosse, *Masses and Man,* 11.

134. Ibid., 163.

135. Ibid., 11.

136. Mosse, "Toward a General Theory of Fascism," 160.

137. Mosse, *Masses and Man,* 12.

138. Mosse, *The Nationalization of the Masses,* 215.

139. Ibid., 215–26

140. Mosse, *Masses and Man,* 11.

141. Ibid., 183–84.

142. Ibid., 178.

143. See Mosse, "Fascism and the Avant-Garde."

144. Mosse, *Masses and Man,* 182.

145. Ibid., 173.

146. See George L. Mosse, "The Community in the Thought of Nationalism, Fascism, and the Radical Right," in *Community as a Social Ideal,* ed. Eugene Kamenka (London: Edward Arnold, 1982), 27–42.

147. Mosse, *Masses and Man,* 168.

148. Ibid., 178, 169.

149. George L. Mosse, "Fascism and the French Revolution," *Journal of Contemporary History* 24, no. 1 (1989): 5–26.

150. Mosse, "Toward a General Theory of Fascism," 165.

151. Ibid., 175.

152. Ibid., 177.

153. Ibid., 183.

154. Ibid., 194–96.

155. Steven E. Aschheim, "Between Rationality and Irrationalism: George L. Mosse, the Holocaust and European Cultural History," in *Simon Wiesenthal Center Annual* 5 (Chappaqua, Rossel Books: White Plains, N.Y., 1988), 194–95.

156. Mosse, *The Culture of Western Europe* (1961), 347.

157. Mosse, *The Fascist Revolution,* ix.

158. George L. Mosse, "Norbert Elias: The Civilizing Process," *New German Critique* 15 (Autumn 1978): 182.

159. See Emilio Gentile, *Fascismo: Storia e Interpretazione* 3rd edition (Roma: Bari, 2003), 54–73.

160. Stanley G. Payne, *A History of Fascism, 1914–1945* (Madison, 1995), 5.

161. Mosse, "Toward a General Theory of Fascism," 1.

Withstanding the Rush of Time

The Prescience of Mosse's Anthropological View of Fascism

Roger Griffin

"You know, the sky here's strange. I often have the sensation when I look at it that it's a solid thing up there, protecting us from what's behind." Kit shuddered slightly as she said: "From what's behind?"
"Yes."
"But what *is* behind?" Her voice was very small.
"Nothing, I suppose. Just darkness. Absolute night."

Paul Bowles, *The Sheltering Sky*

Introduction

In his elegantly concise introduction to *The Fascist Revolution*, George Mosse claims that the ten essays it brings together, published between 1961 and 1996, "present a coherent picture"[1] based on an approach to the nature of generic fascism that is "finding increasing favour with contemporary historians."[2] As one of the historians mentioned in this context, I would like to take the opportunity offered by this collection of essays on Mosse's academic legacy to highlight a central characteristic of this approach, namely, its affinity with an "anthropological" understanding of modern history. I will then draw attention to an aspect of Mosse's approach that has a particular bearing on my own research, namely, its temporal implications. I will use this example to suggest that Mosse's peculiarly eclectic methodology highlights aspects of the dynamics not only of fascism but of a wide range of political phenomena in the era of high modernity whose full sociological significance has yet to be fully grasped by historians and social scientists.

The Genesis of Mosse's Anthropological Approach to the History of Fascism

It is possible to identify five structurally related components that characterize Mosse's approach to the historical reconstruction of fascism: first, his belief in "methodological empathy" as the cornerstone of historiography;[3] second, the centrality of culture in the sense of the values, mind-set, and worldview of the agents of historical processes;[4] third, the crucial role played by myth as a causal factor in the historical process;[5] fourth, a dialectical view of how the inner and outer worlds of human beings interact in the form of "myth and social forces";[6] and fifth, the belief that fascism constituted a "national revolution with its own ideology and its own goals."[7]

The heuristic strategy for investigating fascism which Mosse derived from these premises meant that, at a time when scholars regularly saw it in terms of nihilism or anti-culture, Mosse realized that a primary causal factor in the dynamics of Nazism was "the aspirations and dreams" of ordinary Germans which the Nazis had somehow been able to "capture."[8] At the same time, a major focus of research into generic fascism had to be the way that under it "the liturgy of nationalism moved to the forefront,"[9] so that "considerations of beauty usually not thought of as an element of politics" came to play a crucial role in its attempt to "encompass the entire man or woman, to address, above all, the senses and emotions."[10]

Prima facie, a historian who places so much emphasis on myth and its expression in the political liturgy of a new political community is giving historiography an anthropological orientation. Mosse recognized this himself when he stated, "the longer I work the more I become convinced that the idea of myth is a very important one, not just for anthropologists but also for historians. The historian's function must be to understand the myths that people live by, because these myths have often a tenuous link to reality, though they are placed within reality."[11] It was the feat of the pioneers of cultural and social anthropology, such as W. H. R. Rivers, Bronislaw Malinowski, Margaret Mead, and Franz Boas, to attune themselves to the inner lives of people—and hence their values, beliefs, and cosmology—who belonged to a culture utterly alien to their own. On this basis they reconstructed the belief system/worldview that structured the culture's "normality," to the point of providing rational accounts of their social behavior, no matter how irrational it seemed to an untrained Western or ethnocentric eye. Mosse may not have been unique in applying this technique to major episodes in modern Western history. After all, Mona Ozouf and Lynn Hunt both brought a similar methodology to unpack the historical significance of the rich mythological and festive dimension of the French Revolution contemporaneously with Mosse's work on the liturgy of German nationalism.[12] Rather, the striking feature of his work is that he applied such a methodology to the hidden mainsprings of extremely recent events not only associated with human suffering inflicted on an unimaginable scale but ones that had had such a potentially traumatic effect on his own existence.

Perhaps the key to this achievement lies in Mosse's *Sonderweg* to fascist studies. For one thing, having completed his higher education in the United States, he did not consciously set out to be a specialist in the study of Nazism in order to deal vicariously with the forces that had shattered his own family and cultural life. On the contrary, in Madison he seems to have found both a physical and psychological asylum from the horrors of contemporary war-torn and atrocity-scarred Europe, and he poured his intellectual energy initially into a wide subject area that can be seen as providing a safe refuge from events that were too close for comfort. He cut his pedagogic teeth on preparing survey histories that traced the broad sweep of movements in religious and political ideas fueling the power struggles, violence, and waves of fanaticism of early modern Europe. His first publications were on sovereignty (*The Idea of Sovereignty in England,* 1946) and Protestantism ("Puritanism and Reason of State," 1952; *The Reformation,* 1953; *Calvinism,* 1957).

Nevertheless, however remote the world of Luther may seem from that of Hitler, Mosse's first specialism provided illuminating case studies in the inextricable relationship between the inner world of belief systems and the outer world of political events. The age of the Counter Reformation was particularly rich in examples of the role of myth and ritual in shaping society and conditioning politics. As Mosse himself commented in his discussion with Michael Ledeen: "The Baroque is full of myth, theatre, and symbols which carry you away from the reality of this world. But the very success of the Jesuits was that while carrying you away from this world they were really integrating you into their political system."[13] He implied in the same interview that the insights gained in studying the Jesuits helped him later understand the power of Wagner and Hitler. Indeed, it is tempting in retrospect to see his forensic examination of how Europe tore itself apart with religious and dynastic struggles as an ideal apprenticeship for his bid to resolve the question that he had experienced, as they say in German, "on his skin," namely, how the Third Reich could have become a political reality, why the heavens did not darken. The transition to his new "problematic" is heralded by *The Culture of Western Europe: The Nineteenth and Twentieth Centuries,* published in 1961. In it he applies to the modern world the insights into the role of ideological currents and the general zeitgeist in conditioning the broad evolution of historical events that he had gained from his study of Reformation Europe.

It is thus no coincidence that the same year saw the publication of Mosse's first specialist contribution to fascist studies, "The Mystical Origins of National Socialism."[14] In it he outlined the basic strands of the late-nineteenth-century revolt against positivism, especially the highly diffuse *völkisch* movement which helped prepare the ideological ground for Nazism. As with his earlier work, the essay still owes more to the traditional history of ideas and political thought than to anthropology as such. This is consistent with what can be gleaned about the formative influences on his approach to historiography from a passage in his interview with Michael Ledeen about Nazism published in 1978. None of his mentors are anthropologists, but each made a major contribution to the history of ideas and culture.[15] Instead of citing anthropologists, he singles out Dutch historian Johan Huizinga, who wrote a major work on the zeitgeist of the declining Middle Ages;[16] and, via social historian George Lichtheim, Hegel, the doyen of idealist philosophers of history, who discerned dialectical patterns of thesis and antithesis structuring historical events on an epic scale; and Benedetto Croce, Italy's foremost idealist philosopher, who was as prolific a scholar as Mosse and wrote several survey histories informed by his belief in the primacy of ideas and values in shaping reality.[17]

However, at the risk of cultural stereotyping, I would like to suggest that another factor in his intellectual makeup helped Mosse to achieve his sophisticated understanding of the centrality of dreams and beliefs to the dynamics of fascism. In proposing this factor, which I have yet to see referred to in tributes to him, I should stress that I am operating from within a category that exerted considerable fascination on Professor Mosse, namely the outsider. Because I never had the privilege of meeting him, I was denied that rite of passage of intimacy which would have made him simply "George," and so I must rely on "methodological empathy" with him on the basis of his writings to reconstruct speculatively his private cosmology. Nevertheless, I see in his writings the hallmark of a peculiarly Jewish brand of scholarship. A number of interwar Jewish intellectuals approached the crisis of culture of the time and the rise of Nazism that it brought about with a blend of icy skepticism and warm-blooded fascination, an ability to see through the dense shrouds of mythology spun by Nazism yet give due weight to the power it derived from appearing to satisfy the very psychological and mystic longings it helped foment. I have in mind such figures as Walter Benjamin, Erich Fromm, and particularly Ernst Bloch. Bloch's *The Heritage of Our Time*[18] comprehensively demystifies what he sees as the revolutionary facade of Nazism, while *The Principle of Hope*[19] offers an exhaustive exploration of how millenarian anxieties and utopian fantasies persist in the political motivations and aspirations of contemporary human beings, no matter how secularized and "Westernized" their conscious minds. It is tempting to speculate that such an approach is second nature to those brought up to have a deep empathy and intimacy with the Jewish religious and mystic tradition yet who are excluded from full participation in it by a secular intellect steeped in Enlightenment rationalism.

I would argue that Mosse's specifically Jewish cast of mind inoculated him against even the most ephemeral collusion with the forces of ultranationalism that tarnish the intellectual careers of the likes of Carl Gustav Jung, Emile Cioran, or Mircea Eliade (not to mention fully paid up members of the Conservative Revolution such as Martin Heidegger). At the same time, his genuinely historiographical instincts precluded both the exclusive preoccupation with the history of ideas and championing of liberalism to which fellow Jews Karl Popper and Isaiah Berlin owe their fame, and the temptation to reduce Nazism simplistically to reactionary sociological, economic, and psychological categories which led Wilhelm Reich, Erich Fromm, Herbert Marcuse, and Theodor Adorno astray. It was thus a confluence of different intellectual currents which gave Mosse that peripatetic urge to move between different subject areas, different sources both primary and secondary, and different methodologies without ever allowing himself to become trapped in a narrow specialism or weighed down by a cumbersome theory. A rolling Mosse gathers no stones. It was an approach that enabled him to be outstanding at reconnoitering new terrain, which meant that he sometimes left it to the troops to bring up the extra supplies of empirical material or to resolve the tangled methodological issues he had raised so that it could be properly occupied.

The Development from a Cultural to a More "Anthropological" Approach to Fascism

Whatever its precise origins, Mosse's idiosyncratic emphasis on ideas and myths as causal factors in the genesis of revolutions bore fruit in "The Mystical Origins of National Socialism," published in 1961. At a time when fascist ideology was still widely regarded as reducible to Mussolini's megalomania[20] and a major English historian could still dismiss Nazism as "bestial Nordic nonsense,"[21] two years before Ernst Nolte's cryptic ruminations concerning fascism's "resistance to transcendence" and over a decade before Zeev Sternhell's brilliant exploration of the roots of fascist ideology in the cultural crisis of late-nineteenth-century Europe, which omitted Nazism altogether,[22] this article explored how Nazism was shaped by "a more complex cultural development long before it crystallized into a political party. At the very centre of this development were ideas both of a national and of a romantic nature, part of the revolt against positivism which swept Europe at the end of the nineteenth century."[23]

Over the next ten years Mosse devoted considerable energy to mining this rich vein in the cultural prehistory and history of the Third Reich, organizing the seminar *The Intellectual Foundations* of National Socialism" in 1963 and publishing two seminal books—*The Crisis of German Ideology* (1964) and *Nazi Culture: Intellectual, Cultural, and Social Life in the Third Reich* (1966)—as well as a number of germane articles.[24] Although these were primarily exercises in intellectual and cultural history, there are signs that by the mid-1960s he was becoming increasingly alive to the importance of the nonverbal, liturgical, ritual aspects of Nazism and their relevance to fascism as a generic phenomenon. His contribution to the first issue of the *Journal of Contemporary History* in 1966, the article "The Genesis of Fascism," while primarily written from a history of ideas perspective, stresses the "liturgical element" of fascism expressed in "slogans, choruses, and symbols"[25] and asserts that a corollary of the fascist emphasis on the primacy of the spiritual was that "cultural expressions of the new community moved to the forefront as symbols of the new society."[26] In 1969 he wrote a brief review of three recent publications on the history of anthropology under the title "History, Anthropology, and Mass Movements."[27] It soon becomes clear that Mosse was far less interested in this article in the contents of the three books purportedly under review than in using them as a pretext for articulating his debt to such theorists as Ernst Cassirer and Claude Lévi-Strauss in coming to realize the value of anthropology to historians. In particular, he argues that its insights equip historians to use the "existence of myths and symbols" as "an entry wedge" that keeps them from sliding into the reductionist fallacies of either "idealist or materialistic positions" in explaining sociopolitical realities. More important, myths and symbols provide the key to understanding how "totalitarian movements 'imposed' themselves upon their people by using . . . festivals, mass meetings, and symbolic representation."[28]

This review crystallized Mosse's maturation from intellectual history and history of ideas to an anthropologically informed historiography (or rather a historiography informed by a certain *idea* of anthropology and certainly not by a rigorous anthropological school of thought or theory). It was followed in 1971 by "Caesarism, Circuses, and Monuments,"[29] which argues that a "new politics" had emerged by the end of the nineteenth century that "substituted leader and led, festivals and symbols, for the traditional institutions of Europe"[30] and demonstrates how extensively the realm of the nonverbal, the visual, and the liturgical has moved to the forefront of Mosse's concept of generic fascism. This new orientation is signaled even more clearly in 1973 in the article "The Poet and the Exercise of Political Power: Gabriele D'Annunzio"[31] and in the chapter "Mass Politics and the Political Liturgy of Nationalism."[32]

But it is *The Nationalization of the Masses,* first published in 1975 and immediately translated into German and Italian, that underlines the quantum leap that has occurred in Mosse's "cultural" understanding of fascism. It applies rigorous scholarship to demonstrating the debt which the political form and style eventually adopted by Nazism owed to the cultic forms of German nationalism that had proliferated ever since the Napoleonic Wars, thereby making it possible only for scholars possessed by what Edgar Allen Poe called the imp of the perverse—or, worse still, by revisionist intent—to maintain that Hitler's movement was exclusively the product of the aftermath of World War I and the Russian Revolution.[33] The key to the fascist worldview is, for Mosse, no longer ideas and ideology but self-representation and performative acts. This point was not lost on Michael Ledeen, who in his extensive interview with Mosse two years later put it to him that the focus in *The Nationalization of the Masses* on the expression of the myths of German nationalism in the form of social celebrations represented "something quite new and might be said to represent an anthropological approach to history."[34] Mosse agreed, and he would make a similar observation on the significance of the book two decades later in his autobiography: "To my mind, the real breakthrough in putting my own stamp upon the analysis of cultural history came with *The Nationalization of the Masses* . . . which deals with the sacralization of politics: the Nazi political liturgy and its consequences."[35]

It was precisely in this highly productive period of Mosse's involvement with fascist studies that he was beginning to see that the anthropological approach was not just important for explaining fascism's genesis but held the key to the fascist minimum, something scholars still routinely regarded as a conundrum just as much as when he edited the first issue of the *Journal of Contemporary History* in 1966.[36] In *Nazism* he talks confidently to Ledeen of the centrality to fascist thought of nationalist mystique, the regenerated community, the new man, and the revolution of the spirit, which he now sees primarily enacted not in words but in ritual: "There is in all fascism a sense that it is a door into a utopia of tolerance, of happiness, of productivity," a utopia "brought before the people in mass movements, ceremonies, and symbols."[37] A year later he published "Toward a General Theory of Fascism,"[38] one of three convergent definitions of the revolutionary nature of fascist ideology to be published in the late 1970s, which made these years such a seminal one for the development of fascist studies into a mature discipline.[39] Mosse's theory highlights as a denominator common to all fascist movements: the drive toward creating a "third way" in modern politics, the key to which was the creation of a powerful mythic sense of belonging to a regenerated national community that would be experienced in a spirit of collective redemption from national decadence and cultural decay. Fascism was thus not just a new ideological movement but a revolutionary one that could not be understood outside the context of the rise of nationalism as a civic religion in nineteenth-century Europe, the collective psychological trauma created by World War I, and the profusion of utopian fantasies generated by the sustained interwar crisis of European society. A significant feature of Mosse's definition is the emphasis it places on the continuity between fascist dreams of a new man and a new order and the millenarian fantasies that proliferated in the wake of the Reformation.

Until the end of his life, all of Mosse's studies on fascism or its roots in currents of nationalism or culture display the hallmark of his anthropological approach.[40] It provides the matrix of almost all the essays collected in his two anthologies, *Masses and Man: Nationalist and Fascist Perceptions of Reality* (1980) and *The Fascist Revolution: Towards a General Theory of Fascism* (1999). Moreover, the introduction he wrote to the latter now reads as a methodological "last testament" to a future generation of students of fascism, exhorting them to empathize with the inner world of fascists and to treat fascism's "self-representation" as the key to its political goals and social programs as well as to its crimes against humanity.

Mosse's Legacy to Fascist Studies

The two published collections of essays also serve as testimonies to the prescience of Mosse's "cultural understanding of fascism." His prolific publications contributed to a paradigm shift in fascist studies which is now so complete that it is difficult to realize just how far a number of his earlier essays were out of step with orthodox scholarship when they were first published. For example, the crucial role played in the genesis of Nazism by the *völkisch* movement and the German revolt against positivism was recently explored in considerable depth in a work that, a quarter of a century later, fully vindicates Mosse's original analysis.[41] Similarly, there no longer seems to be anything aberrant about Mosse's stress on the way Nazism functioned as a political religion.[42] Nor do scholars investigating aspects of fascist artistic or intellectual life have to write an elaborate apologia for taking fascist culture seriously. Indeed, the burgeoning of studies published in this area in recent years has been so dramatic that one critic sees "culturalism" as the dominant approach to the interpretation of Mussolini's regime.[43]

However, it would be misleading to portray Mosse as having been the founding father of this approach to fascism. Indeed, an interesting paradox arises when we turn our attention to assessing his impact on fascist studies. Even if he is now coming to be justly regarded as a major pioneer of many of the assumptions that now operate with regard to the scholarly understanding of fascism and Nazism, it is difficult to document a high degree of direct influence, and there does not seem to be (and this is a surely a mercy) a discrete "Mossean" school of fascist studies. Certainly his editorship of the *Journal of Contemporary History* from the mid-1960s and his contacts with scholars such as Walter Laqueur, Stanley Payne, and Juan Linz meant that he helped steer fascist studies in the "right" direction, but it was more through osmosis and synergy than through "influence." As a result, it is rare to find scholars citing Mosse's theory of fascism or particular insights into the significance of its liturgy. For example, it is symptomatic of what now seems like a case of serious neglect that none of the four editions of Ian Kershaw's magisterial survey of the debate on key issues in the study of the Third Reich, *The Nazi Dictatorship,* make any reference to Mosse's works (nor does his two-volume biography *Hitler*). Mosse is similarly ignored by the major Anglo-Saxon historians of Italian Fascism such as Denis Mack Smith, Edward Tannenbaum, and Philip Cannistraro.

As for the non-Anglophone world, despite the early availability of his seminal works in translation, Mosse had no perceptible influence on the continuing debate within Germany and Italy over the genesis and nature of indigenous fascism (*Fascismo*). The only exceptions to this are a brief tribute to Mosse's pioneering work on Nazi ideology in Pier-Giorgio Zunino's *L'Ideologia del Fascism*[44] and several references to him in Emilio Gentile's studies of fascism as a "political religion," including an homage to Mosse in his introduction to *Il culto del littorio.*[45] Gentile's awareness of the potential value of Mosse's work to fascist studies as a whole is very much the exception, however, despite his growing worldwide reputation as one of the major fascist scholars of his generation. Far more typical of the general neglect of Mosse's significance in practical terms that prevailed until the 1990s is the fact that the eminent specialist in Third Reich studies, Tim Mason, gave a paper in 1988 deploring the absence of a concept of generic fascism that would enable Nazism to be studied in a comparative framework, seemingly oblivious of how effectively Mosse had provided a solid basis for one in 1979 in the essay "Toward a General Theory of Fascism," published in *International Fascism.*[46]

In short, Mosse cannot be credited for creating the "culturalist" approach to fascism. Instead, the current vogue of analyzing aspects of fascist culture has much more to do with the "linguistic turn" brought about by the impact of French poststructuralism and postmodernism on the Anglophone social sciences, which, in contrast with the conventional empiricist tradition, placed "myth," "discourse," and "representation" at the center of the analysis of historical phenomena.[47] It is notable in this respect that the main contributors to the new vogue in engaging with fascist culture make no discernible use of Mosse's actual theory of fascism or of an explicitly anthropological approach to their subject, even if they acknowledge him in footnotes.[48] It is perhaps symptomatic of a more general phenomenon, then, that my own work on fascism, which also makes its cosmological dimension central to its genesis, definition, and dynamics, was not influenced directly by Mosse's writings, largely because of his reluctance to resolve his highly discursive characterizations of fascism into a concise, heuristically useful ideal typical definition of it: the "toward" in the title of his essay on generic fascism is telling. This is why it is more appropriate to talk of his "prescience" than of his "formative influence" in this context.

Mosse's failure to have a direct contemporary impact on the conceptual framework used in comparative fascist studies is a fate common to all the formulators of sophisticated theories of fascism before the 1990s. A. James Gregor, Juan Linz, Eugen Weber, Henry Turner, Zeev Sternhell, and Ernst Nolte all became well known for having elaborated approaches to resolving the "fascist conundrum," but none of their theories were used by practicing historians in investigating specific aspects of fascism. The only partial exception to this pattern was Stanley Payne, whose "typological description" (published in 1980) was sometimes invoked, largely because it provided a concise three-point checklist of definitional features stressing fascism's revolutionary nature. Now that "culturalism" is all the rage in approaching fascism, it is my earnest hope that Mosse's legacy will be to exert a benign influence on its scholarly fruits by steering it away from the tendency to volatize all empirical phenomena into an intangible "discourse" or "myth" and relate "culture" back to the spheres of concrete economic and political phenomena in the genuinely historiographical spirit articulated so persuasively by Richard Evans in his broadside against the pernicious abuse of "postmodernist," In Defence of History.[49] I hope that this book will contribute to the "historicization" of culturalism and to the injection of genuine anthropological insights and methodologies into the project of reconstituting the cosmological premises that informed and shaped fascist policies and practices.

Perhaps the most potent sign that this reorientation had taken place would be the publication by a representative of the new generation of students of fascism of an equivalent of Gentile's *Sacralization of the State in Fascist Italy* written on Nazi Germany. It would offer a comprehensive analysis of how Nazism functioned as a "political religion" which completes the story Mosse started with *The Nationalization of the Masses*, taking into account the ritual and liturgical aspects of the Third Reich as well as its cultural and social policies as manifestations of a "totalitarianism" bent on inducing national rebirth. Gentile has already provided a clear conceptual framework for such an undertaking by postulating a profound nexus between the concepts "totalitarianism," "political religion," and "palingenesis."[50] At this point a confluence could come about between several powerful currents of concern with the history of ideas: the theories of fascism of Walter Benjamin and Ernst Bloch, with their stress on the "spectacular" and "specular" aspect of the Nazi regime; the theories of modern nationalism of Jacob Talmon and George Mosse, which stressed its secular religious content; and the sophisticated insights into the role of myth and ceremony in sustaining the political that can be gleaned from anthropologists such as Victor Turner and Clifford Geertz.[51] Should such a confluence or synergy come about between different disciplines in a way that enriches rather dilutes the orthodox historiographical reconstruction of events under the Third Reich represented by the likes of K. D. Bracher and Ian Kershaw, then it will signal a remarkable turnabout from the days when Mosse was such a pariah within conventional Nazi studies. There is a story about a doting parent who, while watching his son take part in an army cadet parade, comments to his wife, "Look! Everyone is out of step except our Harry." Once the full heuristic value of Mosse's approach to fascism is realized, it may become legitimate to ask which scholars were actually adopting eccentric, aberrant approaches to Nazism between the 1960s and the 1990s. Perhaps everyone was out of step except our George!

Arguably the most important writings in which Mosse indisputably established himself as the precursor of later orthodoxies are those relating to the definition of generic fascism itself. His 1966 essay "The Genesis of Fascism" suggests that the appeal of fascism lay in its success in being identified with the myth of the new man, the cult of youth, and an organic view of the world. Its appeal lay in the fact that at a time when Western society was undergoing a major structural crisis, it held out the prospect of putting an end to anomie and alienation by restoring a sense of belonging and rejuvenating the life of the spirit, thereby bringing about the moral rebirth of society. In characterizing fascism this way, Mosse became the first scholar to provide a coherent description of it as an attempted revolution of the nation's political, aesthetic, and ethical culture. This definition is fully consistent with what I have portrayed elsewhere as the "new consensus" on fascism that began to emerge in the 1990s and has now gained enough ground to ensure that the essays assembled in *The Fascist Revolution* would now hardly raise the eyebrows, let alone the hackles, of most contemporary historians of fascism.[52]

Yet there is one area in which I believe academia has yet to catch up with Mosse and recognize the profundity of another of his largely intuitive insights that derived directly from his anthropological approach to fascism. I am referring to the temporal theory implicit in his analysis. Here, as in so many other aspects of his theorizing, Mosse was a discursive thinker, loath to deliver rigorous formulae or succinct definitions (again something he shares with Benjamin and Bloch). Nevertheless, it is possible to infer from his sporadic allusions to the topic a coherent theory of the relationship between the experience of time under modernity and the appeal of fascism, one whose heuristic value to fascist studies has yet to be fully appreciated.

Fascism as a Temporal Revolution

From the outset, Mosse's pioneering work on the role played by the revolt against positivism in the genesis of fascism stressed the centrality to the fascist mind-set of the utopian myth of rebirth from decadence, or what I call "palingenesis." This already involves recognizing that fascism saw as part of its mission the inauguration of a new phase of civilization and a new experience of time. Hence in his very first contribution to fascist studies Mosse emphasizes Nazism's debt to the "artistic outlook upon the world" promulgated by the likes of Langbehn, Klages, and von List, which held out the prospect of "an all-encompassing national renewal" that would prevent modern civilization from "drowning" the soul of man.[53] Thus, while Nolte was developing his theory of fascism as "resistance *to* transcendence," Mosse was investigating the fascist impulse *toward* transcendence (albeit using the word in a less idiosyncratic way), one associated with a "new world of beauty and of aesthetic form."[54] In the same essay, for example, he is already writing lucidly about the fascists' sense of decadence and their urge to "transcend reality."[55]

Significantly, as Mosse's "cultural" approach to fascism matured into a genuinely "anthropological" one a few years later, the temporal aspect of this analysis becomes explicit and the outlines of a cogent theory of the temporal dimension of the fascist revolution begin to be discerned. The 1973 essay on Gabriele D'Annunzio presents the stream of rites and ceremonies that the poet staged as the basis of his legitimacy in Fiume as the dress rehearsal for the spectacular liturgical style of politics perfected by fascism and Nazism. He attributes the success of the "new politics" to the fact that "men longed to escape from the banality of daily life," a longing that "had already given impetus to public festivals in most European nations as an accompaniment of national self-consciousness."[56]

A year later Mosse published "Death, Time, and History: Volkisch Utopia and Its Transcendence," a sustained exploration of the link between the Nazi myth of the new order and an "apocalyptic view of history." The hallmark of such a view is that it saw earthly cataclysms as heralding the advent of a utopia, which meant that history itself would be overcome and "death, too, lost its sting, as merely one episode in the rush of time to obliterate itself."[57] Christian mystics who promulgated this view, such as Jakob Böhme of the seventeenth century, were perpetuating an ancient tradition which held that some hidden essence lay "beneath the passage of time."[58] Under the impact of secularization and the rise of nationalism as a civic religion, ancient longings for the revelation of this essence were no longer projected onto the second coming of Christ but onto the imminent rebirth of Germany. Thus the first half of the twentieth century was characterized by "the constant hope stated in apocalyptic terms that dawn was about to break," a dawn that was no longer religious and metaphysical but political and cultural (though pervaded with religiosity).

A deep-seated mythic reflex thus meant that Germany's catastrophic defeat in World War I brought to the surface a latent collective longing for a redemptive utopia that was fueled by something endemic to the West, namely "the ever-present fear of modernity, of unrest and chaos, which was the mark of the rapid passage of time."[59] The kingdom of God thus became conflated with the Third Reich, whose realization embodied "the eternal quality of the Volk and of nature," thereby "ending the rush of time."[60] For Nazis, once the blood of Germanic ancestors coursed once more within the regenerated *Volksgemeinschaft,* "the flow of time was safely imprisoned in its riverbed."[61]

After this breathtakingly original essay on Nazism, a preoccupation with time was to become a fundamental feature of Mosse's anthropological view of history, and he became the first scholar to recognize the attempt to bring about a temporal revolution as a definitional feature of generic fascism. His discursive characterization of fascism composed for *International Fascism* (1979) picks up a central theme of the earlier essay on "Death, Time, and Utopia" by drawing attention to the "mystical and millenarian dynamic" of fascism, identifying it with the human urge to "overcome," which the Marxist revolutionary Ernst Bloch[62] saw as "the 'hidden revolution' essential to the realization of the true socialist revolution." This leads to the assertion that "it was the strength of fascism everywhere that it sheltered [people] within the national community against the menace of rapid change and the all too swift passage of time."[63]

It is also in this period that Mosse assembled under the title *Masses and Man* fifteen essays whose common theme he identified as "the mobilization of private discontent into collectivities that promised to transcend the anxieties of the modern age. Nationalism was the most important such collectivity, promising a happy and healthy world protected against the rush of time."[64] He would return to this theme in the essay "Fascism and the Avant-Garde" (1980), where he talks of the Nazi appropriation of "all that was eternal, the mountains, the sky, and the nation."[65] In "Fascism and the French Revolution" (1989) Mosse again refers to Bloch's theory of the "hidden revolution"[66] and asserts that "fascism sought to abolish death just as it attempted to make time stand still."[67] Nor did he see the time-defying function of a fanatical ideology as exclusive to fascism. His theory of racism includes the insight that the search for racial roots and ethnic purity fulfilled "a longing for immutability and certainty in a world of rapid social change,"[68] which is why racism so readily drew on anthropology, history, and aesthetics for legitimation.

Overcoming Time

It is a tribute to the prescience of Mosse's earliest work on fascism that his insights into the revolutionary, utopian, cultural, aestheticizing, liturgical form of politics now seem self-evident. The temporal implications of his work on modern politics have yet to become part of the standard paradigm in historiography, however, though there is every reason to think that this will happen "in time." For one thing, in the last ten years a number of scholars have independently recognized how deeply the theatrical,[69] aesthetic,[70] and sacral[71] aspects of interwar fascism imply a transformation in the experience of time. There is also a wealth of scholarship in other disciplines that would enable Mosse's intuitions about the fascist urge to transcend time to be further refined into a comprehensive, genuinely interdisciplinary theory. However, as I have implied earlier, this would involve anchoring fascist studies more securely in the academic anthropology of culture, festivity, ritual, and time than Mosse's restless, roaming, homeless intellectual instinct ever allowed him to do. What follows is a tentative thumbnail sketch of the contours that such a theory might assume when fully elaborated.

Human beings have an instinctive horror of meaningless, amorphous, linear (and hence irreversible) time and an in-built drive to give it meaning, boundaries, shape, and fixity.[72] An important technique that enables them to do this is ritual in its various forms (festivity, rites, ceremony, liturgy, spectacle, sacrifice, etc.), which creates a subjective differentiation between profane and sacred time, normal and special time, individual and transcendent time, linear and cyclic time. Metaphorically, it creates the sense that human life takes place under a sky that is solid on its foundations. A major feature of human societies has been that times of social crisis have triggered a "temporal panic" in which history is experienced as being out of joint, that time itself is running out for the whole community.[73] It is a deeply distressing sensation which in premodern societies regularly unleashed waves of intense ritualistic behavior,[74] such as bouts of animal and even human sacrifice as well as "revitalization movements"[75] whose social purpose was to metaphorically and metaphysically prevent the sky from falling.[76] (The Christian tradition of millenarianism takes on an important supra-European dimension in this context.)[77]

Since modern human beings have the same temporal needs as premodern ones, even if mediated in different ways, the myriad disembedding forces of Western modernity[78] have had the effect of generating deep temporal or existential insecurity, producing ingenious social, intellectual, aesthetic, political, and religious strategies for finding new stability and boundaries. One example is political revolution, which is experienced subjectively by its protagonists and supporters as the renewal of history itself.[79] Moreover, a common denominator of many apparently unrelated phenomena that emerged at the end of the nineteenth century, such as the occult and Catholic revivals, racism, aesthetic modernism, revolutionary politics, and war fever, can be seen in the way they offer individuals a refuge from being engulfed by meaningless time.[80]

Once the Third Reich is located in this context, it becomes a serious historiographical proposition[81] to suggest that what unleashed the demons of Hitler's charisma after 1929 was a collective temporal panic triggered by the collapse of Weimar's viability both as an objective economic, social, and political system and also as the psychological basis for communal existence and social meaning.[82] Nor does it smack of New Age speculation to suggest that individual events in Nazi liturgy, such as the "cathedral of light" created by Albert Speer at one Nuremberg rally, formed part of a vast undertaking not just in social engineering but also in psychological and temporal engineering. It was primarily based not on brainwashing and terror but rather on the power of ritual to re-embed the Germans in time and space. The overriding concern of the Third Reich was to recenter a society cut adrift from its metaphysical anchor and to make the foundations of the sky solid once more so that "time could begin anew."[83] Such an approach gives an extra heuristic dimension to Ian Kershaw's brilliant two-volume biography of Hitler, which relates his charismatic power after 1929 to collective hopes for the renewal of Germany, and hence of time itself.[84] It also fully complements and amplifies Michael Burleigh's somewhat half-hearted interpretation of Nazism as a political religion, giving extra resonance to the Nazi painting he chose as the cover of the book. In kitsch neo-Baroque style it depicts a vast sea of men in SA uniforms flocking toward a huge, luminous swastika bursting through the clouds, some of them already transported aloft like an angelic host and soaring toward their immortality in the reborn nation.[85]

At the risk of succumbing to palingenetic longings myself, I would suggest that an exciting new phase—not just in fascist studies but in the academic understanding of a wide range of political and social events in the modern age—would open up once historians regularly take into account the temporal dynamics of collective social behavior and of revolutionary politics as casual factors helping to shape processes and events. If it one day comes to be generally recognized that a determining factor in the success or failure of a particular manifestation of fascism is the degree to which history is experienced as ontologically distressing, it would be yet another testimony to Mosse's extraordinary intuitive powers as a historian; to his prescience, which at times bordered on pre-science but which always illuminated the terrain ahead like a reconnaissance flare; and to his gift for conceptualizing the historical process in a way which took full account of its nonrational aspects in a spirit that extended, not subverted, the Enlightenment humanist tradition. It would be particularly fitting if this were to happen, since I am convinced that a preoccupation with the rush of time, which he experienced not as a metaphysical theory but as a gut emotion, fueled his innate tendency to be a geographical and academic Ahasverus. Reading Mosse convinces me that what Eliade calls the "terror of history"[86] was as close to his core existential concerns and obsessions as his Jewishness or his sexual preference. The last words of his autobiography read: "I had rejected the worlds of my past and had sought to transform myself, but in my anxieties, fears and restlessness I was still a child of my century."[87] Perhaps a subtext of the title *Confronting History* is that he experienced being a historian as a Promethean challenge to the pitiless time gods who inhabit the nothingness beyond our all-too-human-made skies.

Fortunately for the humanities and for humanity, Mosse found a palliative to the pain of persecution and anguish in the face of all-consuming *chronos,* not in some private fanaticism or collective utopia but in the task of making academically intelligible the fanaticism and utopianism of his would-be persecutors. Indeed, from his own anthropological perspective, the three days of talks, lectures, and convivial meals held at the University of Wisconsin that formed the basis of this book were less an academic conference than a time-defying ritual commemorating the work of George Mosse, a collective act of homage to his manifold scholarly and pedagogic gifts. It also symbolically celebrated the triumph of the ideals of humanism over the fascist attempt to supplant it with an ersatz utopia forged in the fires of nationalist fervors, fires that were devastating but not eternal. It is to be hoped that volcanoes of national, religious, and cultural passions that started erupting so horrifically in New York and Washington two days after the conference ended will wreak far less havoc on humanity, and that the voice of passionate reason which Mosse embodied will in the long run prevail over cold fanaticism.

Notes

1. George L. Mosse, *The Fascist Revolution* (New York: Howard Fertig, 1999), xvii.
2. Ibid., x.
3. For example, "Empathy is for me still at the core of the historical enterprise, but

understanding does not mean withholding judgement"; *Confronting History: A Memoir* (Madison: University of Wisconsin Press, 2000), 172. See his stress on the need to "see fascism as it saw itself and as its followers saw it, to attempt to understand the movement in its own terms" so as to "penetrate fascist self-understanding" (*The Fascist Revolution*, x–xi).

4. In his autobiography Mosse refers to "culture" as "a state or habit of mind which is apt to become a way of life intimately linked to the challenges and dilemmas of contemporary history" (*Confronting History*, 177). His emphasis on the phenomenology of fascism as a lived experience for its protagonists means that, at a time when Nazism was still widely equated with reaction, nihilism, and barbarism, he was already treating it not just as a form of ultra-nationalism but as a "cultural movement" bent on the transformation not of a particular sphere or section of society but of life itself conceived "as a whole, a totality" (*The Fascist Revolution*, xii). Clearly, the concept and significance of "culture," "myth," and "ritual" are as contested within cultural anthropology as any other term in the human sciences (and the very term "cultural anthropology" is contested). Mosse's approach to culture corresponds broadly to what one textbook (Roger Keesing and Andrew Strathern, *Cultural Anthropology: A Contemporary Perspective*, 3rd ed. [Fort Worth: Harcourt Brace, 1998]) calls "an ideational concept of culture." In other words, culture is an "ideational system," "a system of shared ideas, systems of concepts and rules and meanings that underlie and are expressed in the ways that humans live" (16). The chapter on "Religion: Ritual, Myth, and Cosmos" contains the following statement that has a direct bearing on Mosse's attempt to understand Nazism "from within": "Anthropologists have learned the hard way that to understand belief systems they must discard as many rigid definitions as possible and consider the *cosmology*–in other words, find out how another people conceptualize their universe, see the place of humans in it, and relate to and communicate with unseen beings and powers," an exercise that "demands every ounce of one's analytical and intuitive powers, and often more" (305).

5. See, for example, George L. Mosse, *Nazism: A Historical and Comparative Analysis of National Socialism* (New Brunswick, N.J.: Transaction Books, 1978), 29: "The historian's function must be to understand the myths that people live by, because these myths have often a tenuous link to reality, though they are placed within reality." See the importance he placed on the "aspirations and dreams" of historical actors as causal factors (*Confronting History*, 177).

6. See, for example, *Nazism*, 30–31, where Mosse presents Hitler as unable to maintain the balance between dream and reality beyond a certain point, after which he, like Mussolini, "retired more and more into his dream world."

7. Mosse, *The Fascist Revolution*, x–xi.

8. Mosse, *Confronting History*, 177.

9. Mosse, *The Fascist Revolution*, 12.

10. Ibid., 10.

11. Mosse, *Nazism*, 29.

12. Mona Ozouf, *La fête révolutionnaire, 1789–1799* (Paris: Gallimard, 1976); Lynn Hunt, *Politics, Culture, and Class in the French Revolution* (Berkeley: University of California Press, 1981).

13. Mosse, *Nazism*, 31.

14. George L. Mosse, "The Mystical Origins of National Socialism," *Journal of the History of Ideas* 23, no. 1 (1961): 81–96; reprinted in *Masses and Man* (197–213) and also in *The Fascist Revolution* under the title "The Occult Origins of National Socialism," 117–35.

15. This point is corroborated by Jeffrey Herf in "Mosse's Recasting of European Intellectual and Cultural History," *German Politics and Society* 18, no. 4 (2000):18–29.

16. Johan Huizinga, *The Waning of the Middle Ages,* trans. F. Hopman (London: Penguin, 1955).

17. For example, Benedetto Croce, *A History of Italy, 1871–1915,* trans. Ceclia M. Ady (New York: Russell & Russell, 1963).

18. Ernst Bloch, *The Heritage of Our Times,* trans. Neville and Stephen Plaice (Cambridge, England: Polity Press, 1991).

19. Ernst Bloch, *The Principle of Hope,* trans. Neville Plaice, Stephen Plaice, and Paul Kight (Cambridge, Mass.: MIT Press, 1986).

20. An approach most fully elaborated in Mack Smith, *Mussolini* (London: Weidenfeld & Nicolson, 1981).

21. Hugh Trevor-Roper, "The Phenomenon of Fascism," in *European Fascism,* ed. Stuart J. Woolf (New York: Random House, 1968; reprint, London: Weidenfeld & Nicolson, 1970), 55.

22. Zeev Sternhell, "Fascist Ideology," in Walter Laqueur, *Fascism: A Reader's Guide* (London: Wildwood House, 1976), 325–406.

23. Mosse, "The Mystical Origins of National Socialism," in *Masses and Man,* 197. Mosse was not the first serious scholar to recognize the importance of the *völkisch* movement in preparing the ground for Nazism. In 1961 Fritz Stern published *The Politics of Cultural Despair* (Berkeley: University of California Press). Significantly, however, Stern seems oblivious of the revolutionary, palingenetic thrust of Nazism's so-called cultural pessimism.

24. See, for example, "Culture, Civilization, and German Anti-Semitism," *Davar* (1961): 47–64; *The Intellectual Foundations of National Socialism,* seminar held at Stanford University, European Studies Seminar Center, autumn 1963, conducted by George Mosse (Stanford, Calif.: n.p., 1964); and "Fascism and the Intellectuals," in *The Nature of Fascism: Proceedings of a Conference Held by the Reading University Graduate School of Contemporary European Studies,* ed. Stuart J. Woolf (London: Weidenfeld & Nicolson, 1968), 205–26.

25. George L. Mosse, "The Genesis of Fascism," *Journal of Contemporary History* 1, no. 1 (1966): 17.

26. Ibid., 19–20.

27. George L. Mosse, "History, Anthropology, and Mass Movements," *American Historical Review* 75, no. 2 (1969): 447–52.

28. Ibid., 452.

29. George L. Mosse, "Caesarism, Circuses, and Monuments," *Journal of Contemporary History* 6, no. 2 (1971): 167–84; reprinted in *Masses and Man,* 104–18.

30. Mosse, *Masses and Man,* 118.

31. George L. Mosse, "The Poet and the Exercise of Political Power: Gabriele D'Annunzio," *Yearbook of Comparative and General Literature* 22 (1973): 32–42.

32. George L. Mosse, "Mass Politics and the Political Liturgy of Nationalism," in *Nationalism: The Nature and Evolution of an Idea,* ed. Eugene Kamenka (Canberra: Australia National University Press, 1973), 38–54.

33. I have in mind Ernst Nolte's *Der europäische Bürgerkrieg* ([Berlin]: Propyläen Verlag, 1987).

34. Mosse, *Nazism,* 34.

35. Mosse, *Confronting History,* 177. The passage continues: "The book's success was

slow in coming, but eventually the work was regarded as innovative for no longer referring dismissively to Nazi propaganda but instead talking of Nazi self-representation, which interacted with the hopes and dreams of a large section of the population. This was no longer a book in the tradition of the history of political thought as I had been taught at Harvard . . . instead it used the definition of culture as the history of perceptions which I had offered in my *Culture of Western Europe.*"

36. For example, Hugh Seton-Watson, "Fascism, Right and Left," *Journal of Contemporary History* 1, no. 1 (1966): 183: "Twenty years after the destruction of the Third Reich, the essence of fascism is still elusive."

37. Mosse, *Nazism,* 34.

38. Mosse wrote this essay as the editor of *International Fascism: New Thoughts and New Approaches* (London: Sage, 1979).

39. That is, Sternhell, "Fascist Ideology"; Stanley Payne, *Fascism: Comparison and Definition* (Madison: University of Wisconsin Press, 1980).

40. See esp. "The Community in the Thought of Nationalism, Fascism, and the Radical Right," in *Community as a Social Ideal,* ed. Eugene Kamenka (London: Edward Arnold, 1982), 27–42; "The Political Culture of Italian Futurism: A General Perspective," *Journal of Contemporary History* 25, nos. 2–3 (April–July 1990): 253–68; "National Anthems: The Nation Militant," in *From Ode to Anthem: Problems of Lyric Poetry,* ed. Reinhold Grimm and Jost Hermand (Madison: published for Monatshefte [by] The University of Wisconsin Press, 1989), 86–100; "Fascism and the French Revolution," *Journal of Contemporary History* 24, no. 1 (1989): 5–26; and *Fallen Soldiers: Reshaping the Memory of the World Wars* (New York: Oxford University Press, 1990).

41. Uwe Puschner, *Die völkische Bewegung im Wilhelminischen Kaiserreich* (Darmstadt: WBG, Wissenschaftliche Buchgesellschaft, 2001).

42. For example, the concept "political religion" is central in Michael Burleigh's *The Third Reich: A New History* (New York: Hill and Wang, 2000). Mosse's claim that *The Nationalization of the Masses* "led to the first serious analyses of various aspects of the Nazi cult, as well as the first book that treated the sacralization of politics in Italian fascism, written by Emilio Gentile" (*Confronting History,* 177), may be overstated, given the publication of Hans-Jochen Gamm's *Der braune Kult; das Dritte Reich und seine Ersatzreligion* (Hamburg: Rütten & Loening) in 1962 and Klaus Vondung's *Magie und Manipulation: Ideologischer Kult und politische Religion des Nationalsozialismus* (Göttingen: Vandenhoeck & Ruprecht) in 1971. Both arrive at Mossean perspectives without necessarily having been influenced by him. Gentile seems to also have arrived at his view of fascism as an attempt to sacralize the state largely independently of Mosse.

43. See R. J. B. Bosworth, *The Italian Dictatorship: Problems and Perspectives in the Interpretation of Mussolini and Fascism* (London: Arnold, 1998), 24–29. See also Sergio Luzzatto, "The Political Culture of Fascist Italy," *Contemporary European History* 8, no. 2 (1999): 317–336 , which reviews several books on fascism that embody this trend.

44. Pier-Giorgio Zunino, *L'Ideologia del Fascismo* (Bologna: Il Mulino, 1985).

45. Emilio Gentile, *Il culto del littorio* (Rome: Laterza, 1993).

46. Tim Mason, "Whatever Happened to Fascism?" in *Nazism, Fascism, and the Working Class: Essays by Tim Mason,* ed. Jane Caplan (Cambridge: Cambridge University Press, 1995), 331.

47. See James Vernon, "Who's Afraid of the 'Linguistic Turn'? The Politics of Social History and Its Discontents," *Social History* 19 (1994): 81–97.

48. For example, Jeffrey Schnapp, who has written important studies of fascism's aes-

thetic culture, ignores Mosse; Ruth Ben-Ghiat cites him in her *Fascist Modernities* (Berkeley: University of California Press, 2000). Simonetta Falasca-Simonetta in *Fascist Spectacle* (Berkeley: University of California Press, 1997), Mabel Berezin in *Making the Fascist Self* (Ithaca: Cornell University Press, 1997), Emily Braun in *Mario Sironi and Italian Modernism* (Cambridge: Cambridge University Press, 2000), and Thomas Linehan in *British Fascism, 1918–1939* (Manchester, Manchester University Press, 2000) all make fleeting references to him without explicitly adopting any aspect of his theory of fascism. The exception is Matthew Affron and Mark Antliff, who in their introduction to *Fascist Visions* (Princeton, N.J.: Princeton University Press, 1997) use Mosse's "The Political Culture of Futurism" in elucidating the ambivalent nature of fascism's reaction to modernity (13–14). Intelligent applications of Mosse's concepts of political culture, time, and the liturgical to creating a sophisticated conceptual framework for comparative fascist studies are conspicuous by their absence.

49. Richard Evans, *In Defence of History* (London: Granta Books, 1997). See p. 3: "Instead of causes . . . the 'linguistic turn' has given us discourses." However, Evans himself concedes that "At its best, the work that is now appearing under the influence of postmodernist theory provides a new dimension of understanding that moves well beyond the limitations of social history. Studies of popular mentalities, of memory, commemoration and celebrations, of the cultural dimensions of power and authority, of gender and the micropolitics of everyday life, and of many other subjects, have added significantly to historical knowledge. The achievement of cultural history in the postmodern mode is not merely additive; it has helped reorient our understanding of many areas of politics and social history, from the French Revolution to the First World War and beyond" (184).

50. Emilio Gentile, "The Sacralisation of Politics: Definitions, Interpretations, and Reflections on the Question of Secular Religion and Totalitarianism," *Totalitarian Movements and Political Religions* 1, no. 1 (2000): 18–55.

51. I have in mind such works as Clifford Geertz, *The Theatre State in Bali* (Princeton: Princeton University Press, 1980) and "Centers, Kings, and Charisma: Reflections on the Symbolics of Power," in *Rites of Power,* ed. S. Wilentz (Philadelphia: University of Pennsylvania Press, 1985); and Victor Turner, *The Anthropology of Performance* (New York: PAJ Publications, 1988), *Dramas, Fields, and Metaphors: Symbolic Action in Human Society* (Ithaca: Cornell University Press, 1974), and *Blazing the Trail: Way Marks in the Exploration of Symbols,* ed. Edith Turner (Tucson: University of Arizona Press, 1992).

52. On the new consensus and its "culturalist" thrust see particularly Roger Griffin, "The Primacy of Culture: The Current Growth (or Manufacture) of Consensus within Fascist Studies," *Journal of Contemporary History* 37, no. 1 (2002): 21–63.

53. George L. Mosse, "Fascism and the Intellectuals," in *The Nature of Fascism;* reprinted in Mosse, *The Fascist Revolution,* 118–19.

54. Mosse, *The Fascist Revolution,* 98.

55. Ibid., 106.

56. Mosse, *Masses and Man,* 103. This passage goes on to make an important methodological observation when it endorses Brasillach's comment that fascism was not just a revolt of the mythic against the rational but "a revolt of the senses against political philosophy. Fascism itself saw itself in this light, and this is why it cannot be evaluated through the criteria of formal political thought."

57. Ibid., 96.

58. Ibid., 70.

59. Ibid., 71.

60. Ibid., 79.

61. Ibid., 85.

62. Mosse's citing of Bloch underlines the affinity which, I suggested earlier, links the approach the two men had to political phenomena.

63. Mosse, *The Fascist Revolution*, 8.

64. Mosse, *Masses and Man*, 1. In a similar vein, Mosse states: "The nation appropriated the past, preindustrial myths and symbols to veil the actual speed of time. . . . The native landscape with its flowers, woods and mountains stood outside the rush of time and the nervousness of the age." He goes on to argue that the new political religion of nationalism was fed by the longing of men and women who "increasingly perceived the world in which they lived through myth, symbol, and stereotype" "for a new wholeness in their lives." "The longing for totality was accompanied by a strong urge to appropriate immutabilities: the landscape, national traditions and even the sky. All of these were thought to stand outside the rush of time, helping men keep control, introducing something of the sacred into individual lives" (ibid., 11–12).

65. Mosse, *The Fascist Revolution*, 142.

66. Ibid., 86.

67. Ibid.

68. Ibid., 55.

69. Günter Berghaus, "The Ritual Core of Fascist Theatre: An Anthropological Perspective," in *Fascism and Theatre*, ed. Berghaus (Providence, R. I.: Berghahn Books, 1996), 39–71.

70. Jeffrey Schnapp, "Epic Demonstrations: Fascist Modernity and the 1932 Exhibition of the Fascist Revolution," in *Fascism, Aesthetics, and Culture*, ed. Richard Golsan (Hanover, N.H.: University Press of New England, 1992), 30; Linda Schulte-Sass, *Entertaining the Third Reich: Illusions of Wholeness in Nazi Cinema* (Durham, N. C.: Duke University Press, 1996).

71. For example, Robert Pois, *National Socialism and the Religion of Nature* (London: Croom Helm, 1986); Klaus Vondung, *Magie und Manipulation: Ideologischer Kult und politische Religion des Nationalsozialismus*, (Göttingen: Vandenhoeck & Ruprecht, 1971).

72. For example, Mircea Eliade, *The Sacred and the Profane* (New York, Harcourt, Brace, 1959); Alfred Gell, *The Anthropology of Time* (Oxford; Providence: Berg, 1992).

73. Giorgio de Santillana and Hertha von Dechend, *Hamlet's Mill: An Essay on Myth and the Frame of Time* (Boston: Gambit, 1969); Richard Fenn, *The End of Time: Religion, Ritual, and the Forging of the Soul* (London: SPCK, 1997).

74. William Sullivan, *The Secret of the Incas: Myth, Astronomy, and the War against Time* (New York: Crown, 1998), shows an entire civilization indulging in ritual sacrifice to stop time from ending. Parallel symbolic wars against the ending of time fought through intense ritual behavior have been postulated as occurring toward the end of the civilizations of the Aztecs, the Maya, and the Andean Nasca people, and the obsession with the decay of "immortal" Rome led to a cultural obsession with its *renovatio*, which was also associated with ritualistic activity: see Mircea Eliade, *The Myth of Eternal Return*, trans. Willard R. Trask (Princeton, N.J.: Princeton University Press, 1971), chaps. 2 and 4.

75. Victor and Edith Turner, *Celebration: Studies in Festivity and Ritual* (Washington, D.C.: Smithsonian Institution Press, 1982).

76. David Freidel et al., *Maya Cosmos* (New York: W. Morrow, 1993), shows contemporary descendants of the Maya still carrying out elaborate centering ceremonies (e.g., chap. 2) using stones to reproduces a scheme of the universe that not only denotes a new

calendar but reenacts the creation of the universe, the renewal of time itself. One such ritual is called "raising the sky" and continues until it rains.

77. Norman Cohn, *The Pursuit of the Millennium* (London: Temple Smith, 1993); Damian Thompson, *The End of Time* (London: Minerva, 1997); Frederick Baumgartner, *Longing for the End* (Basingstoke: Macmillan, 1999); J. F. C. Harrison, *The Second Coming: Popular Millenarianism, 1780–1850* (London: Routledge & Kegan Paul, 1979).

78. Marshall Berman, *All That Is Solid Melts into Air* (New York: Simon and Schuster, 1982); Anthony Giddens, *Modernity and Self-Identity* (Cambridge: Polity Press in association with Basil Blackwell, 1991); David Harvey, *The Condition of Postmodernity* (Oxford: Blackwell, 1989).

79. See Richard Stites, *Revolutionary Dreams, Utopian Vision, and Experimental Life in the Russian Revolution* (New York: Oxford University Press, 1989); Igor Golomstock, *Totalitarian Art* (London: Collins Harvill, 1990). The creation of instant traditions and liturgies is not just a feature of openly illiberal revolutions, since they occurred both in the French Revolution and in the nation-building processes that followed the collapse of the Soviet Empire, for example in the Ukraine; see Roger Griffin, "Modernity under the New Order: The Fascist Project for Managing the Future," *Thamesman Publications* (Oxford Brookes School of Business imprint), 1994 (available at http://www.brookes.ac.uk/schools/humanities/staff/moderni.txt).

80. This perspective puts the highly contested concept of "modernism" in a fresh light, underlining the recurrence of the theme of renewal and regeneration in the modernist mind-set. For one example among many see Mark Antliff, "The Fourth Dimension and Futurism: A Politicized Space," *Art Bulletin* 82, no. 4 (2000):720–23 . It also underscores the link between a modernist such as Kafka and an existentialist such as Paul Bowles, whose book *The Sheltering Sky* was made into a film by Bertolucci.

81. As opposed to the "alternative history" made popular in the 1960s by the likes of Erich von Däniken and Immanuel Velikovsky; see William I. Thompson, *At the Edge of History* (New York: Harper & Row, 1971).

82. See in particular Fenn, *The End of Time;* Gerard M. Platt, "Thoughts on a Theory of Collective Action: Language, Affect, and Ideology in Revolution," in *New Directions in Psychohistory*, ed. Mel Albin (Lexington, Mass.: Lexington Books, 1980), 69–96 ; and the references to the temporal aspects of modernity in Mark Antliff's seminal essay "Fascism, Modernism, and Modernity," *Art Bulletin* 84, no. 1 (2002): 148–69. For my own contributions to this theme see "'I am no longer human. I am a Titan. A god!' The Fascist Quest to Regenerate Time," Electronic Seminars in History (History of Political Thought), at http://www.ihrinfo.ac.uk/esh/quest.html (May 1998); "Party Time: Nazism as a Temporal Revolution," *History Today* 49, no. 4 (1999): 43–50; and "'Shattering Crystals': The Role of 'Dream Time' in Extreme Right-Wing Political Violence," *Terrorism and Political Violence* 15, no. 1 (2003): 57–94.

83. Hermann Broch, *The Sleepwalkers* (New York: Grosset & Dunlap, 1964), 647.

84. Ian Kershaw, *Hitler*, vol. 1, *Hubris* (London: Allen Lane, 1998), esp. chap. 11.

85. Burleigh, *The Third Reich.*

86. Eliade, *The Myth of Eternal Return,* pt. 3.

87. Mosse, *Confronting History*, 219.

Mosse's Influence on the Historiography of the Holocaust

Saul Friedländer

Pension Biederstein, Munich, September 1961. The sound was persistent and unmistakable: the relentless typing of an invisible neighbor. I identified him at one of our breakfasts in the small dining room of the guest house and inquired about the compelling task that engendered so much noise. It was George, you will have guessed, working at what was to become *The Crisis of German Ideology*. With characteristic generosity, he described his work at length to the graduate student that I was. We became friends, and that friendship lasted to the end of his life.

I shall begin this essay by discussing *The Crisis of German Ideology*, which was not only Mosse's first major work on his new path—after he increasingly turned from early modern history to the history of the cultural, ideological, and political movements of the nineteenth and twentieth centuries that led to fascism and Nazism—but also a lasting reference point for much further research in this domain. I will then turn to the evolution of Mosse's interpretations of the origins of the Final Solution, and finally I shall consider some of the major issues left open in his later attempts at a general synthesis of nationalism, "respectability," outsiderdom, and extermination.

The Crisis of German Ideology in Its Epoch

In his memoirs, Mosse was somewhat dismissive about the significance of *The Crisis*, published in 1964, defining it as "part of a traditional history of political thought."[1] If this had been the case, why does *The Crisis* remain, almost forty years after its publication, one of Mosse's "most successful books," in his own words?[2] In fact, for those of us who, in the mid-1960s, started teaching modern history, particularly the history of

Nazism, Nazi anti-Semitism, and the origins of the Final Solution, *The Crisis* opened new vistas.

We had all been impressed by the brilliance of Hannah Arendt's *Origins of Totalitarianism*. However, as stimulating as it was, the book seemed too idiosyncratic in both argument and construction. As for *Eichmann in Jerusalem*, its polemical strength was unquestionable, but otherwise—so I thought at the time—it mainly used (and also misused) Raul Hilberg's *The Destruction of the European Jews*. Hilberg's own magisterial volume, published in 1961, was on all counts the most important single study of the Holocaust; yet something essential was missing: a historical background that would explain the triggering of the bureaucratic wheels of destruction. Hitler was hardly mentioned and no ideological current was evoked, except for a list of anti-Jewish measures taken by the popes, the church councils, and other Christian institutions throughout the centuries. More historical depth was clearly needed.

Some elements were on hand. Paul Massing had analyzed German political anti-Semitism at the end of the nineteenth century, and Fritz Stern had delved into the "ideological system" of three major *völkisch* figures: Paul de Lagarde, Julius Langbehn, and Arthur Möller van den Bruck. It was Mosse, however, who unveiled the ideological current that best seemed to fill the historical gap. In *The Crisis* he presented the multiple aspects of a movement that partook of both high and popular German culture, of best-selling novels—some of them masterpieces—and of cranky pamphlets that nonetheless (or therefore) seeped into the minds of part of the German middle classes throughout the second half of the nineteenth century and onward. The intellectual/cultural evolution he described was not a powerful force before 1918, but it carried a threatening potential in years of crisis. Its core concepts are well known: the *Volk*, the race, the Jew. In this system, Mosse showed, the Jew was central.

Mosse was the first, I think, to point to the necessary link in the *völkisch* imagination between blood, soil, and cosmos, body and soul, physical appearance and character—all the components, in short, of the oxymoronic "metaphysics of rootedness." On all counts, the rootless Jew appeared as foreign, repulsive, and dangerous. For Aryan Germandom, this antitype was the enemy per se. Mosse clearly perceived the function of such a representation once it was adopted by a political leader of Hitler's ilk. He wrote in his introduction to *The Crisis*:

Ultimately, the Nazi revolution was . . . a "revolution of the soul" which actually threatened none of the vested economic interests of the middle class. Instead, völkisch thought concentrated upon another enemy within. . . . [T]he Jew. It can be justly argued that the attitude toward the Jew provided much of the cement of this thought and gave it a dynamic it might otherwise have lacked. Hitler gave focus to his "German revolution" by making it into an anti-Jewish revolution. In a situation where revolutionary social and economic changes were excluded, the Jew became a welcome and necessary substitute toward which the revolutionary fervor could be directed.[3]

The Crisis became a staple of graduate seminars in our domain.

Mosse failed to consider the possibility that some of the best-selling *völkisch* novels attracted their reading public quite independently of the Aryan or Jewish characteristics of their main protagonists, or of any other ideological message for that matter. It made them particularly insidious in most cases, but harmless in some. This was driven home to me in 1968, in Jerusalem, in a small stationery store owned by a couple of German Jews—"Yekkes" in local parlance. I noticed that the elderly lady at the cash register was engrossed in a book that she read eagerly between one customer and the next: it was a much perused copy of Felix Dahn's *Kampf um Rom*. In *The Crisis*, Mosse had characterized this 1867 novel as "overflowing with an enthusiastic passion for the Volk and the fatherland." The author bore "responsibility for having drawn popular attention to a glorified German past in which the mythology, the moral, ethical, and social values, and the physical qualities of the Goths were extolled."[4] All of this must have been lost on the enthusiastic Jerusalemite who readily confessed to me that this was one of her favorite books.

In the Bundesrepublik, *The Crisis of German Ideology* appeared in an a priori unfavorable ideological and historiographical context. It dealt with neither totalitarianism nor fascism—the competing concepts of the day in the interpretation of Nazism. Instead it focused on cultural roots, and in particular on German and Nazi anti-Semitism, a topic—so was the consensus—that was already perfectly well known and thus of little further interest. The young historians who were not hostile to a *Sonderweg* interpretation were delving into analytic social history, grappling with institutional dynamics, social and political structures, and the defensive behavior of traditional elites. This new Left-oriented generation—the Wehlers, the Mommsens, the Broszats, the Schieders—had little interest in the kind of cultural history that Mosse excavated, and generally speaking *völkisch* ideology and Nazi anti-Semitism were not their main concern. As for the conservative historians of the Gerhard Ritter brand, they did not like Mosse's interpretation of the ideological roots of National Socialism: it sullied the German past. (If I am not mistaken, 1964 saw the culmination of the "Fischer controversy" at the Historikertag in Berlin.)

Mosse did not like their approach either. "Gerhard Ritter," he wrote in the introduction to *The Crisis*, "was far from the mark when he asserted that the ideological evolution that led to National Socialism was not typically German and that other countries also contained such movements. . . . German völkisch thought showed a depth of feeling and a dynamic that was not expressed elsewhere. . . . January 1933 was not an accident of history but was prepared long beforehand."[5] A few years after the publication of *The Crisis*, Karl Dietrich Bracher, in his *Die Deutsche Diktatur*, would adopt an approach similar to Mosse's regarding the cultural/intellectual origins of Nazism; even so, the aim of their query was ultimately different. Bracher mainly wished to understand 1933; Mosse's gaze was essentially directed to 1942.[6]

In reminiscing about the atmosphere at his elite boarding school, Salem, Mosse tells how one of the school's goals was to foster leadership qualities among its students, to create "an aristocracy not of birth but of character." One of the virtues constantly invoked was *Zivilcourage*, "which involved speaking out against injustice, standing up for what you consider just." Then comes a telling remark: "This notwithstanding, some three hundred alumni joined the Hitler Youth, the SA and SS, the latter itself an elite organization."[7] The word "notwithstanding" may not have been the right one from the viewpoint of the young men who, in droves, joined the party and its elite organizations. They believed their cause was just; they became its fanatic propagandists and implementers.

Almost half of *The Crisis of German Ideology* deals with the channels that carried the *völkisch* ideas into post-World War I German society: the youth movement, the schools, the universities. "Education," Mosse writes, "pre-eminently institutionalized the ideology. Prior to 1918, no political organization or group of like-minded people was as important as educators in anchoring the German faith within the Germanic nation."[8] And some of that spirit, certainly its anti-Semitic and nationalist ingredients, was, as Mosse recalls, rampant at Salem as well. If we add "scientific racism" to the ideological syncretism carried through the educational channels of Weimar Germany, the spreading of this deadly mixture among the country's elites is easily accounted for.

In this context, Mosse may have understated the role of the universities in the Weimar years—particularly that of the student associations. They are mentioned in a few pages of *The Crisis*, but nonetheless the youth movement has pride of place. Later studies demonstrated the student associations' crucial role in the propagation of Nazism. More recently, Michael Wildt's 1996 volume on the Jewish policies of the SD (the Security Service of the SS) and especially his study on the Reichsicherheitshauptamt (RSHA), the SS Main Office for the Security of the Reich, show that most members of the second-tier leadership of the RSHA, the hub of the Final Solution, were university-educated and partook of an anti-Semitic ideology acquired in part during their student years.[9]

New Queries, New Interpretations

"The Holocaust was never far from my mind," Mosse wrote in the final page of his memoirs. "I could easily have perished with my fellow Jews. I suppose that I am a member of the holocaust generation and have constantly tried to understand an event too monstrous to contemplate. All my studies in the history of racism and *völkisch* thought, and also those dealing with outsiderdom and stereotypes, though sometimes not directly related to the Holocaust, have tried to find the answer to how it could have happened; finding an explanation has been vital not only for the understanding of modern history, but also for my own peace of mind."[10]

Indeed, if fascism, Nazism, and, above all, Nazi anti-Semitism, as the core of Hitler's worldview, were the essential domains of Mosse's historical investigations, the Holocaust, about which he never wrote in any detail, was nonetheless the visible center of his research. He approached this center from several angles and most directly in *Toward the Final Solution*. Whereas *The Crisis of German Ideology* essentially focused upon German racism and anti-Semitism, Mosse's 1978 study encompassed Europe as a whole. Increasingly, France and the Anglo-Saxon countries were drawn into the picture, and at times, as far as the late nineteenth century and the years preceding World War I were concerned, France moved to center stage. But Mosse was also aware that in France, countervailing forces—far too weak in Germany—ultimately neutralized the political spillover of the racist, ultra-nationalist, anti-Jewish current, at least until June 1940. Moreover, whereas in *The Crisis* Mosse had stressed the mystical and mythical dimensions of *völkisch* thought, in *Toward the Final Solution* "science" and "aesthetics" became the core elements in a much wider conception of race. Mosse's approach now highlighted the use of visual stereotypes and the centrality of the aesthetic dimension. Such an approach underscores even more strongly than beforehand the fundamental dichotomy of racial types and antitypes: on the one hand, the physical qualities closest to the Greek ideal of beauty; on the other, the physical ugliness of the racial antitype. In this conception of race, the beauty of the body necessarily expressed the moral qualities of the soul that resided in it.[11]

Particularly important in view of the historiographical trends of those years was Mosse's juxtaposition of the "science of race" and the "mystery of race." In the 1980s the surge of historical studies on scientific racism was directly linked to the interpretation of Nazism and Nazi racism as offspring of the rational-scientific spirit of the Enlightenment and of modernity. Intent on reversing the traditional interpretations that had foregrounded the irrational and anti-modern dimension of Nazism—its *völkisch* origins, in other words—the historiography of the 1980s immersed itself in eugenics, racial anthropology, and all the trappings of scientific modernity, often seen as the true matrix of genocidal policies. As for the image of the Jew, which in the new framework lost much of its salience to become one facet of racial-biological thinking among many, it was no less transformed. "The Jewish microbe," in Detlev Peukert's words, replaced the "Eternal Jew," the mythical "Ahasverus."[12]

Mosse was certainly not aiming at such an extreme historiographical shift. In fact, in the penultimate chapter of *Toward the Final Solution* he quoted Hitler's use of the very metaphor that Peukert had considered as jettisoned by the Nazis. Mosse reminds us that in January 1944, during the annual commemoration of the *Machtergreifung*, "the myth of Ahasverus, the wandering Jew who wants to destroy Germany through bolshevism . . . was evoked and presented as reality."[13] What Hitler depicted in fact was the fate of Europe in the event of a German defeat. After describing the devastation of the continent and its culture, the deportation of its populations and the murder of its elites, the Nazi leader evoked the triumph of Ahasverus: "Der verwüstete jüdische Ahasver aber könnte dann das zerstörte Europa in einem zweiten triumphierenden Purim-Fest feiern."[14]

Whereas *The Nationalization of the Masses* was a splendid contribution to our understanding of "political religion" as the sacralization of politics that started with the French Revolution and found its most accomplished expression in the cult and rituals of National Socialism, it is *Nationalism and Sexuality*, published in 1985, that is often considered Mosse's most original work, and particularly so in regard to our theme. This is indeed a work of wide-ranging scholarship and powerful synthesis of many historical strands woven around a highly innovative thesis.

The Jew remains the main victim in Mosse's rethinking of the modern dynamics of persecution, but his fate becomes fully comprehensible only when considered alongside that of other categories of outsiders. Neither Germany nor any other European country singled out these outsiders a priori. Rather, according to Mosse's new approach, outsiderdom was created and increasingly stereotyped as a result of the fateful alliance of modern nationalism and bourgeois moral "respectability." This respectability embraced all aspects of middle-class morality, particularly its sexual norms. Manliness, among other markers, became a central aspect of bourgeois self-definition. As one commentator on *Nationalism and Sexuality* pointed out, "this alliance (between nationalism and bourgeois respectability) became increasingly totalized, insistent on assigning everyone a fixed place: healthy and degenerate, manly men and effeminate homosexuals, sane and insane, productive and lazy, native and foreigner. 'Bourgeois society,' Mosse contended, 'needed its dialectical opposite in order to exist.'"[15] And, Mosse argued further, as we move into the twentieth century, these bourgeois norms became the norms of "everyone's morality."

Does Mosse's interpretation cast its net too widely once it addresses the specific historical context of the Final Solution? At the end of *Nationalism and Sexuality*, Mosse attempts to tighten his argumentation: "The Jews were to experience at its most cruel and cynical the power of society and the state to make myth come true, actually to transform those branded as outsiders into their own stereotype."[16] In *Confronting History* he rephrased his argument in compelling terms: "Respectability and Nationalism needed discernable and visible foes for their own self-definition. I came to believe that the existence of outsiderdom was built into modern society and a prerequisite for its continued existence and the self-esteem of its insiders. The insider and the outsider are linked; one cannot exist without the other, just as there can be no ideal type without its anti-type."[17] Yet it seems to me that the interpretive move from extreme nationalism to Nazi extermination policies demands a more complex elaboration, and so does Mosse's attempt to apply the same general theory of outsiderdom to all the victims of National Socialism.

In the chapter on "Fascism and Sexuality," Mosse quotes at length Himmler's November 1937 Bad Tölz speech against homosexuality in which the Reichsführer SS enumerated the dangers of homosexuality for the *Volksgemeinschaft*. Himmler reminded his audience of the old Germanic habit of drowning homosexuals in swamps. Mosse compares the death of the homosexual described by Himmler to the drowning of the Jew Veitel Itzig in a dirty river in Gustav Freytag's *Soll und Haben* and then comments: "Himmler wanted the homosexual to drown in a swamp and the Jew to suffocate without human assistance in the gas chamber." And, closing the circle of his general argument, he adds: "For the outsider himself, such a way of dying must be placed against the background of the comfortable death which was the bourgeois ideal. The 'snuffing out of life' (*Auslöschung*) was diametrically opposed to death in the service of a noble cause on the battlefield or death as the conclusion of a virtuous life."[18]

Rethinking Mosse's General Theory of Outsiderdom and Extermination

When considering the evolution of Mosse's work toward a generalized theory of persecution, we faced two separate issues: first, the role of the bourgeoisie as the bearer of the alliance of nationalism and respectability, and its corollary, the status of the insider as opposed to that of the outsider; and second, the comparison of the various categories of outsiders and the identity or heterogeneity of their exclusion and ultimate fate, mainly in Nazism.

Most commentators of Mosse's work note that the role of the bourgeoisie in his interpretation of fascist ideology and politics was practically reversed from *The Crisis of German Ideology* to *Nationalism and Sexuality*. In the former, the liberal bourgeoisie was the target of the *völkisch* revolution, and that revolution was quintessentially German; in the latter, the bourgeoisie became the bearer of the nationalist-racist consensus, and that consensus was European, as was fascism itself. Nazism, in turn, becomes the most extreme case of this general evolution.

Mosse manifestly started pondering about the link between bourgeois "respectability," nationalism, and the fascist revolution as he was writing *The Crisis:* "Bourgeois respectability and traditionalism were successfully woven into the ideological fabric of the Nazis," he stated in the conclusion of his study.[19] In his 1966 critique of Ernst Nolte's *Three Faces of Fascism* he returned to the issue at greater length: "Nolte ignores a vital aspect of fascism . . . bourgeois transcendence may have been transformed, but bourgeois morality was accepted. Emphasis upon 'respectability,' family relationships and hard work was used to tame a potentially dangerous activism."[20] The same theme appears in Mosse's comment on an SA text in his 1966 *Nazi Culture:* "[The Nazi worldview] was anchored in an idealization of the past which included an emphasis upon bourgeois morality. The taming of the activism through an 'embourgoisement' of the SA was accomplished by stressing the importance of founding a family—the wife must be regarded as a comrade."[21] Mosse's comment takes on its full significance if one keeps in mind that the SA had, until 1934, a notoriously homosexual leadership. In other words, Mosse chose this 1937 Hans Anderlahn story, entitled "The Bonds of Family," to show how, after the liquidation of its leadership in June 1934, the SA toed the line and was set on combating sexual deviance in the name of bourgeois morality and family values.

It is the function of major interpretive frameworks to launch an entirely new line of thinking and research. In many ways *Nationalism and Sexuality* has opened such new vistas, but the linkages, the comparisons, and even some of the more basic assumptions demand to be carefully examined. The relationships among middle-class respectability, nationalism, and the social construction of antitypes as outsiders is compelling, and the transfer of these structures to fascist movements and regimes seems to apply, notwithstanding differences arising from diverse historical backgrounds (the Jews were not particularly branded as outsiders by Italian fascism, at least not until 1938, and only very marginally so afterward). Comparative studies of fascist and communist morality (mainly during the Stalinist period) could point to similar patterns in very diverse social-ideological contexts. However, the major difficulties appear once Mosse moves another step forward and includes Nazism in his general framework.

As we saw, Mosse quoted Himmler's 1937 speech about homosexuality to make the point that, under Nazism, both the "sexual deviant" and the Jew could expect *Auslöschung,* extermination. Such was to be the fate of other outsiders as well: the mentally ill, the "asocials," and the Gypsies. But, notwithstanding these forays into specific contexts, the impression remains that Mosse, intent upon making a general statement about the fate of the outsiders, did not perceive the difficulty that the argument would create in terms of his own theory of "respectability" once the Final Solution was more closely examined.

Himmler openly discussed the extermination of the Jews on several occasions. The most telling of these blunt addresses was an oft-quoted passage of his address to several hundred SS generals in Posen on 4 October 1943. They knew, Himmler told them in referring to what he called "the most difficult issue of his life," the extermination of the Jews, "how hard it was to see 100 corpses, 500 corpses, 1000 corpses," in other words to murder immense numbers of Jewish men, women and children. But, the Reichsführer declared, to have accomplished this and "remained morally upright" was "the most glorious page of German history . . . yet one that has remained unwritten and was never to be written." Himmler went on to threaten with immediate execution anyone who stole from the victims, be it a watch or even a cigarette.[22] Mass murder was glorious but should remain hidden; the fight against corruption, on the other hand, no doubt fitted "everyone's morality."

From our point of view, Himmler's speech is ambiguous. Not only does the SS chief extol the common virtue of honesty (no stealing), but in regard to mass murder he insists that having achieved this with no harm to the moral character of his men should be a source of pride. Yet what manifestly dominates the Reichsführer's exhortation is the imperative of everlasting secrecy. Even future generations, steeped in "everyone's morality," would not comprehend a transgression of such enormity. In other words, Himmler was aware of and pointed to a thorough incompatibility between the extermination of the Jews and any accepted norms of respectability. He may, however, have misjudged the attitude of a majority of the German population.

Thanks to the work of (mainly German) historians on the crimes committed by the Wehrmacht of the Eastern front, we know quite conclusively—notwithstanding a few minor misinterpretations of some photographic material—that ordinary Wehrmacht soldiers and officers, possibly in the tens of thousands, participated alongside SS units and "ordinary men" from the police battalions in the mass murder of Jews. Many more watched the proceedings and took pictures as mementos and entertainment for the folks back home. We also know that details of the mass-murder operations soon spread to the Reich and beyond and were quite openly discussed. A minority expressed compassion, larger numbers supported the killings, but most people seem to have been indifferent. In any case, as far as Jews and Gypsies were concerned there was no public protest except for that of the "Aryan" wives of Jewish detainees, in Berlin, in 1943. In that sense, Himmler underestimated most Germans' capacity for indifference to the fate of those whom they came to see as outside the pale of the *Volksgemeinschaft*.

However, the reaction to the killings of the mentally ill was different. The mentally ill were, by all standards of Nazi medical propaganda, irretrievably diseased beings, "lives unworthy of living." In other words, according to the regime's norms they were to be considered total outsiders. Yet popular and religious protest compelled Hitler to modify the euthanasia program in August 1941. These outsiders were, in some way, considered by the population as part of the national/racial community, and the norms of "bourgeois respectability" regarding their ultimate status were not clear. Were there similar protests regarding the treatment of German homosexuals in the camps? I do not know whether, in this particular case, studies of popular reactions are available. Finally, some Germans, even high-ranking party members, were ill at ease regarding the deportation and massacre of German Jewish war veterans, especially bearers of the Iron Cross.

Thus one must establish a clear distinction between the categories of outsiders perceived as such by the Nazi hard core and those perceived— or not perceived—as such by the majority of the German population that shared the norms of "everyone's morality." Simply put, the rules varied from one category of outsider to another. For a majority of the population as well as for the party faithful, the Jews were the outsiders; the mentally ill, possibly the homosexuals, were less easily categorized. Thus, Mosse remains right in general terms, but a major difficulty nonetheless subsists in the definition of degrees of "outsiderdom" in a regime such as Nazism.

As a matter of fact, the Nazis themselves established distinctions: the "asocials" and the homosexuals were mainly persecuted for exhibiting deviant *behavior*, whereas the Jews, the mentally ill, and the Gypsies were doomed by the fact of their very *existence*.[23] And there was a "logic" behind this differential treatment. Let us return to Mosse's definition of the outsider, this time in its 1993 formulation in *Confronting the Nation:* "The concept of race chiefly affected Jews, but the . . . stylization of the outsider into a medical case placed all of them firmly beyond society's norms. The mentally ill, habitual criminals, homosexuals, and Jews were ever more firmly fixed within their so-called abnormality by means of the concept of illness."[24] If so, how did the Nazis establish their criteria of differentiation?

In a lecture on Nazi anti-Semitism delivered in May 2001 at Oxford, Philippe Burrin, a Swiss historian of French fascism and of the Holocaust, identified three clusters of concepts and metaphors around which Nazi anti-Semitism crystallized: health, power, and culture.[25] Following that distinction, one could argue that all outsiders represented a threat to the health of the *Volksgemeinschaft*, some because they were diseased in essence (the racially different and the mentally ill), others when they acted in a way that could threaten the health of the community (the homosexuals and the asocials). But in Nazi eyes, only one group among all the outsiders competed with Germandom and Aryan humanity for power and domination (world domination) and also threatened the racial community's culture at its core: the Jews; they, ultimately, had to be fought without compromise, and ultimately they had to disappear to the very last.

At the end of the penultimate chapter of his memoirs, entitled "Journey to Jerusalem," Mosse, the twofold outsider for a good part of his life, concludes as follows: "Indeed, I have been extraordinarily lucky throughout my life and this autobiography, as I wrote it, seems to contain much more light than shadow, which may detract from its interest but not from my happiness."[26] Yet the very last chapter, "The Past as Present," ends on a different note. After evoking the constant awareness of the Holocaust in his life and in his constant sense of being a "survivor," Mosse added these final lines: "The crimes of the Third Reich were writ large in my consciousness . . . a past which had to be faced. I had rejected the worlds of my past and had sought to transform myself, but in my anxieties, fears and restlessness I was still a child of my century."[27]

In his personal life, in this great university, in Jerusalem, in London, George certainly found the love, the friendship, and the intellectual nourishment he longed for. But, he also told us, the crimes of the Third Reich were writ large in his consciousness; attempting to understand the

Holocaust was an imperative he could not escape, a vital quest not only for understanding modern history but also for his own peace of mind. And that peace of mind may well have eluded him. Could it be, therefore, that the past he strove to exorcize by understanding it was even more present in his life than he recognized? Could it be that aside from intellectual understanding, something in and of that past fed both the "anxieties, fears and restlessness" and *also* the powerful constancy of his quest, something that George shared with many Jews of his generation and beyond? And couldn't that unacknowledged source of anxiety *and* of energy have been an intangible yet unmasterable sense of guilt for having survived the destruction of his world and the murder of his fellow Jews?

Notes

1. George L. Mosse, *Confronting History: A Memoir* (Madison: University of Wisconsin Press, 2000), 177.

2. Ibid.

3. George L. Mosse, *The Crisis of German Ideology: Intellectual Origins of the Third Reich* (New York: Grosset & Dunlap, 1964), 7–8.

4. Ibid., 70.

5. Ibid., 8.

6. Incidentally, the Jewish historians of Mosse's generation were wary about delving into the Nazi era (apart from very few exceptions). The Leo Baeck Institute, established in 1956 to study the history of Germany Jewry, did not venture beyond 1933 until its Berlin meeting in 1985.

7. Mosse, *Confronting History*, 65–66.

8. Mosse, *The Crisis of German Ideology*, 152.

9. Michael Wildt, *Die Judenpolitik des SD, 1935 bis 1938* (Munich: Oldenbourg, 1995); and Wildt, "Generation des Unbedingten: Das Führungskorps des Reichsicherheitshauptamtes" (Hamburg Edition; Hamburg, 2000). Incidentally, Wildt's studies and others refute the notion that the SS leadership was essentially a group of non-ideological technocrats of deportations, enslavement, and extermination.

10. Mosse, *Confronting History*, 219.

11. Steven E. Aschheim, *In Times of Crisis: Essays on European Culture, Germans, and Jews* (Madison: University of Wisconsin Press, 2001), 160.

12. Deltev J. K. Peukert, "The Genesis of the 'Final Solution' from the Spirit of Science," in *Reevaluating the Third Reich*, ed. Thomas Childers and Jane Caplan (New York: Holmes & Meier, 1993), 274–99.

13. George L. Mosse, *Toward the Final Solution: A History of European Racism* (New York: Howard Fertig, 1978), 214.

14. Max Domarus, ed., *Hitler: Reden und Proklamationen, 1932–1945* (Neustadt a.d. Aisch: Gesamtherstellung und Auslieferung Schmidt, 1962–63), 2:2083–84 ("And then the desiccated Jewish Ahasverus could celebrate the destruction of Europe in another triumphal Purim festival").

15. Aschheim, *In Times of Crisis*, 162–63.

16. George L. Mosse, *Nationalism and Sexuality: Middle Class Morality and Sexual Norms in Modern Europe* (Madison: University of Wisconsin Press, 1985), 190.

17. Mosse, *Confronting History*, 181.

18. Mosse, *Nationalism and Sexuality*, 169–70.

19. Mosse, *The Crisis of German Ideology*, 309.

20. George L. Mosse, "E. Nolte on *Three Faces of Fascism*," *Journal of the History of Ideas* 27, no. 4 (1966): 624.

21. George L. Mosse, ed., *Nazi Culture: Intellectual, Cultural, and Social Life in the Third Reich*, trans. Salvatore Attanasio (1966; New York: Grosset & Dunlap, 1981), 19.

22. *Nuremberg Document, PS-1919, Trial of the Major War Criminals before the International Military Tribunal* (Nuremberg, Germany: [s.n.], 1947–49). Two days after the speech to the SS generals, Himmler repeated his arguments about the extermination of the Jews in almost identical terms in a speech to the Reichsleiter and Gauleiter, also in Posen. Bradley F. Smith and Agnes Peterson, eds., *Heinrich Himmler Geheimreden, 1933 bis 1945* (Frankfurt: Propylän Verlag, 1974), 169 ff.

23. For the persecution of the "asocials" see mainly Wolfgang Ayass, *"Asoziale" im Nationalsozialismus* (Stuttgart: Klett-Cotta, 1995). The persecution and extermination of the Gypsies is best presented in Michael Zimmermann, *Rassenutopie und Genozid: Die Nationalsozialistische "Lösung der Zigeunerfrage"* (Hamburg: Christians, 1996), and in Gunter Lewy, *The Nazi Persecution of the Gypsies* (New York: Oxford University Press, 2000). For a detailed study of the persecution of the homosexuals see Burkhard Jellonek, *Homosexuelle unter dem Hakenkreuz* (Paderborn: Ferdinand Schöningh, 1990). As to the extermination of the mentally ill, the historical literature is vast; see in particular Michael Burleigh, *Death and Deliverance: "Euthanasia" in Germany, 1900–1945* (Cambridge: Cambridge University Press, 1994), and Henry Friedlander, *The Origins of Nazi Genocide: From Euthanasia to the Final Solution* (Chapel Hill, N. C.: University of North Carolina Press, 1995).

24. George L. Mosse, *Confronting the Nation: Jewish and Western Nationalism* (Hanover, N.H.: Published [for] Brandeis University Press by University Press of New England, 1993), 111.

25. Philippe Burrin, "Nazi Antisemitism," unpublished MS.

26. Mosse, *Confronting History*, 202.

27. Ibid., 219.

Part 3
Comparative History, Nationalism, and Memory

George Mosse's Comparative Cultural History

Jay Winter

I want to take this opportunity to take stock of the state of cultural history today, and by doing so to assess aspects of George Mosse's contribution to it. I will consider his work on "the myth of the war experience" and on the mobilization of "fallen soldiers," in particular those of World War I, in the years that followed the war.

The Great War

Mosse came to the Great War late; it is not a significant element in much of his earlier work on the nationalization of the masses or the crisis of German ideology. But when he decided to consider its impact, he did so in ways that have been of fundamental importance to the field. George was one of the founding members of the Historial de la grande guerre at Péronne, on the river Somme. The museum opened in July 1992, in the presence of Ernst Jünger among others. But three years earlier a group of forty historians from around the world had established a research center in the not-yet-completed museum. This group helped design the museum and (if I may be presumptuous) prevented its atrophy in the decade that followed. George was among these founding fathers, and his imprint on it is deep. What may not be apparent is how, since 1997, George's influence on French historical scholarship has come buoyantly to the surface. The work of the co-directors of the Historial's research center, Stéphane Audoin-Rouzeau and Annette Becker, on the brutalizing effects of war service could not have been done without George's lead.[1] What Jean-Jacques Becker has called "la banalisation de la guerre"[2] fit perfectly with Mosse's discussion in *Fallen Soldiers* of the process of trivialization, or the "cutting

151

[of] war down to size so that it would become commonplace instead of awesome and frightening." All kinds of kitsch helped to "disguise and control" the reality of war,[3] and many of these objects are on display in the Historial. I could cite other instances of French borrowings of Mosse's vocabulary and approach; they gave George great pleasure, undiminished by the fact that this recognition was outrageously delayed, in a manner the French have turned into an art form. But now that his work on the Great War and fascism is in French,[4] his ideas have begun to appear in many different corners of scholarship—literary, historical, and cultural.

Reflecting on this recent recognition of George's significance as a scholar enables me to open a more general discussion of a problem in contemporary scholarship. I want to make two points, and although they may appear at first glance to be entirely inconsistent, I hope to show that this is not the case. The first is that George was a comparative cultural historian and that comparative cultural history is a quixotic enterprise, almost impossible to do. The second is that George did it anyway and that the obstacles to truly comparative work in European cultural history are lower today because of what he did and who he was.

Let me try to make this two-part case with respect to George's work on the Great War. His most important intervention in this field is *Fallen Soldiers,* a book that moved from commemorations of the Great War back into the nineteenth century and forward to World War II. It incorporates American, British, French, Italian, and German material in comparative perspective, but it ultimately used evidence from numerous sources to elucidate the German case. This strategy, I believe, was not one that George adopted arbitrarily. It may be built into the nature of comparative history itself. George's work in general may be described as a set of experiments in comparative cultural history. But the obstacles to comparison must be faced. Are national cultural histories comparable? Is there a transnational unit of study, in the manner of European cultural history, or is such a subject as remote as a United States of Europe? Do Europeans have an irreducible "uncollective memory" of the past, a memory that is fragmented into national units? The fact that George's work posed rather than solved this set of problems is hardly a criticism; it just indicates that he had the vision to help set the agenda we now have to face.

Comparative Cultural Histories

One way to characterize George's approach to this set of problems is to see it as an exercise in what might be termed comparative cultural histories. Why the plural? Because the way cultural history has developed over the last decade or so, in the Historial and elsewhere, suggests that comparative cultural history does not in fact exist. I want to raise the disconcerting possibility that it may never exist in full. The comparative approach abounds, but its fundamental and unavoidable purpose is to offer insights that enrich rather than displace national histories.

Perhaps this return to the national unit as the necessary destination of comparative cultural history is inevitable. Archival sources are rarely strictly comparable in two (let alone three) nations. There are exceptions, to be sure. In my field there are valuable studies of trench journalism[5] and war memorials,[6] but outside these cases the study of parallel historical processes in cultural history (as opposed to economic history, demographic history, or labor history, e.g.) is very limited, observed more in exhortation than in practice.

The neighbors have some advantages, though as I will suggest in a moment, those advantages are limited too. Cultural history does not have the benefit of a fixed set of theoretical findings that provides the framework within which comparative economic history, for example, operates. Amartya Sen's attack on rational choice theory and his elaboration of an alternative way of configuring entitlements, capabilities, and functionings is a case in point.[7] Economic historians can examine harvest failure and market failure in particularly fruitful ways across a number of instances because Sen's theory is there to guide them.

Another instance of the way social-scientific research has informed a branch of comparative history is in the field of demography. Ansley Coale and Paul Demeny constructed model life tables—standardized descriptions of the way in which, under given fertility and mortality conditions, populations age over time. That is, in every year, each member of a society has a particular likelihood of dying before reaching his or her next birthday.[8] These model life tables have been particularly useful in providing demographic historians with the parameters of population growth in the past. Once some data can be found on some vital statistics, the rest can be calculated with some degree of confidence.[9] Demographer Louis

Henry set up a model of fertility decline based on the experience of an un-usual community, the Hutterites of the American Midwest and the plains of Canada, who did everything possible to maximize fertility in their com-munity.[10] This Hutterite fertility schedule provided an end point, an ex-treme case, of what Henry described as "natural fertility" against which the reproductive behavior of any population can be measured. Using this standard, the Office of Population Research at Princeton produced a massive set of studies of European fertility decline in which every na-tional case was measured in terms of the "out-rider," the society in which fertility was at a maximum.[11]

Comparative social history draws its models less from mathematical or formal analysis than from what may be termed the sociology of politi-cal struggles. Hidden agendas developed by the powerless can under-mine the powerful in ways that make sense not only of contemporary up-heavals but of historical movements.[12] The comparative history of slavery is a well-trodden field;[13] so is the comparative history of women's move-ments or (of particular interest to Mosse) of homosexuality.[14] The history of labor movements has, in the past, followed an emancipatory model, though in recent years, comparative studies of working-class culture have escaped from a political framework they never really fitted in the first place.[15] Substructure and superstructure were never sufficiently differ-entiated to permit such statements as to how "culture" (however defined) accounts for "politics" (however defined). Now that Marxism has frag-mented, the comparative history of working people has either retained its national emphases or moved into transnational or diasporic histories, in which migration and hybridity are central phenomena.[16]

And yet, even in well-developed areas of social-scientific history, prob-lems have emerged. In many cases, the payoff of comparative studies aris-ing out of theoretical or empirical work in other disciplines has been called into question. The bottom line is that the great promise of social-scientific history has never been fully realized. Indeed, the law of diminishing re-turns has been at work here. There has been a mountain of number-crunching and more and more elaborate modeling of historical behavior, but such research, while valuable in and of itself, has not on the whole led to fundamental revisions of historical interpretation. Yes, fertility rather than mortality is the driving force of English population growth, but the Industrial Revolution is still where it was. And yes, we now know that the introduction of railroads was not a revolutionary event in the economic history of most developing countries (canals and roads might have done about as well),[17] but scholarly life has gone on just the same. Slavery may or may not have been profitable, but the literature of the Civil War has not shifted much one way or the other accordingly.[18] But even so, the broader narratives of modern historical development have not been radically altered by this exciting, and yet to a degree disappointing, phase of historical research.

In addition, there is a kind of hubris associated with social-scientific theory—what might be called the pride of prediction—that has come home to haunt it. Theory means prediction, but too many lapses have emerged to enable theorists to take pride in the "scientific" nature of their models or equations. Many models of economic growth or fertility decline or class consciousness have been unable to predict sharp and at times abrupt changes in behavior. The Clinton years played havoc with trade cycle theory; no one could have predicted the downturn following 11 September 2001; the radical decline in fertility from the mid-1960s on was a surprise, as was the popular uprising that destroyed the satellite states of the Warsaw Pact and then the Soviet Union itself. Comparison on the basis of theoretical work in the social sciences has not had a happy time in recent years.

The question arises as to whether comparative cultural history has avoided these pitfalls. The answer is mixed. On the positive side, in most cases, cultural historians make more modest claims than many social scientists do; cultural historians study forms of representation and symbolic language that change only slowly, if at all. Endurance rather than rapid transformation is the hallmark of much work in this field. The very slowly moving, almost glacial, character of the phenomena studied by cultural historians makes their findings less prone to making headlines or disappointing expectations.

But on the down side, comparative cultural history has not really lived up to its own agenda. One reason for this is linguistic. The nuances of particular historical notation make comparison both essential and maddeningly difficult. Think of the difficulty of translating the phrase "shell shock" or in rendering the shadings of meaning in the phrase "war memorial" into other European languages. Shell shock is not *choc traumatique*, and war memorials are not *monuments aux morts*.[19] Poetry is fundamentally untranslatable, which is one reason why the works of Wilfred Owen, for example, iconic in Britain, have only very recently been translated into

French. The receptors are different; what James Joll called the "unspoken assumptions" are different.[20]

The locus classicus of this set of barriers to the construction of comparative cultural history is the study of the history of "memory." The term itself has entirely different shadings and connotations in different European languages. The classic studies of Halbwachs and Bloch on memory are profoundly French, infused with a set of assumptions about *la mémoire collective* that precludes any translations of the term simply as "collective memory"; it is both more and less than that. The French term is embedded in a literary, political, and cultural terrain of a very particular kind.[21]

Is it possible that the best way to move forward from this point is not to give up the effort but to treat comparison in a different way, one in which it discloses the ineluctable, irreducible differences and particularities of national cultures? Comparative history may be the path to our understanding of what may be termed "uncollective memory," those bits that do not make it across borders and cultural frontiers.

Then what kinds of comparisons can be made in the field of cultural history? My guess is that the ones which will last are those that are framed around questions of particular national experience. That is, comparative history is a branch of national history and not a different field at all.

George Mosse's scholarship in the field of twentieth-century cultural history demonstrates the force of this argument in compelling ways. The comparisons he was interested in were configured around Germany and German history. Other historians do the same with their particular preoccupations and then call their national histories comparative, since the comparisons always return to the primal scene, as it were.

For this reason (among others), what I would like to suggest, in part as a devil's advocate—a stance Mosse loved to take—is that the agenda of comparative cultural history is both futile and fertile. It is an ideal type, one that can never be realized but whose very existence as an ideal helps to enrich national cultural histories in profoundly important ways.

Fallen Soldiers and Comparative History

I have taken precisely this kind of insight from Mosse's work on the remembrance of war in twentieth-century Europe. The ideal type of the "myth of the war experience" has served an extremely important purpose by enabling us to investigate the following question: How, after the carnage of the Somme and Verdun, was another war possible—how was it thinkable? It would seem that the most natural response to war after 1918 would be to treat it with total and unshakable revulsion, to put its recurrence outside the boundaries of the imaginable. But we know that that outcome was precluded by other outcomes, in part determined by how men and women remembered the war and the men who died in it. The German part of this story is well known, but it is equally clear that the nature of what George called "the myth" and the sense of "war experience" were very different in different countries. That difference is not highlighted in *Fallen Soldiers*, but because of George's work we can see it more clearly today.

Consider two instances of the limits of comparison in this context. The first is personal. Mosse wrote in *Fallen Soldiers* that war cemeteries were "shrines of national worship," places where the nation worshiped itself. Consequently, war cemeteries strictly segregated bodies into national groups and buried them in different places, even though they fell together.[22] After the founding meeting of the Historial de la grande guerre in 1989, we took a trip to the battlefields in the French sector of the Western front near Noyons; Annette Becker guided us to three French cemeteries in which French and German war dead were buried side by side.

I cite this incident not to point out error, which George acknowledged immediately with his characteristic generosity of spirit, but to indicate how it discloses much that is of value in his approach to comparative history. His central point is that cemeteries were sacred spaces and, as such, could not accommodate those who took French lives alongside those Frenchmen who gave their lives in a holy cause. His argument does not fit the evidence in this case, but that does not destroy its validity. Counterexamples simply establish the limits of his interpretation. And those limits were set by the German experience. In German cemeteries, where *Heldenhaine* (Heroes' groves) were constructed, the symbolism of endurance and cultural continuities in spite of defeat was evident. Boulders represented *Urkraft* (primeval power). The linden tree symbolized the emperor. Other pastoral forms were adopted by the Imperial (now Commonwealth) War Graves Commission. In contrast, French cemeteries were vast and, in comparison, largely unadorned. The two Allied examples highlight what German commemorative art and architecture did *not* say and did *not* do. Comparison provides emphasis, not argument.

The argument lies elsewhere, and in Mosse's case that was almost always on the east bank of the Rhine.

Relational History and National Interpretations

This one instance highlights my general point about comparative history. Perhaps a better way of capturing both the spirit and the utility of Mosse's work is to describe it as *relational history.* That is, the subject is national, but the salient features of the national case are brought into relief by juxtaposing them to other, distinctive national cases. Thus what matters in *Fallen Soldiers* is neither the French form of funerary architecture in war cemeteries nor the British approach to the problem, which they resolved in terms of the ambience of an English country garden. What matters is the German case, the one that Mosse returned to throughout his life.

I suspect that much work which falls under the rubric of comparative history is very similar to this asymmetrical geometry of Mosse's historical argument, in which one point dominates the topology in view. My claim here is that it is best for comparative historians to come out of the closet and admit what is really in their hearts: that they are doing national history in imaginative, sometimes daring ways.

National Schools of Comparative Cultural History

This brings me to another point related to Mosse's contribution to the field: its nationally distinctive features help account for the different ways in which his work has been received in the scholarly world. Speaking very broadly, today there are three schools of cultural history in Europe; all three are robust and thriving, but they have little incentive to join together in something truly European. Mosse's work emerged from one of them, but it took time before it has became important in a more general sense. I want to define these schools in terms of how each lives with its neighbors, that is, how cultural history borrows from and contributes to cognate disciplines.

The first is the German case, in which cultural history (like George himself) came out of intellectual history but then emerged either as a branch of historical sociology, either Weberian or Marxian, or as an outgrowth of linguistic analysis. In the former case, which is closer to Mosse's writings, cultural history is contained within and directed toward an explanation of political phenomena. In effect, from this perspective, cultural life is always political in character and is never separate from the state and its institutions. In some studies in this tradition, the boundaries between social history and cultural history are blurred; one can speak of "social and cultural history" as one continuum, since the state is a point of reference for both.[23]

In the second case, what may be termed the French school, cultural history privileges different neighbors—anthropology, in the study of *mentalités*, or philosophy, as in the study of representations and discursive practices, elaborated by, among others, Louis Marin,[24] Michel de Certeau,[25] Michel Foucault,[26] and Roger Chartier.[27] The state is there, but as one player among many.

In the third, Anglo-Saxon case, cultural history has gained much from cross-fertilization with literary studies, and in the study of wartime cultural history, literary scholars like Paul Fussell[28] and Samuel Hynes[29] have led the way. The analysis of representations, now a category of intense scholarly interest, has virtually eclipsed the study of *mentalités*, and in this new paradigm literary scholars such as Stephen Greenblatt have been particularly influential.[30] In the Anglo-Saxon branch of the discipline, cultural history is unthinkable without reference to the literary imagination, be it through the work of Northrop Frye[31] or Edward Said[32] or Fredric Jameson.[33] In this very varied school, politics matters, but always in an indirect and framing manner.

Although overlaps and exceptions exist, it is still the case that national intellectual frontiers describe the different domains within which cultural history develops largely in tandem rather than collaboratively. This divided landscape of international scholarship helps us both to place Mosse's work in context and to account for the varied reception of that work over the last thirty years. It is only when the French began to consider the significance of both German and Anglo-American historical writing (and even agreed to read it in the original) that Mosse's scholarship became accessible and significant to a number of them. Of course it was there all the time, but its national characteristics (in the sense of national schools of cultural history) made it very difficult to translate into the language of a very different scholarly tradition.

Comparison, I am arguing, highlights difference, and for Mosse the difference that mattered most was German. Although George was intensely American, in his scholarly assumptions and methods he never left Germany. His approaches and emphases were German in character, something that helped him find a very congenial home in Jerusalem, which is (so I was told thirty years ago) the site of what may be the last German university in the world. His comparative work always migrated toward an understanding of the national case, his national case, the case of the German catastrophe. His use of non-German evidence was by and large directed toward highlighting essential features of German history. Britain and France were there in large part to show what Germany was not.

George did not draw on French cultural history for his methods or his style, and he was not impressed (justifiably) by some practitioners in the field of cultural studies in the United States or Britain. His intellectual origins were where his heart was and where the deepest sources of his work must be found. And that always led back to Germany.

At this point, two qualifications must be made. The first concerns George and Italy. Gentile's remarks in this volume help us to appreciate the complexities of the reception of Mosse's work in Italy. It is certainly true that George treated the case of Italian fascism on its own terms and not as one that simply replicated or illuminated the German model; on the contrary, his discussions of Italian fascism stood on their own. The second exception to the argument I am developing about the national destination of his work concerns the history of masculinity and sexuality, which truly transcends national boundaries.

In his work on modern European cultural history, though, it is clear that what Mosse helped create was less *comparative* history than *relational* history. That is, national cases could be understood by placing them geometrically in a kind of solar system, where they would "orbit" around the one central case at the core of the historical study. For George, I believe, that core was almost always Germany, but the constellation around it changed depending on the problem and the evidence at hand. What gave his work its force was its capacity to illuminate many historical instances by these sometimes jarring juxtapositions.

For instance, George enjoyed placing Israeli history in this kind of relational context. Germany was at the center, but in a number of studies he placed different national histories in relation to the German experience—with sometimes surprising results. The cult of manliness among elements of the fascist movement became something else when put

alongside the highly gendered nature of Israeli society. So too did the rituals and symbols of the Nazis—the flags, the uniforms, the invocations of
fallen brethren—when elided with the ceremony Israeli paratroopers
shared when they get their "wings" (or insignia of service) on Masada.
Here it was not only George's innate sense of fun, at times a bit barbed,
that was at work. It was also (and more importantly) his belief that history
had no consoling force; the more it disturbed, the more it alerted the
scholar or the student, the better. And this was nowhere more strikingly
evident than in the powerful presence he occupied in Jerusalem and in
the enduring effect he had on several generations of Israeli students and
colleagues.

To my knowledge, George was the only professor at the Hebrew
University of Jerusalem who was not obliged to teach in Hebrew. This
enabled him to use his wit to bring Israeli students into the discussion
of their tortured history by placing it in a relational context. That is,
analogies between Israeli nationalism and the Nazis are repugnant and
unacceptable, but seeing Israeli politics *in relation to* the cultural forms
the Nazis (or other Europeans) developed was and remains deeply in-
structive. There is no other explanation for the fact that *Fallen Soldiers*
remains a best-seller in Hebrew; George's approach brought many Israelis up abruptly against the jagged edges of their own history. And he
knew it.

George's contribution as a cultural historian was therefore multifac-
eted and deep. That there were limits to his insights is only to say that he
was like everyone else. But in other respects, his touch was singular; what
he had to say in his sonorous baritone could only have been said by him.

These remarks are in no sense offered in a critical spirit; on the contrary. My central point is simply that George explored the limits of cultural history and pushed them about as far as they could go. It is both the
strength and the limitation of the discipline that it has emerged from national intellectual and political traditions and that, despite its cosmopolitan character, in seeking evidence wherever it can be found, cultural history still uses comparative statements (as George did) primarily to deepen
national ones. In his early scholarship on the Reformation this may not
have been the case, but when he returned to European history in the
modern period and produced the work for which he will be remembered
most, he illustrated a more general point. European history, like European unity, is both eminently desirable and probably impossible. As long

as that is the case, George Mosse the German cultural historian will be read, celebrated, and profoundly missed.

Notes

1. Stéphane Audouin-Rouzeau and Annette Becker, *14–18, retrouver la guerre* (Paris: Gallimard, 2000).

2. Jean-Jacques Becker, *Les français dans la Grande Guerre* (Paris: Editions Robert Laffont, 1980).

3. George L. Mosse, *Fallen Soldiers: Reshaping the Memory of the World Wars* (New York: Oxford University Press, 1990), 126–27.

4. George L. Mosse, *De la Grande Guerre au totalitarisme: La brutalisation des sociétés européennes,* preface by Stéphane Audoin-Rouzeau, trans. Edith Magyar (Paris: Hachette littératures, 1999).

5. Stéphane Audoin-Rouzeau, *Men at War, 1914–1918: National Sentiment and Trench Journalism in France during the First World War,* trans. Helen McPhail (Providence: Berg, 1992); John G. Fuller, *Troop Morale and Popular Culture in the British and Dominion Armies, 1914–1918* (Oxford: Clarendon Press, 1990).

6. See, among others, Ken S. Inglis, *Sacred Places: War Memorials in the Australian Landscape* (Carlton, Vic.: Miegunyah Press, 1998).

7. Amartya Sen, *Poverty and Famines: An Essay on Entitlement and Deprivation* (Oxford: Clarendon Press, 1981).

8. Ansley J. Coale and Paul Demeny, *Regional Model Life Tables and Stable Populations* (Princeton: Princeton University Press, 1966).

9. E. A. Wrigley and R. S. Schofield, *The Population History of England, 1541–1871: A Reconstruction* (Cambridge: Harvard University Press, 1981); E. A. Wrigley et al., *English Population History from Family Reconstitution* (Cambridge: Cambridge University Press, 1997).

10. Louis Henry, *Demographie* (Paris: LeSeuil, 1972).

11. Ansley J. Coale and Susan Cotts Watkins, eds., *The Decline of Fertility in Europe: The Revised Proceedings of a Conference on the Princeton European Fertility Project* (Princeton: Princeton University Press, 1986).

12. James C. Scott, *Weapons of the Weak: Everyday Forms of Peasant Resistance* (New Haven: Yale University Press, 1985).

13. For a starter see Robin W. Winks, ed., *Slavery: A Comparative Perspective: Readings on Slavery from Ancient Times to the Present* (New York: New York University Press, 1972); and Marie-Christine Rochmann, ed., *Esclavage et abolitions: Mémoires et systèmes de représentation: Actes du colloque international de l'Université Paul Valéry, Montpellier III, 13 au 15 novembre 1998* (Paris: Karthala, 2000).

14. Again, for an aperitif, see Jeffrey Weeks, *Making Sexual History* (Malden, Mass.: Polity Press, 2000).

15. Ira Katznelson and Aristide R. Zolberg, eds., *Working-Class Formation: Nineteenth-Century Patterns in Western Europe and the United States* (Princeton: Princeton University Press, 1986).

16. For a guide to recent publications see *Diaspora: A Journal of Transnational Studies.*

17. For but one instance of this kind of work see Gary R. Hawke, *Railways and Economic Growth in England and Wales, 1840–1870* (Oxford: Clarendon Press, 1970).

18. For the classic argument see Robert William Fogel and Stanley L. Engerman, *Time on the Cross: The Economics of American Negro Slavery* (Boston: Little, Brown, 1974).

19. The January 2000 special issue of the *Journal of Contemporary History*, dedicated to George Mosse, addresses the subject of the comparative history of shell shock.

20. James Joll, *1914: The Unspoken Assumptions; An Inaugural Lecture Delivered 25 April 1968* (London: Weidenfeld & Nicolson, 1968).

21. See Maurice Halbwachs, *On Collective Memory*, ed., trans., and with an introduction by Lewis A. Coser (Chicago: University of Chicago Press, 1992); and Patrick H. Hutton, "Collective Memory and Collective Mentalities: The Halbwachs-Ariès Connection," *Historical Reflections/Réflexions Historiques* 15, no. 2 (1988): 311–22.

22. Mosse, *Fallen Soldiers*, 92.

23. See, e.g., Jurgen Kocka, *Sozialgeschichte: Begriff, Entwicklung, Probleme* (Gottingen: Vandenhoeck & Ruprecht, 1986).

24. Louis Marin, *Utopics: Spatial Play*, trans. Robert A. Vollrath (Atlantic Highlands, N.J.: Humanities Press, 1984), 2.

25. Michel de Certeau, *L'écriture de l'histoire* (Paris: Gallimard, 1975).

26. Michel Foucault, *L'Archéologie du savoir* (Paris: Gallimard, 1969).

27. Roger Chartier, *Au bord de la falaise: L'histoire entre certitudes et inquiètude* (Paris: Albin Michel, 1998).

28. Paul Fussell, *The Great War and Modern Memory* (New York: Oxford University Press, 1975).

29. Samuel Hynes, *The Soldiers' Tale: Bearing Witness to Modern War* (New York: A. Lane, 1997).

30. See Stephen Greenblatt, *Marvelous Possessions: The Wonder of the New World* (Chicago: University of Chicago Press, 1991).

31. See Northrop Frye, *The Critical Path; An Essay on the Social Context of Literary Criticism* (Bloomington: Indiana University Press, 1971).

32. See Edward Said, *Culture and Imperialism* (New York: Knopf, 1993).

33. See Fredric Jameson, *The Political Unconscious: Narrative as a Socially Symbolic Act* (Ithaca: Cornell University Press, 1981).

George Mosse and
"Destination Culture"

Rudy Koshar

Introduction

Tourism is the biggest industry in the world, now employing more people globally than the oil industry, and arguably causing even greater environmental harm. Last year more than seven billion tourists took to the roads, the airways, and the sea routes. If there can be little doubt that tourism has had a massive impact on contemporary cultural perceptions, the nature of that impact remains a matter of dispute. Henry James once argued that just three words describe tourist culture: "vulgar, vulgar, vulgar." American cultural critics of the 1920s warned against becoming permanently infected with the tourist's disease, *Bacillus wanderlusticus*.[1] Present-day scholars, active tourists all, are less likely to accept such characterizations, but they are more divided than ever as to how the tourist experience should be analyzed.

A book by performance scholar Barbara Kirshenblatt-Gimblett entitled *Destination Culture*[2] provides one of the more useful recent approaches to the subject. Its concern is the "political economy of display" that has evolved with considerable influence in the past quarter century in the Euro-American world. How do contemporary cultures transform "locations" into "destinations," asks the author, who ranges across a number of topics, including tourism, museums, kitsch, and what we now call the heritage industry. Her answer has to do with patterns in how the world is staged as a museum of itself. Contemporary "destination cultures" rely on tourism to transform life-worlds into sites to be displayed and consumed; they compel museums, strapped for funds and viewers, to emulate the experience of travel in constructing exhibitions; and they raise the expectation that what will be produced is something called "heritage." In this recourse to the past, which is mediated by memory, "authenticity" and "identity" do not merely result—they are *performed.* The artifact plays a central role in such performance, as a chunk of the Berlin Wall, a vintage car, or Jerusalem dust is called on to enact a ritual of cultural display far afield from the point of origin. Throughout this process, heritage does more than provide a pleasant refuge from everyday concerns or enhance civic education. Rather, through the touristic experience, heritage offers a new viability to ways of life, places, and objects whose previous meanings and uses have decayed or died. In this sense, one could say that history really does repeat itself, the first time as tragedy, the second time as a tourist site.

Kirshenblatt-Gimblett's book does not stand alone in the recent theoretical work on tourism. In researching my book on the history of German tourist guidebooks, I was impressed to find a broad array of sociological, anthropological, geographical, and ethnological studies of tourism, to say nothing of the vast policy literature generated by the tourist industry itself.[3] Among the best recent academic works are the Swedish ethnologist Orvar Löfgren's *On Holiday,* which discusses "elsewhereness" as a human pursuit, and British sociologist John Urry's *The Tourist Gaze,* which offers the historian important theoretical insights, shaped in part by Michel Foucault's work on modern perception and modalities of power.[4] In the worst cases, however, the theoretical literature is highly specialized and extremely limited in its willingness to connect the evolution of tourism with broader trends in cultural or political history. Focused analysis of the relationship between tourism and the heritage industry such as that provided in *Destination Culture* is the exception that proves the rule in this scholarship.

Even so, for all its clutter, the theoretical literature seems highly developed and lively compared to historical research on the subject of European tourism.[5] Except for a rather advanced scholarship on travel literature, for which we have our colleagues in literature and language departments in particular to thank, historical study of European tourism as a significant cultural practice is highly uneven. As John Walton remarked in a review article several years ago, "tourism has not been accepted into the charmed circle of acceptable themes in European history."[6] Pockets of activity in British and French social history contrast with a paucity of serious work in my field, late modern German history. Without rehearsing this scholarship, I should emphasize that historical research on the long-term evolution of tourism in German-speaking

Europe as well as more specialized studies of its impact in particular time periods and regions are sorely needed. The subject of tourism in the former East Germany, to say nothing of eastern-bloc countries more generally, is virtually terra incognita, a recent edited volume of essays by the Berlin scholar Hasso Spode notwithstanding.[7] What is more, much historical scholarship lacks the very dimension that informs Kirshenblatt-Gimblett's insights, namely a rigorous focus on how tourism appropriates and implements the past.[8]

George Mosse was not a scholar of the history of tourism. As the papers in this conference make clear, Mosse's oeuvre is known more for its emphases on mainstream topics in European history such as the Holocaust and the rise of fascism. This focus is understandable, of course, given Mosse's life experience, the state of the historical discipline, and the political climate in which he worked. Nonetheless, not only in his *Fallen Soldiers*,[9] in which World War I battlefield tourism is an important topic, but also in his earlier research, such as *The Nationalization of the Masses*,[10] one finds that issues of display and showing inform the analysis in ways that remain unacknowledged by cultural historians. Mosse's purchase on such issues was neither as sociologically focused nor as theoretically developed as Kirshenblatt-Gimblett's, but as I will argue, Mosse's work anticipated some of the key questions in recent historical scholarship on tourism, heritage, and practices of visual culture. In this essay I will outline some of those anticipations and consider how they are manifested in several areas of recent scholarship.

The history of destination culture as a global phenomenon remains to be written, though its outlines may be gleaned from the already briefly mentioned studies of the evolution of tourism as a formalized cultural practice. Geographer David Lowenthal's *The Past Is a Foreign Country* and his more recent *Possessed by the Past* are also relevant to the topic.[11] Not to be overlooked are the important connections between the formation of destination cultures and the history of imperialism and colonialism. A worldwide political economy of display depended in part on the showing of the exotic Other to European and American travelers and scholars.[12] In the Euro-American world, the past quarter century is central to the evolution of a heritage industry, as Lowenthal makes clear, but one can see its outlines well before this time. One of the key shortcomings of Kirshenblatt-Gimblett's study is its general inattention to such long-term historical precedents. The genealogy (if not the origin) of a "Western" culture of display and showing may be traced back quite far, but the late eighteenth and early nineteenth centuries represent a constitutive moment for understanding the late modern period.

Not coincidentally, this is also the moment when something like a modern form of tourism evolved, first in the guise of English romantics, who not only traipsed around the British Isles but also embraced the Rhineland. In doing so they encouraged that cult of the ancient artifact on German soil which later gave rise to the historic preservation movement. Not long after, the iron network of the railway system began crisscrossing German-speaking Europe, creating a market for a new brand of tourist guidebook, based less on speculation and cultured anecdote than on the prospect of organized encounters with rail schedules, hotels, carriages, and tourist sites along the way. The appearance in the 1830s of Karl Baedeker's first guidebooks to the Rhineland signaled the rise of a burgeoning middle-class tourist market on the Continent. The itineraries described in the new genre of tour guides were not unlike those that shaped the Grand Tour, a ritualized practice enjoyed by the aristocracy and upper middle class. Although the Grand Tour had educative goals for the scions of European elites, it often deteriorated into rounds of drunkenness and rowdy debauchery. But it shared with the later middle-class travel itinerary a love for the cherished destinations of northern Italy and Greece, Switzerland, the Rhineland, and Paris.[13]

Not a few of those middle-class tourists were inspired by the nationalist symbolism that Mosse analyzed in his *Nationalization of the Masses.* In this book, Mosse sought the historical roots of Nazism's aestheticization of politics. He found them in the period of the Napoleonic Wars and the rise of nationalist movements. Surveying an array of topics, from nature to historical ruins, from national monuments to gymnastics organizations and trade unions, Mosse analyzed the long-term evolution of a nationalist culture of display. Through this culture, the German nation, still politically fragmented and economically underdeveloped in the early nineteenth century, not only performed itself in front of the masses but also incorporated those masses into an economy of showing. In addition, the German nationalist movement drew on memory of the past, combining classical Greek influences, Germanic myths, and fragments of that *völkisch* ideology which Mosse had so skillfully analyzed in *The Crisis of German Ideology.*[14]

Kirshenblatt-Gimblett argues that the modern heritage industry gives "second life" to places, objects, and peoples whose original meanings have weakened or been eviscerated.[15] A dilapidated mining town, a down-and-out urban neighborhood, even the site of a former concentration camp—all derive a "second chance" when they are marketed as heritage. Germany's landscape of venerable castle ruins and medieval towns indeed gained a second life in the evolution of the new culture of display. On the one hand, they were made to operate as political symbols of a rising national movement; on the other hand, they functioned as economic resources in a country just entering the age of modern industrialization and commercialization. In either case, the adaptation of nature and history to the modern process of nationalization was also an act of conquest. The modern gained dominance over tradition and heritage, although its dominance was most often expressed in the rhetoric of love or veneration for the past. Although heritage ostensibly references bygone ages, it is highly modern and contemporary, a product of the here and now.

In present-day underdeveloped countries, heritage is mobilized to present nations as museums of themselves. This self-archaeologization results not only in the influx of tourist dollars (or pounds, euros, and yen) but also, presumably, in an increase in national memory and, quite possibly, national pride. In this sense, Mosse's work helped us to understand Germany as the world's first developing nation, although he never put the matter in quite these terms. The German nation was not only the site of a growing nationalist movement, intensely threatened by French and English power, but also home to a nascent heritage industry, which, before the rise of a modern industrial system, attracted British and French (and not a few American) tourists to the lovely castles and towns of the Rhineland, the scenic natural attractions of Alpine regions, or the classically inspired national monuments dotting the landscape. Even after industrialization had taken off later in the nineteenth century, the process of self-archaeologization continued, and Germany was recognized for its prominence in transforming historic towns into attractive (and profitable) tourist sites.[16] This prominence was registered in the tourist guidebooks, which even touted Berlin, a city notably lacking in historical architecture, as a site of romantic effect and historical ambience.[17] But by rendering itself as a destination, Germany also developed highly ambivalent relations with "colonial" powers. Anti-Americanism and the critique of Western commercial society were by-products of this ambivalence, which rested on borrowing and implementing colonial models while also resisting or criticizing them. This contradictory process lay at the heart of that "crisis" of German ideology which Mosse had discussed.

Germany developed a destination culture only in part through the display of historical places and objects. As Mosse's research made clear, this process entailed popular self-display as well. Mosse was most interested in the manner in which nationalist festivals and other events created venues through which the populace both imagined and admired itself as a national entity. Such self-admiration was often inspired by images of "ideal" beauty, derived in part from classical Greek culture. As Mosse pointed out in *Nationalism and Sexuality,* such images gained impetus from evolving middle-class notions of respectability and sexual norms.[18] Moreover, ritualized self-admiration would take on politically more dangerous forms, as when it regulated the idea that the nation as a racial body needed to remove threats to its collective health. After World War I, the culture of display and popular self-admiration took its cue from technology, as the Greek-inspired ideals of the nineteenth century gave way to motorized, militarized bodies capable of unprecedented violence. The "rhythm of the blood" and the "tempo of the machine" were to be conjoined in a new, hypernationalist hybrid.[19] Accordingly, a machine aesthetic regulated much of that nationalist self-display for which Albert Speer's creations at National Socialist rallies became signature elements.

But Germans put themselves on display for the colonizers as well. Whether as Bavarian peasants going about their quotidian tasks or as tourist-conscious promoters of "folk" festivals, local theater performances, and other kinds of "environmental performance,"[20] Germans helped construct the destination culture in the context of their everyday lives. Even militarized bodies could perform this function. Wilhelm II's armies and Hitler's storm troopers had obvious internal political and military roles to play, but they also functioned as tourist spectacles for both domestic and foreign consumers, as the descriptions in pre-1914 Baedeker guidebooks or in interwar guidebooks to Germany make abundantly clear.[21] (Jakob Vogel's recent book on popular militarism does a good job of analyzing Wilhelmine and French Third Republic military festivals as public spectacles.)[22] Not that the exhibition of people as living rarities was a new phenomenon. Eskimos were exhibited in Bristol, England, in 1501, and subsequent centuries produced many examples of ethnographic displays through which "exotics" came under the scrutiny of the "civilized."[23] Yet modern destination cultures take this interaction a step further, often transforming whole ways of life, whether of peasant villages or armies, into display exhibits. The line between observer and observed becomes extremely blurry in such contexts, just as definitions of "exotic" and "indigenous" do.

As the foregoing suggests, destination cultures are intensely visual. Since the mid-1990s, poststructuralists, colonial studies scholars, feminists, and many others have criticized the masculinist "hegemony of vision" that has been said to regulate Western culture for centuries. Such critique has been part of a growing scholarly interest in visuality/perception as both a historical phenomenon and a theoretical-philosophical problem.[24] This is not the place to enter into these often recondite debates over what one scholar had the courage to call "the problematics of anti- and post-ocularcentric positions in the field of visual experience,"[25] but one of the great advantages of Mosse's work—and a distinguishing characteristic in comparison to most historical research on German nationalism in the 1970s—was its resolute attention to visual aesthetics and symbolism, indeed, to how German nationalist culture *looked.* At the time *Nationalization of the Masses* appeared, only Thomas Nipperdey, most notably in a 1968 essay on national monuments, had made a serious statement on the role of the visual in nineteenth-century German-speaking nationalist movements.[26] Significantly, that essay is still cited often, despite the outpouring of research on national monuments that has occurred since the late 1980s. Whereas scholars of medieval and early modern history had long understood the importance of visual cultures, students of late modern European political and social history had virtually ignored this aspect at the time Mosse wrote. Walter Benjamin's discussion of fascism as the aestheticization of politics was well known to scholars of modern German culture, of course, as were Siegfried Kracauer's writings on the "mass ornament."[27] For the Nazi period, moreover, Barbara Miller Lane's still influential book on German architecture and the rise of National Socialism was available.[28] But a long-term and more synoptic historical analysis of nationalist cultures of display did not exist.

In more recent scholarship on late modern German history, the visual occupies pride of place. Among German-language scholars, Peter Reichel's study of the "beautiful look" of the Third Reich demonstrated how the Nazi regime "staged" itself for public consumption through architecture, Nazi Party rallies, the autobahn, entertainment, military display, and many other cultural practices.[29] Historians of the Nazi period share a growing belief

that the Third Reich was a highly modern "audiovisual" nation whose impact on the perception of ordinary people is still only incompletely understood. As I show in my two books on monument preservation and historical
sites in Germany, the maintenance and representation of historical buildings provide clues to how Germans imagined themselves as a nation.[30] In
Germany's Transient Pasts the subject was the formation of a "national optics" that served to regulate preservationist discourse from the late nineteenth century into the 1970s.[31] Although I cannot claim that Mosse's earlier work was my main influence, it would be difficult to argue that my
interest in the field of nationalist visuality would have developed quite as
strongly as it did without Mosse's example in the background. In other recent works in German cultural history—for example, Alon Confino's *The
Nation as a Local Metaphor*—the optics of identity formation also appears
as a central narrative thread, if not necessarily as a significant conceptual
problem.[32] In Janet Ward's recent study of "Weimar surfaces," visual culture in the form of architecture, advertising, film, and commercial window
displays becomes the direct object of analysis, though here the goal is not
an understanding of the heritage industry or nationalist culture but rather
1920s urban modernism.[33] Finally, in recent studies of Holocaust memory,
as in Cornelia Brink's analysis of photographs of the concentration camps
taken after 1945, or Dagmar Barnouw's excellent book on U.S. Army Signal Corps photography of Germany at the end of the war, or in debates on
the controversial Wehrmacht exhibit photographs, the visual element takes
center stage.[34] The point is not that Mosse's scholarship directly influenced
this recent work but rather that it anticipated a cultural-historical scholarship on visuality in German history that is just now acquiring a certain depth
and precision. Why the turn to visuality in German historiography happened when and how it did is a more complex issue that cannot be addressed here.

If *Nationalization of the Masses* looked to the future, Mosse's more recent work was even more relevant to a discussion of the visual as a key element in late modern cultural and political history. A central feature of
modern destination cultures is that they deploy objects and artifacts that
have no distinctive visual interest of their own. National monuments were
made to be visually striking, even commanding, but they were not the
only buildings or artifacts that attracted tourists. In some cases, not
only quite ordinary objects but also ugly landscapes, such as World War I
battlefields or former concentration camps, entered the touristic canon.

What is it that makes us look at vast, open, treeless stretches of land, bordered in some cases (Buchenwald, for example) only by rusting barbed-wire fences? It is certainly not the intrinsic visual appeal of the objects or sites themselves, which for the most part look entirely banal and ordinary, even those that witnessed unspeakable cruelty. It is rather the meaning we ascribe to them and the history in which we have embedded them that matter. As Kirshenblatt-Gimblett maintains, artifacts do not exist, they are made, and displays of artifacts "are also exhibits of those who make them."[35]

It is the mundane artifact that attracts Mosse's attention in his analysis of the "trivialization" of World War I memory in *Fallen Soldiers,* published in 1990. In this book, Mosse argues that a mythic sense of the war experience used nature and religion to derive positive meaning from an event whose sine qua non was senseless slaughter. But the process of coming to terms with the Great War also consisted of turning it into something commonplace and everyday rather than frightening and distant. To use Nietzsche's oft-quoted conceptualization in *Untimely Meditations,* the war became an antiquarian rather than monumental species of history.[36] War memory engaged not just the mountain peaks of accomplishment or sublime defeat but also the valleys of daily existence and dogged survival. In doing so, it also engaged artifacts and objects that were the stuff of trivia and everyday life. Mosse recounts how a 1916 exhibition by the Red Cross on "War, Volk, and Art" included needle cushions, matchboxes, and candy wrappers decorated with the Iron Cross; a cigarette case with a picture of a trench; and inkstands and bath toys designed as German soldiers. In addition, real battlefield objects—shells, helmets, and cartridges—were on display. After the war, these trinkets and artifacts were sold to pilgrims and tourists on the battlefields.[37] (After World War II, objects such as shell casings and steel helmets were sold as household appliances in an effort to both domesticate and recycle the implements of destruction.) In this same analysis, Mosse examined the history of picture postcards with World War I themes as well as military board games and toys manufactured to look like tanks, weapons, and soldiers. World War I battlefields became destinations, using graves and cemeteries, nature, landscapes, and other features in the process of catering to increasing numbers of tourists. This too was an original and provocative approach to the subject of war memory, one that has now finally begun to receive more systematic treatment, as, for example, in David W. Lloyd's book on battlefield tourism and World War I commemoration in Britain, Australia, and Canada.[38]

Mosse was explicit about the effects of all this. "The reality of war was transcended once more," he concluded, "not by absorbing war into a civic religion, but by making it mundane and reducing it to artifacts used or admired in daily life and co-opted by those who wanted to satisfy their curiosity about the fighting. The process of trivialization did not uplift or soothe the mind, but instead gave men and women the feeling of dominating events."[39] Even when tourists visited World War I battlefields not as curiosity seekers but as pilgrims and mourners, Mosse argued, the organization of their itineraries, the amenities of their stay, and the broader commercial mediation of the sites and objects of war weakened the impact of memory.

I have taken issue with Mosse's argument that the display of such mundane objects distorted war memory. I state in *From Monuments to Traces* that the representation of everyday objects was not a distortion of the past but rather consistent with the nature of the Great War.[40] From the beginning, the conflagration had been a spectacle, overwhelming in its massive, inexplicable destruction and its ability to touch almost every individual or family in the belligerent nations. But precisely because it touched everyday life so deeply, its otherworldiness was often manifested in the most mundane or trivial ways. Cultural studies scholars have effectively demonstrated the connection between spectacle and kitsch. In the United States in particular, where such things as Elvis Presley memorabilia probe the depths of human understanding of life, death, and redemption, it should not be difficult to grasp this relationship. Battlefield tourism, war memoirs, films, postcards, mass-produced monuments, everyday utensils, pillows, matchboxes, children's war games—all reproduced the effect of a historical phenomenon both overwhelming and fascinating to the human imagination yet rendered meaningful through seemingly degraded artifacts or "things." Memory called up this theme of sublimity even after the battlefield sites had been plowed over and the war monuments integrated as symbols in ritualized myth. It was this impulse to which the seemingly trivial activities of the tour guides, monument builders, and hotel keepers appealed as well.

Such issues also take us into the realm of reception. Recent scholarship by Vanessa Schwartz and others points out that modern visual cultures presuppose and construct spectators whose appropriation of

images, directives, or objects may occur in a manner that does not coin-
cide with the intentions of producers.[41] The complexities whereby particular images, objects, and ideas circulate through the "scapes" and
"flows" of modern society remained more or less unexplored in Mosse's
work.[42] What did "nationalization" entail for the patriots, consumers, and
spectators affected by the process once it was a matter not of grand monumental displays and rousing speeches but of implementing such ideas
in daily life? How were commercialized and seemingly trivial artifacts of
the German tourist industry, of war commemoration, or of the nationalist and (much later) National Socialist movements actually used once
they entered the homes, schools, or offices of the German people?[43] Did
the various "scopic regimes of modernity," to use Martin Jay's evocative
phrase,[44] clash or compete with one another when it came to embracing
or rejecting the visual elements of particular war memorials? What did
mourning mean once it was removed from public commemorations and
marble plaques and practiced in the context of individual and familial experience? (Jay Winter's work on the European culture of mourning provides a valuable response to this question.)[45] In a seminal essay on the
history of the Italian motor scooter, cultural studies scholar Dick Hebdige argued that no idea, image, or artifact can be studied in its full complexity unless it is seen at three key "moments": production, mediation,
and consumption.[46] In Hebdige's perspective, the real goal of cultural
analysis is unraveling these moments, demonstrating the interaction and
mutual dependence of the manufacture, distribution, and social appropriation of artifacts and objects. In general, Mosse's work remained focused on the first moment, just as most cultural and social history on late
modern Europe concentrates on the production rather than full social
itinerary and disposition of objects and images. In this regard, the blind
spots of Mosse's analysis are illustrative of a larger analytical problem in
contemporary scholarship, in which, as one scholar has remarked, "the
history of consumption as production is still, to some extent, waiting to
be written."[47]

The problem of trivialization is a controversial one, weighing heavily
in recent debates on Holocaust commemoration. For good reasons,
scholarship on Holocaust memory is particularly sensitive not only about
what topics constitute the analytical canon but what modes of representation ought to be deployed. Saul Friedländer's *Reflections of Nazism* set
the agenda for many such current discussions on the topic, although I

would argue that it is too pessimistic about popular media's role in shaping the memory of genocide.[48] Should scholarly monographs and solemn historical commemorations be regarded as the most appropriate mode of representation? What of oral testimony as compared to critical historical analysis? If film is to be allowed into the canon, then is *Shoah* preferable to *Schindler's List* or *Life Is Beautiful*? How do we assess the relative merits of each different kind of representation when they are placed side by side, as they so often are in everyday life (but not, unfortunately, in scholarly analysis)?[49] For example, how do we assess the comment of the teenager who, after touring the Sachsenhausen concentration camp site, told a friend that "*Schindler's List* was better"?[50] Is the piling up of certain mundane objects—such as former concentration camp victims' shoes or the issuing of "identity cards" to visitors at the Holocaust Museum in Washington, D.C.—a cheapening of the memory of the victims? What of the rendering of Holocaust memory in comic books such as *Maus*[51] or, as in the 1970s, in the Sex Pistols' rock song "Holidays in the Sun," where lead singer Johnny Rotten expresses his desire to go to "new Belsen" for a vacation?[52]

In asking such questions, it is worth noting that both *Maus* and the Sex Pistols can hardly be considered kitsch. Art Spiegelman's work is analytically demanding, and even though punk often relied on the safety pin and the dog collar as fashion statements, it was based on a highly stylized and self-conscious ransacking of contemporary mass culture. Maybe the television situation comedy *Hogan's Heroes*, neither self-conscious about its thematic scope nor ambitious in its cultural reach, would be a better place to start for assessing examples of popular media culture's representation of traumatic events like World War II and the Holocaust. But there are of course more recent (and more dangerous) examples, as in recent neo-punk rock music performed by groups with racist political intentions.

It is worth citing a passage from Kirshenblatt-Gimblett, who devotes an entire chapter to the problem of "taste" in contemporary destination cultures. "What do aerosol cheese, Liberace, tattoos, Chihuahuas, and feminine hygiene spray have in common?" she asks.

The diverse social locations from which such instances of "bad taste" come make Spam, ant farms, facelifts, low riders, and Lawrence Welk incommensurable as a set. They have nothing in common but their relationship to the canon of good taste. Bad taste is one of the ways in which good taste announces itself—the finger that points to the breach in the rule. The connoisseurship of bad taste must therefore be read back on itself, for it reveals more about the arbiter than the offender. As Meyer Shapiro is said to have said, "Kitsch is chic spelled backwards."[53]

The point is not to adjudicate the battle over good or bad taste, either in the question of World War I memory or in the more controversial subject of Holocaust memory. But Kirshenblatt-Gimblett's approach to the subject reminds us that the matter of taste is quite culturally specific. Different memory cultures—indeed, different generations or social groups within ostensibly coherent memory cultures—may have recourse to the past in a variety of seemingly incommensurable ways. That incommensurability may be a key to understanding the richness of contemporary destination cultures, whether the subject is the Holocaust or, to take an issue more specifically "American," the representation and preservation of Ellis Island—also a subject of interest in *Destination Culture*. To choose one modality of memory as the "correct" approach to the past is to miss the valuable cultural energy that is generated when conflicting viewpoints and opinions clash.

If the balance of Mosse's analysis of trivialization is rather mixed, it nonetheless takes us onto a terrain that is, once again, both productive and contentious in contemporary cultural theory and history. The question of how commercial goods and consumer society relate to memory cultures has only recently received the kind of attention it should, and then more by cultural studies scholars than by historians. Kirshenblatt-Gimblett argues that certain consumer goods give shape to time.[54] Although commodities may have more accelerated temporalities than museums or historical spaces and buildings do, they nonetheless assist in the process of temporal indexing that is so central to relating past, present, and future. The phenomenon of the incessant rise and fall of certain fads—from hula hoops to automobile fins—provides a useful example. Evanescence is as important to the process of situating the Self and Other in time as durability or persistence are. In societies in which acts of purchase have become constitutive of a broad range of both personal and collective identities, it would seem that memory cultures might demonstrate a particularly strong reliance on—or perhaps an anxious resistance to—the commodity as an index of the past. But this possibility has rarely received full analytical treatment from scholarship on Euro-American memory in general and German memory in particular; and when it has, it tends to resemble Mosse's trivialization model. A rather glaring example of such scholarly inattention is the recent first volume of a multivolume project on German "places of memory" edited by the distinguished historians Etienne François and Hagen Schulze and designed to be a German-language rejoinder to Pierre Nora's massively influential collection on French *lieux de mémoire*.[55] More than seven hundred pages long, *Deutsche Erinnerungsorte* has just one essay on a commercial object that was significant to the formation of German memory cultures. It is an interesting piece on the Volkswagen by Erhard Schütz, a Germanist and cultural studies scholar rather than a historian.[56]

Recently the study of material culture has gone mainstream, as academic historians have turned to a field that until the past decade or so was the province mainly of folklorists or museum scholars. This scholarship has concentrated increasingly on commercial objects, from low-status commodities such as zippers and mirrors to more expensive things such as furniture or even historical artifacts. I think Leora Auslander's book *Taste and Power,* which deals with French furniture design and middle-class culture over two centuries, is a model of analysis in this genre.[57] (Auslander has now undertaken a most interesting research project on household inventories of Berlin and Parisian Jews during the Holocaust. Her data on Jewish material possessions come from a particularly poignant source, namely inventories collected by the Nazis as they expropriated people slated for transport to the camps.)[58] It would seem useful for scholars of twentieth-century memory cultures in particular to take account of this "material turn." In one respect this has already occurred, if recent research by Detlef Hoffmann and others on concentration camp relics and sites is any indication of current concerns.[59] Yet this work, the title of which in English is *The Memory of Things: Concentration Camp Relics and Monuments, 1945–1995,* remains largely unreflective on the status of commercial objects as such in the formation of collective and personal memory. This is a significant oversight, if for no other reason than that anyone who has walked into the information center of a former concentration camp site in Europe will have to confront the commercial mediation of those very relics and monuments Hoffmann's contributors discuss.

Whence the reluctance to broaden the range of "vectors of memory" included in historical study to encompass the commodity?[60] In part, particularly in scholarship on German-speaking Europe, preoccupation with the representation of past trauma as such has diverted attention from the everyday workings of memory cultures, including the way in which "getting and spending" shapes those cultures. But if the foregoing discussion on trivialization is accurate, then there is an even more deep-seated unwillingness to consider how the memory of trauma may be evinced in allegedly "low-class" or inappropriate attitudes and contexts. In German historiography, this reticence may still be connected with a long-standing discourse of *Kultur,* the alleged profundity of which disallows commercialism and consumer objects as appropriate topics of scholarly research.[61] But it would be unfair to single out German scholars on this score. Even in American academic culture there is a long-standing and rather extraordinary ambivalence among scholars about accepting commodity culture as a legitimate focus of scholarship,[62] much less as an appropriate vehicle for understanding the memory of war or genocide. In short, we are dealing here with the politics of a historiography that has not, apparently, ever gotten over the analytical hangover that resulted from Karl Marx's evocative discussion of the "fetishism" of commodities. In this still influential analysis, Marx argued that the only way to find an analogy to the relationship between things qua commodities was to "have recourse to the mist-enveloped regions of the religious world."[63]

An even broader reason for scholarship's inability to see its way into commercial culture as a medium of memory formation has to do with the concept of identity deployed by historians and other scholars. Still largely derived from nineteenth-century notions of national territoriality and bounded spaces, the regnant analytical concept of identity favors sessility rather than movement, fixedness rather than flow.[64] Scholarship on memory concentrates on those sites and practices that seem to have ensured a degree of perdurability in otherwise rapidly changing societies. Relatively stable or more slowly changing topographies seem to offer a better point of analytical entry in the study of memory cultures than do evanescence or fluidity. The national state has most often regulated this analytic of sessility, not least because of the investments it has made in territorial boundedness and longevity.

But movement and dispersal, which together constitute the sine qua non of twentieth-century societies, do not preclude the formation of relatively stable (or perhaps identifiable) orientations to both the past and the future. Such orientations may crystallize more regularly around different objects and practices, however, than those that have occupied scholars.

They may be less predictable from prior historical developments and less lasting in their effects than are other objects. Memory sites that "travel" in corporeal, social, cultural, and transnational terms are as important to the understanding of memory cultures as fixed spaces and sites are (which are themselves deceiving in terms of the stability or boundedness they ostensibly embody). How these sites travel, what itineraries they describe, and how their movements relate to processes of remembering and forgetting across a whole range of individual and collective experiences—these issues are central to our understanding of the formation of destination cultures.

Conclusion

My goal in this essay has been to focus on attributes of George Mosse's oeuvre that have received relatively little attention from the many scholars who have been influenced by his work. I have purposely avoided discussing Mosse's contributions to scholarship on German-Jewish relations, to gender and gay studies, and to the history of the Holocaust. I have only briefly touched on his scholarship on National Socialism and fascism. In portraying Mosse as a historian of the culture of display in late modern Europe, however, I hope to draw attention to the possibilities of his work for scholars whose interests extend into the field of cultural studies. In particular, as he has in so many of the more mainstream fields of contemporary European historiography, Mosse anticipated debates that have only now become unusually productive. In his emphasis on nationalist visuality; his often unintentional contributions to scholarship on display and traditions of showing; his remarks on kitsch and memory; his discussions of material culture; and his attention to commercial objects—in all this there was a profound commitment to broadening the conceptual and topical ambit of scholarship, focusing on the unexpected, and drawing connections between ostensibly unconnected phenomena. From my point of view, Mosse's work always opened the door to the noncanonical, even the idiosyncratic. Scholars committed to stepping through that door will continue to find much to offer them in his research.

Notes

1. Warren James Belasco, *Americans on the Road: From Autocamp to Motel, 1910–1945* (Cambridge: MIT Press, 1979).

2. Barbara Kirshenblatt-Gimblett, *Destination Culture: Tourism, Museums, and Heritage* (Berkeley: University of California Press, 1998).

3. See Rudy Koshar, *German Travel Cultures* (Oxford: Berg, 2000), esp. 11–15.

4. Orvar Löfgren, *On Holiday: A History of Vacationing* (Berkeley: University of California Press, 1999); John Urry, *The Tourist Gaze: Leisure and Travel in Contemporary Societies* (London: Sage, 1990).

5. Koshar, *German Travel Cultures*, 12–15; Koshar, "'What Ought to Be Seen': Tourists' Guidebooks and National Identities in Modern Germany and Europe," *Journal of Contemporary History* 33, no. 3 (1998): 323–40, esp. 324–26.

6. John Walton, "Taking the History of Tourism Seriously," *European History Quarterly* 27 (1997): 563–71, quote on 563.

7. Hasso Spode, ed., *Goldstrand und Teutonengrill: Kultur- und Sozialgeschichte des Tourismus in Deutschland 1945 bis 1989* (Berlin: Verlag für universitäre Kommunikation, 1996); see also József Böröcz, *Leisure Migration: A Sociological Study on Tourism* (Oxford: Elsevier Science, 1996).

8. See Alon Confino, "Traveling as a Culture of Remembrance: Traces of National Socialism in West Germany, 1945–1960," *History and Memory* 12, no. 2 (2000): 92–121, for an informed perspective on this subject.

9. George L. Mosse, *Fallen Soldiers: Reshaping the Memory of the World Wars* (New York: Oxford University Press, 1990).

10. George L. Mosse, *The Nationalization of the Masses: Political Symbolism and Mass Movements in Germany from the Napoleonic Wars through the Third Reich* (New York: New American Library, 1975).

11. David Lowenthal, *The Past Is a Foreign Country* (Cambridge: Cambridge University Press, 1985); Lowenthal, *Possessed by the Past: The Heritage Crusade and the Spoils of History* (New York: Free Press, 1996).

12. See Edward Said, *Orientalism* (New York: Pantheon, 1978); James Clifford, *Routes: Travel and Translation in the Late Twentieth Century* (Cambridge: Harvard University Press, 1997).

13. Koshar, *German Travel Cultures*, 20–28.

14. George L. Mosse, *The Crisis of German Ideology: Intellectual Origins of the Third Reich* (New York: Grosset & Dunlap, 1964).

15. Kirshenblatt-Gimblett, *Destination Culture*, pt. 2, which is titled "A Second Life as Heritage."

16. See Celia Applegate, *A Nation of Provincials: The German Idea of Heimat* (Berkeley: University of California Press, 1990); Alon Confino, *The Nation as a Local Metaphor: Württemberg, Imperial Germany, and National Memory, 1871–1918* (Chapel Hill: University of North Carolina Press, 1997).

17. Koshar, *German Travel Cultures*, 54–55.

18. George L. Mosse, *Nationalism and Sexuality: Middle-Class Morality and Sexual Norms in Modern Europe* (Madison: University of Wisconsin Press, 1985).

19. The terms were used by the engineer Karl Arnhold, as cited by Anson Rabinbach, *The Human Motor: Energy, Fatigue, and the Origins of Modernity* (New York: Basic Books, 1990), 287.

20. The term is from Kirshenblatt-Gimblett, *Destination Culture*, 59. On the formation of a German tourist culture in a single region see Helena Waddy Lepowitz, "Pilgrims, Patients, and Painters: The Formation of a Tourist Culture in Bavaria," *Historical Reflections/ Réflexions Historiques* 18 (1992): 121–45.

21. See also Angela Schwarz's discussion of British travelers' responses to Nazi public culture in *Die Reise ins Dritte Reich: Britische Augenzeugen im nationalsozialistischen Deutschland (1933–1939)* (Göttingen: Vandenhoeck & Ruprecht, 1993).

22. Jakob Vogel, *Nationen im Gleichschritt: Der Kult der "Nation in Waffen" in Deutschland und Frankreich, 1871–1914* (Göttingen: Vandenhoeck & Ruprecht, 1997).

23. Kirshenblatt-Gimblett, *Destination Culture*, 41.

24. John Urry, *Sociology beyond Societies: Mobilities for the Twenty-first Century* (London: Routledge, 1999), 80–93.

25. Ian Heywood and Barry Sandywell, "Introduction: Explorations in the Hermeneutics of Vision," in *Interpreting Visual Culture: Explorations in the Hermeneutics of the Visual*, ed. Heywood and Sandywell (London: Routledge, 1999).

26. Thomas Nipperdey, "Nationalidee und Nationaldenkmal in Deutschland im 19. Jahrhundert," *Historische Zeitschrift* 206 (1968): 529–85.

27. Walter Benjamin, "The Work of Art in the Age of Mechanical Reproduction [1936]," in *Illuminations: Essays and Reflections*, ed. Hannah Arendt (New York: Schocken, 1969); Siegfried Kracauer, "The Mass Ornament [1927]," in *The Mass Ornament: Weimar Essays*, ed. Thomas Y. Levin (Cambridge: Harvard University Press 1995).

28. Barbara Miller Lane, *Architecture and Politics in Germany, 1918–1945* (Cambridge: Harvard University Press, 1968).

29. Peter Reichel, *Der schöne Schein des Dritten Reiches: Faszination und Gewalt des Faschismus* (Munich: Carl Hanser, 1991).

30. Rudy Koshar, *Germany's Transient Pasts: Preservation and National Memory in the Twentieth Century* (Chapel Hill: University of North Carolina Press, 1998); Koshar, *From Monuments to Traces: Artifacts of German Memory, 1870–1990* (Berkeley: University of California Press, 2000).

31. Koshar, *Germany's Transient Pasts*, 18–29.

32. See n. 16 above.

33. Janet Ward, *Weimar Surfaces: Urban Visual Culture in 1920s Germany* (Berkeley: University of California Press, 2001).

34. Cornelia Brink, *Ikonen der Vernichtung: öffentlicher Gebrauch von Fotografien aus nationalsozialistischer Konzentrationslagern nach 1945* (Berlin: Akademie Verlag, 1998); Dagmar Barnouw, *Germany 1945: Views of War and Violence* (Bloomington: Indiana University Press, 1996); Hannes Heer and Klaus Naumann, eds., *Vernichtungskrieg: Verbrechen der Wehrmacht, 1941–1944* (Hamburg: Hamburger Edition, 1995).

35. Kirshenblatt-Gimblett, *Destination Culture*, 2.

36. Friedrich Nietzsche, "On the Uses and Disadvantages of History for Life [1874]," in *Untimely Meditations* (Cambridge: Cambridge University Press, 1983).

37. Mosse, *Fallen Soldiers*, 127.

38. David W. Lloyd, *Battlefield Tourism: Pilgrimage and the Commemoration of the Great War in Britain, Australia, and Canada, 1919–1939* (Oxford: Berg, 1998).

39. Mosse, *Fallen Soldiers*, 156.

40. See Koshar, *From Monuments to Traces*, 104–5.

41. Vanessa Schwartz, *Spectacular Realities: Early Mass Culture in Fin-de-Siècle Paris* (Berkeley: University of California Press, 1998).

42. On scapes and flows see Urry, *Sociology beyond Societies.*

43. Primary source material for exploring popular appropriations of nationalist symbols under Nazism were provided in the still useful collection *Nazi Culture: A Documentary*

History, ed. George L. Mosse (New York: Schocken, 1966), but no extended analysis of this topic was offered.

44. Martin Jay, "Scopic Regimes of Modernity," in *Modernity and Identity,* ed. Scott Lash and Jonathan Friedman (Oxford: Blackwell, 1992), 178–95.

45. Jay Winter, *Sites of Memory, Sites of Mourning: The Great War in European Cultural History* (Cambridge: Cambridge University Press, 1995).

46. See Dick Hebdige, "Object as Image: The Italian Scooter Cycle," in *Hiding in the Light: On Images and Things* (London: Routledge, 1988).

47. Daniel Roche, *A History of Everyday Things: The Birth of Consumption in France, 1600–1800* (Cambridge: Cambridge University Press, 2000), 250.

48. Saul Friedländer, *Reflections of Nazism: An Essay on Kitsch and Death* (New York: Harper & Row, 1984).

49. See David Crew, "Remembering German Pasts: Memory in German History, 1871–1989," *Central European History* 33, no. 2 (2000): 233.

50. The comment is recounted by Caroline Wiedmer, *The Claims of Memory: Representations of the Holocaust in Contemporary Germany and France* (Ithaca: Cornell University Press, 1999), 166. Crew, "Remembering German Pasts," 233, also highlights the remark.

51. Art Spiegelman, *Maus: A Survivor's Tale,* vol. 1, *My Father Bleeds History,* and vol. 2, *And Here My Troubles Began* (New York: Pantheon, 1986).

52. See Rudy Koshar, *"Hitler: A Film from Germany:* Cinema, History, and Structures of Feeling," in *Revisioning History: Film and the Construction of a New Past,* ed. Robert A. Rosenstone (Princeton: Princeton University Press, 1995), 166.

53. Kirshenblatt-Gimblett, *Destination Culture,* 259.

54. Ibid., 273–74.

55. Pierre Nora, ed., *Realms of Memory: Rethinking the French Past,* 3 vols. (New York: Columbia University Press, 1996–98).

56. Erhard Schütz, "Der Volkswagen," in *Deutsche Erinnerungsorte,* vol. 1, ed. Etienne François and Hagen Schulze (Munich: Beck, 2001).

57. Leora Auslander, *Taste and Power: Furnishing Modern France* (Berkeley: University of California Press, 1996).

58. See Leora Auslander, "'Jewish Taste'? Jews and the Aesthetics of Everyday Life in Paris and Berlin, 1920–1942," in *Histories of Leisure,* ed. Rudy Koshar (Oxford: Berg, 2002).

59. Detlef Hoffmann, ed., *Das Gedächtnis der Dinge: KZ-Relikte und KZ-Denkmäler, 1945–1995* (Frankfurt: Campus, 1998).

60. For the concept of vectors of memory see Henry Rousso, *The Vichy Syndrome: History and Memory in France since 1944* (Cambridge: Harvard University Press, 1991).

61. For a consideration of German historiography's belated turn to studies of consumer culture, see Alon Confino and Rudy Koshar, "Regimes of Consumer Culture: New Narratives in Twentieth-Century German History," *German History* 19, no. 2 (2001): 135–61.

62. For a balanced attempt to critique this ambivalence while also retaining its useful insights, see Gary Cross, *An All-Consuming Century: Why Commercialism Won in Modern America* (New York: Columbia University Press, 2000).

63. Karl Marx, *Capital: A Critique of Political Economy,* vol. 1, *A Critical Analysis of Capitalist Production* (New York: International Publishers, 1967), 72.

64. See Urry, *Sociology beyond Societies,* esp. chap. 2.

Mosse, Masculinity, and the History of Sexuality

Robert A. Nye

In recent years, historical work on bodies, sexuality, and desire has become both more theoretically sophisticated and more respectful of how these subjects have figured in the history of popular culture. One thinks of the work of George Chauncey, Joanna Bourke, Susan Bordo, Marjorie Garber, Sander Gilman, and many more scholars who have employed Michel Foucault, Pierre Bourdieu, psychoanalysis, and various poststructuralist theorists to explore not only visual culture and the literary and documentary record but also television sitcoms, pornography, women's magazines, and health and diet faddists. The best of this work has not neglected high culture but has sought in addition to reveal the reciprocal exchanges between the different levels and spaces in which cultural production and cultural practices occur. One need not be a historian to do this sort of thing; anthropologists, sociologists, and literary scholars are constructing, deconstructing, and reconstructing the bodies and pleasures and phobias of past generations, though for many of them scrupulousness about time and place is also an indication of the subversive relativizing of their agendas, their scorn for universals.

The history of the body and the history of sexuality have emerged as scholarly and teaching fields only in the last two decades or so, thanks in part to the pioneering work of George Mosse, who has influenced many of us in some measure but who also benefitted in this last scholarly phase of his life from the work of students, friends, and colleagues. I hope to accomplish several things here. I will of course look at Mosse's work for evidence of the themes that eventually blossomed into his cultural history of bodies and sexuality, and I will make some elementary observations about George's personal interest in them. I also hope to place Mosse's work on sexuality, the body, and respectability in a scholarly context by assessing the contributions Mosse made to some important critical work on race and sex in imperial and global history. But I will begin with an anecdote that demonstrates a few things about George and the way he was able to turn ordinary things into opportunities for deeper understanding.

In the late 1970s, the University of Oklahoma invited Mosse to lecture and to teach an undergraduate seminar, at which I figured as the local faculty participant. Of course George wanted to see real Indians, whose poverty I think troubled him, and the Western history museum, where he reveled in the frontier kitsch. The seminar was devoted to race. Mosse singled out a blond, blue-eyed student named Greg Heidrich and asked him about his idea of physical beauty and ugliness, both in women, which was fairly easy, and in men, which was like pulling teeth. Mosse was relentless and did not leave off until he had revealed the aesthetic foundations of the poor lad's concept of beauty, with examples mostly drawn from popular culture that were conventionally white, and which hovered around the kinds of norms Mosse has shown Western societies take for granted. He adroitly exposed the disingenuousness of other students' politically correct objections to these norms until a consensus emerged which revealed to them all the stunning power that physical and behavioral norms play in shaping attitudes and values. Thus chastened, they enjoyed a very productive week together.

This little tour de force summed up for me Mosse's great originality as a cultural historian. He did not privilege ideas or movements in any hierarchy of significance, giving Hegel, say, pride of place over Father Jahn, or ranking Richard Wagner over Karl May. Nor was he interested in simple vulgarization, but rather in reciprocity, in the connections between the arcane hermeticisms of elites and the slogans and propaganda of mass movements. In his cultural history Mosse was generally a lumper, not a splitter. If he drew attention to difference it concerned how the tensions of difference worked to reinforce norms, both in individuals and in nations. In his cultural history Mosse was always after a convincing account of the origins of what historians and sociologists used to call "mass society," in particular the symbols and sentiments that have nourished the great ideological currents in modern nation-states.

Mosse discovered early on that (male) bodies did cultural work. They served as paradigmatic ideals, symbolized the "otherness" of outsiders, provided raw material to be sculpted into heroic forms, and served as icons in the memorials and festivals of national ritual. The "culture book," as we used to call it, was first published in 1961; there was already ample evidence of Mosse's interest in the ideals of manliness he found in English liberals like Charles Kingsley, Thomas Hughes, and Samuel Smiles, in the bonds of eros that united German youth in the *Wandervögel*, in the explorations of unconventional sex and homosexuality in Mann, Gide, and Baudelaire, and the poetic brotherhood of Stefan George. His account already appreciated the remarkable tension present between the homo-eroticism of antibourgeois youth and respectable society.[1]

Mosse had also discovered J. J. Winckelmann and his serene and aestheticized notions of corporeal beauty, and Cesare Lombroso and Max Nordau, popularizers of the hideousness of the degenerate body. His take in those days was that positivist science had discovered a language about bodies that somehow articulated middle-class fears of departures from the ideals of "Greek" beauty, "clarity," and "symmetry" assimilated earlier in the nineteenth century, but he did not dwell overlong on this point, and elsewhere his discussion of medicine and medical matters is a fairly conventional treatment of public health and hygiene as a general goal of the improving bourgeoisie.[2] Nude bodies and male eros get more attention in *The Crisis of German Ideology* (1964), but here Mosse also makes the links to *völkisch* nationalism, if not to Nazism, more explicit. The chapter "Leadership, *Bund*, and Eros" is his most extended discussion of the erotics of male sexual bonding before *Nationalism and Sexuality*. Mosse's reading in *The Crisis* of Hans Blüher's wartime text on "Männlichen Gesellschaft" accepts a Freudian notion of male bonds as sublimations or deflections of "surplus" homosexual impulses that would otherwise be wasted in mere carnality.[3] Mosse also, albeit briefly, explains how women and the principle of femininity fit into the *völkisch* worldview as silent wives and mothers with distinctly inferior qualities and abilities.[4]

The Nationalization of the Masses (1975) explored masculine and feminine principles in art and architecture, but other than poor, unloved Germania, the emphasis is almost wholly on males: male beauty in the expanded sections on Winckelmann, male shooting, choral and gymnastic societies and the manly virtues they encouraged and symbolized, and the masculine virtues of ancient and contemporary heroes celebrated in monuments all over the Reich.[5] But here Mosse explicitly speaks about "the transformation of the human being into a symbol" in connection with the manipulation of representations of the Führer and his role as a male leader of a *Männerbund* who could not afford to water down the image of his virility in familial *Gemütlichkeit*.[6]

Mosse had already shown his familiarity with (and horror of) Otto Weininger's *Sex and Character* (1903) as early as *The Culture of Western Europe*. He mentions it again in *The Nationalization of the Masses*, and then he expands his coverage in *Toward the Final Solution* (1978), linking Weininger directly to a set of stereotypes about the femininity of (male) Jews that fortified Hitler's own prejudices on this issue. This section prefaced another in which Mosse explored perceptions of racial "others" as sexual predators and referred to the "sexual fantasies" that were stimulated by putatively foul-smelling, disease-bearing Jews and blacks.[7] It was in his history of European racism that Mosse first decisively consolidated his account of a European hierarchy of race based on aestheticized and now profoundly gendered values. Manliness, always important in his early work, becomes in this book decisively linked to body morphology and embedded in racial and national ideologies. Winckelmann, Blumenbach, Lavater, and other Enlightenment figures are the sources for a kind of *Ur*-stereotype of serene masculinity against which everything else is measured.

Mosse published two essays in 1982 in the *Journal of Contemporary History* in a special issue on "Sexuality in History" that consolidated his forays into the history of masculinity and sexuality. Gert Hekma has written me that this particular issue of the *Journal* excited great interest in the Netherlands when it came out; indeed, 1982 was a kind of *annus mirabilis* for the history of sexuality, since that was the year John Boswell's brilliant exposition appeared in *Salmagundi* and set out the essentialist/social constructionist debate that still agitates the field.[8] In these pieces and in his later book, Mosse both sums up what he has learned about aesthetics, male bonds, and nationalism and adds new material on the symbiosis of nationalism and respectability taken from medical discourse.

The notes to *Nationalism and Sexuality* acknowledge a flood of new influences, not least, to my knowledge for the first and last time, Michel Foucault and Norbert Elias, but also Peter Cominos, John Boswell, Jeffrey Weeks, Vern Bullough, Théodore Tarczylo, Jim Steakley, Sander Gilman, and many other pioneers of the history of sexuality. It would be interesting to speculate on who was not cited—Klaus Theweleit, to be sure, but also Benedict Anderson, whose *Imagined Communities* appeared in 1983.[9] Although they rely on completely different disciplinary and documentary foundations, there is much in common in Mosse's notion of the nationalization and embodiment of manners and morals and Anderson's conception of nationalism as a "deep horizontal comradeship" based on solidarities that relied on idioms of kinship and home. As Anderson put it, "Both idioms denote something to which one is naturally tied. As we have seen earlier, in everything 'natural' there is always something unchosen. In this was nation-ness assimilated to skin-colour, gender, parentage and birth-era—all those things one can not help. And in these 'natural ties' one senses what one might call 'the beauty of *Gemeinschaft.*' To put it another way, precisely because such ties are not chosen, they have about them a halo of disinterestedness."[10]

Chided gently in 1982 by Isabel Hull and perhaps nudged by Sander Gilman and others, Mosse devotes more space to women in *Nationalism and Sexuality,* acknowledging the social and symbolic roles that women played in a culture of respectability.[11] This material is later smoothly integrated into *The Image of Man* (1996), but one has the feeling that, although he fully appreciated the "otherness" that women and embodied femininity played in a dialectical relationship to men and masculinity, Mosse did not really have his heart in the business of exploring the feminine side of the European gender system; this was always an underdeveloped side of his work. But by 1985 what many considered absent in his earlier work, a genuine socially based explanation of the origins of respectable morality, is now present. Although he undoubtedly learned from Elias, Foucault, and Gilman about the evolution and medicalization of bourgeois sexuality, Mosse's surprising claim is that a bourgeois sexuality of pathology and norm had to be "rescued," as he put it, by nationalism, which "absorbed and sanctioned middle-class manners and morals and played a crucial part in spreading respectability to all classes of the population, however much these classes hated and despised one another."[12]

Mosse's personal and historical experience made it impossible for him to imagine cultural developments that were not somehow tied up with the mythmaking activities of modern nationalism. The alliance of bourgeois morality and nationalism spawned a set of symbols that mediated between voluntary organizations and the state, private and public life, to make bourgeois morality "everyone's morality," as he puts it, and which became available eventually to ultra-nationalist political movements willing to exploit it. Mosse's repeated use of the phrase "onslaught of respectability" (which began in 1961 and is repeated in virtually all his texts thereafter) suggests that the gentle percolation of civilized manners and morals à la Elias, or the discursive dalliances that enmeshed individuals in networks of power and knowledge à la Foucault, cut no ice with him. Respectability was a flood, a forcing house, a character-building place like Salem with its rigors and discipline, obsessiveness about hygiene, physical terrors, and soldierly mission.[13]

Nationalism and Sexuality has been widely praised as a pioneering work. The editors of *Nationalisms and Sexualities,* an influential volume published in 1992, lauded Mosse for being among the first to break "with prevailing academic paradigms that treat nation and sexuality as discrete and autonomous constructs." Mosse, they write, resisted the standard approach of conflating "national" with "public" identity and the "private" with "sexual" identity.[14] As several of the contributors indicated, the construction of sexual "others" varied with time, place, and circumstance, being in one place an ethnicity, in another a religious minority, a language group, or a class, sometimes disadvantaged, sometimes not. A sexual stereotype informed by medical or biological discourse was an invariant aspect of these sexual "others," as Mosse, Gilman, and others pointed out in the early and mid-1980s. Sexual identities were protean constructions easily yoked to other suspect traits such as criminality, alcoholism, race, or salient behavior like prostitution or violence and "explained" as symptoms of biological degeneration that threatened individuals and nation-states alike.[15]

National histories of sexuality that consider sexual stereotypes and practices as parts of the process of constructing and reconstructing national identities have since become commonplace. Some studies anticipated the trend, as did Jeffrey Weeks's pathbreaking 1981 book on sexual regulation in modern Britain.[16] Such national surveys have been attempted for Britain and the United States, though these are less tied to nationalism than one might like.[17] But a number of fine studies on the dialectic of sexual and national identities have been done that examine how sexual stereotypes both shape and serve nationalist discourse. I am thinking here, just to mention work in English, of Daniel Pick, for Britain, France, and Italy; Joanna Bourke for Britain; David G. Horn for Italy; Mary Louise Roberts, Mary Lynn Stewart, and Robert A. Nye for France; and Atina Grossman, Isabel Hull, and Jim Steakley for Germany.[18] The best of these studies, such as Isabel Hull's book on early modern Germany, also consider the history of sexuality in connection to categories of citizenship, a subject that did not interest many of the first writers on nationalism and sexuality, including Mosse.[19]

More recently, studies of nations and sexuality have laid less stress on politics and ideology and more on culture. *Sexual Cultures in Europe: National Histories* (1999), without forgetting the nation-state or regulation, focuses on the diversity of sexual cultures within European societies, considering religious, urban-rural, generational, or regional differences and the impact of immigration and demography.[20] This volume of essays demonstrates that historians are shifting their attention away from the national community and toward both smaller and larger settings: toward the sexual practices and beliefs of religious, ethnic, and regional populations within Europe and outward toward their colonial, global, or transnational brethren. This development coincides with a growing conviction that as traditional forms of sexual life are gradually supplanted and as new human solidarities and new sexual practices spread, we must accordingly change our *optique* and methods to adjust to them, which is perhaps a better strategy for sociologists or anthropologists than it is for historians.

Not all students of the history of sexuality or of nationalism have profited from the insights of Mosse and his colleagues about the interactions between nationalism and sexuality. Peter Gay devoted a couple of volumes to sexuality and the body in his gigantic history of the European bourgeoisie, in which he discusses his subjects against a homogeneous backdrop of European middle-class life largely unvexed by national difference. In these volumes, Gay is trying to pin down a class psyche that mystifyingly transcends the sexual experiences of nationalist bourgeoisies in a continent of nation-building states.[21] On the other side of the coin, some students of nationalism have not always made use of the history of sexuality in ways that might broaden and deepen their accounts of the culture of nationalism. Tzvetan Todorov's study of modern French racism explores the great texts of the genre without seeing sexual others beneath the scrim of race; sexuality, or rather eroticism, only emerges in the "exotic" texts of French travelers to lands beyond the *métropole*.[22]

Eric J. Hobsbawm is eloquent on race, languages, ethnicity, religion, and all the other ways that nationalism can be sliced and diced, but his text is innocent of any references to gender, much less sex, with one exception, which makes a nice contrast with Mosse's treatments of the same subject. On the matter of interwar sport as a stimulant to competitive national feelings and identities, Hobsbawm writes: "What has made sport so uniquely effective a medium for inculcating national feelings, at all events for males, is the ease with which even the least political or public individuals can identify with the nation as symbolized by young persons excelling at what practically every man wants, or at one time in his life has wanted, to be good at. . . . The individual, even the one who only cheers, becomes a symbol of his nation himself."[23] What an irony that George Mosse, the non-sportive man, should see so much more complexity and meaning in sport and physical culture than a man who, at the end of the passage quoted above, fondly recalls the radio broadcast and final score of the first Anglo-Austrian football international in 1929![24]

The Image of Man, Mosse's last book in this genre, is both a personal and a scholarly culmination for him. He reminds the readers of his memoirs that he was a "double outsider," homosexual and Jew, whose "image" was related symbiotically to what he called "the all-American boy or the blond Nordic man."[25] Type and antitype would be his theme. The chief trope animating this insightful book is pathos: the pathos of lost opportunities, crushed hopes, and self-betrayal, a narrative not unlike the tragic saga of liberalism that occupies Mosse in so much of his work. Johann Joachim Winckelmann is the pivot of this book, in more ways than one can say. In writing about the beauties of the male athletes and graceful ephèbes of ancient statuary, Winckelmann conflated the artistic conventions of the "classic" style with what he and his contemporaries imagined to be the equilibrium, moderation, and disciplined self-control of Greek culture at the height of its power and influence. All the late-Enlightenment figures—from Goethe to the painter Jacques-Louis David—who took up this theme helped establish a language and an iconography that enabled later generations to inscribe cultural ideals on bodies and to permit body discourse to invent metaphors for society and nation.[26]

In the course of the nineteenth century, this set of aestheticized principles was medicalized, so that the beauty of the well-shaped body could signify the health and well-being of both individuals and the body politic. The triumphs and weaknesses of Imperial Britain, Republican France, or newly united Italy and Germany could be explained as the successes and failures of the pedagogical techniques and disciplines that shaped men and women for national tasks. Stereotypical "others" were maintained to stimulate male elites to distinguish their strong and disciplined bodies from the weak, emotional, and "disorderly" bodies of women, effeminate men, Jews, or criminals. As Mosse convincingly demonstrates, the power of these normative ideals subverted even the most self-conscious efforts to overturn or replace them with counter-ideals. Thus, many of the sexologists who sought legal reform in behalf of homosexual men in the late nineteenth century did so by claiming that homosexuals were different from the masculine norm only in their choice of sexual object. The socialist activists who sought to create a caring, pacifistic, socialist man ended by adopting the same standards of aggressive and willful manliness held by their class enemies. Even the early Zionists, tormented by a heritage of racist imagery that held Jews to be feeble or subhuman monsters, opted to showcase a new Jewish man who had muscles and courage in abundance.[27]

Mosse's history of the male body since the Enlightenment acknowledges the body as a palimpsest upon which supplementary meanings could be inscribed: a medicalized body upon an aestheticized one. But Mosse's "image" of man continued to bear the serene and symmetrical shape of its neoclassic origins, and in this his body history runs against the grain of some recent scholarship. Postmodern treatments of the body stress the transitory and insubstantial nature of the body, how easily it is penetrated, fragmented, transformed from within and without, and how it is responsive to varied settings and subjectivities. There has been a radical historicization and deconstruction of bodies that favors microanalysis, discursive breaks, and, in opposition to a base/superstructure model of the sort favored by Mosse, an interactive model of bodies shaping and being shaped by environments.[28] These developments have coincided, not surprisingly, with the construction of the human genome, the discovery of the flexibility and mutability of the immune system, and the successful application of surgery to everything from cosmetic interventions to sex-change operations. Biomedicine has transformed our conception of the body from a fortified castle to a congeries of processes and particles.[29]

There is an irony in these developments, however, that I think reveals the soundness of Mosse's notion of a remarkably stable and historically coherent "image of man" (and woman) in Western societies. The history of endocrinology and the history of cosmetic and sex-change surgery reveal that an increasing capacity to alter or reshape the body and its processes has probably strengthened traditional gender identities, not weakened them. As recent studies have pointed out, cosmetic surgeons have collaborated with their patients and with popular images of beauty to eliminate so-called bodily imperfections and to shape bodies according to norms that cleave to standard masculine and feminine body types: breasts, tummies, hips, noses, and lips are puffed out or slimmed down to conform to notions of symmetry and proportion as old as Western culture itself.[30]

Sex-change operations are now said to cure a situation known as gender dysphoria, in which a man feels himself to be trapped in the body of a woman (or vice versa), language that curiously replicates various nineteenth-century efforts to describe the dilemma of homosexuals as male or female "souls" in bodies of the opposite sex. In any case, the passage from one sex to another involves a remaking of the body that must measure up to all the cultural prerequisites of gender, including sexual function. Anne Bolin quotes one of her transsexual informants as wanting surgery "so my body conforms to my spirit. It is discomforting to see yourself in a mirror with male genitalia and know it isn't right. Surgery will complete my external image."[31] As Bernice L. Hausman writes of these procedures, "The history of plastic surgery and the development of cosmetic surgery services in the early to mid-twentieth century demonstrates that plastic surgeons were actively involved in the delineation of the semiotic field in which they practiced. Unwilling to settle for patients who would come to them due to accidents, car wrecks, or congenital deformities, cosmetic surgeons decisively rewrote the code of normal appearance to enhance their practices."[32]

Finally, males and females in the West receive hormone treatments in order to put their bodies on their "correct" growth or developmental trajectories. Thousands of young men ingest dangerous steroidal hormones in order to build strength and muscle mass, and millions of young women risk their health by dieting. More millions of our aging contemporaries request hormone "therapy" in order to maintain a youthful appearance and to keep sexual function in operation long after it might have otherwise disappeared. Some of these individuals have pathological conditions for which there is no other medical option; far more are taking these treatments in order to attain or retain a "body image" and correlative functions that may vary with time and place, that may even flirt with androgyny, but which persistently have hovered around gender norms that insist upon sexed minds and bodies.[33]

In his memoir Mosse reproaches himself for not defending Jewish classmates and for his lengthy reticence about his own homosexuality. As a historian and critic of anti-Semitism and in his antifascist activism, he more than expiated his youthful neutrality on "racial" issues. But I would also say that he presented a positive if limited account of homosexuality from his very earliest work, and he later represented homosexuals and their allies as vigorous resisters of anti-homosexual stereotypes, indeed as exponents of a worthy alternative love that would eventually stretch the borders of respectability without, for all that, breaking them.[34]

There has been a spirited debate among historians of sexuality about the extent to which adopting a medical frame of analysis of the history of homosexuality, as Mosse often does, entails accepting the notion that medicalized stereotypes were assumed as identities without resistance by men and women who consulted medical authorities or texts for personal enlightenment. In *Rewriting the Soul,* Ian Hacking has laid out a kind of middle ground that explains sexual identity as a reciprocal negotiation between social experience and medical authority, and the best scholarship has reflected that formulation, most particularly the beautifully nuanced book of Harry Oosterhuis on Richard Von Krafft-Ebing and his patients.[35] Mosse's reliance on the explanatory power of medical stereotypes is clear enough, but so is his willingness to identify the cultural and personal sources of resistance to medical authority.

Finally, I would like to analyze the derivative but nonetheless important influence of Mosse's work on nationalism and sexuality for imperial and postcolonial studies of sexuality and identity. Mosse himself dwelled only briefly on how the shaping of men for nationalist tasks was equally useful for imperial ventures, but important aspects of his work on nationalism and sexuality were later adapted to explanations of sexuality in colonial domains.[36] First, as the contributors to the volume *Nationalisms and Sexualities* understood, the "other" of the nation could be many things indeed. It could be, as Eve Sedgwick wrote, "the pre-national monarchy, the local ethnicity, the diaspora, the trans-national corporate, ideological, religious, or ethnic unit, the sub-national locale or the ex-colonial, often contiguous unit; the colony may become national vis-à-vis the homeland, or the homeland become national vis-à-vis the nationalism of its colonies; the nationalism of the homeland may be co-extensive with or oppositional to its imperialism; and so forth."[37] Viewed this way, the construction of otherness was utterly situational and therefore historical, depending on a set of typical mechanisms to bend materials at hand to satisfy the prevailing psychology.

From the beginning, the strength of Mosse's characterization of otherness in nationalist discourse was his realization that such stereotypes did not arise from a hegemonic impulse but rather from efforts by social formations in insecure circumstances seeking more affirmative identities. *Völkisch* nationalists were not—or ever, for that matter—in a numerical majority, nor were Freikorps members, Männerbundists, or even Nazis. The concessions such groups made to respectability, Mosse points out, were psychologically strategic; their primary loyalties were to their comrades. Mosse was convinced that the emotional bonds that united such groups were essentially "between men" and served to buffer them against what he called the "chaos" of industrialization and modernity. The construction of a discourse of otherness was thus always for Mosse a cultural process that took place largely outside and sometimes against the authority of the state.

Mosse's treatment of these themes in German history prefigured the development of the critique of orientalism by Edward Said and the rise of postcolonial and subaltern studies generally. The subject of this scholarship was Western imperialism and the ideologies and discourse that sustained it—not just as a theory of dominion, but also as a set of correlative practices. A central concern of this work has been to understand how sex and gender operated within imperial discourse and how, dialectically, colonial nationalisms formed themselves in opposition to imperial culture. Postcolonial theory has made liberal use of stereotypes and fetishization, and historians have made an effort to incorporate some of these concepts into their accounts of the imperial process.[38]

Early theory incorporated the Sartrian notion that master-slave discourses like those that nurtured imperialism were driven by an internal logic of cognitive dependence: master needed slave to know himself as master, and vice versa. Theorists added the sexual elements of "fascination" and "repugnance" to show that what or who is reviled becomes also an object of desire because it is the presence of the dominated that justifies their continued domination.[39] Mosse had already arrived at this fundamental insight without going, so far as we know, through these theoretical steps. He had also explained that the homoerotic attachments that united *völkisch* nationalists and their political heirs could not be acknowledged as such and were accordingly neutralized by reaction formations of homophobic and misogynous sentiments. This fundamental ambivalence has been employed by Mosse, by Klaus Theweleit, and later by other historians to explain the gender and sexual dynamics of youth movements, *völkisch* nationalists, and Nazi-era paramilitary organizations.[40]

By transferring these primordial psychic processes to different geographical places, historians of imperialism have shown their potential for explaining a vast number of developments.[41] Although the proportion of the members of middle class and aristocracy varied in European imperialisms, recent scholars have pictured the process of transplanting European culture to the colonies as a bourgeois cultural phenomenon. Citing Mosse, Irvin Schick demonstrates how colonists attempted to produce the national culture in the colonial space by using sexualities "to draw boundaries between 'us' and 'them' in the manner of the respectable bourgeoisie of Europe."[42] This maneuver, reinforced by custom and law, had the additional benefit of concealing the class and other social and educational boundaries among the Europeans that were more visible in the homeland.[43] The assimilation of "other" sexualities to race operated in the colonial domain much as it did with Jews and other outsiders in Europe: black and Arab men embodied the contradictory traits of hypervirility and effeminacy, women those of lasciviousness and puritanical unresponsiveness. These apparently simple binaries generated a number of rich semiotic and practical alternatives, but invariably, as Shick observes, it is the contrast with European identities that counted the most, not the apparent contradictoriness of stereotypes. As he writes, "mutually contradictory stereotypes can co-exist without undermining one another's effectiveness; indeed, they reinforce each other even while they reciprocally contradict or negate one another."[44]

The chief task of the colonial enterprise was to preserve the national culture in an exotic place, which meant in practice exercising a constant boundary vigilance against "going native," miscegenation, or internal "degeneration." As Ann Laura Stoler has argued, European identity in the colonies was protean, under constant siege, and in constant need of disciplined management. The Dutch East Indian colonials she has studied "confused the equation of whiteness and middle-class sensibilities in a discourse that legitimated the state's interventions in how all Europeans raised their children and managed their domestic and sexual arrangements. . . . It prompted new institutional initiatives and government policies that made claims to racial superiority *dependent* on middle-class respectability for the entire European population. It made linguistic competence in Dutch the marker of cultural 'suitability' for European middle-class norms. It implicitly tied the quality of maternal sentiment and parental care to racial affiliation and nationality."[45]

The reciprocal dependence of respectable European sexual norms and the exotic sexual "otherness" of colonial peoples is a common theme in recent work. With respect to male desire for women, what Schick calls xenological thinking ranges between contrasting the "dirty oriental woman" with the "clean and proper" hygienic standards of colonialism, on the one hand, and the exotic image of oriental harem women spending whole days in washing, grooming, and perfuming their bodies.[46] Each trope satisfied the dual "repugnance" and "fascination" requirements of the male Western colonial's relation to the sexual other.

With respect to male-male relations there is a similarly complex range of response. Operating within the traditional pederastic model, mid-nineteenth-century men of letters made minimal distinction between sexual contacts with boys or "girls," an aspect of colonial exoticism that, as Mosse has noted, continued into the 1880s with André Gide's generation. However, the invention of adult male same-sex love as inversion, and later homosexuality by the 1890s, required a rereading of the sexual ethnography of colonial domains. The new reading pronounced male-male relations to be endemic in tropical lands, a primitive aspect of native "promiscuity," as the evolutionary paradigm would have it. As Rudi Bleys has argued, racialist discourse proved decisive in constructing sexual analogues to homosexuality in the West. He writes: "Representations of the presence of male-to-male sexual praxis among less developed people eventually consolidated the analogical structure of human anthropology in an evolutionary context. More specifically, it sanctified the newly conceptualized medical stigmatization of same-sex praxis at once as a sign of inferior evolutionary status ('endemic sodomy/pederasty') and of 'degenerate,' pathological heritage ('homosexuality')."[47]

Many of those who have written on colonial sexuality have noted that after an initial period of laxness about interracial and intrasexual activity, most colonial regimes applied more rigid standards of sexual respectability and amalgamated them with the nationality of "Englishness," "Frenchness," "Dutchness," and the like, so that by 1914, as Hyams has written, "almost no sexual interaction between rulers and ruled occurred."[48] The same could not be said about European societies, where there had been, if anything, some relaxation in these matters and perhaps greater tolerance for independent women and sexual minorities in general. But the "[heterosexual] white man's burden" was heavier and the stakes higher in the European empires, where racism and strictures against fraternization or miscegenation were strictly enforced, where racial and sexual otherness, in other words, were most intimately conjoined. As John Noyes has argued, when the inevitable revolt of racial "others" began, it simultaneously heightened sexual fears and stimulated masochistic fantasies in which power relationships were imaginatively inverted and men were the willing playthings of women and blacks.[49] It also stimulated the masochist's propensity to slide into sadistic explosions in defense of a masculine gender identity under siege, and in twentieth-century Europe that reaction was often less fantasized than real.

Finally, some postcolonial studies acknowledge that the new nations that emerged from the debris of decolonialization have simply borrowed the conceptual and psychic apparatus of Western nationalism in charting their own destinies. They have "internalized" rather than "problematized" nationalism and so remain vulnerable to the same racialist, dichotomizing outlook that has characterized the history of Western nation-states.[50] Rather than compose for themselves a "subaltern" history that reflects the realities of the colonial period, the literary elites of new nations write histories about oppressors and glorious resisters, compressing complex social, ethnic, and religious realities into familiar binary categories. At least one result has been the enforced silence of women and sexual minorities in national revolutions, but also, certainly, the marginalization of religious and ethnic minorities from inclusion in the new "national" synthesis.[51] The dangers inherent in the turn of this particular wheel is something Mosse has noted with respect to Israel, the only postcolonial nation with which he had much experience.

The analytical utility of Mosse's work on nationalism and sexuality has transcended the largely German historical context in which it was originally imagined by him and that he demonstrated could be applied generally to modern European societies. Mosse's understanding of the process in which national identities provided cultural support for the administrative structures and symbolic trappings of nation-states has also shown its value when applied to the extended domain of imperial relations. His pioneering use of race and sexuality as categories that permitted the national community to define itself in the process of identifying racial and sexual "others" has been widely taken up by historians and anthropologists of nationalism, sexuality, and gender and by students of both imperial and postcolonial societies. As I have tried to show here, George Mosse's contributions to the history of sexuality in the modern nation-state existed in latent form in his earliest work. To reach their fullest flowering, they only needed to be acknowledged for what they had been all along.

Notes

1. I have taken these references from the third edition of George L. Mosse, *The Culture of Western Europe: The Nineteenth and Twentieth Centuries* (Boulder: Westview Press, 1988), 113–18, 130, 215, 229–30, 243–44, 306–8.

2. Ibid., 66, 88, 214–16, 285–86.

3. Mosse singles out these passages in his memoirs, one of the few times he actively claims precedence for an interpretation. See *Confronting History: A Memoir* (Madison: University of Wisconsin Press, 2000), 179.

4. George L. Mosse, *The Crisis of German Ideology: Intellectual Origins of the Third Reich* (New York: Grosset & Dunlap, 1964), 204–17.

5. George L. Mosse, *The Nationalization of the Masses: Political Symbolism and Mass Movements in Germany from the Napoleonic Wars Through the Third Reich* (New York: Howard Fertig, 1975), 23–30, 53, 74–100, 127–60.

6. Ibid., 203.

7. George L. Mosse, *Toward the Final Solution: A History of European Racism* (New York: Howard Fertig, 1978), 108–12.

8. Boswell's essay is reprinted in Martin Duberman, Martha Vicinus, and George Chauncey, eds., *Hidden from History: Reclaiming the Gay and Lesbian Past* (New York: NAL Books, 1989), 17–36.

9. Nor does Theweleit cite Mosse, an oversight partly mitigated by Anson Rabinbach and Jessica Benjamin's foreword to *Male Fantasies: Psychoanalyzing the White Terror,* vol. 2, by Klaus Theweleit, trans. Erica Carter and Chris Turner (Minneapolis: University of Minnesota Press, 1989), ix–xxv.

10. Benedict Anderson, *Imagined Communities: Reflections on the Origins and Spread of Nationalism* (London: Verso, 1983), 143.

11. See Isabel Hull, "The Bourgeoisie and Its Discontents: Reflections on 'Nationalism and Respectability,'" *Journal of Contemporary History* 17 (1982): 247–68.

12. George L. Mosse, *Nationalism and Sexuality: Respectability and Abnormal Sexuality in Modern Europe* (New York: Howard Fertig, 1985), 9.

13. Mosse, *Confronting History*, 53–70.

14. Andrew Parker, Mary Russo, Doris Sommer, and Patricia Yaeger, introduction to Parker et al., eds., *Nationalisms and Sexualities* (London: Routledge, 1992), 2.

15. See in particular Sander Gilman, *Difference and Pathology: Stereotypes of Sexuality, Race, and Madness* (Ithaca: Cornell University Press, 1985), esp. 37–128; also J. Edward Chamberlin and Sander L. Gilman, *Degeneration: The Dark Side of Progress* (New York: Columbia University Press, 1985); Robert A. Nye, *Crime, Madness, and Politics in Modern France: The Medical Concept of National Decline* (Princeton: Princeton University Press, 1984).

16. Jeffrey Weeks, *Sex, Politics, and Society: The Regulation of Sexuality since 1800* (London: Longman, 1981).

17. John D'Emilio and Estelle Friedman, *Intimate Matters: A History of Sexuality in America* (New York: Harper and Row, 1988); Michael Mason, *The Making of Victorian Sexuality* (Oxford: Oxford University Press, 1994) and *The Making of Victorian Sexual Attitudes* (Oxford: Oxford University Press, 1995).

18. Daniel Pick, *Faces of Degeneration: A European Disorder* (Cambridge: Cambridge University Press, 1989); Joanna Bourke, *Dismembering the Male: Men's Bodies, Britain, and the Great War* (Chicago: University of Chicago Press, 1996); David G. Horn, *Social Bodies: Science, Reproduction, and Italian Modernity* (Princeton: Princeton University Press, 1994); Mary Louise Roberts, *Civilization without Sexes: Reconstructing Gender in Post-War France, 1917–1927* (Chicago: University of Chicago Press, 1994); Mary Lynn Stewart, *For Health and Beauty: Physical Culture for French Women, 1880s–1930s* (Baltimore: Johns Hopkins University Press, 2001); Robert A. Nye, *Masculinity and Male Codes of Honor in Modern France* (New York: Oxford University Press, 1993); Atina Grossman, *Reforming Sex: The German Movement for Birth Control and Abortion Reform* (New York: Oxford University Press, 1995); Isabel Hull, *The Entourage of Kaiser Wilhelm II, 1888–1918* (Cambridge: Cambridge University Press, 1982); Jim Steakley, "Iconography of a Scandal: Political Cartoons of the Eulenberg Affair," *Studies in Visual Communication* 9 (1983): 20–51; See also the recent issue devoted to "Im Inneren de Männlichkeit," *Osterreichische Zeitschrift für Geschichtswissenschaften* 11, no. 3 (2000).

19. Isabel Hull, *Sexuality, State, and Civil Society in Germany, 1700–1815* (Ithaca: Cornell University Press, 1996).

20. Franz Eder, Lesley Hall, and Gert Hekma, eds., *Sexual Cultures in Europe: National Histories* (Manchester: Manchester University Press, 1999).

21. Peter Gay, *The Bourgeois Experience: Victoria to Freud*, vol. 1, *The Education of the Senses*, vol. 2, *The Tender Passion* (New York: Oxford University Press, 1984, 1986).

22. Tzvetan Todorov, *On Human Diversity: Nationalism, Racism, and Exoticism in French Thought*, trans. Catherine Porter (Cambridge: Harvard University Press, 1993), 314–18.

23. Eric J. Hobsbawm, *Nations and Nationalism since 1780: Programme, Myth, Reality* (Cambridge: Cambridge University Press), 143.

24. Rogers Brubaker is similarly mute on sex and gender in his treatment of race and immigration issues in his book on French and German citizenship, *Citizenship and Nationhood in France and Germany* (Cambridge: Harvard University Press, 1992).

25. Mosse, *Confronting History*, 181.

26. George L. Mosse, *The Image of Man: The Creation of Modern Masculinity* (New York: Oxford University Press, 1996), 25–39.

27. Ibid., 77–154.

28. For scholarship on the themes of interactionism and body deconstructions see Gail Weiss, *Body Images: Embodiment as Intercorporeality* (London: Routledge, 1999); Rose Weitz, ed., *The Politics of Women's Bodies* (New York: Oxford University Press, 1998).

29. For a particularly astute account of how recent medical and biological knowledge has changed the concept of the body see Emily Martin, *Flexible Bodies: Tracking Immunity in American Culture—From the Days of Polio to the Age of AIDS* (Boston: Beacon Press, 1994), 21–112. The best work on the anatomy and physiology of the constructed "gendered" body is Anne Fausto-Sterling, *Sexing the Body* (New York: Basic Books, 2000).

30. The secondary literature on these phenomena is growing rapidly. Among some important recent books see Joan Brumberg, *The Body Project: An Intimate History of American Girls* (New York: Random House, 1997); Maurizia Boscagli focuses on the

neoclassical inspiration for the aestheticized male body at the turn of the century in *Eye on the Flesh: Fashions of Masculinity in the Early Twentieth Century* (Boulder: Westview Press, 1996), 21–54; see also Lynne Luciano, *Looking Good: Male Body Image in Modern America* (New York: Hill and Wang, 2001).

31. Anne Bolin, *In Search of Eve: Transsexual Rites of Passage* (South Hadley, Mass.: Bergin & Carvey, 1988), 180.

32. Bernice L. Hausman, *Changing Sex: Transsexualism, Technology, and the Idea of Gender* (Durham, N.C.: Duke University Press, 1995), 62. On the history of cosmetic surgery see Elizabeth Haiken, *Venus Envy: A History of Cosmetic Surgery* (Baltimore: Johns Hopkins University Press, 2001); Sander Gilman writes the prehistory of modern cosmetic surgery as "aesthetic" surgery, which, as he demonstrates, was linked to the nineteenth-century habit of thinking in terms of idealized racial "types." Like Mosse, he traces the roots of the ideals of outer physical and moral "inner" beauty to Winckelmann. Gilman, *Creating Beauty to Cure the Soul: Race and Psychology in the Shaping of Aesthetic Surgery* (Durham, N.C.: Duke University Press, 1998), 39–48.

33. For an interesting example of the ways that a prolactin hormone imbalance in a young man was interpreted by him in terms of gender and sexual stereotypes, see Ken Baker, *Man Made: A Memoir of My Body* (New York: Putnam, 2001).

34. See Mosse's chapters on "The Decadence" and "The Normal Society of Men," in which he relates the reforming efforts of Magnus Hirschfeld, mentions the resistence of Oscar Wilde to British legal authority, and represents medical stereotypes as constructions of bourgeois and nationalist inspiration. Mosse, *The Image of Man*, 77–106, 133–54; see also *Nationalism and Sexuality*, 24–47, 104–13.

35. See Ian Hacking, *Rewriting the Soul: Multiple Personality and the Sciences of Memory* (Princeton: Princeton University Press, 1995), 21–38; Harry Oosterhuis, *Step-children of Nature: Krafft-Ebing, Psychiatry, and the Making of Sexual Identity* (Chicago: University of Chicago Press, 2000).

36. Mosse, *Nationalism and Sexuality*, 84–85, and *Image of Man*, 134–36.

37. Eve Kosofsky Sedgwick, "Nationalisms and Sexualities in the Age of Wilde," in Parker et al., *Nationalisms and Sexualities*, 241.

38. See, e.g., Robert Young, *White Mythologies: Writing History and the West* (London: Routledge, 1990), esp. 119–213.

39. Peter Stallybrass and Allon White, *The Poetics and Politics of Transgression* (London: Methuen, 1986), 5.

40. See Harry Oosterhuis and Hubert Kennedy, eds., *The Youth Movement: The Gay Movement and Male Bonding before Hitler's Rise* (New York: Haworth Press, 1991); Nicholas Stargardt, "Male Bonding and the Class Struggle in Imperial Germany," *Historical Journal* 38 (1995): 175–93; Harry Oosterhuis, "Medicine, Male Bonding, and Homosexuality in Nazi Germany," *Journal of Contemporary History* 32 (1997): 187–205. Joanna Bourke strikes a different note in her analysis of male bonding among British troops in the Great War. She sees male bonding as innocently uncomplicated by doubts or fears of homosexual transgressions, conceding only, perhaps, that it proved a meager substitute for the feminine love objects the men increasingly came to desire. See Bourke, *Dismembering the Male*, 124–70.

41. On the importance of place and space see Rob Shields, *Places on the Margin: Alternative Geographies of Modernity* (London: Routledge, 1991).

42. Irvin Schick, *The Erotic Margin: Sexuality and Spatiality in Alterist Discourse* (London: Verso, 1999), 57.

43. Inderpal Grewal, *Home and Harem: Nation, Gender, Empire, and the Cultures of Travel* (Durham, N. C.: Duke University Press, 1996), 87–88.

44. Schick, *The Erotic Margin*, 100.

45. Ann Laura Stoler, *Race and the Education of Desire: Foucault's History of Sexuality and the Colonial Order of Things* (Durham, N. C.: Duke University Press, 1995), 106–7.

46. Schick, *The Erotic Margin*, 101.

47. Rudi Bleys, *The Geography of Perversion: Male-to-Male Sexual Behaviour outside the West and the Ethnographic Imagination, 1750–1918* (New York: New York University Press, 1995). Bleys cites Mosse on the link between respectability and nationalism, p. 152.

48. Ronald Hyams, *Empire and Sexuality: The British Experience* (New York: St. Martin's, 1990), 1; Bleys, *The Geography of Perversion*, 147–50; Stoler, *Race and the Education of Desire*, 95–136.

49. John K. Noyes, *The Mastery of Submission: Inventions of Masochism* (Ithaca: Cornell University Press, 1997), 106–7.

50. R. Radhakrishnan, "Nationalism, Gender, and the Narrative of Identity," in Parker et al., *Nationalisms and Sexualities*, 86–88.

51. Gayatri Spivak, "Woman in Difference: Mahasweta Devi's 'Douloti the Bountiful,'" in Parker et al., *Nationalisms and Sexualities*, 97.

The Body in Modern Warfare

Myth and Meaning, 1914–1945

Joanna Bourke

When George Mosse turned his mind to the history of modern warfare, he instinctively focused his gaze on the male body. Without dispute, the body is everywhere in war. Whether battered and bruised in some trench or flying majestically above the clouds, the corporeal self has been the central target of battle: humanity's entire wrath focuses upon puny skeletons. Historians have access to two main forms of representation of the corporeal self in war. The first is the written testimony of combatants in or immediately behind the front lines. Their letters and diaries are the historian's most direct interpretative tool for cutting through the fundamental glossolalia of combat. This was Mosse's initial tool when, in 1995, he published an essay entitled "The Knights of the Sky and the Myth of the War Experience," in which he used literary accounts and memoirs from World War I to examine myths about airmen. In this essay I will turn to letters and diaries written closer to the front lines, asking the question, Do they confirm his analysis about the function of the "myth of the war experience"? Second, historians have images. One of the questions addressed by Mosse in *The Image of Man: The Creation of Modern Masculinity* (1996) is, How was the body visually represented in war? Although Mosse was primarily concerned with official images, such as the male hero in posters, in the modern period, war's fury is nowhere more evident than in the everyday photographic snapshots taken by men in battle. Indeed, shooting the body at war has never had more multiple meanings and, in all its meanings, has never been easier. Technological modernity has given us the machine gun, the bomb, and the artillery shell along with the camera, enabling us to frame our destructiveness simply and cheaply. Images of "total war"—dictated by science and driven by the urge to slaughter en masse—can now be captured on the prosaic fabric of film, serving as mementoes of our personal contribution to the enterprise of war. As the main wars of the twentieth century started, ended, and started again we have become progressively less dependent upon the "official" image for representations of the body in battle. The "snapshots," taken by ordinary men, and sometimes women, in the combat zones, tell us more than we may want to know about our society's heart of darkness. What do these diaries and these photos, inscribed and snapped by "tourists in hell," have to tell us, both about representations of the male body in war and the multiple ways in which, in Mosse's words, "the reality of war was masked and made bearable"?[1]

Myth

The most obvious point of all is that war service alters bodies. Mosse referred to the "general feeling" prevailing in western Europe during World War I that a "new type of man had emerged from the trenches." According to him, these new men were defined largely in terms of an alteration in outward appearance: they had "supple, lean, muscular bodies."[2] In war, men's shapes literally shifted: muscles elbowed out fat, scars appeared, limbs disappeared. Military training, coupled with the rigors of front-line service, facilitated this remarkable change in the male physique.[3] The magazine *Health and Efficiency* reported the change in July 1919: "Now before the war, though I still say we are a nation of sportsmen, there was an enormous mass of men who talked sport, read sport, looked on life through sport spectacles . . . but—practised no form of sport themselves." With the war, the average man (known as "John Jones") was "jerked out of an office or mill into the Army . . . John Jones went through trying times for a few weeks. He literally endured the pangs of a new birth. 'Physical jerks,' drills, fatigues, marches, gradually sweated the beef off him and sweated the muscles on, reddened his pale blood and gave his walk a spring. John cursed and went through it all. He was a Briton and a sportsman. He was training for the Great Game, and when at last with a clear eye and a cool hand he crossed the sea, we saw how he played it."[4]

Men's subjective experience of their body also underwent a transformation. One of the most common statements about bodies made in letters from the front lines concerned heightened fitness. As Basil Hart wrote in a letter to his parents in 1914, while in training: "I get fitter &

fitter every day & the life is is [sic] doing wonders for me,"⁵ or in the words of C. B. Stokes, writing to his wife from the front line: "We are all very fit indeed, as for myself, I am burnt black several [sic] fellows here have re-marked on my fitness, chaps I have not seen for a few weeks, they all re-mark on my complexion!"⁶

Such boasts to parents and spouses were part of an assertion of mas-culinity. War was one of the major rites of manliness; it was a "test of man-liness" and "projected so-called old-fashioned virtues associated with manliness."⁷ Combatants frequently commented on the rite of passage from boyhood to manhood that took place in wartime. Thus, in a letter to his girlfriend on 11 September 1915, Norman Austin observed: "To be quite frank with you, my dear Eileen, I am both older & sadder & cer-tainly graver as you can see by my rediculously [sic] sober letter—I am not in the least amusing—buffonery [sic] as of old ceases to entertain me—in fact your curly, golden headed little dream-boy is no more & the strong, silent man has taken his place."⁸

Despite the popularity of this myth of manly virility, even the heroic bodies of "strong, silent men" carrying out their duty to their nation lasted only a short period in contact with battle in the trenches. Disillusionment rapidly set in. After all, there was little role for the manly body in actual war. As Alfred Bland wrote in a letter to his wife on 16 May 1916: "In the trenches one's activity is so passive. If one is hit, it is no trial of strength, no result of skill—but pure mischance. That constitutes part of the strain of trench life. A casual shell, a rifle-grenade, a canister, a spent bullet—these may hit or miss. . . . This is no war for *men,* but for automata—and yet it is *men* who will win and lose."⁹ Time and again, the male body was described as a machine. As I argue elsewhere, killing machines were not only the embodiment of human ingenuity but also the physical mecha-nism and the linguistic trope used to disembody the human.¹⁰ During wartime the rhetoric of men-machines was extremely popular, and nowhere was it more influential than in E. G. Boring and Marjorie Van de Water's classic *Psychology for the Fighting Man* (1943). This book was prepared for the National Research Council and sold 380,000 copies (at the time, the widest sale for any book by academic psychologists). One of their main arguments was that

fear is the body's preparation for action. The heart pounds faster, pumping blood more rapidly to the arms and legs and brain, where the oxygen is needed. The lungs do their part by quickened breathing. Blood pressure goes up. Adrenaline, which is nature's own "shot in the arm," is poured liberally into the blood to act as fuel for the human fighting machine. Subtle changes in body chemistry, automatically effected by powerful emotion, serve to protect the soldier in action in ways he would never think of, if he had to plan for himself. His blood clots more readily. He loses temporarily the sense of fatigue even though he may have been dog tired.[11]

In the words of the chief of the U.S. Applied Psychology Panel in 1946, wars were fought, not by machines or men alone, but by "man-machine units."[12]

It was a transformation that men at the front observed in themselves—albeit slowly. For instance, Lieutenant A. B. Scott starts his front-line horror all too conscious of his physical vulnerability. His terror is audible in his diary for 17 July 1918 when he admits that he is "going all to pieces." He confesses, "my imagination is killing me. Last night I was alone inspecting the wire when for some Hellish reason I saw a picture of myself disabled by a bullet and lying for hours until I bled to death—days it would have been for my vitality is tremendous. For several minutes I couldn't move, covered with a clammy sweat and paralysed with fear." It only took a month in the front lines for him to change his tune. He had just experienced some extremely heavy fighting when, on 18 August, he wrote: "Slowly and surely I am breaking up, and now I am so far gone that it is too much trouble to go sick. I am just carrying on like an automaton, mechanically putting up wire and digging trenches while I wait, wait, wait for something to happen—relief, death, wounds, anything, anything in earth or hell to put an end to this, but preferably death—I am becoming hypnotised with the idea of Nirvana—sweet, eternal nothingness."[13] Fear had killed off his imagination, transforming him into just one further "automaton" of war.

But there was one part of war where the aesthetics of the man-machine was radically different. As Mosse argued, in the air force the myth of man-machine took on a new meaning. Enthusiasm might have "cooled in the trenches," as Mosse put it, but high above the bloody, muddy trenches were the airmen, who saw themselves as fighting a clean war, raining death on a filthy foe below.[14] Mosse's chapter "The Knights of the Sky and the Myth of the War Experience" (1995) remains the clearest exposition of this war aesthetics. The chapter begins with a statement about the role of myth: myth is crucial to the process of masking "the reality of war" and cleansing its memory.[15] In other words, myth made war bearable, both in the present and in the future.

In Mosse's hands, the aesthetics of flight in wartime is a terrifying story, combining as it does both idealism and murder. During World War I, the vast majority of people experienced the soaring beauty of flying machines for the first time. Airmen were the "cavalry of the clouds."[16] Mosse dissects the ways World War I airmen coped with combat. They engaged in a process of "distilling its adventure, exaltation and vitality" while "sublimating its horrors." During World War II, an identical process took place. For instance, Roderick Chrisholm, a night fighter in the Royal Air Force, destroyed two enemy aircraft on 13 March 1941. The experience, he wrote, could "never be equalled": "For the rest of that night it was impossible to sleep; there was nothing else I could talk about for days after; there was nothing else I could think about for weeks after. . . . [I]t was sweet and very intoxicating."[17] Equally, a Spitfire pilot, Flight-Lieutenant D. M. Crook, described the "moments just before the clash" as "the most gloriously exciting moments of life." He was "absolutely fascinated" by the sight of a plane going down and could not pull his eyes away from the sight. The day after shooting down his first plane, he bragged about it to his wife ("she was delighted") and "with considerable pride" also informed his family of his success.[18] Kenneth Hemingway dive-bombed Japanese soldiers on the ground: "Oh, boy. . . . Og [*sic*], Boooyy!" he yelled, describing his "exhilaration" as similar to the joy of drinking champagne on a sunny spring morning. He felt "ruthlessly happy—quite an atavistic orgy!"[19] After a "kill," pilots admitted that they "all felt much better," and there would be "a good deal of smacking on the back and screaming of delight."[20] Shooting down a plane made the crew "frightfully excited" so that they recited the phrase "it was wizard" repeatedly.[21] There are innumerable snapshots of men posing in front of downed planes, and these also inevitably include photographs of the injured or dead enemy— with the men who shot the plane down towering above. Although the sight of mutilated and dead Germans staining the rear cockpit of their planes might be described as "sad and beastly," airmen admitted that they had felt "elated then."[22]

What was it about the language of killing from the air that could aestheticize killing? Mosse argued that air warfare was conceptualized as being in line with certain chivalrous codes (or recognized formalities, ceremonies, and courtesies) involving honorable exchange, compassion, and altruism at the same time as invoking reckless adventure and a high-minded disdain of death. Combatants manipulated knightly grammar to describe their actions. Aerial combat linked modernity with old-fashioned chivalry. Fighter pilots were, according to Lloyd George, the "knighthood of this war." He continued, "Every flight is a romance; every record an epic. . . . They recall the old legends of chivalry."[23] W. N. Cobbold, in a poem called "Captain Albert Ball, V. C., D. S. O." (1919), waxed lyrically and at great length (there were thirty-two stanzas) about the "knight-errant of the clouds above" who drove his chariot across the heavens, single-handedly combating squadrons of Huns and evading scores of antiaircraft guns.[24] In "The Revival of Knighthood," published in the same volume, Cobbold claimed that the spirit of the knight had been revived in the fight in the air. The airman was equated with the calvary of old: he was the "glorious Horseman of the clouds" roaming among the clouds and speeding through fields of space. The fight was "mount against mount," and airmen drove "steeds of steel and wire." Once again, there was "single combat," a "romantic adventure," a duel in which the true warrior either conquered or died.[25] In a less poetic vein, fighter pilot Cecil Lewis made the same point. Aerial warfare enabled the combatant to

be alone, to have your life in your own hands, to use your own skill, single-handed, against the enemy. It was like the lists of the Middle Ages, the only sphere in modern warfare where a man saw his adversary and faced him in mortal combat, the only sphere where there was still chivalry and honour. . . . You did not sit in a muddy trench while someone who had no personal enmity against you loosed off a gun, five miles away, and blew you to smithereens—and did not know he had done it! That was not fighting; it was murder. Senseless, brutal, ignoble. We were spared that.[26]

Airmen lived and fought "like gentlemen."[27]

Most importantly, however, these ways of killing symbolized individual prowess in anonymous, technologically driven warfare. Despite attempts by the Royal Flying Corps command to insist upon the interdependency of each individual and joint responsibility for victories, they failed to halt the romanticization of individual aviators.[28] Night fighters at a Royal Air Force Fighter Station might not have seen battle, but they spoke and dreamed of the soon-to-come event as an affair of "man against man" rather than "squadron against squadron." Battle was an "individualistic experience" for them.[29] The one-to-one fight of the air was "fair," since "his chances were as good as mine."[30] It was a "sporting" way of killing.[31] Airmen going to their first battle were going to be "blooded."[32] Men watching air fights reported that it was "the most thrilling event I have ever seen" and described it in terms of "rounds" between two contestants.[33] The "old delight of battle" was possible in fighter planes because of the speed and skill of the killing.[34] In 1942, Roderick Chrisholm reflected (after shooting down a Heinkel), that this type of combat was "a big-game hunt, and thought was focused on personal achievement. In the aftermath it was satisfactory to know that the enemy bomber force had been reduced by one, but immediately it was the elation of personal success."[35] This romanticization of the individual fighter meant that the rewards were individual too, particularly for the pilot who drew the "first blood" of the day.[36]

The skill involved in aerial warfare was crucial in understanding the pride of aerial combat. "On the ground," one World War II fighter pilot commented, "the clash of armour and lead and tommy gun and flamethrower dragged down man's internecine struggles to the level of some martian obscenity; up high it was individual skill and luck, and more luck. The aeroplane, far more than any other machine of war, in its element becomes a living thing, a Pegasus that makes every gyrating air battle an adventure."[37] The gunner "felt no antagonism. . . . [He] felt as a boxer or duellist might feel, pitting his skill against that of his opponent."[38] Consequently, airmen might express dissatisfaction if the destruction was too easily wrought because the enemy was flying inferior planes.[39]

The premium placed on individual skill tended to generate a sense of respect between pilots, irrespective of nationality.[40] Mosse observed that airmen really did treat their foe with some degree of chivalry. He reminded his readers that those who shot down German ace Manfred von Richthofen gave him a solemn funeral, photographs of which were then dropped behind German lines.[41] This was an important theme in the letters and diaries of combatant airmen during both world wars. World War II fighter pilot Paul Richey described how he was "fascinated" watching a plane he had just hit go into a spin: "I remember saying, 'Oh God, how ghastly!' as his tail suddenly swivelled sideways and came right off, while flames poured over the fuselage. Then I saw, with relief, a little white parachute open beside it. Good." When an enemy pilot was captured, Richey explained, "we all felt that this German had put up a damned good show, and as a tribute to the spirit that all pilots admire, we determined to have him to dine with us as our guest," and they treated the pilot to the best dinner and clothes they could muster.[42] Similarly, Wing Commander Roland Beaumont discovered that he was incapable of killing a German pilot whom he had downed during the Battle of Britain. He wrote: "I could not bring myself to fire at this man who had just put up such a beautiful exhibition of flying." The downed pilot was thus able to destroy his plane before saluting Beaumont and walking into captivity.[43]

As Mosse observed, such recollections reveal a relative absence of hatred of the enemy, both in the air and on the ground. Indeed, "hatred of the enemy was only occasionally used as a means of coping," Mosse insisted.[44] This is confirmed time and again in the letters and diaries of combatants. For instance, during World War I the fighter pilot Cecil Lewis honored his foe. He noted that combatants did not "love" the enemy "in the conventional sense," but they certainly honored and respected them. He continued:

> Besides, there is, as everybody who has fought knows, a strong magnetic attraction between two men who are matched against one another. I have felt this magnetism, engaging an enemy scout three miles above the earth. I have wheeled and circled, watching how he flies, taking in the power and speed of his machine, seen him, fifty yards away, eyeing me, calculating, watching for an opening, each of us wary, keyed up to the last pitch of skill and endeavour. And if at last he went down, a falling rocket of smoke and flame, what a glorious and heroic death. What a brave man! It might just as well have been me.[45]

Similarly, during World War II, in a series of interviews of successful combatants in the U.S. Eighth Air Force, it was found that less than 30 percent expressed any sense of personal hatred for the enemy.[46] Indeed, civilians were most prone to articulating virulent hatred toward the enemy, leading many commentators to conclude that reading or writing about killing was more likely to stimulate hateful feelings than actually participating in the slaughter.[47] While pilots and their crew admired and respected their victims, often burying them with full military honors, civilians felt only contempt for the enemy, declaring courteous rites as analogous to according respect to Jack the Ripper.[48] Thus, when Captain Albert Ball (the ace pilot personally responsible for downing forty-seven German planes) was encouraged by his father to "let the devils have it," Ball replied that he did not see the enemy as devils. "I do not think anything bad about the Hun. He is just a good chap with very little *guts*, trying to do his best," he informed his father.[49]

Of course, it must be remembered that this truly was "myth." After all, there was little that was truly chivalrous about war from the air. By World War II, flying machines had transformed themselves into the chief agents of death. The fact that civilians accounted for 65 percent of the deaths between 1939 and 1945 is largely due to the advances in the technology of flying and killing from the skies. The age of "total war" was ushered in by the flying machine. In Mosse's words: "Wartime aviation presented a climax of the myth of the war experience."[50]

Meaning

Nowhere was the myth of the war experience more evident than in its visual representations. Mosse was one of only a handful of historians who inspired a generation of scholars to use images to understand history.[51] His focus was always on the heroic body—the virile, masculine image of official photography, poster art, and propaganda. On the surface, such images were the opposite of the war snapshots taken by men in or near the front lines. In the snapshot, a different masculinity was revealed—an uglier one—but one that shared with its heroic counterpart the need to mask war and make it bearable.

It is striking how often camera lenses linger over the broken corpses of the enemy. This has often been observed in connection with the Vietnam War in part because by that time the technology of photography allowed for a proliferation of gruesome images. Because cameras of the World War I period were cumbersome, few "ordinary soldiers" possessed them, and it was a capital offense to be caught with a camera in the front lines. Photographs were much more likely to be "official," sponsored by the War Office or government, and many were explicitly linked to some propagandist agenda. It is hardly surprising that dismembered corpses hardly feature in this canon. In their stead we have official photographs, typically portraying British servicemen in chivalric poses, emphasizing that this is a civilian army made up of honest folks defending the world against "Prussian" militarism.

It was not until the 1930s that a really compact camera entered the market, and even then it was not cheap. This affected the types of images we have from World War II. Thus, the Imperial War Museum's photographic archive has around 100,000 photographs of World War I but well over two million for World War II. From the late 1950s, the first really low-priced cameras, designed for a mass market, entered the scene—just in time for the Vietnam War. This partially explains why photographs from the Vietnam War seem so different from those we have for earlier conflicts. Everyday "grunts" could frame the war in ways not dreamt about by government agencies. In other words, shifts in the technology of photography have distorted comparisons between the Vietnam War and other conflicts, such as the war in the Pacific during World War II, encouraging myths that the Vietnam War was *particularly* strewn with dismembered corpses. It was only during the Vietnam War that the combat photograph came into its own, snapping apart representations of the body at war from the heroic one common to official war photography to the dismembered one of the "snapshots." Nevertheless, photographs exulting in the "deadness" of the enemy were not rare during the two world wars as well. In any number of everyday photograph albums from the war, there are photographs of World War I and World War II soldiers posing among the skulls.

Such photographs, of which there are thousands, were not "about" the horror of war. Many, if not most, were part of a glorification of war and of killing. There is no question that many of these snapshots were taken by people who were *pleased* by what they were seeing or by what they had done. They were mementoes, memorializing proud actions. The attitude of such soldiers was summed up by John Henry Ewen, who found himself in combat in Bougainville in 1944:

I can remember Uncle Jack telling me about the skeleton in the last war [World War I] with a dog-biscuit in his hand, so a few days ago, when I ran across this Jap skeleton near the track, I could not resist the temptation to use it. I was putting up track-signs at the time, so I propped him up under the sign-post and fixed his arm so that he was pointing up the track. A few bits of dry grass for hair and his tin hat stuck on him and he looked pretty good. I was wishing I had a camera.[52]

The photographs were called "trophies."

This language of photography has a familiar ring to it, echoing other forms of dehumanization evident in representations of the enemy's body. By classifying the Germans or Japanese as inhuman, they all became fair game. Indeed, the most popular metaphor used to describe mass killing was that of hunting. The enemy were "specimens" to be "bagged." Going to war was the equivalent of being "blooded." This game-hunting metaphor held certain attractions. In the British context, the hunting metaphor ennobled bloody fighters by linking it with traditionally upper-class activities; in America and Australia, it was related to the "frontier" or "outback." In each case, it enabled a certain degree of emotional distancing—relationally and temporally. Furthermore, it tied in to ideas in common circulation about "human nature" and warfare: it was in man's instincts to kill. There was no point in feeling guilty for what was inherent in human nature.

But it is easy to take this argument about dehumanization too far. After all, time and again, combatants insisted on the need to *humanize* the enemy. As I argued in *An Intimate History of Killing* (1999), combatants were often particularly upset by those occasions of killing when the enemy could not be seen.[53] An Australian soldier fighting in New Guinea during World War II expressed this fear:

There are mists creeping over the trees all day, and sometimes you can't see your hand in front of your face under the cover of the jungle. Most of our chaps haven't seen a Jap! You don't even see the Jap who gets you! It's like fighting the invisible man. Those Japs are tough, hard fighters and their camouflage is perfect. They can move through scrub or tall grass without making a sound and without showing a sign except—if your eyes are good—an occasional stirring in the vegetation.[54]

Such forms of warfare were particularly difficult for combatants who longed for a face-to-face encounter with human beings, albeit in the stereotyped form described by Mosse in *The Image of Man.*

In addition, dehumanization could be counterproductive, as philosopher William Hocking noted in 1918: "It is never wise to make him out less than human. For anger . . . runs in the opposite direction; it personifies and attributes conscience to even inanimate things. If we dehumanize the foe we remove him from the reach of instinctive indignation."[55] In other words, portraying the enemy as a different species could diminish any sense that the enemy should be held accountable for his actions, yet it was precisely this accountability that sustained condemnation. During the war against the Japanese in World War II, excessive dehumanization of the enemy ended up being questioned by certain sections of military command. In a report in 1944 on morale in the Far East, Major General Lethbridge warned that atrocity stories might merely make combatants frightened of combat or of having to bail out of their airplanes if hit.[56] Dehumanizing the enemy could increase levels of fear by transforming the enemy into "mysterious wraiths": men yearned for the reassurance that their foes were "flesh and blood" even if this induced feelings of remorse. Photographing a clearly defeated enemy, slouched in a trench with head blown apart, could provide reassurance to the soldier that victory was possible.

However, images were not only about the relationship between the dead and the living. They were also part of a dialogue between the living and the living. Photographic images were central to display behavior. They gave two signals. During the Second World War, there are snapshots of enemy skulls, hung on trees or set outside dugouts by British and American soldiers. One soldier explained such actions by saying that "decapitation and stuff" was done "not so much for souvenirs as for terror. I thought everyone was doing it. I really did. I'd cut their head off and put it outside my hole at night."[57] Such tactics were intended to scare off the enemy: it was a way of saying "Don't mess with me!" It was also an assertion of power over the vanquished enemy, and it may have helped alleviate the fear of the enemy who was thus portrayed as broken.

The other signal was to comrades and civilian audiences. Photographs of men posing on the battlefield was the best evidence that a man had seen active combat and thus had proved himself on the field of battle. For instance, during World War I, George Coppard admitted that a "ghoulish curiosity" initially led him to collect souvenirs. But then he recalled that the Pickelhaubes was the favorite souvenir, "as the mere display of one of these when you were on leave sort of suggested that you had personally killed the original owner."[58] Others took pictures of themselves posing with other signs of their combatant prowess. One such photograph showed a British soldier posing in front of a fin from an enemy airplane he had shot down. The soldier was leaning on a walking stick, on which he had made notches for every "Nazi" he claimed to have "personally" killed. The original caption for this photograph read: "At Chateaudun on 14 June, just before being flown to England, I pose before the ME110 fin I had collected and presented to the Squadron after our battle on 11 May: nine notches on the stick and one of my neck." In other words, the photograph was a way this soldier retained his souvenir, which was too large to cart home with him. The photographic image was a way of asserting power over the living for many years to come: those back home could admire the walking stick with its notches indicating persons killed and the photographic souvenir of death, both of which bore witness to his status in war.

As with all souvenirs, photographic souvenirs conferred immense power upon the serviceman. In the words of one World War II soldier, it was "a little transfer of power."[59] At a political level, these rituals of collecting and remembering performed a crucial function in enabling men to cope with the problem of the transition from an identity based upon the commandment "Thou shalt not kill" to one in which killing was the measure of identity and self-worth. Carnivalesque rites of killing could be enjoyable: they helped create individual identity as a "warrior" engaged in a life-and-death struggle, and they helped cement group bonds—comradeship between men, all of whom were "set apart" from both their prewar personas *and* civilian society "back home" by acts of violence. This was why, in combat, cruel and often carnivalesque rites constituted what Mikhail Bakhtin called "authorized transgression":[60] military authorities officially disapproved of gruesome photographs and "fooling around" with enemy corpses, but they "turned a blind eye" to such antics, accepting them as necessary for "effective combat performance." Despite threats by the military that stern disciplinary action would be taken if a man was caught with a part of an enemy's body,[61] offenders seldom were even mildly rebuked. For the combatant, such photographic mementoes were proof of combat effectiveness and their status as "combatant men." In the grotesque, men were able to confront (and survive) "the horror, the horror." The photograph (and the diary account of battle) not only framed cruelty, it enabled it.

Put another way, the innumerable photographs of dead bodies—like the bloody accounts of slaughter recorded in diary entries and letters home—were one way of coming to terms with random, omnipresent death. It was a way of grasping something oppressive, crushing, and profoundly significant, something for which men could find no adequate signifiers. Julia Kristeva put this particularly well in *Powers of Horror* when she referred to the state of "abjection."[62] Using this term, writing about and photographing the horrors of war were a way of coping with "a reality that, if I acknowledge it, annihilates me, [the] object and abjection are my safeguards." This is clearly one of the functions of war writing: it is part of the struggle to find a language—not in an attempt to "approximate" "reality," an impossible feat in the horror that is combat, but precisely to integrate it into some sequence that refers to the self. After all, although it may be important to engage in war, at some stage peace must break out again. In this latter shift, the act of narration or photographically "framing" extremes of violence can be integral to the process of enabling the perpetrator to assimilate his or her acts into a peacetime "self." It is no wonder that so many war memoirs have been written.

Those who failed to find some way of assimilating their combat experiences into a linguistic or visual framework simply went mad. In "Shell-Shock as a Social Disease" (2000), Mosse discussed society's "other," that is, men who threatened society's values through behavior that defied its ideal types. The most stigmatized of such men were those who, in the midst of war, refused (or proved unable) to act as "true men."[63] These were men whose starkly emotional sentences attest to how "the sights cannot cannot be explained in writing. Writing is not my line. No fighting either For them that wants to let them fight Because I will never like it no no never" (as one stammered from hospital) or, as another terrorized private who spent time in a military mental hospital put it, "I admit I am a coward. A bloody, bleeding coward, and I want to be a live Coward than a dead blasted Hero."[64] There are many such accounts, including more poignant descriptions of fear like the one a private sent to his mother after the Battle of the Somme, simply saying: "It makes my head jump to think about it."[65] World War II poet and combatant Shawn O'Leary put it best in his poem of 1941 when he wrote:

And I—
I mow and gibber like an ape.
But what can I say, what do?—
There is no saying and no doing.[66]

Society's rejection of such "pathetic specimens of manhood" could be pitiless. As Mosse noted, they were "the enemies of settled society and because men so afflicted were thought to be effeminate, they endangered the clear distinction between genders which was generally regarded as an essential cement of society."[67] Soldiers were expected to be able to cope with battle: techniques aimed at cultivating a certain indifference to death and horror, as evident in the many letters, diaries, and photographs of "effective combat personnel," clearly failed for those who "broke" under the strain. Their lack of willpower and self-control dealt a fatal blow to their manliness and (more importantly) to the myths of "civilized society." After all, as Mosse continually emphasized, "Although the warrior image of masculinity had existed ever since the French Revolution and the Napoleonic wars, the Great War further accentuated certain aspects of masculinity that of themselves did not have to be warlike but—like willpower, hardness, or perseverance—were qualities that peacetime society prized as well."[68] In other words, "the fears engendered by a presumed attack on the fundamental pillars of society—strong nerves, willpower and a clear separation of sexes—all relevant to the comprehension of shell-shock, were increased by the threat of degeneration which had haunted society and culture ever since the turn of the century."[69] Men who failed to find a way—whether through language or through visual representation—to "make sense" of what was often senseless violence in combat were "incomplete men"[70] who, by their very existence, weakened the social fabric.

Exhortations to "be a man" have been "all pervasive in Western culture," as Mosse observed in the first sentence of his *The Image of Man* (1996). Never was this so powerful as in the context of war, when the male body and the masculine ideal became society's central symbol of personal and national regeneration. Whether examined in the context of literature and official images (as in Mosse's work) or in the less formal medium of letters, diaries, and photographic "snapshots," representations of the male body proliferated. The heroic body, as mythologized in the image of the airman, drew its force as much from its ability to imitate fantastic visions of "olden time chivalry" as it did by its ability to differentiate itself from the muddied frame of the soldier crouching in the trench. The struggle to maintain the myth was always present, however: airmen could not avoid recognizing that their work was brutal and bloody. As a consequence, in words and in pictures, even the heroic body slipped further away from the landscape inhabited by its past selves. For combatants who possessed an "after" to war, remarkable feats of imagination were needed to enable them to survive (emotionally and psychologically) their ordeal in battle. Nevertheless, even in the midst of the inexplicable unreasonableness of mass, modernized death, most combatants found a linguistic "truth" or a way of pinning down the confusion of combat into an image that could be taken home to remind them of who they were when they were "tourists in hell" and who they were now. In Mosse's memorable words: the myth of war was the way "the reality of war was masked and made bearable."[71]

Notes

1. George L. Mosse, "The Knights of the Sky and the Myth of the War Experience," in *War: A Cruel Necessity? The Bases of Institutional Violence,* ed. Robert A. Hinde and Helen E. Watson (London: Tauris Academic Studies, 1994), 132.

2. George L. Mosse, *The Image of Man: The Creation of Modern Masculinity* (New York: Oxford University Press, 1996), 115.

3. For further discussion see Joanna Bourke, *Dismembering the Male: Men's Bodies, Britain, and the Great War* (London: Reaktion Books, 1998).

4. C. Ranger Gull, "The Great Sport Revival," *Health and Efficiency,* July 1919, 146.

5. Basil Hart to his parents, undated [1914], in Sir Basil Liddle Hart, Liddle Hart Centre (London), call number 7/1914/4.

6. C. B. Stokes, "Papers," letter to his wife, dated 28 June 1915, file CBS 4/5, Imperial War Museum, London (hereafter IWM). Punctuation as in original.

7. Mosse, "Knights of the Sky," 133, 134, 140; and Mosse, *The Image of Man,* 111.

8. Captain Norman Austin Taylor to Eileen Irvine, 11 September 1915, IWM.

9. Captain Alfred Bland to his wife, 16 May 1916, IWM; emphasis in original.

10. Joanna Bourke, "The Emotions in War: Fear and the British and American Military, 1914–45," *Historical Research* 74 (August 2001): 314–30.

11. E. G. Boring and Marjorie Van de Water, *Psychology for the Fighting Man* (Washington, D.C.: National Research Council, 1943), 298–99.

12. Water S. Hunter, "Psychology in the War," *American Psychologist* 1 (1946): 479.

13. Entries for 17 July and 18 August 1918, Lieutenant A. B. Scott, "The Diary," in *Thirty-second Division, Artillery and Trench Mortar Memories* (London: Unwin Brothers Ltd., 1923), 66, 96.

14. Mosse, "Knights of the Sky," 133.

15. Ibid., 132.

16. David Lloyd George, "A Nation's Thanks," 29 October 1917, in George, *The Great Crusade: Extracts from Speeches Delivered during the War* (London: Hodder and Stroughton, 1918), 148.

17. Roderick Chrisholm, *Cover of Darkness* (London: Chatto and Windus, 1953), 71.

18. Flight-Lieutenant D. M. Crook, *Spitfire Pilot* (London: Faber and Faber, 1942), 28, 30–31, 75.

19. Kenneth Hemingway, *Wings over Burma* (London: Quality Press Ltd., 1944), 41–42, 68–69.

20. See the interview of K. O. Moore and Alec Gibb in Squadron Leader Hector Bolitho, "Two in Twenty-two Minutes," in *Slipstream: A Royal Air Force Anthology,* ed. R. Raymond and David Langdon, (London: Eyre and Spottiswoode, 1946), 10–11.

21. Ibid., quoting from a letter from the pilot "John," no date but probably January 1940.

22. Hector Bolitho, *Combat Report: The Story of a Fighter Pilot* (London: B. T. Batsford, 1943), 54, quoting from a letter from pilot "John," 10 April, probably 1940.

23. George, "A Nation's Thanks," 148–49.

24. W. N. Cobbold, "Captain Albert Ball, V. C., D. S. O.," *Poems on the War: March 21st to November 11th, 1918 and after the Armistice* (Cambridge: published by the author, 1919), 2–5.

25. "The Revival of Knighthood," in Cobbold, *Poems on the War,* 10–11.

26. Cecil Lewis, *Sagittarius Rising* (London: Peter Davies, 1936), 45.

27. Boyd Cable, *Air Men O'War* (London: John Murray, 1918), 139–40.

28. For a discussion see John H. Morrow, "Knights of the Sky: The Rise of Military Aviation," in *Authority, Identity, and the Social History of the Great War,* ed. Frans Coetzee and Marilyn Shevin-Coetzee (Providence: Berghahn Books, 1995), 316–17.

29. T. T. Paterson, *Morale in War and Work: An Experiment in the Management of Men* (London: Max Parrish, 1955), 88.

30. Wing-Commander Athol Forbes and Squadron-Leader Hubert Allen, *The Fighter Boys* (London: Collins, 1942), 97.

31. See Walter A. Briscoe, *The Boy Hero of the Air: From Schoolboy to V. C.* (London: Humphrey Milford, 1921), throughout; Crook, *Spitfire Pilot,* 41–42; Rev. E. J. Kennedy, *With the Immortal Seventh Division,* 2nd ed. (London: Hodder and Stroughton, 1916), 114.

32. Quoting John Beede, in *The War in the Air, 1939–1945: An Anthology of Personal Experience,* ed. Gavin Lyall (London: Hutchinson, 1968), 278.

33. Canadian Field Comforts Commission, *With the First Canadian Contingent* (Toronto: Hodder and Stroughton, 1915), 76–77.

34. Letter by Lieutenant Leslie Yorath Sanders, 4 March 1917, in *War Letters of Fallen Englishmen,* ed. Lawrence Housman (London: Victor Gollancz, 1930), 231.

35. Chrisholm, *Cover of Darkness,* 73; also see 71.

36. Bolitho, *Combat Report,* 45, 58.

37. Kenneth Hemingway, *Wings over Burma* (London: Quality Press Ltd., 1944), 76.

38. Flight-Lieutenant Richard Charles Rivaz, *Tail Gunner* (London: Jarrards, 1943), 74.

39. "H. G.," *R. A. F. Occasions* (London: Cresset Press, 1941), 41.

40. Bolitho, *Combat Report,* 133; Walter A. Briscow, *The Boy Hero of the Air: From Schoolboy to V. C.* (London: Humphrey Milford, 1921), 50; *Universal Military Training—No!* (N.p.: n.p., 1919), 8.

41. Mosse, "Knights of the Sky," 135.

42. Paul Richey, *Fighter Pilot: A Personal Record of the Campaign in France* (London: B. T. Batsford, 1944), 11, 42.

43. The diary of Wing Commander Roland Beaumont, in Edward Lanchbery, *Against the Sun: The Story of Wing Commander Roland Beaumont, D. S. O., O. B. E., D. F. C. Pilot of the Canberra and the P.1* (London: Cassell, 1955), 56–57.

44. Mosse, "Knights of the Sky," 137.

45. Lewis, *Sagittarius Rising,* 45–46.

46. D. W. Hastings, D. G. Wright, and B. C. Glueck, *Psychiatric Experiences of the Eighth Air Force* (New York: New York Army Air Forces, 1944), 137–39.

47. Oliver Elton, *C. E. Montague: A Memoir* (London: Chatto and Windus, 1929), 197; G. C. Field, *Pacifism and Conscientious Objection* (Cambridge: Cambridge University Press, 1945), 67; Frederic Hillersdon Keeling, *Keeling Letters and Recollections* (London: G. Allen and Unwin, 1918), 285.

48. James Molony Spaight, *Air Power and War Rights* (London: Longmans, 1924), 319; *London Weekly Dispatch,* 10 September 1916; *London Daily Mail,* (London) 4 and 7 May 1918.

49. R. H. Kiernan, *Captain Albert Ball* (London: John Hamilton, 1933), 60; emphasis in original.

50. Mosse, "Knights of the Sky," 132.

51. Others include Peter Burke, Sander Gilman, and Roy Porter.

52. Sergeant John Henry Ewen, "Bougainville Campaign," book 1, 1944, 68, Australian War Memorial PR89/190, Canberra, Australian Capital Territory, Australia.

53. For further discussion see Joanna Bourke, *An Intimate History of Killing: Face-to-Face Killing in Twentieth-Century History* (London: Granta, 1999).

54. An Australian soldier, quoted in George H. Johnston, *The Toughest Fight in the World* (New York: Duell, Sloan and Pearce, 1944), 127.

55. William Ernest Hocking, *Morale and Its Enemies* (New Haven: Yale University Press, 1918), 56–58.

56. "Morale (Far Eastern) Inter-Services Committee. Interim Report: Second Draft," 1944, p. 4, PRO WO32/11195. Also see "Morale (Far Eastern) Inter-Services Committee. Minutes of the Eighth Meeting Held in Room 433, Hobart House, on Wednesday, 16th August, 1944," pp. 4 and 7, PRO WO32/11195.

57. Donald Hedges, interviewed in J. T. Hanson, A. Susan Owen, and Michael Patrick Madden, *Parallels: The Soldiers' Knowledge and the Oral History of Contemporary Warfare* (New York: Aldine de Gruyter, 1992), 95.

58. George Coppard, *With a Machine Gun to Cambrai* (London: Imperial War Museum, 1980), 73, 90.

59. Michael Herr, *Dispatches* (London: Pan Books, 1978), 52.

60. Mikhail Bakhtin, *Rabelais and His World*, trans. Helene Iswolsky (Cambridge, Mass.: MIT Press, 1985).

61. For a discussion see Paul Fussell, *Wartime: Understanding and Behaviour in the Second World War* (Oxford: Oxford University Press, 1989), 117.

62. Julia Kristeva, *Powers of Horror* (New York: Columbia University, 1982), 23.

63. George L. Mosse, "Shell-Shock as a Social Disease," *Journal of Contemporary History* 35, no. 1 (2000): 101.

64. Unnamed soldier in convalescent hospital, in Miss Dorothy Scholes, "Papers of Miss Dorothy Scholes," unpaginated, Wigan Archives Service D/DZ.EHC, and Joanna Bourke, ed., *The Misfit Soldier* (Cork: Cork University Press, 1999), 32. In both, punctuation and capitalization as in original.

65. Private Arthur H. Hubbard, "Letters Written May–November 1916," IWM.

66. Shawn O'Leary, "Shell Shock," in *Spikenard and Bayonet: Verse of the Front Line* (Melbourne: published by the author, 1941), 20.

67. Mosse, "Shell-Shock as a Social Disease," 103.

68. Mosse, *The Image of Man*, 115.

69. Mosse, "Shell-Shock as a Social Disease," 104.

70. The phrase is Mosse's; see ibid.

71. Mosse, "Knights of the Sky," 132.

Part 4
Mosse and Jewish History

German Jewish History

Back to *Bildung* and Culture?

Shulamit Volkov

It was at Berkeley, during the second half of the 1960s, that I first encountered the work of George Mosse. These were years of intense political upheaval on campus but also a time of exhilarating intellectual exchange. While we, graduate students of the history department, were part witnessing and part contributing to the general unrest, we also part witnessed and part contributed to the emergence of a new—or rather renewed—kind of history: social history. From today's perspective it is easy to see how inflated was our self-consciousness as pioneers, how exaggerated our self-esteem as innovators. Yet we were truly immersed in the enthusiasm of it all, practicing history in a new way—"from below" as it were—a history that would naturally complement our political vision and fit in with our youthful, perhaps utopian, worldview. Particularly committed were those among us who read European history. These were the days of E. P. Thompson's magnum opus *The Making of the English Working Class*, of George Rudé's and Eric Hobsbawm's books on "the crowd," of new experiments with quantitative history, and of bold approaches, borrowing heavily from the social sciences.[1] For the "elect" who were admitted to Hans Rosenberg's seminars, these were also the days in which we could watch him complete his break with his own mentor, Friedrich Meinecke.[2] *Ideengeschichte*, Meinecke's in particular, became a thing of the past for us. I was by then writing a dissertation on the handicraft masters in Germany of the "great depression."[3] My best friend, Maura Kealey, who had come to Berkeley with a B. A. from Madison, wrote about the coal miners' strikes at that time.[4] We seemed to be handling the real stuff of history, finding ways to "give voice"—though this expression had not yet been coined—to the simple, undistinguished people: men and women, to be sure, the inarticulate, the clearly nonintellectual.

It was then, while searching the library for books on anti-Semitism, which seemed rampant among "my" artisans, that I ran into two relatively new books. One was Fritz Stern's *Study in the Rise of the Germanic Ideology,* under the ringing title *The Politics of Cultural Despair;* the other was George Mosse's *The Crisis of German Ideology,* subtitled *Intellectual Origins of the Third Reich.*[5] On the face of it, Stern and Mosse went about attacking the old *Ideengeschichte* just as fiercely as we were then doing at Berkeley. However, at that time they seemed to belong to another camp. Theirs was no longer the intellectual history à la Meinecke, nor did they follow in the footsteps of Arthur Lovejoy or of our own teacher at the time, Carl Schorske, whose magnificent weekly lectures were still ringing in our ears from our undergraduate days.[6] But they were no social historians. For us, armed with the methods of a new discipline, everything that smacked of the old one was suspect, and for some reason, while Stern's book was mildly appreciated, Mosse's seemed rather unpalatable.[7] He could not be picked up as a model in our milieu.

And what a shame, in fact, it was—especially for me. As I moved on to deal ever more explicitly with anti-Semitism and began to study the history of German Jewry, Mosse's name repeatedly reemerged. His significance for my new field of interest had been apparent even before I first met him—rather briefly—in March of 1981 at the inauguration of his chair at the Hebrew University in Jerusalem.[8] I was by then still vigorously fighting my way through the promised land of social history, cherishing a sense of belonging to a younger generation of rebel-historians. And I still believed that Mosse's interests and mine were at bottom very different, despite the apparently converging themes.

All this now seems ages ago. It has been fascinating and enlightening to go over George's work on German Jewish history in preparing this paper. One encounters real treasures, and it is painful indeed to think of all the shortcuts one could have taken—but missed. From a distance of two decades, there is still no excuse for that early arrogance. But while my— or should I say our—posture was surely an outcome of that modern *Streit der Fakultäten* (*Contest of Faculties,* Kant), it also had something to do with Mosse's attitude toward Jewish history, his own way of handling it. As if against his own temperament, Mosse seemed to approach this subject matter cautiously, as if not quite so willingly. By the late 1950s he was apparently trying to go beyond his original research interests in early modern Europe.[9] As he was seeking a new niche for himself, he almost intuitively—so it seems—went back to the materials he knew best. In 1957 he contributed his first essay to the *Leo Baeck Institute Year Book,* entitled "The Image of the Jews in German Popular Literature," and almost simultaneously published another piece in *Judaism,* likewise dealing with anti-Semitism as an aspect of German culture.[10] But as anti-Semitism, to be sure, is not merely—not even primarily—a subject matter of Jewish history, Mosse's new move in this direction still left him comfortably within the boundaries of German history. For him it was conspicuously and emphatically a chapter in German history. *The Crisis,* too, being after all a book on the sources of National Socialism, was meant to be a book on Germans and only marginally about Jews. It belongs among Mosse's works on fascism, on National Socialism, partly also on anti-Semitism, but not really on German Jews. They were clearly on his mind by then, but he still kept his distance.

Here is how he chose to approach the matter: in 1965 he wrote an extended piece on the German Right and the Jews, followed by a full-fledged essay on the influence of the *völkische Bewegung* on the Jews themselves.[11] In 1966 he wrote a general essay on the German Left between the two world wars and only then added a study of their attitudes toward the Jews.[12] He worked intensively on World War I before he was ready to write on German Jews at the time.[13] He published widely on nationalism before he turned to deal with Zionism, and he was for long preoccupied with the failure of German liberalism before he wrote *German Jews beyond Judaism*—that hymn to the Jewish devotion to *Bildung* and to the principles of humanistic liberalism.[14] He was approaching the matter of Jewish history with a great deal of circumspection.

Moreover, at this stage Mosse was no rebel methodologically, too. During the 1960s and the early 1970s, he still felt indebted to a kind of *Ideengeschichte—his* kind, to be sure. We were perhaps not entirely wrong to doubt his drive for innovation. After all, his chief contribution by then—still focusing, as he himself said, on the "world of ideas"—was not really in breaking away from the old discipline but rather in widening its scope and enriching its palate. The inclusion of less illustrious thinkers, of those considered "second class" writers, of forgotten intellectuals, whose effect was not in their genius but in their accessibility—all that did not constitute a complete turnabout. Social historians at that time seemed to be testing less familiar grounds. In Germany, Reinhard Rürup was working on the Vormärz protocols of the various south German parliaments, debating the position of Jews in their slowly modernizing states. Monika Richarz then wrote a dissertation on the entry of Jews into the academic professions. Stefi Jersch-Wenzel concentrated on the local citizenship rights of the Jews.[15] And in Israel, Jacob Katz and his doctoral students were sketching a theory of Jewish social history and examining its practical parameters.[16] Both their language and their pronounced purposes seemed at that time far more revolutionary than Mosse's.

But like Mosse, they too were still clearly focusing on the non-Jewish Germans. They all wrote mainly on attitudes toward Jews, though not only on anti-Semitism, and on the Jews' image, not about their unique history. Even Katz was by then working on such monographic themes as the history of Jews in the Freemasons' lodges in Europe, in addition to his general expositions of Jewish-Gentile relationships.[17] The grand theme at the time was clearly assimilation. This was also Mosse's main interest, until his *Fragestellung*, like that of so many of his colleagues in social history, began to shift, slowly but consistently. By the 1970s he was no longer exclusively interested in the special German "gaze," as we might call it today, but in Jewish life itself. Mosse was by then weighing the place of Jews within those special discursive worlds he had been investigating—the Right, the Left, and the liberal middle—and it was from that perspective and at a relatively late date that his interest in Jewish history proper began to grow.

Here too, however, his deep attachment to old historical idioms cannot be overlooked. As was indeed so common among liberal historians of German Jewry throughout the immediate postwar years, there was an undisguised note of apologetics in Mosse's writing about the Jews. Despite the tale of his youth as a rebel, despite his distance from his immediate family, despite his sharp, critical mind, Mosse was attached to the world he had lost. He never ceased to seek the Jews' dignified and admirable sides. He never ceased to try to exonerate them of explicit and often implicit reproach. Jewish right-wing tendencies, according to Mosse, never went as far as those of their German counterparts. Even the young Buber, speaking of *Volkgeist* and the community of blood, was a cosmopolitan humanist to Mosse. Max Nordau, preaching the need for a "New Jew"—vigorous and physically rejuvenated—was interpreted as a true liberal, while Gershom Scholem's Zionism had been rooted, according to Mosse, in the highest principles of *Bildung* and in strictest scientific rationalism.[18]

Mosse's writings on Jewish nationalism are doubtless the most striking example. Having exposed the extent of the influence exerted by the
völkische Ideologie upon German Jews, he repeatedly made sure to differentiate between them and their German counterparts. Jewish men
and women were always at bottom true humanists, even when they were
carrying the banners of regeneration, participating in a variety of group
rituals, romanticizing the countryside, admiring the open landscape of a
beloved *Vaterland,* extolling vital masculinity, even the forces of ethnicity
and of ancient blood ties. In later essays, especially those written during
the 1990s, Mosse was even willing to transpose this claim onto the Israeli
scene. Unlike some former supporters and later critics of Zionism,
Mosse's strong ties to Israel made him uphold even *its* human, enlightened face—a most unusual stance in this day and age, indeed.

This was also the line he took in his only work fully dedicated to Jewish history "from within," so to speak. The message of *German Jews beyond Judaism* was clear: Jews entered German culture at the "autumn of
Enlightenment."[19] They remained loyal to its principles and to the guide-
lines of *Bildung* till the bitter end. It was surely this book that contained
Mosse's credo regarding the history of Germany Jewry between emancipation and destruction. It was here that he summarized two decades of
research into this subject, here that he finally intended to summarize
what he considered the centerpiece of their narrative—more even: their
true, lasting legacy.

Using a similar methodology, even some of Mosse's closest followers
were capable of a more critical posture. Most emphatically, it seems to
me, it is Steven Aschheim who, while clearly following Mosse's lead, repeatedly touches upon some of the raw nerves of that liberal, open-
minded, enlightened Jewry. A student of Mosse, he began his academic
career with a book about the attitudes of these very Jews toward their presumed brothers from the East—at best an ambivalent tale.[20] Later on,
perhaps as a sideline of his work on Nieztsche's intellectual reception,
Aschheim further brought out those Jewish intellectuals whose concept
of *Bildung* during the Weimar Republic was by no means still that pre-
scribed by Humboldt.[21] Zvi Bacharach, to give another example, belonging to another historical school, recently exposed yet another group of
Jewish intellectuals at that time, suspicious of democracy, hostile to liberalism, and fearful in confronting modernity.[22] In an earlier lecture in
Madison, I also suggested that Jews were part and parcel of the overall in-

tellectual scene in Germany. They were no more dedicated to true old-fashioned *Bildung* than others and no less prone to embrace German nationalism—despite its affinity to racism and its inherent anti-Semitism.[23]

Be that as it may, while Mosse continued to dwell—in his own way, to be sure—on the history of *Bildung,* social historians developed their own craft along two other, parallel routes. One of these, like Mosse's, upheld the main *Fragestellung* focusing upon the age of emancipation, while seeking new methods and different sources for finally providing a better explanation for these familiar issues. True to its Marxist roots, German social history of that brand continued to ask questions about the origins of National Socialism—for instance, about Germany's *Sonderweg.* The Bielefelder Schule, for instance, led by Hans-Ulrich Wehler, was busy thinking about grand structures of inequality and the overall processes of modernization.[24] It focused upon previously neglected aspects of society, indeed, but it was still dealing with the same old global issues. My own work on the German handicraft masters was surely a case in point, too. It dealt with a much neglected social group but was in fact yet another study on the origins of National Socialism.[25]

The other line of social historical research, though, took off in another direction. This was partly an outcome of minute daily work on the German working class, on the Mittelstand, or on the ever more intensely discussed Bürgertum. While researching into the history of all these, new issues presented themselves: some related to demography, some to family history, to urbanization, to the various sides of industrialization, and to women's own story too, of course. Historians occasionally became so deeply involved in these matters that they lost sight of their original interest. It is surely a common procedure in the history of historiography. In addition, influence of the French *Annales* began to be felt among us. Long-term changes, oral history, even *Alltagsgeschichte* now supplemented the more conventional sociopolitical history. It implied the treatment of another cluster of new, different themes. Some of these could still be tied to the familiar major questions that shook the historians' guild since 1945, but many could no longer refer to them. Inequality in death and sickness, to take one example, now became central, though it could hardly contribute to solving the puzzle of fascism. Research on workers' popular culture, on the rise of entrepreneurs, on the free professions—all had their own independent rationale.[26] The issues of Nazism, of totalitarianism, and of the global power structure were addressed only marginally, if at all.

For a long time, the social history of German Jewry was particularly strong on the first line of research I just mentioned and particularly weak on the second. Why, we all wanted to know, did the project of emancipation in Germany collapse so miserably? Why did assimilation never seem to be enough for achieving full integration? Why and how did the anti-Semites, considered in civilized circles to be nothing but remnants of medieval backwardness, survive and thrive both before and after World War I? How did it all culminate, so unexpectedly and so tragically, in the Final Solution?

But German Jewish history too fell prey to the inner dynamics of research and the multitude of international influences. Gradually, one began to ask questions that made little or no sense in the context of that famous triad of emancipation, assimilation, and anti-Semitism. One discovered Jewish demography, the life of Jewish women, questions concerning occupational stratification, social and welfare organizations, leisure activities, and so forth. Like German history in general, German Jewish history too had undergone a thorough transformation, but much has been changed since then.

Let us look at today's research in that apparently ever more prospering subdiscipline of German Jewish history. It was in March of 2000 that I was invited to open a workshop sponsored by the Leo Baeck Institute in Jerusalem to which some twenty-five young researchers, mostly from Germany, had been invited. In preparing my talk, seeking to address this new generation of historians with what may seem most relevant to their work, I first examined the provisional program of the workshop itself. And here is what I found: the first session was to be dedicated to religion and the Wissenschaft des Judentums. The second meant to deal with some inter-European comparisons. However, among the first six lectures, only one focused on the interrelationships between Jews and Germans; the rest reported on research into inner conflicts within the famous Verein für Kultur und Wissenschaft der Juden, on the history of international Jewish welfare organizations, and on internal community matters in Germany, in America, and even in Denmark. The third session was entitled "Religious Pluralism among German Jews between 1815 and 1933," and the fourth was to deal with some of the special professional groups active within the congregations: the dayans, the cantors, the *Religionslehrer,* and the rabbis. Further down the list came lectures on Jewish autobiographies, both during the early days of eighteenth-century Haskalah and later on, during times of emigration and exile. There followed the obligatory lecture on

Jewish commemoration of the dead, and the last full-length session was reserved for problems of identity formation and identity transformation among Jews in the modern world.

These details are quite telling. There was no lecture on anti-Semitism in this workshop, nothing directly on assimilation or on problems of social and cultural integration. Likewise, no word was uttered on social or oc-cupational stratification, for instance, on demography, or on any of the "classical" social historical themes. Neither the issues that captured the imagination of Mosse's generation nor the ones that seemed so central to historians like myself were to be handled in Jerusalem. The young re-searchers in this field, one had to conclude, were clearly presenting a new agenda. Finally, the workshop included no programmatic statements by any of the participants. They simply took for granted the change of para-digm. I seemed outdated even in pointing this out.

Not everyone, however, is so unselfconscious. Take a look, for in-stance, at the book of essays recently published to celebrate Reinhard Rürup's sixty-fifth birthday, *Juden, Bürger, Deutsche*. It was jointly edited by three of the most outstanding younger German historians of German Jewry today: Andreas Gotzmann, Rainer Liedtke, and Till van Rahden.[27] Gotzmann recently published his *Habilschrift*, on the reception of the Halacha in Germany, and has likewise published a new book on German Jewish "discourse of modernization"—so the fashionable title reads. Liedtke received his Ph.D. with a dissertation comparing Jewish welfare organizations in Hamburg and in Manchester between 1850 and 1914. And van Rahden has made a name for himself by publishing a number of "revisionist" essays on anti-Semitism as well as a dissertation on Jews, Protestants, and Catholics in Breslau between 1860 and 1925.[28] Aside from their own contributions, the Rürup Festschrift includes thirteen ad-ditional articles on a variety of topics. Some of them address what we might consider good old-fashioned themes, but all are written in the new language of cultural history. Their authors display an admirable theoreti-cal versatility as well as occasional knowledge of Yiddish or even He-brew. They are all clearly capable of dealing not only with German Jew-ish interrelations but with that complex, *internal* history of German Jewry, too. In the context of German historiography, this is a promising novelty.[29]

Just as some thirty years ago a new, independent social history, with its own separate agenda, sprang both out of confrontations with daily prob-

lems of research and through the influence of practicing historians elsewhere, so does the new cultural history of today grow in response to the
failing of previous research strategies and in line with new theoretical and
methodical trends. In its own time, let us not forget, social history often
had to struggle in order to secure its place in the field of German Jewish
history, and this despite the fact that this field was clearly no subject matter for old-style political or diplomatic history. But once we got our way
and no longer needed to defend ourselves, many of us began to drift away.
Observe the inner tensions that were revealed almost at the outset.
Monika Richarz published a three-volume selection of memoirs written
by German Jews.[30] Her introductory chapters were models of social historical presentation. She offered a multitude of important data, some representative tables, some vital statistics, details on occupation, income, and
stratification—all clearly and straightforwardly set forth. The primary
sources that followed, however, seemed to deal with another cosmos.
They told the story of everyday life, dealt with religious customs and daily
norms, with the pains of integration, with assimilation—successful or
otherwise, and with the ever present issues of identity. In short, they dealt
with the typical subject matters of cultural history. Marion Kaplan, to take
another example, began her career with a pioneering book on the Jewish
Women's Association in Germany—an obvious offshoot of social history,
combining institutional history with the by then new concern for women's
affairs. Her second book, though, dealing with the Jewish *Mittelstand*
family, originally likewise a sideline of social history, ended up handling
above all the various aspects of acculturation—clearly not a typical strategy for a *social* historical project.[31] Take some of my own works, too. I
have written two essays on German Jewish scientists, for instance.[32] In
1985 I started out by searching for the social origins of Jewish success in
the natural sciences, relying primarily on data for familial background and
on a variety of socioeconomic factors. I ended up some ten years later
writing an essay on *Denkstyl*, clearly now a cultural concept, a study in the
intellectual makeup of the men under investigation.

Social history, in fact, seemed to have failed to respond to what most
urgently interested us even at the time, or perhaps we simply failed in
making a proper use of it. Above all, we failed in our efforts to turn German *Jewish* history into an integral part of *German* history. We failed in
our efforts to use it for breaking away from what we sensed as our un-
justified marginality. And this is precisely where social history failed, let

me remind you, elsewhere too. The case of women's history is most telling. In an essay titled "Language, Gender, and Working-Class History," Joan Scott describes the cool reception of women's social history even among the presumably most progressive and open-minded labor historians. The relegation of gender "to a set of descriptive social roles," she claims, "vitiated the theoretical interest and the analytic force feminist history could have."[33] She then goes on to argue that it is perhaps through the study of language that gender too can come into its own. Social history may have indeed managed to make labor history an integral part of the general, overall historical narrative. It did not manage to do the same either for women's history or for Jewish history. Could the "linguistic turn" do the trick? Or could at least some other form of a new cultural history accomplish the task?

The first step taken by the new historians, as we saw, just as in the case of women's history before, was to move away from the general German context and concentrate on the Jewish one—a kind of consciousness-raising exercise. Young historians are now getting nearer to their subject matter, as I showed before. They seem to be more interested in the Jews themselves than in their interaction with others. They learn to appreciate the significance of Jewish life experience and to give proper weight to internal Jewish affairs and interaction. Jews are finally active players in their narrative, an integral part of the world they shared with others, not simply some outsiders whose only desire was to fit in. They now move to center stage, and this cannot be done without studying in depth the internal dimensions of both their private and their public life.

The second step consisted in openly adopting the new cultural history. Those who write on German Jewry today continue to rely occasionally on some of the methods characteristic of social history, but they claim to be far less bogged down by its inherent determinism. They set out to reread old and new texts in different ways and give the "words themselves," so to speak, their true significance. They now consider "discursive codes," to use van Rahden's terminology, and not only "social practices," cultural and not only socioeconomic factors.[34]

But is this such an entirely new road, taken by a bold new generation, or is it a return to older practices? Are we not finally moving back to George Mosse? I have already sketched above the ways through which he too gradually moved from the periphery of Jewish history to its center, from dealing with it by proxy to handling it as the main theme. In some ways he too accomplished this move by applying a new kind of cultural history. One may go back to one of Mosse's partly forgotten book reviews, published in 1969 by the *American Historical Review*.[35] Interestingly enough, it does not deal with a book on the Reformation or with any new work on fascism. Some six years prior to the publication of *The National-ization of the Masses* and more than a decade before his *Toward the Final Solution,* this review clearly documents Mosse's originality. In it he dis-cusses two publications dealing with the history of anthropology. Having moved from high culture to popular culture in the early 1960s, Mosse was apparently ill at ease with his own methodology. "In the analysis of popu-lar culture or mass politics," he wrote, "the irrational seems to predomi-nate, and the historian needs different tools to capture the structure of the popular mind." This declaration, however, did not lead him in the footsteps of Le Bon, for instance, or the more modern social psychologists at the time. He instead turned to seek help from anthropology. "Here an-thropology can be of great help," he explained, "for not only have anthro-pologists concerned themselves with the analysis of folkways and com-munity customs, but their use of myths and symbols can provide useful ways to penetrate the mind of modern as well as primitive man."[36] But in order to facilitate the intrusion into this unknown land, Mosse sought comfort in a more familiar terrain. After all, a number of philosophers too have dealt with myths and symbols, and it was finally to Ernst Cassirer that he turned for help. Cassirer believed, Mosse writes, "that men com-prehend the reality within which they live through the mediation of sym-bolic systems such as language, religion, and learning." And while Cas-sirer applied his insight to "a kind of intellectual history that he conceived as a series of philosophical systems . . . his conception of how men medi-ate between their own minds and reality is useful at all levels of historical analysis."[37]

By 1977, as I was contemplating an essay on the historiography of anti-Semitism for the *Leo Baeck Institute Year Book*, rushing from the li-brary with a bag full of books, I ran into a colleague at Tel Aviv University. He wanted to know what I was up to, and as I told him he suggested in passing that I read Clifford Geertz. It was thus that my article on "Anti-semitism as a Cultural Code" took shape.[38] But had I been better read, I could have easily taken my clue from George ten years earlier. Mine is usually considered an *early* attempt to move away from the constraints of social history to some other kind of historiography that has had as yet no name. But Mosse, not having gone at all through the stages of social history, had moved in this direction much earlier. As always, throughout his career, he did it in his own way: sophisticated without being theoretically too self-conscious, renovating without insisting on revisionism. Still, there remains a deep gap between him and the new cultural historians—especially, it seems to me, in the field of German Jewish history—and that gap is not to be found in matters of theory or methodology but rather, as one might have suspected by now, in ideology.

The ideological poles in writing German Jewish history are familiar enough: Liberalism on the one hand, Zionism on the other. The old conflict between members of the Central-Verein and Jewish nationalists seemed to have colored the historical narrative of a whole century. Historians tended to behave as if one was forever arguing about the pros and cons of emancipation or about the most proper way of refuting anti-Semitism. Everyone was caught in this anachronistic, magic circle. Mosse was no exception. But he, quite particularly, must have felt torn within it. Unlike many other committed liberals, he long felt a deep respect for Jewish nationalism. Although he was above all a true *Bildung*-humanist, he felt attracted to Zionism. He could never fit comfortably into either of the alternatives offered by Jewish historiography. Thus, he repeatedly tried to make the Zionists into pronounced liberals and the liberals into proud, self-conscious Jews. There was, I believe, much truth in this unorthodox construction, but above all it was crucial in undermining the repetitiveness and self-assurance of the old historical discourse. The final demise of this historiography, however, could only come with the emergence of a full-fledged *new* ideology. Postmodernism and multiculturalism—despite all their failings—seem to have provided an anchor for the new cultural historians, an anchor Mosse too was perhaps reaching for during his last years. It now seems possible to approve of Diaspora life while cherishing one's ethnicity, to uphold liberalism while setting bounds to assimilation. Mosse always sensed that this could be done. The new historians of today, however, are moving comfortably within an ideology that legitimizes such combinations and operate easily within such complex parameters. You would not find them apologizing—whether Jews, Germans, or Americans. You would not find them struggling to square the circle. Their intellectual environment is different. Their context is far less constricting.

Finally, these new historians still need to prove that their newly gained ideological freedom is really conducive to more open-minded and refined historiography. They seem to be on a promising track. Although not all of us can follow suit, we will surely watch them closely going along it, wishing them—as George Mosse invariably did—further and lasting success.

Notes

1. E. P. Thompson's book was first published in 1963, and see George Rudé, *The Crowd in the French Revolution* (Oxford: Clarendon Press, 1959), as well as his *The Crowd in History: A Study of Popular Disturbances in France and England, 1730–1848* (New York: Wiley, 1964); also Eric Hobsbawm, *Primitive Rebels: Studies in Archaic Forms of Social Movement in the Nineteenth and Twentieth Centuries* (Manchester: Manchester University Press, 1959).

2. For Rosenberg's approach to social history see especially his *Bureaucracy, Aristocracy, and Autocracy: The Prussian Experience, 1660–1815* (Cambridge: Harvard University Press, 1958; Boston: Beacon Press, 1966), and *Probleme der deutschen Sozialgeschichte* (Frankfurt am Main: Suhrkamp, 1969).

3. Shulamit Volkov, *The Rise of Popular Antimodernism in Germany: The Urban Master Artisans, 1873–1896* (Princeton, N.J.: Princeton University Press, 1978).

4. Her dissertation has not been published, but see, e.g., Maura Kealey, "Kampfstrategien der Unternehmerschaft im Ruhrbergbau seit dem Bergarbeiterstreik vom 1889," in *Glück auf, Kameraden! Die Bergarbeiter und ihre Organisationen in Deutschland*, ed. Hans Mommsen and Ulrich Borsdorf (Cologne: Bund-Verlag, 1979), 175–98.

5. Stern's book was published by California University Press in 1961, while Mosse's *Crisis* was published in 1964 by the Universal Library, New York.

6. Although Schorske was teaching a general course on European intellectual history, we were by then avid readers of his *German Social Democracy, 1905–1917* (Cambridge, Mass.: Harvard University Press, 1955). But see now Schorske's *Fin-de-siècle Vienna: Politics and Culture* (New York: Vintage Books, 1981), and *Thinking with History: Explorations in the Passage to Modernism* (Princeton, N.J.: Princeton University Press, 1998).

7. My guess is that Stern's treatment of Nietzsche's case, especially in the conclusion of his book, made it attractive even to those who were skeptical concerning his methodology.

8. For a collection of the papers that were presented during the inauguration festivities, see Moshe Zimmermann, ed., *Crises of German National Consciousness in the Nineteenth and Twentieth Centuries* [Hebrew] (Jerusalem: Hotsa'at sefarim 'al shem Y. L. Magnes, ha' Universita ha'Ivrit, 1983).

9. The best source on Mosse's development as a historian, including the various issues treated here, is his autobiography, *Confronting History: A Memoir* (Madison: University of Wisconsin Press, 2000).

10. George L. Mosse, "The Image of the Jew in German Popular Culture: Felix Dahn and Gustav Freitag," *Leo Baeck Institute Year Book* 2 (1957): 218–27; Mosse, "Culture, Civilization, and German Anti-Semitism," *Judaism* 7 (1958): 256–67.

11. See George L. Mosse, "Die deutsche Rechte und die Juden," in *Entscheidungsjahr 1932: Zur Judenfrage in der Endphase der Weimarer Republik. Ein Sammelband*, ed., Werner Eugen Mosse and Arnold Paucker (Tübingen: Mohr, 1965), 183–246; Mosse, "The

Influence of the Völkisch Idea on German Jewry," in *Studies of the Leo Baeck Institute*, ed. Max Kreuzberger (New York: Frederik Unger, 1967), 81–115.

12. George L. Mosse, "Left Wing Intellectuals between the Wars," *Journal of Contemporary History* 1 (1966) ; Mosse, "German Socialists and the Jewish Question in the Weimar Republic," *Leo Baeck Institute Year Book* 16 (1971): 123–51. In between see also his *Germans and Jews: The Right, the Left, and the Search for a "Third Force" in Pre-Nazi Germany* (New York: Howard Fertig, 1970).

13. George L. Mosse, "1914: The Coming of the First World War," *Journal of Contemporary History* 1, no. 3 (1966) ; Mosse, *The Jews and the German War Experience, 1914–1918*, Leo Baeck Memorial Lecture 21 (New York: Leo Baeck Institute, 1977).

14. Mosse began to publish on nationalism around 1973. By 1975 he published *The Nationalization of the Masses: Political Symbolism and Mass Movement in Germany from the Napoleonic Wars through the Third Reich* (New York: Howard Fertig), followed by a string of books and articles on this topic. He first touched upon Zionism as early as 1968 in his introduction to a new edition of Max Nordau's *Degeneration*. Later he only rarely treated the topic, but see his collection of essays *Confronting the Nation: Jewish and Western Nationalism* (Hanover, N.H., and London: Published [for] Brandeis University Press by University Press of New England, 1993). His *German Jews beyond Judaism* (Bloomington and Cincinnati: Indiana University Press and Hebrew Union College Press) appeared in 1985.

15. Reinhard Rürup's early essays are reprinted in his *Emanzipation und Antisemitismus: Studien zur "Judenfrage" der bürgerlichen Gesellschaft* (Göttingen, Vandenhoeck und Ruprecht, 1975); and see also Monika Richarz, *Der Eintritt der Juden in die akademischen Berufe: Jüdische Studenten und Akademiker in Deutschland, 1678–1848* (Tübingen: Mohr, 1974); and Stefi Jersch-Wenzel, *Jüdische Bürger und kommunale Selbstverwaltung in preußischen Städten, 1808–1848* (Berlin: de Gruyter, 1967).

16. The main Hebrew publications have been translated, either partially or in full. See Jacob Katz, *Exclusiveness and Tolerance: Studies in Jewish Gentile Relations in Medieval and Modern Times* (London: Oxford University Press, 1961) and *Tradition and Crisis: Jewish Society at the End of the Middle-Ages* (New York: Schocken Books, 1971); Jacob Toury, *Die Politische Orientierung der Juden in Deutschland: Von Jena bis Weimar* (Tübingen: Mohr [Siebeck], 1966), and see also his later books and articles, all within the genre of social history, listed in *Tel Aviver Jahrbuch für Deutsche Geschichte* 20 (1991): 469–85; likewise see Mordechai Eliav, "Jüdische Erziehung im Zeitalter der Aufklärung und der Emanzipation," *Bulletin des Leo Baecks Institute* 11 (1959): 207–15.

17. Jacob Katz, *Jews and Freemasons in Europe, 1723–1939* (Cambridge, Mass.: Harvard University Press, 1970).

18. In addition to Mosse's essays on Nordau and on Scholem, reprinted in *Confronting the Nation*, see his "Deutscher Patriotismus und Jüdischer Nationalismus," in *Deutschlands Weg in die Moderne: Politik, Gesellschaft, und Kultur im 19. Jahrhundert*, ed. Wolfgang Hardtwig & Harm-Hinrich Brandt (Munich: Beck, 1993), 161–69.

19. See George L. Mosse, "Jewish Emancipation: Between 'Bildung' and Respectability," in *The Jewish Response to German Culture: From the Enlightenment to the Second World War*, ed. Jehuda Reinharz and Walter Schatzberg (Hanover, N.H.: Published for Clark University Press by the University Press of New England, 1985), 1–16. For a fuller critique of Mosse's position on these matters, see my "The Ambivalence of Bildung: Jews and Other Germans," in *The German-Jewish Dialogue Reconsidered: A Symposium in Honor of George L. Mosse*, ed. Klaus L. Berghahn (New York: Peter Lang, 1996), 81–98.

20. Steven E. Aschheim, *Brothers and Strangers: The East European Jews in German and German-Jewish Consciousness, 1800–1923* (Madison: University of Wisconsin Press, 1982).

21. I rely here directly on a Hebrew paper by Aschheim, *German Jews beyond Bildung and Liberalism: The Radical Jewish Revival in the Weimar Republic* (Ramat-Gan: Bar-Ilan University, 1995). But also see his *Culture and Catastrophe: German and Jewish Confrontation with National Socialism and Other Crises* (New York: New York University Press, 1996) and now *In Times of Crisis: Essays on European Culture, Germans, and Jews* (Madison: University of Wisconsin Press, 2001).

22. Zvi Bacharach, *The Challenge: Democracy in the Eyes of German Professors and Jewish Intellectuals in the Weimar Republic* [Hebrew] (Jerusalem: Hotsa'at sefarim 'al shem Y. L. Magnes, ha' Universita ha'Ivrit, 2000).

23. See my "The Ambivalence of Bildung."

24. The most comprehensive example is indeed Wehler's *Deutsche Gesellschaftsgeschichte*, 3 vols. to date (Munich: C. H. Beck, 1987–95).

25. See Volkov, *The Rise of Popular Antimodernism.*

26. For a view of the various dimensions of social history in Germany, including both major trends, see the essays in *Sozialgeschichte in Deutschland*, ed. Wolfgang Schieder and Volker Sellin, 4 vols. (Göttingen: Vanderhoeck und Ruprecht, 1986–87), or—more fully—the numerous volumes of *Geschichte und Gesellschaft: Zeitschrift für die historische Sozialwissenschaft* (1975–).

27. *Juden, Bürger, Deutsche: Zur Geschichte von Vielfalt und Differenz*, ed. Andreas Gotzmann, Rainer Liedtke, and Till van Rahden (Tübingen: Mohr, 2001).

28. For their own work and for a full listing of new works on German Jewry, especially those published in Germany, see the bibliography attached to the collection of essays, ibid., 419–32.

29. Knowledge of the relevant languages and interest in internal Jewish affairs was often required among German scholars in the theological and philosophical faculties. It had been, however, rather rare among historians.

30. Monika Richarz, *Jüdisches Leben in Deutschland: Selbstzeugnisee zur Sozialgeschichte*, 3 vols. (Stuttgart: Deutsche Verlags-Anstalt, 1976–82).

31. Marion Kaplan, *The Jewish Feminist Movement in Germany: The Campaigns of the Jüdischer Frauenbund, 1904–1938* (Westport, Conn.: Greenwood Press, 1979) and *The Making of the Jewish Middle Class: Women and German-Jewish Identity in Imperial Germany* (Oxford: Oxford University Press, 1991).

32. Both articles are now to be found—separately—in my two books of essays, published in Germany by Verlag C. H. Beck: *Antisemitismus als kultureller Code* (Munich, 2000) and *Das jüdische Projekt der Moderne* (Munich, 2001). An English version of both is now available in *Aleph: Historical Studies in Science and Judaism* 1 (2000): 215–81.

33. A first version of Scott's article was published in *International Labor and Working-Class History* 31 (1987): 1–13. It is now available in her *Gender and the Politics of History* (New York: Columbia University Press, 1988), 53–67, quote on 55.

34. See Till van Rahden, "Words and Actions: Rethinking the Social History of German Antisemitism, Breslau, 1870–1914," *German History* 18, no. 3 (2000): 413–38, quote on 416.

35. George L. Mosse, "History, Anthropology, and Mass Movements," *American Historical Reviews* 75, no. 2 (1969): 447–52.

36. Ibid., 448.

37. Ibid.

38. It is with pleasure that I use this opportunity to thank, yet once again, my friend and colleague Hagai Hurwitz. See my "Antisemitism as a Cultural Code: Reflections on the History and Historiography of Modern Antisemitism," *Leo Baeck Institute Year Book* 22 (1978): 25–45.

George Mosse and the Israeli Experience

Emmanuel Sivan

The Silver Platter

In 1977, toward the end of his semester in Jerusalem, George Mosse agreed to give an annual public lecture on nationalism. He relished the irony that this endowed series was funded by the South African Jewish friends of an ultra-right-wing Knesset member who had recently died. He mused maliciously about the kind of lesson he should teach them, and finally he chose as his topic "The Commemoration of Fallen Soldiers after the Great War."

As I sat listening to him in the packed lecture hall, I could not avoid feeling that he was actually speaking about us Israelis, even though he had always protested, rather coyly, that he did not know enough about the country to be directly relevant to its concerns. George was speaking of the fallen all being dubbed "heroes," in a country where many a town has a street named after *Ha-Giborim*, the heroic fallen of the 1948 war. He analyzed the Pietà-like icon of the mother country holding in her lap a dying soldier, while its exact analogue, with no Christian connotations to speak of, could be found on many an Israeli monument to the fallen. The altar he described in monuments and in paintings recurs in their Israel counterparts, though there with the particular Old Testament twist referring to the sacrifice of Abraham, which, for the first twenty-five years of Israel's existence, stood (in poetry and plastic arts) as the ultimate symbol of the price in blood paid for independence. He waxed rhapsodic and ironic when discussing the myth of camaraderie in virtually the exact terms of the Israeli notion of *Re'ut*, which had supposedly been born out of the underground activity of the volunteer Palmach troops in the 1940s and later in their crucial role in 1948. The German

239

origin of this allegedly *Echt*-Israeli notion was unsettling (all the more so as the song "Re'ut" has been for the last half century the most popular in the Hebrew hit parades).

And yet there was more to it, I felt. From a certain point on I heard humming in my head bits and pieces of a text. This was so unnerving that when I came home later that early summer evening I went straight to the bookcases, took out a tattered poetry volume, and indeed there it was— "The Silver Platter," a poem by Natan Alterman, a prominent poet, published in a Tel Aviv daily in December 1947, three weeks after the beginning of the war, and which in the following gloomy months was to become spontaneously a part of the burial ritual of many of the fallen soldiers, in addition to the traditional Kaddish. After the end of the war (in March 1949) it was turned into the standard recitation to be read aloud on Memorial Day and learned by heart by all Israeli schoolchildren.

Rereading the familiar text through Mosse's eyes, so to speak, I perceived that what I had taken to be a sort of secular prayer for the dead was actually a piece of national liturgy. It was the nation rather than the fallen that was glorified, sanctified by their sacrifice. Sacralized politics were not the belated product of the post-1967, messianic Right of Gush Emunim, as we, liberal secular Israelis, tended to think. It had its origins in the sacralized politics of the civic culture, the Zionist Left, that Alterman spoke for: the nation, hence the fledgling nation-state, was the historically consecrated, quasi-transcendental embodiment of the Jewish quest for redemption.

I verified my impression on a second and third reading. Obviously shaken by foreboding fears of heavy losses, the poet foresees the day hostilities would end, the guns fall silent, and the smoke peter out slowly over the reddened sky. The nation, draped as a female figure, appears upon the scene:

. . . heart torn, but still breathing,
Ready to accept that unique miracle
. . . preparing herself for the ceremony,
Exalted and horrified . . .
And then a boy and a girl
Come forward
Slowly walking towards her.

Clad in army fatigues,
Heavy boots,

Silently they ascend the path.
They had not had the leisure
To change their dress,
To wash the traces
Of mud, blood and fire.

Tired to the bone . . .
Still smelling of the dew
Of Hebrew youth,
They stop, stand at attention.
And there is no way of knowing
Whether they are dead or alive.

Asks the Nation,
Her eyes flooded
With tears and enchantment:
Who are you?
And the two quietly retort:
We are the silver platter
Upon which was served unto Thee
the State of the Jews.

Thus spake the two,
Falling at her feet
Covered by shadow.
The rest would be told
in the history books.[1]

Several colleagues and students, all veterans of the Yom Kippur war, with whom I talked in the days after the lecture shared this discovery that our cult of the fallen is not a funerary rite but a nationalist ceremony. Some were greatly disturbed by finding that Alterman's poem leaves moot the question of whether the fallen have actually died. Mosse discussed the same characteristic with regard to postwar England and Germany and surmised that it might indicate a sort of pathological bereavement, providing neither resolution nor closure. Was it, they asked themselves, an Israeli expression of denial of death, entertaining the illusion that human losses are immaterial? What kind of nation is ours if it cherishes such delusions?

Let us note that the same theme appears in other war poems, like the famous one by Haim Guri, the laureate of the younger generation, who

wrote about the famous slaughtered platoon of thirty-five students (commemorated in street names all over Israel) that they "would resurrect
as red poppies" on the road to Jerusalem.[2] Resurrection is a Christian
theme; can it be transformed into a Jewish one?

The success of this lecture, which turned into the talk of the day in
those turbulent weeks preceding the Camp David summit of Carter, Sa-
dat, and Begin, explains why its somewhat different written version, published in the *Journal of Contemporary History* in 1979, entered into university syllabi almost instantaneously and was soon translated into
Hebrew.[3] The relevance of Mosse's thinking on this sensitive topic for a
society at war may account for the great success that *Fallen Soldiers* had
with the educated Israeli public when it appeared in translation (1993),
its success exceeding by far that of *Toward the Final Solution*, his only
other work that was translated into Hebrew.

Civil Society

A much deeper relevance can be perceived in the scholarly output inspired by *Fallen Soldiers*, where one can observe the interplay of the factors of space and time.

Space: Israel is a small country with half a dozen research universities; a charismatic teacher could have a ripple effect in a matter of months. Word of
mouth of a new discovery, a new method, travels fast.
Time: The 1980s and 1990s were a moment when major Israeli myths were
coming up for reconsideration; the myth of the fallen, given its centrality in
the national mythology was bound to be a favorite target, especially during
the controversy over the Lebanon war and the first Intifada.

Yet it was not just the topic; it was also the method. Israeli historiography was dominated at the time by political and intellectual history, and
thus it was no wonder that whatever research on the fallen—or for that
matter on other types of commemoration—had been conducted was concerned above all with the role the state (as well as leading intellectuals)
had played therein. Not that this approach had no merit. The political institutions of the pre-1948 Yishuv, and even more so of the state, constituted a major "agent of memory," endeavoring to shape the historical dimension of the Zionist civic culture.

The fallen, being mostly soldiers (though one-fifth of the 1948 war dead were civilians), were quite naturally, following the models of Western Europe, Russia, and Poland, "nationalized" and incorporated into the founding mythology. No effort was spared to this end: public speeches, funerals, and parades, painstaking planning of sites and rites, allocation of material resources.

The culmination of this effort is the way the fallen are integrated into the sacred civic calendar: beginning with Passover (the fourteenth of the Jewish month of Nissan), followed by Holocaust Memorial Day (the twenty-seventh of Nissan, the day the Warsaw Ghetto revolt broke out), the memorial day of the fallen of Israel's wars (the fourth of Iyyar), and on the day after, Independence Day (which, according to Jewish custom, starts at dusk on the day before). The first of the four is the oldest Jewish festival, announcing the exodus from enslavement to freedom, and is steeped in a three-millennium tradition. The other three were decreed by the state as official holidays and represent the path to freedom through the tragedy of destruction and sacrifice of youth. The state is both a guarantor that genocide would not take place again and an event paid for by extra bloodshed. The way the fourth and fifth of Iyyar are joined together makes their linkage all the more "natural." The historical continuum of the national ethos—from extermination to the struggle for independence and its attainment—fits in with the rhythm of Jewish cultural time—from darkness to light—in actual and metaphorical terms (in the creation act in the Book of Genesis, in the way the day of the Jewish calendar goes from sundown to sundown, the rhythm of the week through six profane days to the sanctity of the "glowing" Shabbat).

The same holds true in physical terms for the sacred space, especially if one reads it with the help of the tools Mosse pioneered in his studies of *The Nationalization of the Masses.* This space was invented *in* the western part of Jerusalem in the 1950s (when the Old City was in Jordanian hands) on the highest ridge in that part, Mount Herzl, a sort of pantheon that begins on a western slope with the Yad Vashem memorial complex, set somewhat apart, and moving up to the military cemetery, and thence to the summit, the burial ground of Theodor Herzl and the dignitaries of the state and of the Zionist movement.

Deliberate integration between the spatial elements is evident at the ritualistic level as well. State ceremonies open at different sacralized spots: Holocaust Day at Yad Vashem, Memorial Day at the Western Wall (as from 1968), Independence Day near Herzl's tomb. The Holocaust ceremony can be read semiotically as representing a primordial chaos, the Jewish experience of cosmic extinction, while that of Memorial Day is rigidly constructed as the negation of chaos, superseded by the monolithic uniformity of the nation-state, incarnated by a single image—the fallen, whose sacrifice made it possible. It is the culmination of Jewish history as represented by the Western Wall—a sort of metonymy for the Temple and a metaphor for the Jewish people. Only the families of the war dead (the so-called Family of Bereavement) have access to the ceremony, apart from government ministers and top army brass. (Independence Day ceremony, by contrast, is relaxed, joyful, open to all, decentralized and stressing heterogeneity of origin of the population.)

The two wings of the "sacred complex"—the military cemetery and Yad Vashem—celebrate death and absence, but the state planners have seen to it that different modes of symbolic representation are employed so as to create different types of rituals of death, hence different types of secular sanctity. As the military cemetery contains the bodies of the fallen (*noflim* in Hebrew, but also called *hallalim*, a term that signifies both "killed" and "vacuum" or "absence"), there is no need for an elaborate symbolic representation. There is a simple stone tomb with the name and a uniform text. The tomb is a metonymy, a continuation of the dead soldier it covers. The body inside is linked with the national-state territory. Monuments to the dead in this complex are usually for MIAs (e.g., sailors whose ships or submarines were sunk in battle), hence they need a greater dose of metaphorical representation in order to bring the bodies into presence.

When we move to Yad Vashem, we also deal with dead who were "nationalized," although they had lived and died elsewhere (and were made into Israeli citizens retroactively). But here the dimension of absence is much more prominent and can by no means be moderated by authentic relics (as in stones from the battlefield, damaged military vehicles, or mangled weaponry to be found in some monuments). Therefore the metaphorical representation is greatly magnified, especially in the closed spaces: the Yizkor Tent, the Temple of the Child, the Vale of Exterminated Communities. There is something incongruous about them—physically and symbolically—while the military dimension is smoothly integrated into the scenery.

The state's major agent of indoctrination, the elementary and secondary school system, was effectively marshaled to foster the commemorative effort. As Independence Day was a holiday, commemoration of the war dead was combined in schools with that of independence, with the former clearly overshadowing the latter due to its greater emotional charge.[4]

The state seems to have monopolized the memory of the fallen. Or has it really? Studies by Israeli scholars inspired by Mosse turned toward civil society—where he had dug such rich source material—and found that in the Israeli case the role of society was even more salient than in Europe. This was particularly true in the formative period of the cult of the fallen, when the state moved in a rather slow and cumbersome manner and, on the whole, was quite sensitive to what was on society's mind, acutely aware of the gaping wounds created by war casualties—an awareness due in part to the fact that the political elites had lost an even greater proportion of their sons than the rest of the citizenry.[5]

Even with regard to the state-controlled aspects of the cult, one discovers that civil society had a say. The portentously symbolic date of the fourth of Iyyar was actually chosen (in 1950) at the urgent behest of the organization of bereaved parents, a powerful and vociferous lobby, while the state had originally preferred two other, far-flung dates (the tenth of Teveth, a minor religious fast day, or the twentieth of Tammuz, the anniversary of Herzl's death as well as Army Day). The bereaved parents, incidentally, soon found a way to participate in school commemorations, putting their imprint on them in a manner that many a child would not easily forget. No less palpable was how the uniformity of the military tombs was disrupted in a rather anarchic manner when the families began to embellish them with plants, ceramics, earthenware pots, and so forth, thus endowing the tombs with quasi-individual characteristics. Largely helpless before this tide of initiatives, the authorities did manage for a while to prevent the families from adding personal lines to the official inscriptions. However, as a result of the Supreme Court of Justice in the mid-1990s, they were compelled to allow one personal line to be inscribed at the bottom of the official headstone.

The vitality and creativity of social commemoration can best be detected elsewhere: in the almost one thousand non-official monuments (about one for every nineteen of the fallen) and in the nearly one thousand Yizkor booklets (about a soldier or group of soldiers) published by family, friends, and comrades-in-arms. The breakthrough was achieved in the first decade after the 1948 war, when about one-third of the total number of these monuments and booklets were erected or printed, even as the official initiatives concentrated on Memorial Day. A sort of frenetic activity of relatives, buddies, and small localities produced these artifacts, which adorn the urban and rural landscape and can be found on many a private bookshelf.

Collectivism and Individualism

The tone of commemoration was thus set early on: death is in a way nationalized, but the dead belong also to their families and social circles. They are to be remembered not just as part of a mobilized mass but also as individuals. Even in the heyday of collectivism this individuality was recognized and given its strongest expression in the booklets.

Here is how the febrile commemoration activity is described in one such case—in the summer of 1967, in a gathering during the seven days of mourning:

Words. Commonplace words and unforgettable words. Tearful words. And also unspoken words . . . it is impossible, ineffable . . . we cannot explain. There are things, moments, deeds; yet we are unable to name them. There once was a boy in Jerusalem, we loved him, we still love him, we cannot let go of him. How little can we say about him. We remember moments, laughs, conversations. . . . They talk in confusion. Cutting into each other's words, repeating themselves. Dazed by the dazzling sword of death . . . here, now, what can we say. *Now there will be a Yizkor booklet.* (emphasis added)[6]

It was indeed during the traditional week (or month) of mourning that the decision about the commemorative initiative was often made, as an integral part of the "work of grieving." Yet it took time and persistence for it to be brought to fruition. Funds had to be raised (onerous in the case of many of the monuments, less so for booklets and other artifacts and sites of mourning discussed below). Artists, contributors, editors, gardeners, artisans, and others had to be commissioned. Thousands were involved in the work of remembrance in the wake of any cycle of hostilities. The decision was made spontaneously, and that at the level of basic social cells, yet it follows patterns set by secondary elites (teachers, cultural activists in kibbutzim and trade unions) and diffused by copycat and example. Monuments follow the Western (and Eastern) European model set already in the pre-1948 Yishuv, in line with nationalist models of the pioneering immigrants. Yizkor booklets were a secularized adaptation of a medieval Jewish genre, originally designed to commemorate communities hit by persecutions, expulsions, and pogroms. From 1912 on, the genre was converted in Palestine into a sort of literary memorial for those killed in the violent confrontations with the native inhabitants of the land the Jews claimed as theirs.

Other social modes soon followed suit: funerary gardens or groves (a combination of the romantic vision of death with the Zionist pioneering ideal of cultivating the ancestral soil), endowed scholarships and concerts. From the early 1970s, with the return to religion and the inclusion of more traditional (namely Sephardi) social strata in the commemorative endeavor, one witnesses the rise to prominence of Torah scrolls or other objects of ritual for synagogues, endowed Psalm prayers or study groups of Mishnah and Talmud on the anniversary day of death. All in all, this old Jewish mode of commemoration, now applied to soldiers as a kind of martyrs, is currently third in popularity after booklets and monuments.

The commemorative booklets and monuments have retained their secular, maybe even profane, character. The transcendental has rarely been mentioned in the work of grief carried through them in the first two decades of Israel's existence. And even today God serves as reference only in a small minority of booklets (Yizkor booklets coming from the national-religious sector are quite different and have a unique structure, coming in two parts: the one, traditional—learned discussion of the Scriptures in honor of the dead; the other, modern—memoirs and evaluations that try to evoke him in all his individuality. In recent years videos produced by family and friends began to replace booklets).

Elegy and Sense of Guilt

These two primary modes carry the heavy imprint of the 1948 war that gave them birth, a war of attrition of sixteen months, with a rate of casualties never attained before or after: 1 percent of the population and 8 percent of the major cohorts (nineteen to twenty-one years old) involved. And because commemoration begins with the groups nearest to the fallen, grief overshadows everything. An elegiac, litany-like style expresses loss in words or stone (and from the mid-1960s in scrapes of metal of scorched jeeps or guns on monuments, representing by metonymy the reality of war).

Small wonder one detects very little triumphalism or spirit of vengeance in these artifacts, with some exceptions, mostly in monuments erected in the immediate wake of the Six-Day War, when trophy Arab tanks served, for instance, to commemorate a battle. The war experience that Mosse found to be so central to the Western European phenomenon is, by contrast, only marginally celebrated in the Israeli booklets and monuments and in the fiction and either in these modes or in the fiction and memoirs written by combat soldiers from 1948 on. (Those who did celebrate the war experience were mostly older writers or journalists.) War is justified, say the writers (at least until the early 1980s), but it is hell.

If commemoration, Israeli-style, is part and parcel of an effort to rehabilitate the bereaved, it is a rehabilitation of a special kind: it intends not only to make meaningful the death of a particular individual; it intends also to endow meaning in society at large. It does not seek to divert one's mind from the dear departed; it rather endeavors, by objectifying their individuality, to transfer their memory in wider social circles. A personal, familial memory is integrated into a collective memory.

Whether the process of commemoration by civil society, which today covers three-fifths of the casualties (as against one-third in 1948), really helps rehabilitate the parents, brothers, and sisters who are the most immediately affected is a moot question. The files of the Israel Defense Forces' archive are bulging with letters of complaint, protest, and anguish written by the bereaved. As one of them summed it up in 1949 in a personal letter to Prime Minister Ben Gurion:

Thousands of bereaved families have been thrown into the vale of death. Their world has been darkened all of a sudden. They are on the decline and die out slowly but surely, having drunk from the chalice of poison. They suffer from a chronic illness; bereavement and nothingness. Most of these miserable persons walk back and forth like shadows in their closed rooms, withdrawn from the world, disoriented, unable to contain their tears, full of piercing pain and scorching anger.[7]

Even the writers of these letters tended (until recently) to accept death in battle as justified, but the comfort they gained therefrom was often very paltry indeed. There was justification but no real solace. Still, they did try to overcome their grief to some extent and hoped against hope that a memory artifact would provide a guarantee that the soldier's individual memory would perhaps not be forgotten.

The irony is that most of the individual soldiers had been or would be forgotten, with the exception of several war heroes or poets, or those about whom best-selling Yizkor booklets were written. Yet the contribution of the booklets and monuments to the collective memory of each generation of combat soldiers (1948, 1956, 1967, 1970, 1973, 1982) is substantial.

More important still is the fact that this social representation of war as an activity bound to produce destruction of human lives—a necessary evil, perhaps, but an evil all the same—helped inoculate society against militarism. This inoculation was certainly an unintended consequence of the literature of loss and of the monuments to grief. Who says war says death, death of our boys.

Pietà-like mothers holding their dying sons abound in monuments, wounded soldiers carried by buddies in paintings and drawings. However, one mother who gave a stiff-upper-lip speech at the funeral of her son would ask three years later in the commemoration booklet: "How can I acquiesce with this loss? Why is it that this being, so full of life and animation lies still, his glowing eyes dimmed, his fresh body turning into earth. Why is it that there will be no joy anymore at my home, no worry for the future any more? But why do I say this, I who have educated you to be a patriot, and even fight if it is necessary? Why do I say this, I who at your open grave declared that I am proud you fell for the homeland? Why?"[8]

For it is not just the sense of loss, permeating this whole endeavor, that drives home this lesson, but also the sense of guilt running deeply through it. The guilty feeling expressed by comrades-in-arms is born out of their survival through sheer chance. The sense of guilt is even more poignant in the parent generation. Parents evince a profound sense of responsibility for the soldier's death, an event viewed as the upshot of their having brought up their children to serve the nation. One father notes in the excruciating diary he kept in the first year of mourning that he had recurring nightmares where his son appears—a blackened hole in the front of his head, another in the corner of his mouth—and accuses him: "You have murdered me."[9]

At times parents and teachers and other adults attest to their own anxieties that the Zionist dream is turning sour, and thus commemoration becomes a sort of antidote to social ills that stem from amnesia about the values on which the state was established and for which they believe their sons have fallen. This complex of feelings is summed up in a telling metaphor—the sacrifice of Abraham. It had first been used in 1930 by the poet Yitzhak Lamdan in order to depict the pioneering effort; then it was adopted by a minor poet, Yehoshua Rabinow, to express his grief over the death of his daughter by enemy fire in early 1948.[10] Rabinow's moral authority endowed the metaphor with a powerful echo in other poetry, in funerary speeches, and in the plastic arts, both popular and avant-garde. It would be common currency for the coming two decades, as long as wars were not controversial. For in the biblical story, father as well as son agree to obey the order, and even in the post-biblical Midrash it is the father who has some doubts (which he overcomes). By the time of the war of attrition against Egypt, gnawing doubts as to the war's ends came to be evinced in public and the use of the imagery of the sacrifice of Abraham was called in question. A young dramatic author, Hanoch Levin, included in a political cabaret show a number that created scandal when performed in the spring of 1970. In it a fallen soldier talks from the grave to his father:

Dear Dad, when you stand at my grave,
Old, weary, and very much childless
And you'll see how they put my body into the earth
And you stand above me, Dad

Don't stand so proud
Don't raise your head, Dad . . .

And don't say you made such a sacrifice
For he who was sacrificed was I,
And don't use high words anymore
For I already lie very low, Dad.

Dear Dad, when you stand at my grave,
Old, weary, and very much childless
And you see how they put my body into the ground
Ask for my forgiveness, Dad.[11]

After the Yom Kippur War, one finds Levin's sarcastic poem in Yizkor booklets alongside more canonical nationalist poems as well as translated pacifist poems (such as Jacques Prevert's "Oh, Barbara, quelle connerie la guerre"). The use of the imagery of the sacrifice of Abraham would soon enter a steep decline, precipitated by the Lebanon war and the first Intifada. In the 1980s and 1990s it would survive only in commemoration artifacts produced by the national-religious sector, especially in circles close to Gush Emunim, where the traditional Zionist interpretation still holds: namely, that ours—the believers—is not to reason why, neither with regard to God nor to the country.[12]

Despite this cleavage, a community of memory is maintained. For both national-religious Israelis (who are Modern Orthodox) and secular Israelis employ the same modes, especially the Yizkor booklet, with its distinctly individualistic bent, as evident in the effort to evoke the fallen friend or son in all his uniqueness. And even some among the secularists donate scrolls of the Law to Reform or Conservative synagogues.

Inclusion and Exclusion

As George Mosse taught us, however, wherever there is community there is also exclusion, for boundaries are crucial. Who was excluded, then, from this community of memory? Obviously, Arabs and Haredim (ultra-Orthodox Jews) who do not serve in the army. Tensions come to a head in this context on Memorial Day, when the media as well as common people react sharply to the refusal of many Haredim to stand at attention during the two minutes of silence following the 11 A.M. siren (less in disrespect to the dead than out of refusal to adopt a non-Jewish custom).

But in Israel's early days the modes of popular commemoration and the preferred status of booklets tended to exclude. People who did not know Hebrew–that is, new immigrants–were excluded. And those among the new immigrants who were Holocaust survivors were often doubly excluded because they laced families, who were the prime movers of commemoration. These immigrants, as well as immigrants from Islamic lands, were not yet integrated into the networks of voluntary associations, neighborhoods, and so forth that raised the funds and provided the organizational basis for much of the commemoration endeavor. It was thus the upper half of the Israeli population—veteran, more articulate, better organized at the grass-roots level—that was included in the commemoration. The others—newcomers, with lesser educational attainment, lower commitment to national history—tended to be forgotten, excluded.

In the 1970s this state of affairs started to change, as the immigrants of the 1950s and their offspring gained access to secondary education and were integrated into social networks, be it older ones or those they established on their own. We have seen above how this resulted in the rise of the synagogue-related memory artifacts, for between the secularists (52 percent of the Jewish population) and the religious (15 percent) there is a vast group of traditionalists, mostly originating from Islamic countries.

Moreover, one finds the second generation of immigrants taking over sites of memory of earlier, veteran generations that had fallen into desuetude, thus giving them a new lease on life. The famous Roaring Lion monument to the victims of the battle of Tel-Hai (1920), neglected by the grandchildren of the founding fathers, was adopted by the neighboring town of Kiryat Shemona, populated mostly by North African immigrants, who see to its upkeep and hold the annual ceremonies. Other localities adopted 1948 sites that the dwindling generation of bereaved parents could no longer care for properly. These small towns are proud to foster local patriotism and endow it with a genealogy linked to the national martyrology.

Another glaring exclusion relates to civilians killed in wars (1,300 of the 5,900 dead of the 1948 hostilities). Given the activism of the Zionist ethos, the Yishuv tended to consider those killed by Arabs not in the active defense of Jewish settlements but accidentally—such as by shots from an ambush or on the roads, let alone in massacres during riots—as a lesser, passive breed of victims, an attitude pursued under the state of Israel toward the overwhelming majority of those killed not in uniform. Not only had they no right to official commemoration, but their families had no right to pensions. These families had so deeply internalized the hegemonic ethos that they did not fight for material compensation, and rarely did they initiate a commemorative effort of their own. It was as though they thought that because of their lesser, passive stature, their loved ones did not really belong among the fallen. (Civilians could not, of course, be buried in military cemeteries, and therefore they were never commemorated there in the local ceremonies held on the morning of Memorial Day.)

It was only in the late 1970s, with the rise of terrorism, that families of terror victims organized a powerful lobby to fight for their rights. Within a few years they succeeded in wrenching pensions for those killed by terror (though smaller than soldiers' pensions and paid by the Social Security Authority and not by the Ministry of Defense). A telling indicator of their sense of symbolic entitlement is that the families and friends of the victims began to erect memorials at the places where they had been killed. Yet a good many of these monuments (such as the one at the country club intersection north of Tel Aviv) depict the civilians as helpless prey.

Concurrently, the families fought hard so that their dead would be commemorated in the central official ceremony on Memorial Day. "Terror is part and parcel of the Arabs' continuing war against Israel" was the claim. This demand was vehemently opposed by the families of the fallen soldiers in the name of the activist, supposedly non-Diasporic ethos. It was only in 2000 that a compromise was found between the two lobbies: "The victims of acts of hostility," as the civilians are officially called, are to be commemorated on Memorial Day, but in a separate ceremony on Mount Herzl, held two hours earlier than the major one consecrated to the soldiers. The civilians are, therefore, part of the fallen, but at the same time they are not. It was, in a way, a typical Israeli compromise, much like the one set in the military cemeteries: uniform rows of uniform tombs, with tombstones surrounded by personalized, rather chaotic shrubbery, alternating with the neglected tombstones of those without families to care for them.

As I was writing the first draft of this essay in early 2001, the two major Israeli television channels broadcast daily the electoral ads of the candidates for the post of prime minister. The fallen figured there quite saliently. "Beware of my opponent, who dragged us into the Lebanese quagmire and cost us more than a thousand dead"; "Only I can deter the enemy, ensure peace and security, and put an end to the shedding of our blood." Each of these former generals swore his commitment to his former soldiers and especially to those comrades who died at his side on the battlefields.

That is the picture of a country where warfare is no longer consensual. Ever since the 1982 invasion of Lebanon it is a matter of bitter controversy. The Family of Bereavement, once the epitome of national unity, takes an active part in the internecine war. The reserve combat officer who launched in 1978 the Peace Now movement spoke of the legacy transmitted to them by their buddies who were killed in the Yom Kippur war. The "Four Mothers" movement for the unilateral evacuation of Lebanon (1996–2000) not only used the moral stature of mothers of draftee soldiers but also had this implicit connotation: we want to prevent our sons from joining the fallen. In the opposing camp, families of the "Association of Victims of Terror" demonstrated in favor of putting an end to the "mirage" of the Oslo Peace Agreements; settlers held sit-ins in favor of an iron-hand policy, carrying mock coffins for those killed by the second Intifada.

The myth of the fallen, more criticized and manipulated than ever, is alive and kicking. It is the kind of construct of the past that is acutely relevant, the very type of past that George Mosse had been obsessed with all through his trailblazing studies of the twentieth century.

Notes

1. Natan Alterman, *The Seventh Column* [Hebrew] (Tel Aviv: Ha-Kibbutz Ha-Meuhad, 1950), 306–7. Reprinted by permission.

2. Haim Guri, *Flowers of Fire* [Hebrew] (Tel Aviv: Sifriyat Poalim, 1949), 78.

3. In *Zemanim* (Tel Aviv: Tel Aviv University, 1983).

4. Avner Ben Amos and Ilana Beth-El, "Memorial Day and Holocaust Day in Israeli Schools," *Israel Studies* 4, no. 1 (1999): 284–358.

5. Esther Lewinger, *Monuments for the Fallen in Israel* [Hebrew] (Tel Aviv: Ha-Kibbutz Ha-Meuhad, 1993); O. Almog, *The Sabra—A Profile* [Hebrew] (Tel Aviv: Am Oved, 1997); I. Shamir, *Commemoration and Memory* [Hebrew] (Tel Aviv: Am Oved, 1996); E. Sivan, "The 1948 Generation" [Hebrew] (Tel Aviv: Ma'arachot, 1991); Ruth Malkinson, Samson Rubin, and Eliezer Witztum, eds., *Loss and Bereavement in Israeli Society* (Jerusalem: Kana, 1993).

6. Amos Oz, *Yizkor—Yigal Wilk* (Jerusalem: published by author, 1968), 4–5.

7. Amiram Harlap, letter of 6 February 1949, Israeli Defence Forces Archive, file 388/580/56.

8. Micha Fisher, *Alim Le-Zichro* (Tel Aviv: published by author, 1952), 52.

9. Moshe Shamir, *Not Far from the Tree* [Hebrew] (Tel Aviv: Devir, 1982).

10. Yehoshua Rabinow, *Before the Mount of Sacrifice* (Tel Aviv: Ha-Kibbutz Ha-Meuhad, 1994).

11. Hanoch Levin, *The Bird Doesn't Care* [Hebrew] (Tel Aviv: Zemora-Bitan, 1987), 92. Reprinted by permission.

12. Rabbi Itzhak Ba-Gad, in *Yizkor* [Hebrew] (Nehalim Yeshiva: n.p, 1974).

A Bibliography of
George L. Mosse's Work

Prepared by John Tortorice

1946

1. *The Idea of Sovereignty in England, from Sir Thomas Smith to Sir Edward Coke.* Thesis, Harvard University, 1946.
2. "Thomas Hobbes: Jurisprudence at the Cross-Roads." *University of Toronto Quarterly* 15, no. 4 (1946): 346–55.

1947

3. In collaboration with William H. Seiler. *Outline and Sources for a History of Western Civilization: Europe and the United States from the Middle Ages to the Congress of Vienna.* Dubuque, Iowa: William C. Brown, 1947.
4. "The Anti-League: 1844–1846." *Economic History Review* 17, no. 2 (1947): 134–42.
5. "Change and Continuity in the Tudor Constitution." *Speculum* 22, no. 1 (1947): 18–28.
6. In collaboration with David Hecht. "Liturgical Uniformity and Absolutism in the Sixteenth Century." *Anglican Theological Review* 29, no. 3 (1947): 158–66.

1948

7. "The Influence of Jean Bodin's 'Republic' on English Political Thought." *Medievalia et Humanistica* 5 (1948): 73–83.

1949

8. "Freshman History: Reality or Metaphysics?" *Social Studies* 40, no. 3 (1949): 99–103.

9. In collaboration with Everett W. Hall and John L. McGalliard. "The Humanities at the State University of Iowa." In *The Humanities in General Education*, ed. Earl J. McGrath, 106–36. Dubuque, Iowa: William C. Brown, 1949.

1950

10. *The Struggle for Sovereignty in England, from the Reign of Queen Elizabeth to the Petition of Right.* East Lansing: Michigan State College Press, 1950.
11. *The Struggle for Sovereignty in England, from the Reign of Queen Elizabeth to the Petition of Right.* Oxford: Basil Blackwell, 1950. [see no. 10]

1951

12. In collaboration with Philip A. M. Taylor. *Outline and Sources for a History of Western Civilization: Europe and the United States from the Congress of Vienna to the Present Time.* Dubuque, Iowa: William C. Brown, 1951. [see no. 3]

1952

13. "Die amerikanische Geschichtsschreibung: Ein überblick." *Die Welt als Geschichte* 12 (1952): 264–73.
14. "Puritanism and Reason of State in Old and New England." *William and Mary Quarterly* 3rd ser., 9, no. 1 (1952): 67–80.
15. "Sir John Fortescue and the Problem of Papal Power." *Medievalia et Humanistica* 7 (1952): 89–94.
16. "Change and Continuity in the Tudor Constitution." In *The Making of English History*, ed. Robert Livingston Schuyler and Herman Ausubel, 187–95. New York: Holt, Rinehart & Winston, 1952. [see no. 5]

1953

17. *The Reformation.* New York: Henry Holt, 1953.

1954

18. "The Assimilation of Machiavelli in English Thought: The Casuistry of William Perkins and William Ames." *Huntington Library Quarterly* 17, no. 4 (1954): 315–26.
19. "Puritan Political Thought and the 'Cases of Conscience.'" *Church History* 23, no. 2 (1954): 109–18.

1955

20. "Christian Statesman." *History of Ideas Newsletter* 1, no. 2 (1955): 2–4.
21. "Puritanism." In *The New Schaff-Herzog Encyclopedia of Religious Knowledge*, 931–33. Grand Rapids, Mich.: Baker Book House, 1955.

1956

22. "A Challenge to Phi Eta Sigma." *Forum of Phi Eta Sigma,* January 1956, 22–23.
23. "The Importance of Jacques Saurin in the History of Casuistry and the Enlightenment." *Church History* 25, no. 3 (1956): 195–210.

1957

24. *Calvinism: Authoritarian or Democratic?* New York: Rinehart, 1957.
25. *The Holy Pretence: A Study in Christianity and Reason of State from William Perkins to John Winthrop.* Oxford: Basil Blackwell, 1957.
26. "The Image of the Jew in German Popular Culture: Felix Dahn and Gustav Freytag." In *Leo Baeck Institute Year Book 2,* 218–27. London: Secker & Warburg, 1957.
27. "The Pragmatism of Freshman History." *Social Studies* 48, no. 8 (1957): 289–92.
28. *Europe in Review: Readings and Sources since 1500.* Ed. with introductions by George L. Mosse et al. Chicago: Rand McNally, 1957.

1958

29. "Culture, Civilization, and German Anti-Semitism." *Judaism* 7, no. 3 (1958): 256–67.

1959

30. "The Hope for Germany." *Progressive* 23, no. 5 (1959): 18–21.

1960

31. "Puritan Radicalism and the Enlightenment." *Church History* 29, no. 4 (1960): 424–39.
32. *The Reformation.* 2nd ed. New York: Henry Holt, 1960. [see no. 17]

1961

33. *The Culture of Western Europe: The Nineteenth and Twentieth Centuries: An Introduction.* Chicago: Rand McNally, 1961.

34. "The Mystical Origins of National Socialism." *Journal of the History of Ideas* 23, no. 1 (1961): 81–96.

35. "Culture, Civilization, and German Anti-Semitism." *Davar* (1961): 47–64. [see no. 29]

1962

36. "'German Kultur of European Spirits': Old Ideology in New Garb." *Wiener Library Bulletin* 16, no. 3 (1962): 48.

37. "Le origini mistiche del nazionalsocialismo." Trans. Alessandro Serpieri. *Il Ponte* 18, no. 1 (1962): 30–40. [see no. 34]

1963

38. *The Culture of Western Europe: The Nineteenth and Twentieth Centuries: An Introduction.* London: John Murray, 1963. [see no. 33]

39. *The Reformation.* 3rd rev. ed. New York: Holt, Rinehart and Winston, 1963. [see no. 17]

1964

40. *The Crisis of German Ideology: Intellectual Origins of the Third Reich.* New York: Grosset & Dunlap, 1964.

41. "The Deputy's Dilemma." *Progressive* 28, no. 6 (1964): 38–41.

42. "Puritanism Reconsidered." *Archiv für Reformationsgeschichte* 55, no. 1 (1964): 37–47.

43. "Romantic and Irrational: Pitfalls of a 'Non-Political' Youth Movement." *Wiener Library Bulletin* 18, no. 3 (1964): 37.

44. *The Intellectual Foundations of National Socialism.* Seminar held at Stanford University, European Studies Seminar Center, autumn 1963, conducted by George Mosse. Stanford, Calif.: N.p., 1964.

45. *Europe in Review: Readings and Sources since 1500.* Ed. with introductions by George L. Mosse et al. Rev. ed. Chicago: Rand McNally, 1964. [see no. 28].

46. "Puritan Radicalism and the Enlightenment." In *The Role of Religion in Modern European History,* ed. Sidney Alexander Burell, 65–77. New York: Macmillan, 1964. [see no. 31]

1965

47. "The Corporate State and the Conservative Revolution in Weimar Germany." In *Gouvernés et gouvernants,* vol. 5, *Période contemporaine,* 213–42. Bruxelles: Editions de la Librairie Encyclopédique, 1965.

48. "Die deutsche Rechte und die Juden." In *Entscheidungsjahr 1932: Zur Judenfrage in der Endphase der Weimarer Republik. Ein Sammel-*

band, ed. Werner Eugen Mosse and Mitwirkung von Arnold Paucker, 183–246. Tübingen: Mohr, 1965.

1966

49. "Comments." In *Seminar on Preservation and Restoration, Williamsburg (Va.), 1963: Historic Preservation Today,* 38–42, 73–77. Charlottesville: Distributed by University Press of Virginia, 1966.
50. "E. Nolte on *Three Faces of Fascism.*" *Journal of the History of Ideas* 27, no. 4 (1966): 621–25.
51. "The Genesis of Fascism." In "International Fascism 1920–1945." *Journal of Contemporary History* 1, no. 1 (1966): 14–26.
52. "International Fascism, 1920–1945." [Editors: Walter Laqueur, George L. Mosse; Assistant Editors: Jane Degras, Ernest Hearst]. London: Weidenfeld & Nicolson, 1966 (*Journal of Contemporary History* 1, no. 1). [see no. 50]
53. "Left Wing Intellectuals between the Wars." [Ed. Walter Laqueur and George L. Mosse]. London: Weidenfeld & Nicolson, 1966 (*Journal of Contemporary History* 1, no. 2).
54. *Nazi Culture: Intellectual, Cultural, and Social Life in the Third Reich.* Ed. George L. Mosse, trans. Salvatore Attanasio et al. New York: Grosset & Dunlap, 1966.
55. "1914." [Editors: Walter Laqueur, George L. Mosse; Assistant Editors: Jane Degras, Ernest Hearst]. London: Weidenfeld & Nicolson, 1966 (*Journal of Contemporary History* 1, no. 3).
56. "Socialism and War. The Dismissal of Jellicoe. Munich: The Czech Dilemma. Russians in Germany, 1900–1914." [Editors: Walter Laqueur, George L. Mosse; Assistant Editors: Jane Degras, Ernest Hearst]. London: Weidenfeld & Nicolson, 1966 (*Journal of Contemporary History* 1, no. 4).
57. *The Crisis of German Ideology: Intellectual Origins of the Third Reich.* London: Weidenfeld & Nicolson, 1966. [see no. 40]
58. "International Fascism, 1920–1945." Ed. Walter Laqueur and George L. Mosse. New York: Harper & Row, 1966 (*Journal of Contemporary History* 1. Harper Torchbooks, The Academy Library). [see no. 52]
59. *Internationaler Faschismus, 1920–1945.* Ed. Walter Laqueur and George L. Mosse. Munich: Nymphenburger Verlagshandlung, 1966. [see no. 52]
60. "The Left Wing Intellectuals between the Wars, 1919–1939." Ed. Walter Laqueur and George L. Mosse. New York: Harper & Row, 1966 (*Journal of Contemporary History* 2. Harper Torchbooks, The Academy Library). [see no. 53]

61. *Nazi Culture: Intellectual, Cultural, and Social Life in the Third Reich.* Ed. George L. Mosse, trans. Salvatore Attanasio et al. London: W. H. Allen, 1966. [see no. 54]

62. "1914: The Coming of the First World War." Ed. Walter Laqueur and George L. Mosse. New York: Harper & Row, 1966 (*Journal of Contemporary History* 3. Harper Torchbooks, The Academy Library). [see no. 55]

1967

63. "Concluding Remarks." In "Education and Social Structure." *Journal of Contemporary History* 2, no. 3 (1967): 217–20.

64. "The Influence of the Völkisch Idea on German Jewry." In *Studies of the Leo Baeck Institute*, ed. Max Kreutzberger, 81–115. New York: Frederik Unger, 1967.

65. "Education and Social Structure." [Editors: Walter Laqueur, George L. Mosse; Assistant Editors: Jane Degras, Ernest Hearst]. London: Weidenfeld & Nicolson, 1967 (*Journal of Contemporary History* 2, no. 3).

66. "History Today in USA, Britain, France, Italy, Germany, Poland, India, Czechoslovakia, Spain, Holland, Sweden." [Editors: Walter Laqueur, George L. Mosse; Assistant Editors: Jane Degras, Ernest Hearst]. London: Weidenfeld & Nicolson, 1967 (*Journal of Contemporary History* 2, no. 1).

67. "Literature and Society." [Editors: Walter Laqueur, George L. Mosse; Assistant Editors: Jane Degras, Ernest Hearst]. London: Weidenfeld & Nicolson, 1967 (*Journal of Contemporary History* 2, no. 2).

68. "Free Speech and the University." *Madison Select*, May 1967, 10.

69. "Religion and Reason of State." In *Interpreting European History*, ed. Brison D. Gooch, 166–71. Homewood, Ill.: Dorsey Press, 1967.

70. "Education and Social Structure in Twentieth Century." Ed. Walter Laqueur and George L. Mosse. New York: Harper & Row, 1967 (*Journal of Contemporary History* 6. Harper Torchbooks, The Academy Library). [see no. 65]

71. "Fascismo internazionale 1920–1945." *Dialoghi del XX*, April 1967, 224. [see no. 52]

72. *Kriegsausbruch 1914,* "Deutsche Buchausgabe," des *Journal of Contemporary History.* Ed. Walter Laqueur and George L. Mosse. Munich: Nymphenburger Verlagshandlung, 1967. [see no. 55]

73. "Literature and Politics in the Twentieth Century." Ed. Walter Laqueur and George L. Mosse. New York: Harper & Row, 1967 (*Journal of Contemporary History* 5. Harper Torchbooks, The Academy Library). [see no. 67]

74. "The New History: Trends in Historical Research and Writing since World War II." Ed. Walter Laqueur and George L. Mosse. New York:

Harper & Row, 1967 (*Journal of Contemporary History* 4. Harper Torchbooks, The Academy Library). [see no. 66]

1968

75. In collaboration with Helmut Georg Koenigsberger. *Europe in the Sixteenth Century.* London: Longmans, 1968.

76. "Fascism and the Intellectuals." In *The Nature of Fascism: Proceedings of a Conference Held by the Reading University Graduate School of Contemporary European Studies,* ed. Stuart J. Woolf, 205–26. London: Weidenfeld & Nicolson, 1968.

77. "Houston Stewart Chamberlain." Introduction to Houston Stewart Chamberlain, *Foundations of the Nineteenth Century.* Translated from the German by John Lees. New York: Howard Fertig, 1968.

78. "Max Nordau and His 'Degeneration.'" Introduction to Max Nordau, *Degeneration,* xi–xxxiv. New York: Howard Fertig, 1968.

79. "The Middle East." [Editors: Walter Laqueur, George L. Mosse; Assistant Editors: Jane Degras, Ernest Hearst]. London: Weidenfeld & Nicolson, 1968 (*Journal of Contemporary History* 3, no. 3).

80. "Reappraisals: A New Look at History. The Social Sciences and History." [Editors: Walter Laqueur, George L. Mosse; Assistant Editors: Jane Degras, Ernest Hearst]. London: Weidenfeld & Nicolson, 1968 (*Journal of Contemporary History* 3, no. 2).

81. In collaboration with Helmut Georg Koenigsberger. *Europe in the Sixteenth Century.* New York: Holt, Rinehart and Winston, 1968. [see no. 75]

82. "The Genesis of Fascism." In *Fascism: An Anthology,* ed. Nathanael Greene, 3–14. New York: Crowell, 1968. [see no. 51]

83. *The Holy Pretence: A Study in Christianity and Reason of State from William Perkins to John Winthrop.* New York: Howard Fertig, 1968. [see no. 25]

84. *Nazi Culture: Intellectual, Cultural, and Social Life in the Third Reich.* Ed. George L. Mosse, trans. Salvatore Attanasio et al. New York: Grosset & Dunlap, 1968. [see no. 54]

85. *Le origini culturali del Terzo Reich.* Trans. Francesco Saba Sardi. Milan: Il Saggiatore, 1968. [see no. 40]

86. *The Struggle for Sovereignty in England, from the Reign of Queen Elizabeth to the Petition of Right.* New York: Octagon Books, 1968. [see no. 10]

1969

87. "History, Anthropology, and Mass Movements." *American Historical Review* 75, no. 2 (1969): 447–52.

88. "The Great Depression." [Editors: Walter Laqueur, George L. Mosse; Assistant Editors: Jane Degras, Ernest Hearst]. London: Weidenfeld & Nicolson, 1969 (*Journal of Contemporary History* 4, no. 4).

89. "Urbanism: The City in History." [Editors: Walter Laqueur, George L. Mosse; Assistant Editors: Jane Degras, Ernest Hearst]. London: Weidenfeld & Nicolson, 1969 (*Journal of Contemporary History* 4, no. 3).

90. From "The Culture of Western Europe." In *A Century for Debate, 1789–1914: Problems in the Interpretation of European History*, ed. Peter N. Stearns, 35–39, 505–11. New York: Dodd, Mead, 1969.

91. In collaboration with Helmut Georg Koenigsberger. *L'Europa del Cinquecento*. Trans. Maria Teresa Grendi. Bari: Laterza, 1969. [see no. 75]

92. "Fascism and the Intellectuals." In *The Nature of Fascism*, ed. Stuart J. Woolf, 205–26. 1st American ed. New York: Random House, 1969. [see no. 76]

93. *Linksintellektuelle zwischen den beiden Weltkriegen.* Ed. Walter Laqueur and George L. Mosse. Munich: Nymphenburger Verlagshandlung, 1969. [see no. 53]

1970

94. *Germans and Jews: The Right, the Left, and the Search for a "Third Force" in Pre-Nazi Germany.* New York: Howard Fertig, 1970.

95. "Changes in Religious Thought." In *The New Cambridge Modern History*, vol. 4, *The Decline of Spain and the Thirty Years War, 1609–48/59*, ed. J. P. Cooper, 169–201. Cambridge: Cambridge University Press, 1970.

96. "The Heritage of Socialist Humanism." In "The Legacy of German Refugee Intellectuals." *Salmagundi* (Fall 1969–Winter 1970): 123–39.

97. "The Rightist Reaction: French Theorists of Law and Order." *Times Literary Supplement*, 14 May 1970, 525–27.

98. "Generations in Conflict." [Editors: Walter Laqueur, George L. Mosse; Assistant Editors: Jane Degras, Ernest Hearst]. London: Weidenfeld & Nicolson, 1970 (*Journal of Contemporary History* 5, no. 1).

99. In collaboration with Helmut Georg Koenigsberger. *L'Europe au XVI siècle*. Trans. S. Chassagne. Paris: Sirey, 1970. [see no. 75]

100. "The Genesis of Fascism." In *Manners, Morals, Movements: The History of European Man, 1500 to the Present*, ed. Werner Braatz et al., 300–302. Berkeley, Calif.: McCutchan, 1970. [see no. 51]

101. *Kriegsausbruch 1914.* Ed. Walter Laqueur and George L. Mosse. Munich: Nymphenburger Verlagshandlung, 1970. [see no. 72]

1971

102. "Die Linke in ihrer Stellung zum Nationalsozialismus—das Jüdische Problem." In *Zur Geschichte der Juden in Deutschland im 19. und 20. Jahrhundert*, 94–100. Jerusalem: Jerusalem Academic Press, 1971.

103. "Caesarism, Circuses, and Monuments." *Journal of Contemporary History* 6, no. 2 (1971): 167–82.

104. "German Socialists and the Jewish Question in the Weimar Republic." In *Leo Baeck Institute Year Book 16*, 123–51. London: Secker & Warburg, 1971.

105. In collaboration with Helmut Georg Koenigsberger. *Europe in the Sixteenth Century.* London: Longmans, 1971. [see no. 75]

106. *Germans and Jews: The Right, the Left, and the Search for a "Third Force" in Pre-Nazi Germany.* New York: Grosset & Dunlap, 1971. [see no. 94]

107. *Germans and Jews: The Right, the Left, and the Search for a "Third Force" in Pre-Nazi Germany.* London: Orbach & Chambers, 1971. [see no. 94]

108. "Mutamenti nel pensiero religioso." In *Storia del mondo moderno,* vol. 4, *La decadenza della Spagna e la Guerra dei trent'anni (1610–1648/59),* ed. J. P. Cooper, 190–228. Milan: Garzanti, 1971. [see no. 95]

109. "I socialisti tedeschi e la questione ebraica durante la repubblica di Weimar." *Storia contemporanea* 2, no. 1 (1971): 17–52. [see no. 104]

110. "The Youth Movement." In *Forces of Order and Movement in Europe since 1815,* ed. Robert J. Scally, 50–70. Boston: Houghton Mifflin, 1971.

1972

111. "Literature and Society in Germany." In *Literature and Western Civilization,* ed. David Daiches and Anthony Thorlby, 2:267–99. London: Aldus Books, 1972.

112. "The French Right and the Working Classes: Les Jaunes." *Journal of Contemporary History* 7, nos. 3–4 (1972): 185–208.

113. "The Heritage of Socialist Humanism." In *The Legacy of German Refugee Intellectuals,* ed. Robert Boyers, 123–39. New York: Schocken, 1972. [see no. 96]

114. *Kryzys ideologii niemieckiej: Rodowód intelektualny Trzeciej Rzeszy.* Trans. Tadeusz Evert. Warszawa: Czytelnik, 1972. [see no. 40]

1973

115. "Mass Politics and the Political Liturgy of Nationalism." In *National-ism: The Nature and Evolution of an Idea,* ed. Eugene Kamenka, 38–54. Canberra: Australian National University Press, 1973.

116. "Comment." In "Hitler's Concept of 'Lebensraum': The Psychological Basis." *History of Childhood Quarterly: The Journal of Psychohistory* 1, no. 2 (1973): 230–32.

117. "Left Wing Intellectuals and the Jewish Problem in the 'Thirties' and in the 'Sixties.'" *Dispersion and Unity* 17–18 (1973): 106–16.

118. "The Marquis de Morés." *North Dakota Quarterly* 73 (Winter 1973): 44–47.

119. "The Poet and the Exercise of Political Power: Gabriele D'Annunzio." *Yearbook of Comparative and General Literature* 22 (1973): 32–41.

120. *La cultura Nazi: La vida intelectual, cultural y social en el Tercer Reich.* Trans. J. C. García Borrón and Enrique de Obregón. Barcelona: Grijalbo, 1973. [see no. 54]

121. "The Genesis of Fascism." In *Western Civilization: Recent Interpre-tations from 1715 to the Present,* ed. C. Stewart Doty, 501–11. New York: Thomas Crowell II, 1973. [see no. 51]

122. "The Genesis of Fascism." In *An Age of Controversy: Discussion Problems in Twentieth-Century European History,* ed. Gordon Wright and Arthur Mejia (alternate edition), 168–77. New York: Dodd, Mead, 1973. [see no. 51]

1974

123. "Was sie wirklich lasen: Marlitt, Ganghofer, May." In *Popularität und Trivialität. 4. Wisconsin Workshop,* ed. Reinhold Grimm and Jost Hermand, 101–20. Frankfurt: Athenäum-Verlag, 1974.

124. "Tod, Zeit, und Geschichte: Die völkische Utopie der Überwindung." In *Deutsches utopisches Denken im 20. Jahrhundert,* ed. Reinhold Grimm and Jost Hermand, 50–69. Stuttgart: Kohlhammer, 1974.

125. Joshua A. Fishman, George L. Mosse, and Laurene J. Silberstein, dis-cussants. "Contemporary Jewish Civilization on the American Cam-pus: Research and Teaching." *American Jewish Historical Quarterly* 63, no. 4 (1974): 369–78.

126. *Historians in Politics.* Ed. Walter Laqueur and George L. Mosse. London: Sage, 1974.

127. *Jews and Non-Jews in Eastern Europe 1918–1945.* Ed. Bela Vago and George L. Mosse. New York: John Wiley, 1974.

128. *The Culture of Western Europe: The Nineteenth and Twentieth*

Centuries. 2nd ed. Chicago: Rand McNally, 1974. [see no. 33]

129. In collaboration with Helmut Georg Koenigsberger. *Europa en el siglo XVI.* Madrid: Aguilar, 1974. [see no. 75]

130. In collaboration with Helmut Georg Koenigsberger. *L'Europa del Cinquecento.* Trans. Maria Teresa Grendi. Rome-Bari: Laterza, 1974. [see no. 75]

1975

131. *The Nationalization of the Masses: Political Symbolism and Mass Movements in Germany from the Napoleonic Wars through the Third Reich.* New York: Howard Fertig, 1975.

132. *Police Forces in History.* Ed. George L. Mosse. London: Sage, 1975.

133. "On Liars and Lying." *Salmagundi* (Spring 1975): 95–111.

134. *La nazionalizzazione delle masse: Simbolismo politico e movimenti di massa in Germania dalle guerre napoleoniche al Terzo Reich.* Intro. Renzo De Felice, trans. Livia De Felice. Bologna: Il Mulino, 1975. [see no. 131]

1976

135. "Die NS-Kampfbühne." In *Geschichte im Gegenwartsdrama,* ed. Reinhold Grimm and Jost Hermand, 24–36. Stuttgart: Kohlhammer, 1976.

136. Comment on "Hitler as the Bound Delegate of His Mother" by Helm Stierlin. *History of Childhood Quarterly: The Journal of Psychohistory* 3, no. 4 (1976): 505–7.

137. "Albert Speer's Hitler, Spandau: The Secret Diaries." *Quadrant* 20, no. 10 (1976): 53–55.

138. "Mass Politics and the Political Liturgy of Nationalism." In *Nationalism: The Nature and Evolution of an Idea,* ed. Eugene Kamenka, 38–54. New York: St. Martin's Press, 1976. [see no. 115]

139. "Mass Politics and the Political Liturgy of Nationalism." In *Nationalism: The Nature and Evolution of an Idea,* ed. Eugene Kamenka, 38–54. London: Edward Arnold, 1976. [see no. 115]

140. *Die Nationalisierung der Massen: Die politische Symbolik und Massenbewegung in Deutschland von den Napoleonischen Kriegen bis zum Dritten Reich.* Frankfurt: Ullstein, 1976. [see no. 131]

141. *La nazionalizzazione delle masse: Simbolismo politico e movimenti di massa in Germania dalle guerre napoleoniche al Terzo Reich.* Intro. Renzo De Felice, trans. Livia De Felice. Bologna: Il Mulino, 1976. [see no. 131]

1977

142. *Intervista sul nazismo.* Ed. Michael A. Ledeen, trans. Giovanni Ferrara. Rome-Bari: Laterza, 1977.
143. *The Jews and the German War Experience, 1914–1918.* New York: Leo Baeck Institute, 1977.
144. "George Lichtheim: Sketch for an Intellectual Portrait." In *Varieties of Marxism,* ed. S. Avineri, 1–6. The Hague: Martin Nijhoff, 1977.
145. *The Nationalization of the Masses: Political Symbolism and Mass Movements in Germany from the Napoleonic Wars through the Third Reich.* New York: Meridian, 1977. [see no. 131]
146. (Michael A. Ledeen, interviewer), "On Nazism." *Society* 14, no. 4 (1977): 69–73. [see no. 142]

1978

147. *Toward the Final Solution: A History of European Racism.* New York: Howard Fertig, 1978.
148. "La sinistra europea e l'esperienza della guerra (Germania e Francia)." In *Rivoluzione e reazione in Europa 1917–1924. Convegno storico internazionale (Perugia, 1978),* 2:151–67. Rome: Mondo operaio-Avanti!, 1978.
149. "Art and Politics in Germany: A Comment." *Central European History* 11, no. 2 (1978): 184–88.
150. "Norbert Elias: The Civilizing Process." *New German Critique* 15 (Autumn 1978): 178–83.
151. *Der nationalsozialistische Alltag: So lebte man unter Hitler.* Königstein/Ts.: Athenäum Verlag, 1978. [see no. 54]
152. *Nazism: A Historical and Comparative Analysis of National Socialism: An Interview with Michael A. Ledeen.* New Brunswick, N.J.: Transaction Books, 1978.
153. *Nazism: A Historical and Comparative Analysis of National Socialism: An Interview with Michael A. Ledeen.* Oxford: Blackwell, 1978.
154. *Rassismus: Ein Krankheitssymptom in der europäischen Geschichte des 19. und 20. Jahrhunderts.* Königstein/Ts.: Athenäum Verlag, 1978.
155. *Toward the Final Solution: A History of European Racism.* London: Dent & Son, 1978. [see no. 147]

1979

156. "Toward a General Theory of Fascism." In *International Fascism: New Thoughts and New Approaches,* ed. George L. Mosse, 1–41. London: Sage, 1979. [see no. 161].

157. *L'opera di Aldo Moro nella crisi della democrazia parlamentare in occidente: Intervista a cura di Alfonso Alfonsi,* trans. Alfonso Alfonsi and Riccardo Duranti. In Aldo Moro, *L'intelligenza e gli avvenimenti. Testi 1959–1978. Con note di Gianni Baget Bozzo, Mario Medici, Dalmazio Mongillo e un intervento di George L. Mosse,* ed. Fondazione Aldo Moro, ix–xlvii. Milan: Garzanti, 1979.

158. "Hitler Redux." *New Republic,* 16 June 1979, 21–24.

159. "National Cemeteries and National Revival: The Cult of the Fallen Soldiers in Germany." *Journal of Contemporary History* 14, no. 1 (1979): 1–20.

160. "Arbeiterkultur." Ed. Gerhard A. Ritter. Überarbeitete deutsche Ausgabe des Heftes "Worker's Culture" der *Journal of Contemporary History* 13, no, 2 (1978), ed. Walter Laqueur and George L. Mosse. Königstein/Ts.: Hain, 1979.

161. *International Fascism: New Thoughts and New Approaches.* Ed. George L. Mosse. London: Sage, 1979.

162. *Ein Volk, ein Reich, ein Führer: Die völkischen Ursprünge des Nationalsozialismus.* Königstein/Ts., Athenäum Verlag, 1979. [see no. 40]

1980

163. *Masses and Man: Nationalist and Fascist Perceptions of Reality.* New York: Howard Fertig, 1980.

164. "Faschismus und Avantgarde." In *Faschismus und Avantgarde,* ed. Reinhold Grimm and Jost Hermand, 133–48. Königstein/Ts.: Athenäum Verlag, 1980.

165. "Soldatenfriedhöfe und nationale Wiedergeburt: Der Gefallenenkult in Deutschland." In *Kriegserlebnis: Der Erste Weltkrieg in der literarischen Gestaltung und symbolischen Deutung der Nationen,* ed. Klaus Vondung. 241–61. Göttingen: Vandenhoeck & Ruprecht, 1980.

166. In collaboration with Steven George Lampert. "Weimar Intellectuals and the Rise of National Socialism." In *Survivors, Victims, and Perpetrators: Essays on the Nazi Holocaust,* ed. Joel E. Dimsdale, 79–105. Washington, D.C.: Hemisphere, 1980.

167. "Zum deutschen Soldatenlied." In *Kriegserlebnis: Der Erste Weltkrieg in der literarischen Gestaltung und symbolischen Deutung der Nationen,* ed. Klaus Vondung, 331–33. Göttingen: Vandenhoeck & Ruprecht, 1980.

168. "La nationalisation des masses, Gymnastique tir et constitution du sentiment en Allemagne." In "Aimez vous les Stades?" *Recherches* 43 (April 1980): 59–75.

169. *Il razzismo in Europa dalle origini all'Olocausto.* Trans. Livia De Felice. Rome-Bari: Laterza, 1980. [see no. 147]

170. *Toward the Final Solution: A History of European Racism.* New York: Harper Colophon, 1980. [see no. 147]

1981

171. "War and the Appropriation of Nature." In *Germany in the Age of Total War: Essays in Honour of Francis Carsten,* ed. Volker R. Berghahn and Martin Kitchen, 102–22. London: Croom Helm, 1981.

172. "Retreat to the Status Quo." In "Left-Wing Fascism." *Society* 18, no. 4 (1981): 39–40.

173. "Amistad y conciencia nacional: Promesa y fracaso de nacionalismo alemán." *Rumbos* 5 (Fall 1981): 29–46.

174. "Razzismo." In *Enciclopedia del Novecento,* 5:1052–63. Rome: Istituto dell'Enciclopedia Italiana, 1981.

175. "Cimiteri nazionali e revival nazionalista: Il culto dei caduti in Germania." *Laboratorio di scienze dell'uomo* 1, no. 2 (1981): 143–60. [see no. 159]

176. *The Crisis of German Ideology: Intellectual Origins of the Third Reich.* New York: Schocken, 1981. [see no. 40]

177. *The Crisis of German Ideology: Intellectual Origins of the Third Reich.* New York: Howard Fertig, 1981. [see no. 40]

178. *Nazi Culture: Intellectual, Cultural, and Social Life in the Third Reich.* Ed. George L. Mosse, trans. Salvatore Attanasio et al. New York: Schocken, 1981. [see no. 54]

1982

179. "The Community in the Thought of Nationalism, Fascism, and the Radical Right." In *Community as a Social Ideal,* ed. Eugene Kamenka, 27–42. London: Edward Arnold, 1982.

180. Introduction to "Sexuality in History." *Journal of Contemporary History* 17, no. 2 (1982): 219.

181. "Friendship and Nationhood: About the Promise and Failure of German Nationalism." In "Sexuality in History." *Journal of Contemporary History* 17, no. 2 (1982): 351–67.

182. "Nationalism and Respectability: Normal and Abnormal Sexuality in the Nineteenth Century." In "Sexuality in History." *Journal of Contemporary History* 17, no. 2 (1982): 221–46.

183. *L'uomo e le masse nelle ideologie nazionaliste.* Trans. Pietro Negri. Rome-Bari: Laterza, 1982. [see no. 163]

1983

184. "Gedanken zum deutsch-jüdischen Dialog: Vortrag zur Eröffnung der Gastprofessur für jüdische Geschichte." In *Chronik der Ludwig-Maximilians-Universität Munich 1982–1983*, 48–58. Munich: Munich University, 1982–83.
185. In collaboration with Helmut Georg Koenigsberger. *L'Europa del Cinquecento*. Trans. Maria Teresa Grendi. Rome-Bari: Laterza, 1983. [see no. 91]
186. "Nationalism and Sexuality in Nineteenth Century Europe." *Society* 20, no. 5 (1983): 75–84. [see no. 182]
187. "Nazionalismo e rispettabilità." *Prometeo* 1, no. 3 (1983): 22–37. [see no. 182]
188. *The Reformation*. Westwood, Mass.: Paperbook Press, 1983. [see no. 39]

1984

189. *Sessualità e nazionalismo: Mentalità borghese e rispettabilità*. Trans. Andrea Zorzi. Rome-Bari: Laterza, 1984.
190. "Political Style and Political Theory: Totalitarian Democracy Revisited." In *Totalitarian Democracy and After: International Colloquium in Memory of Jacob L. Talmon. Jerusalem, 21–24 June 1982*, 1167–76. Jerusalem: Israel Academy of Sciences and Humanities/ Magnes Press/Hebrew University, 1984.
191. "Berlin und die Moderne." In *Berlin um 1900* (Berliner Festwochen 1984. Programm-Magazin), 126.
192. "Bookburning and the Betrayal of German Intellectuals." *New German Critique* 11, no. 1 (1984): 143–55.
193. "Razzismo e omosessualità: Intervista a George L. Mosse." *Sodoma* 1, no. 1 (1984): 93–101.
194. "Race and Sexuality: Bourgeois Society and the Outsider in the Nineteenth Century." In *Onder Mannen, Onder Vrouwen: Studies van homosociale emancipatie*, comp. Mattias Duyves, Gert Hekma, and Paula Koelemij, 79–91. Amsterdam: SVA, 1984.
195. *La nazionalizzazione delle masse: Simbolismo politico e movimenti di massa in Germania, 1815–1933*. Trans. Livia De Felice, Bologna: Il Mulino, 1984. [see no. 131]
196. *Le origini culturali del Terzo Reich*. Trans. Francesco Saba Sardi. Milan: Il Saggiatore, 1984. [see no. 40]

1985

197. *German Jews beyond Judaism*. Bloomington and Cincinnati: Indiana University Press and Hebrew Union College Press, 1985.

198. "Jewish Emancipation: Between 'Bildung' and Respectability." In *The Jewish Response to German Culture: From the Enlightenment to the Second World War*, ed. Jehuda Reinharz and Walter Schatzberg, 1–16. Hanover, N.H.: Published for Clark University Press of New England, 1985.

199. *Nationalism and Sexuality: Respectability and Abnormal Sexuality in Modern Europe.* New York: Howard Fertig, 1985. [see no. 189]

200. "Die Bildungsbürger verbrennen ihre eigenen Bücher." In *Das war ein Vorspiel nur . . .* , ed. Horst Denkler and Eberhard Lämmert, 143–55. Berlin: Akademie der Künste, 1985. [see no. 192]

201. *Nationalismus und Sexualität: Bürgerliche Moral und sexuelle Normen.* Trans. Jörg Trobitius. Munich: Hanser Verlag, 1985. [see no. 189]

202. *Il razzismo in Europa dalle origini all'Olocausto.* Trans. Livia De Felice: Rome-Bari: Laterza, 1985. [see no. 169]

203. "La Sécularisation de la théologie juive." Trans. Pascale and Terrenoire Gruson. *Archives de Sciences Sociales des Religions* 30, no. 6 (1985): 27–41.

204. *Toward the Final Solution: A History of European Racism.* Madison: University of Wisconsin Press, 1985. [see no. 147]

1986

205. "Response." In *George Mosse on the Occasion of His Retirement, 17.6.1985*, xxvi–xxxiii. Jerusalem: The Koebner Chair of German History/The Hebrew University of Jerusalem, 1986.

206. "Rushing to the Colors: On the History of Volunteers in War." In *Religion, Ideology, and Nationalism in Europe and America: Essays Presented in Honour of Yehoshoua Arieli*, 173–84. Jerusalem: Historical Society of Israel and Zalman Shazar Center for Jewish History, 1986.

207. "Deutsche Juden und der Liberalismus. Ein Rückblick." In *Das deutsche Judentum und der Liberalismus/German Jewry and Liberalism: Dokumentation eines internationalen Seminars der Friedrich-Naumann-Stiftung in Zusammenarbeit mit dem Leo Baeck Institut, London*, 173–91. St. Augustin: Comdok-Verlagsabteilung, 1986.

208. "Two World Wars and the Myth of the War Experience." *Journal of Contemporary History* 21, no. 4 (1986): 491–513.

209. *La cultura dell'Europa occidentale nell'Ottocento e nel Novecento.* Trans. Savino D'Amico. Milan: Mondadori, 1986. [see no. 33]

1987

210. "Der Erste Weltkrieg und die Brutalisierung der Politik: Betrachtungen über die politische Rechte, den Rassismus und den deutschen

Sonderweg." In *Demokratie und Diktatur: Geist und Gestalt politis-cher Herrschaft in Deutschland und Europa. Festschrift für Karl Dietrich Bracher,* ed. Manfred Funke, Hans-Adolf Jacobsen, Hans-Helmuth Knütter, and Hans-Peter Schwarz, 127–39. Düsseldorf: Droste, 1987.

211. "Zu Hause in der Maaßenstraße." In *750 Jahre Berlin: Ammerkun-gen, Erinnerungen, Betrachtungen,* ed. Eberhard Diepgen, 226–30. Berlin: Nicolai, 1987.

212. "Anatomy of a Stereotype." *New German Critique* 42 (Fall 1987): 163–68.

213. "Schönheit ohne Sinnlichkeit: Nationalsozialismus und Sexualität." In "1937: Europa vor dem 2. Weltkrieg." *Zeitmitschrift,* Sonderheft 1987, 96–109.

214. *La cultura dell'Europa occidentale nell'Ottocento e nel Novecento.* Trans. Savino D'Amico. Milan: Mondadori, 1987. [see no. 33]

215. *Germans and Jews: The Right, the Left, and the Search for a "Third Force" in Pre-Nazi Germany.* Detroit: Wayne State University Press, 1987. [see no. 94]

216. "German Jews and Liberalism in Retrospect: Introduction to Year Book XXXII." In *Leo Baeck Institute Year Book 32,* xiii–xxv. London: Secker & Warburg, 1987. [see no. 207]

217. *Masses and Man: Nationalist and Fascist Perceptions of Reality.* De-troit: Wayne State University Press, 1987. [see no. 163]

218. *Nationalismus und Sexualität: Bürgerliche Moral und sexuelle Nor-men.* Trans. Jörg Trobitius. Hamburg: Rowohlt, 1987. [see no. 189]

1988

219. "Futurismo e culture politiche in Europa: Una prospettiva globale." In *Futurismo, cultura e politica,* ed. Renzo De Felice, 13–29. Turin: Fondazione Giovanni Agnelli, 1988.

220. "Die lückenlose Geschichte: Ernst Noltes Antwort auf seine Kritiker." In *Ein Büchertagebuch: Buchbesprechungen aus der Frankfurter All-gemeinen Zeitung,* 425–27. Frankfurt: F. A. Z., 1988.

221. "Homosexualité et fascisme français." *Société,* 17 March 1988, 14–16.

222. "The End Is Not Yet: A Personal Memoir of the German-Jewish Legacy in America." *American Jewish Archives* 40, no. 2 (1988): 177–201.

223. "Wagner, the Ring, and History." *Skript* 10, no. 4 (1988): 287–88.

224. *The Culture of Western Europe: The Nineteenth and Twentieth Centuries.* 3rd rev. and enl. ed. Boulder: Westview Press, 1988. [see no. 33]

225. *Il dialogo ebraico-tedesco: Da Goethe a Hitler.* Trans. Daniel Vogel-
mann. Firenze: Giuntina, 1988. [see no. 197]

226. *Nationalism and Sexuality: Middle Class Morality and Sexual Norms
in Modern Europe.* Madison: University of Wisconsin Press, 1988.
[see no. 199]

227. *La nazionalizzazione delle masse: Simbolismo politico e movimenti di
massa in Germania (1815–1933).* Trans. di Livia De Felice. Bologna:
Il Mulino, 1988. [see no. 131]

228. *L'uomo e le masse nelle ideologie nazionaliste.* Trans. Pietro Negri:
Rome-Bari: Laterza, 1988. [see no. 163]

1989

229. "L'autorappresentazione nazionale negli anni Trenta negli Stati Uniti
e in Europa." In *L'estetica della politica. Europa e America negli anni
Trenta,* ed. Maurizio Vaudagna, 3–23. Rome-Bari: Laterza, 1989.

230. "National Anthems: The Nation Militant." In *From Ode to Anthem:
Problems of Lyric Poetry,* ed. Reinhold Grimm and Jost Hermand,
86–100. Madison: Published for Monatshefte [by] The University of
Wisconsin Press, 1989.

231. "Fascism and the French Revolution." *Journal of Contemporary History* 24, no. 1 (1989): 5–26.

232. "Il canto della patria." *Prometeo* 8, no. 29 (1990): 14–21. [see
no. 230]

233. In collaboration with Helmut Georg Koenigsberger and Gerard Q.
Bowler. *Europe in the Sixteenth Century.* 2nd rev. and enl. ed. London: York: Longman, 1989. [see no. 75]

234. *Toward the Final Solution: A History of European Racism.* Tel Aviv:
Everyman, 1989. [see no. 147]

1990

235. *Fallen Soldiers: Reshaping the Memory of the World Wars.* New
York: Oxford University Press, 1990.

236. "Das deutsch-jüdische Bildungsbürgertum im 19. Jahrhundert." In
Bildungsbürgertum im 19. Jahrhundert, vol. 2, *Bildungsgüter und Bil-
dungswissen,* ed. Reinhart Koselleck, 168–80. Stuttgart: Klett-Cotta,
1990.

237. "New Left Intellectuals/New Left Politics." In *History and the New
Left: Madison, Wisconsin, 1950–1970,* ed. Paul Buhle, 233–38.
Philadelphia: Temple University Press, 1990.

238. "Gershom Scholem as a German Jew." *Modern Judaism* 10, no. 2
(1990): 117–32.

239. "Medicine and Murder." *Studies in Contemporary Jewry* 6 (1990): 315–20.
240. "Racism." In *Encyclopedia of the Holocaust*, 1206–17. New York: MacMillan, 1990.
241. "The Political Culture of Italian Futurism: A General Perspective." *Journal of Contemporary History* 25, nos. 2–3 (April–July 1990): 253–68.
242. In collaboration with Helmut Georg Koenigsberger and Gerard Q. Bowler. *L'Europa del Cinquecento*. Rome-Bari: Laterza, 1990. [see no. 75]
243. *Le guerre mondiali: Dalla tragedia al mito dei caduti*. Trans. Giovanni Ferrara. Rome-Bari: Laterza, 1990. [see no. 235]
244. *Rassismus: Ein Krankheitssymptom in der europäischen Geschichte des 19. und 20. Jahrhunderts*. Frankfurt am Main: Fischer Taschenbuch, 1990. [see no. 154]

1991

245. *George L. Mosse, "Ich bleibe Emigrant": Gespräche mit George L. Mosse*. Ed. Irene Runge and Uwe Stelbrink. Berlin: Dietz, 1991.
246. "Beauty without Sensuality: The Exhibition *Entartete Kunst*." In *"Degenerate Art": The Fate of the Avant-Garde in Nazi Germany*, ed. Stephanie Barron, 25–31. Los Angeles: Los Angeles County Museum of Art, 1991.
247. "Über Kriegserinnerungen und Kriegsbegeisterung." In *Kriegsbegeisterung und mentale Kriegsvorbereitung: Interdisziplinäre Studien*, ed. Marcel van der Linden and Gottfried Mergner with Herman de Langen, 27–36. Berlin: Duncker & Humblot, 1991.
248. "'Fin de siècle': Challenge and Response." *Bijdragen en medelingen betreffende de geschiedenes der Nederlanden* 106, no. 4 (1991): 573–80.
249. "Rescuing Marxism." *Salmagundi* (Fall 1990–Winter 1991): 510–14.
250. "The United States: The Dominance of Cultural History." *La Grande Guerre. Pays, Histoire, Mémoire. Bulletin de recherche* 3 (February 1991): 8–9.
251. "George L. Mosse over de Duitslanden en de Duitsers." *Spiegel Historiael* 26, no. 4 (1991): 187–92. [interview by Martijn van Leishout]
252. *The Nationalization of the Masses: Political Symbolism and Mass Movements in Germany from the Napoleonic Wars through the Third Reich* Ithaca: Cornell University Press, 1991. [see no. 131]
253. *Le origini culturali del Terzo Reich*. Trans. Francesco Saba Sardi. 3rd ed. Milan: Il Saggiatore, 1991. [see no. 40]
254. *Die völkische Revolution: Über die geistigen Wurzeln des Nationalsozialismus*. Frankfurt: Anton Hain Verlag, 1991. [see no. 40]

255. *Ebrei in Germania fra assimilazione e antisemitismo.* Trans. Paola and Cristina Candela. Firenze: Giuntina, 1991. [see no. 94]

1992

256. "The Jews and the Civil Religion of Nationalism." In *The Impact of Western Nationalisms: Essays Dedicated to Walter Z. Laqueur on the Occasion of His Seventieth Birthday,* ed. Jehuda Reinharz and George L. Mosse, 319–30. London: Sage, 1992. [see no. 259].

257. "Gli ebrei e il nazionalismo." *Nuova Antologia,* January–March 1992, 63–73.

258. "Max Nordau, Liberalism and the New Jew." *Journal of Contemporary History* 27, no. 4 (1992): 565–81.

259. *The Impact of Western Nationalisms: Essays Dedicated to Walter Z. Laqueur on the Occasion of His Seventieth Birthday.* Ed. Jehuda Reinharz and George L. Mosse. London: Sage, 1992.

260. "Schönheit ohne Sinnlichkeit: Die Ausstellung 'Entartete Kunst.'" In *"Entartete Kunst." Das Schicksal der Avantgarde im Nazi-Deutschland,* ed. Stephanie Barron, 25–32. Munich: Hirmer, 1992. [see no. 246]

261. "Gli ebrei e la religione civica del nazionalismo." In *Stato nazionale ed emancipazione ebraica,* ed. Francesca Sofia and Mario Toscano, 143–54. Rome: Bonacci, 1992. [see no. 256]

262. *Jüdische Intellektuelle in Deutschland: Zwischen Religion und Nationalismus.* Intro. Alida Assmann, trans. Christine Spelsberg. Frankfurt: Campus Verlag, 1992. [see no. 197]

263. *Il razzismo in Europa: Dalle origini all'Olocausto.* Trans. Livia De Felice: Milan: Mondadori, 1992. [see no. 147]

1993

264. *Confronting the Nation: Jewish and Western Nationalism.* Hanover, N.H., and London: Published [for] Brandeis University Press by University Press of New England, 1993.

265. "Deutscher Patriotismus und jüdischer Nationalismus." In *Deutschlands Weg in die Moderne: Politik, Gesellschaft und Kultur im 19. Jahrhundert. In memoriam Thomas Nipperdey,* ed. Wolfgang Hardtwig and Harm-Hinrich Brandt, 161–70. Munich: C. H. Beck, 1993.

266. "Virilità e decadentismo." *Sodoma* 6, no. 5 (1993): 91–101.

267. "Il dibattito sul neo-nazismo." *Nuova Antologia* (April–June 1993): 16–19.

268. *Gefallen für das Vaterland: Nationales Heldentum und namenloses*

Sterben. Stuttgart: Klett-Cotta, 1993. [see no. 235]

269. *Intervista sul nazismo*. Ed. Michael A. Ledeen, trans. Giovanni Ferrara. Milan: Mondadori, 1993. [see no. 142]

270. "Max Nordau and His 'Degeneration.'" Introduction to Max Nordau, *Degeneration*, xv–xxxiv. Lincoln: University of Nebraska Press, 1993. [see no. 78]

271. *Der nationalsozialistische Alltag*. Frankfurt: Anton Hain Verlag, 1993. [see no. 54]

1994

272. "Masculinity and the Decadence." In *Sexual Knowledge, Sexual Science*, ed. Roy Porter and Mikulás Teich, 251–66. Cambridge: Cambridge University Press, 1994.

273. "Souvenir de la guerre et place du monumentalisme dans l'identité culturelle du National-Socialisme." In *Guerre et Cultures, 1914–1918*, ed. Jean-Jacques Becker et al., 278–86. Paris: Armand Colin, 1994.

274. "The Knights of the Sky and the Myth of the War Experience." In *War: A Cruel Necessity? The Bases of Institutionalized Vilence*, ed. Robert A. Hinde and Helen E. Watson, 132–42. London: I. B. Tauris, 1994.

275. "La guerre et l'identité culturelle du National-Socialisme." *Vingtième Siècle* 41 (January–March 1994): 51–59.

276. "National Socialism, Nudity, and the Male Body." *CultureFront* 3, no. 1 (1994): 89–92.

277. *Le origini culturali del Terzo Reich*. Trans. Francesco Saba Sardi. Milan: Il Saggiatore, 1994. [see no. 40]

278. *The Nationalization of the Masses: Political Symbolism and Mass Movements in Germany, from the Napoleonic Wars through the Third Reich*. Tokyo: Takunisato, 1994. [see no. 131]

279. *Fallen Soldiers: Reshaping the Memory of the World Wars*. Tel Aviv: Am Oved, 1994. [see no. 235]

1995

280. "Estetica fascista e societè: Considerazioni." In *Il Regime fascista*, ed. Angelo del Boca, Massimo Legmani, and Mario G. Rossi, 1. Rome-Bari: Laterza, 1995.

281. "Männlichkeit und der Grosse Weltkrieg." In *So ist der Mensch: 80 Jahre Erster Weltkrieg*, 57–69. Vienna: Eigenverlag der Museen der Stadt Wien, 1995.

282. "1915–18: La Madre di tutti gli stermini." *Panorama*, 25 May 1995, 127–34.

283. "Racism and Nationalism." *Nations and Nationalism* 1, no. 2 (1995): 21–31.

284. *Can Nationalism Be Saved? About Zionism Rightful and Unjust Nationalism.* The Weizman Lecture in the Humanities, Weizman Institute, Jerusalem, Nov. 5, 1995.

1996

285. *The Image of Man: The Creation of Modern Masculinity.* New York: Oxford University Press, 1996.

286. *Il fascismo: verso una teoria generale.* Rome: Laterza, 1996.

287. "Manliness and the Great War." In *Genocide, War, and Human Survival,* ed. Charles B. Strozier and Michael Flynn, 165–75. Lanham, Md.: Rowman and Littlefield, 1996.

288. "Fascist Aesthetics and Society: Some Considerations." *Journal of Contemporary History* 31, no. 2 (1996): 245–52.

289. "Central European Intellectuals in Palestine." *Judaism* 45, no. 2 (1996): 131–42.

290. "Il declino della morale." *Prometeo* 14, no. 53 (1996): 6–13.

291. "Max Nordau, le Libéralisme et le Nouveau Juif." In *Max Nordau,* ed. Delphine Bechtel, Dominque Bourel, and Jacques le Rider, 11–29. Paris: Les Editions du Cerf, 1996.

292. "Les deux Guerres de George Mosse." *L'Histoire,* May 1996, 13–14. [interview by Bruno Cabanes]

293. *German Jews beyond Judaism.* Tokyo: Kashana, 1996. [see no. 197]

294. "Zu Hause in der Maaßenstraße." *Jüdische Korrespondenz* 5, nos. 7–8 (July/August 1996): 1. [see no. 211]

295. "Ist der Nationalismus noch zu retten? Über gerechtfertigten und ungerechtfertigten Nationalismus." In *Responsibility and Commitment: Festschrift für Jost Hermand,* ed. Klaus Berghahn et al. Frankfurt: Peter Lang, 1996. [see no. 284]

1997

296. "Politisches Erwachen, Berlin, das Exil und die antifaschistische Bewegung." In *Die Erfahrung des Exils,* ed. Wolfgang Benz and Marion Neiss, 67–82. Berlin: Metropol Verlag, 1997.

297. "The Universal Meaning of the Concept of Bildung." *Zmanin* (published by the School of History at Tel Aviv University) 16, no. 61 (1997–98): 6–10.

298. "Zionism at 100: The God That Did Not Fail" (Symposium). *New Republic,* 8 and 15 September 1997, 19–20.

299. *The Culture of Western Europe: The Nineteenth and Twentieth*

Centuries. With a new preface. Barcelona: Ariel Historia, 1997 (nine-teenth century only). [see no. 33]

300. *Das Bild des mannes: Zur Konstruktion der modernen männlichkeit.* Frankfurt: Fisher Verlag, 1997. [see no. 285]

301. *L'immagine dell'uomo: Lo stereotipo maschile nell'epoca moderna.* Turi: Einaudi, 1997. [see no. 285]

302. *The Image of Man: The Creation of Modern Masculinity.* Seoul: Moonye Publishing, 1997. [see no. 285]

303. *La imagen del hombre: La creación de la mascalinidad moderna.* Barcelona: Talasa Editiones, 1997. [see no. 285]

304. *L'Image del'homme: L'invention de la virilité moderne.* Paris: Abbeville Press, 1997. [see no. 285]

305. "Can Nationalism Be Saved? About Zionism Rightful and Unjust Nationalism." *Israel Studies* 2, no. 1 (1997): 156–73. [see no. 284]

1998

306. "Razzismo e nazionalismo in Europa." In *Integrazione e identità, l'esperienza ebraica in Germania e Italia dall'illuminismo al fascismo,* ed. Mario Toscano, 236–43. Milan: Franco Agnelli, 1998.

307. "De Felice e il Revisionismo Storico." *Nuova Antologia* 113 (April–June 1998): 177–86.

308. "Ein Besuch in Salem nach langer Zeit." *Salem College—Salem 1998,* 35–36.

309. *The Crisis of German Ideology: The Intellectual Origins of the Third Reich.* New York: Howard Fertig, 1998. [see no. 40]

310. *The Crisis of German Ideology: The Intellectual Origins of the Third Reich.* Tokyo: Kasiva Shobo, 1998. [see no. 40]

311. "Le origini occulte del nazionalsocialismo." *I viaggi di erodoto* 12, no. 35 (1998): 24–39. [see no. 34]

1999

312. *The Fascist Revolution: Toward a General Theory of Fascism.* New York: Howard Fertig, 1999.

313. "America 1939–42." *Journal of Contemporary History* 34, no. 3 (1999): 443–56.

314. "Dankesworte." In *Grußworte und Vorträge anläßlich der Verleihung der Ehrendoktorwürde an George L. Mosse am 6. November 1998,* ed. Rektor der Universität-Gesamthochschule Siegen, 35–37. Siegen: presse-und Informationsstelle, 1999.

315. *Fallen Soldiers: Reshaping the Memory of the World Wars.* Paris: Hachette, 1999. [see no. 234]

2000

316. *Confronting History: A Memoir.* Madison: University of Wisconsin Press, 2000.
317. "Shell-shock as a Social Disease." *Journal of Contemporary History* 35, no. 1 (2000): 101–8.
318. In collaboration with Helmut Georg Koenigsberger and Gerard Q. Bowler. *Europe in the Sixteenth Century.* 2nd rev. and exp. ed. London: Longman, 2000. [see no. 75]
319. *De la Grande Guerre au totalitarisme, la brutalisation des sociétés européenes.* Paris: Hachette Littératures, 2000. [see no. 234]

Contributors

Stanley G. Payne is Hilldale-Jaume Vicens Vives Professor of History at the University of Wisconsin–Madison. His last major book was *Fascism in Spain, 1923–1977* (1999). *The Soviet Union, Communism, and Revolution in Spain, 1931–1939* will appear in 2004.

David J. Sorkin is Frances and Laurence Weinstein Professor of Jewish Studies at the University of Wisconsin–Madison. He is the author, most recently, of *The Berlin Haskalah and German Religious Thought* (2000) and coeditor of *The Oxford Handbook of Jewish Studies* (2002). He is working on a book provisionally entitled *Reasonable Belief: Six Faces of the Religious Enlightenment, 1689–1789*.

John S. Tortorice directs the Mosse Program in the Department of History at the University of Wisconsin–Madison.

Steven E. Aschheim holds the Vigevani Chair of European Studies at The Hebrew University, Jerusalem, where he has taught Cultural and Intellectual History in the Department of History since 1982. In 2002–3 he was the first Mosse Exchange Professor at the University of Wisconsin–Madison. He is the author of *Brothers and Strangers: The East European Jew in German and German-Jewish Consciousness, 1800–1923* (1982), *The Nietzsche Legacy in Germany, 1890–1990* (1992), *Culture and Catastrophe: German and Jewish Confrontations with National Socialism and Other Crises* (1996); *In Times of Crisis: Essays on European Culture, Germans and Jews* (2001); *Scholem, Arendt, Klemperer: Intimate Chronicles in Turbulent Times* (2001). He is also the editor of a conference volume, *Hannah Arendt in Jerusalem* (2001).

Joanna Bourke is professor of history at Birkbeck College, University of London. She has published seven books, on Irish history, gender and "the body," the history of psychological thought, and modern warfare. Her books have been translated into Chinese, German, Italian, Portuguese, Spanish, and Turkish. *An Intimate History of Killing: Face-to-Face Killing in Twentieth Century Warfare* (1999) won the Fraenkel Prize in Contemporary History for 1998 and the Wolfson

History Prize for 2000. She is currently completing a book entitled *Fear: A Cultural History of the Twentieth Century.*

Saul Friedländer is 1939 Club Professor of History at UCLA. His latest book is *Nazi Germany and the Jews*, vol.1, *The Years of Persecution, 1933–1939* (1997).

Emilio Gentile is professor of contemporary history at the University of Rome "La Sapienza." He is on the editorial board of *Journal of Contemporary History* and is coeditor of *Totalitarian Movements and Political Religions.* Among his most recent books are *Il culto del littorio: La sacralizzazione della politica nell'Italia fascista* (1993), *La via Italiana al totalitarismo: Il partito e lo Stato nel regime fascista* (1995), *La Grande Italia: Ascesa e declino del mito nazionale nel XX secolo* (1997), *Le origini dell'ideologia fascista*, rev. and enl. ed. (1996), *Fascismo e antifascismo: I partiti italiani fra le due guerre mondiali* (2000); *Le religioni della politica: Fra democrazie e totalitarismi* (2001), *Fascismo: Storia e interpretazione* (2002), *Renzo De Felice: Lo storico e il personaggio* (2003). His latest book, *The Struggle for Modernity: Nationalism, Futurism, and Fascism*, is forthcoming.

Roger Griffin is professor in the history of ideas at Oxford Brookes University and the author of *The Nature of Fascism* (1991), which had a major impact on fascist studies. This was followed by two documentary readers—*Fascism* (1995) and *International Fascism. Theories, Causes and the New Consensus* (1998)— and numerous articles, chapters and encyclopedia entries on interwar and postwar manifestations of the genus of fascism. His forthcoming projects include a five-volume critical anthology of secondary sources relating to fascism (2004), and *Beginning Time* (2005), an investigation of the relationship of modernity and modernism to fascist projects for the renewal of history.

Rudy Koshar is the DAAD Professor of German and European Studies at the University of Wisconsin—Madison. Among his most recent books are *German Travel Cultures* (2000) and an edited volume, *Histories of Leisure* (2002). He is at work on a history of driving and cultures of automobility in twentieth-century Europe and America.

Walter Laqueur is chairman of the International Research Council at the Center for Strategic and International Studies in Washington, D.C. His most recent book is *No End to War: Terrorism in the 21st Century* (2003).

Robert A. Nye received his Ph.D. in 1969 from Wisconsin. He is the Thomas Hart and Mary Jones Horning Professor of the Humanities and Professor of History at Oregon State University. His most recent book is *Sexuality*, an Oxford Reader (1999). He is presently working on *Masculinity and the History of the Professions.*

David Warren Sabean studied with George Mosse from 1960 to 1965, receiving his Ph.D. in 1969, with a dissertation on the social history of the German

Peasant War of 1525. He taught at the University of East Anglia (Norwich, England) and the University of Pittsburgh before spending the years 1976–83 at the Max-Planck-Institut für Geschichte in Goettingen, Germany. He then taught at Cornell University and the University of California–Los Angeles, where he is now the Henry J. Bruman Professor of German History. His work has been in the social history of rural society, family and demographic history, and the history of popular culture. His most recent book is *Kinship in Neckarhausen 1700–1870* (1998). His current project is a study of incest discourse in Europe and America since 1600. He has held a Guggenheim Fellowship and is a fellow of the American Academy of Arts and Sciences.

Emmanuel Sivan is professor of history at The Hebrew University, Jerusalem. Educated in Israel and France, Sivan is the author of *Strong Religion* (2003) and of *The Future of Radical Islam* (forthcoming).

Johann Sommerville is professor of history at the University of Wisconsin–Madison. He is the author of *Royalists and Patriots: Politics and Ideology in England 1603–1640* (1999) and is currently working on the history of political ideas in early modern Europe.

Jay Winter is professor of history at Yale University. From 1979–2001, he was Reader in Modern History in the University of Cambridge and Fellow of Pembroke College–Cambridge. He is the author of many books on the First World War, including *Sites of Memory, Sites of Mourning: The Place of the Great War in European Cultural History* (1995) and, with Jean-Louis Robert, *Capital Cities at War: Paris, London, Berlin 1914–1919* (1997). He was chief historian and coproducer of the television series *The Great War and the Shaping of the Twentieth Century*, first screened on PBS and the BBC in 1996, for which he won an Emmy award.

Shulamit Volkov is professor of modern European history and holder of the Konrad Adenauer Chair for Comparative European History at Tel Aviv University. She publishes in the fields of German social and intellectual history, German Jewish history and the History of Antisemitism. Her most recent book is *The Vicious Circle: Jews, Germans, and Antisemites* (2002) [Hebrew]. She is now preparing a comprehensive essay on the historiography of National Socialism.

Index

Adorno, Theodor, 114
aesthetics, 167, 169, 190; and appeal of
    tourist sites, 171–72; and the body, 139,
    185, 191–92; of fascism, 89–91, 111,
    122–23; of flight in wartime, 205–7; of
    Nazi visual culture, 170–71
alienation: causes of, 58, 85; fascism as cure
    for, 55, 62, 64, 71, 79, 121–22
Alterman, Natan, 240–41
*Ancient Constitution and the Feudal Law,
    The* (Pocock), 33
Anderlahn, Hans, 142
Anderson, Benedict, 186–87
Anglo-Saxon cultural history, 159
anthropology, 83, 124; influence on Mosse's
    work, 79, 111, 117–18, 122–23, 233; value
    to historians, 116, 159
anti-Semitism, 68, 87, 145; and bourgeois
    morality, 91, 101; European, 138–39; and
    formation of stereotypes, 50–51; German,
    135, 225; and *völkisch* ideology, 137–38.
    See also racism
anti-Semitism studies, 135, 224; historians
    losing interest in, 136–37; historiography
    of, 229–30
Arendt, Hannah, 68, 135
Aschheim, Steven, 19, 227
attitudes, 51, 60, 88; of fascism, 73–74; in
    Mosse's historiography, 59–60, 66–67
Audoin-Rouzeau, Stéphane, 151
Auslander, Leora, 177
Austin, John, 29

Austin, Norman, 204
avant-garde, 97
Aydelotte, William O., 51

Bacharach, Zvi, 227
Baedeker, Karl, 167
Bakhtin, Mikhail, 214
Ball, Albert, 209–10
Barnouw, Dagmar, 171
Beaumont, Roland, 209
beauty. *See* aesthetics
Becker, Annette, 151, 157
Becker, Jean-Jacques, 151
Benjamin, Walter, 23, 114, 121–22, 170
Berlin, Isaiah, 114
Bildung, Jewish loyalty to, 23, 225, 227–28
Bildungsbürgertum, 23
Bismarck, Otto von, 22
Bland, Alfred, 204
Bleys, Rudi, 196
Bloch, Ernst, 114, 121–22
Boas, Franz, 111
Bodin, Jean, 31, 34
body, the, 191; enemies', in war photos,
    211–14; as heroic, 210, 216; mutability of,
    191–92; and stereotyped others, 190–91;
    used as symbolic, 184–85; in warfare,
    202–5, 244
Böhme, Jakob, 123
Bolin, Anne, 192
Bolshevism, fascism compared to, 95, 98
"Bonds of Family, The" (Anderlahn), 142

283

GEORGE L. MOSSE SERIES
IN EUROPEAN CULTURAL
AND INTELLECTUAL HISTORY

Series Editors

Stanley G. Payne, David J. Sorkin, and John S. Tortorice

Collected Memories: Holocaust History and Postwar Testimony
Christopher Browning

Nazi Culture: Intellectual, Cultural, and Social Life in the Third Reich
George L. Mosse

What History Tells: George L. Mosse and the Culture of Modern Europe
Edited by Stanley G. Payne, David J. Sorkin, and John S. Tortorice